Words Between Worlds

◆ FriesenPress

One Printers Way
Altona, MB R0G 0B0
Canada

www.friesenpress.com

ISBN
978-1-03-912412-7 (Hardcover)
978-1-03-912411-0 (Paperback)
978-1-03-912413-4 (eBook)

1. TRAVEL, ESSAYS & TRAVELOGUES

Distributed to the trade by The Ingram Book Company

Words Between Worlds

a 1970s travel memoir

JOHN DOMINELLI

)

Table of Contents

Intro

SOMEONE ONCE SAID, "NINETY PERCENT OF IT IS SHOWING UP." I SHOWED up at the ticket counter, and I showed up at the airport. The rest seemed to "just happen."

At the tail end of my teen years, I knew little of *why* I wanted to leave. But I would not take the path whose bends and straight-aways were plain to see and marked by a whole lot of reasonable recommendations, and as many expectations.

So with money in my pocket and hunger all over me I set out on a six-month trip that turned into a year, then three. Road, rail, trail, ferry, canoe, bike, plane, potato truck, rickshaw, and horse carriage carried me on a path of meanders and loops going west around the globe. Along the way I lost my girl, traded in my outlook a few times, and ran into a character or two as rare as a blooming pond in a desert. Add a couple of big-time illnesses and a few psycho- time-bombs, on a journey some would surely describe as an emotional and spiritual joy-ride...

After returning home, and with a child on the way, I took one of those "lifer" railway jobs. Sensing that I was about to take a sharp turn into the solemn lands of parenthood, I asked myself a question: *What have I learned in this life?* I took my time to answer, and I began to write. It soon became clear that early childhood and my travels were stand-out times of intense activity and learning. After a year of scribbling, I looked at my notebooks and observed, *a helluva lotta stuff here; I could write a book.* I chuckled. Me, the son of semi-literate peasants, writing a book. I was more likely to whack away at a cheap guitar or take up a trade than do anything so learned as write. So it seemed, and so it was. I've since become a big fan of travel writing, memoirs and such. On this, my own journey, the traveler had no inkling he would write about it, for he had not yet imagined "writing."

Yet so many unexpected and peculiar turns came my way during my trip that after coming home, the sheer delight in remembering and writing it down, even in continuing to integrate some of the experiences, in these present times, has me wanting to share it. Hence, this book. In the telling I've chosen to include some of the ways and ideas by which this seminal journey of my youth has informed my life. The road has revealed itself as playground, stage and classroom, each in its turn and simultaneously. Many new paths of enquiry were thus encountered, and I have wondered aloud on these fascinating subjects. And so I have drawn liberally from many sources, scholarly and otherwise, with the hope that they simply will serve to pique the reader's curiosity, as they have mine.

Any information herein pertains to the time of my trip, during the 1970s, so things may sound dated here and there. For example, statistics and place names, along with certain terms and pronouns, remain as they were. My hope is in reflecting something of the mood and aura of that time.

As well, some personal names have been changed. And, what with zigzagging and backtracking, the sequence of a few minor events was shuffled for brevity.

Finally, it surely must be true, what they say: that confabulations of the past will tease and tempt the fickle whitecaps of memory, in as many ways as there are viewers. It is against such odds that I have done my best to remain true to the events I here describe.

There are only two mistakes one can make along the road:
not going all the way, and not starting.
—Gautama Buddha

PART 1
West with the Sun

1. Land of New Zeal

you say you wanna start something new[1]

I'M SITTING ON a grassy river bank dangling my feet, having left behind the hiss and moan of airport and city. I'm in a new land, a friendly land, one filled with a generosity of kind and chipper citizens.

Having randomly wandered the streets of this mill town, I've found a river that seems to run strangely fast... for being so eerily quiet. Swollen from spring rains, it tugs at the hanging branches of this sun-mottled forest. The sparkle of rays in the canopy, the musky smells, the lush breeze—I'm emptied by beauty in the river's presence. I, a mere container of thought, awareness, and feelings... I must assure myself that all is well in my towers of fact and fiction, for the question has just occurred to me: "Can a river 'know' it's a river?" Its almost soundless speed and power seems, *yeah, cunning*. If it has a soul it must be the trickster kind, we land dwellers catching sight only of a few of its many faces: mirror, menace, genie of life, hidden realm of fear and myth.

My base of reason has shifted. For I see myself sitting, a reasonably well-trained ape-thing, entertaining some pretty crazy thoughts. A few minutes in and I'm willing to forgo my past, my name tucked away in a pocket somewhere. I am not only in a new land for the first time, but evidently, I'm cast adrift in unfamiliar inner territory as well. Yet I'm keen and curious, and my desire is as green as it is strong. I stare good and hard into the river's fluid, eerie depth, jaw all slack, staring as if into the very essence of the journey I've just begun. Staring, as I feel it, into the heart of the unknown.

---

1   From the song "Wild World" by Cat Stevens.

I shake myself and head back.

It's my first real pause since leaving BC. While I'm out communing with the local geography, my mate Billy is either snoozing in his room, back at the mill where we found jobs, or out with some Kiwi lads on the hunt in Small Town, New Zealand. He began to paint *his* new canvas thusly: not yet an hour on Kiwi soil, still at Auckland Airport, he stopped in his tracks and rifled through his wallet.

"Fuck! I've only got seventy bucks left!" His eyes were sad, droopy. Then a bit pissed.

I'm twenty, he's nineteen. We met recently through friends in Port Coquitlam, our hometown on the outskirts of Vancouver. We knew little of each other except for those commonalities of shared place, a fondness for the same streets where shadows of meaning and the scent of familiarity live in our minds like unheeded messengers. It is the wild west of the West, a land of raw, endless wild that provides a backdrop and energy that charges youths like Billy and me with a hunger for the obscurities of adventure. We are barely familiar with the fathomless land that has graced our lives. We've left our little PoCo far behind, and with it, some powerful unknowns.

Of course, small towns will fill in your blanks with whatever's going around. Having heard of JD's plan to leave town, Billy looked me up. "D'ya mind if I come along?" Told me he'd just had his heart mashed but good by the ruthless hand of romance. *Sounds familiar.* Perfect time for a cool flight into the great blue yonder. I had planned, and was prepared, to go alone. But as the day of departure approached I began to feel uncertain, unready. His request came as a reassuring surprise (I had no idea how much comfort his company would bring in the early, timorous weeks.) I told him that my girl would follow in a few months, that we'd stay maybe a year, and, "Uh, yeah, man, let's start out together, for sure." Allies in our first venture overseas, we are virtual strangers of heart and mind. We barely know ourselves, never mind acknowledge each other's frontier of ignorance.

Seventy bucks? I saved for two years on a slow burn of wanderlust that I could barely wrap my head around. One could say I was diligent, organized, covering my options (and apprehension) with preparedness. The proper way to go about things. Yet in this moment my respect for

Billy jumps with admiration. His gutsy flight into risk, unprepared, looks something like, "I'm outta here—headed to New Zealand for the weekend." A few dollars. Pocket change.

Clearly, my new friend needed a job. And so my rising traveling anxiety was given a welcome cover: that of slinking along in the shadow of *his* job hunt. Shuffling along a city street, we fresh-off-the-plane, Canucklehead yokels found three jobs each in less than an hour—construction site, a bar, the docks—and kept walking into hills as green as our resumés.

Truth is, I missed my girl and my mom as soon as that airplane started rolling. World adventurer? More like a white-knuckle run in a leaky kayak and don't know how to swim. Billy and I have little in common, so hiding behind the "cool dude with guitar" façade (I brought a guitar) is lusciously convenient. Like a lot of guys, I'm an old hand in the mask department.

Kawerau

Less than two weeks in we've found jobs at a pulp mill just a day's thumbing down the main highway. We've traded the city's stimulation and compressed anxiety for the dense vision of industry and capital in a fetid mill town. Kawerau is a planned, one-stop pony a few miles inland from the Bay of Plenty. In Auckland I'd looked at a map and was drawn southeast to a long and graceful arc of shoreline. We arrived at Ohope Beach, a few buildings tucked into a great, blonde curve of sand. With the gentle sea and warm sea breeze, false memories of Paradise were roused at first sight, the serpent and its wily hiss having taken up residence a few miles east at Kawerau's noxious mill. At the beachside restaurant hut we ordered fish and chips and our first "eggburger."

The Tasman Pulp and Paper Mill is a sprawling, faceless complex whose unrelenting mechanical rhythms will at first vex, then aim to consume one's own more buoyant variety. Like any industrial site bulging at the twentieth century's proud midriff, no effort is wasted on pretty lines. The factory's multiple buildings sit like cruddy cubist blisters that seethe continuous streams of gray, steaming nasties. It is the snap and spit of a great beast, the source of the acrid reek we will inhale every breath of every day. *Psychoactive zombie chemistry?* With the

$1.26 per week rent, they manage to keep a buzzing hive of otherwise healthy young men working here. We are paid every Friday in cash with crisp, new bills placed neatly in an envelope. I'm guessing that "social insurance numbers", or some equivalent, are yet to be installed as a governmental people-accounting system. For we are promptly given jobs on a large company's payroll with no mention of numbers, or even a peek at our foreign passports.

Billy and I shovel sawdust like robots until our pace slows to the ambient average, something like sheep on a beer buzz. At this signal, right when we slow down, the jolly supervisor comes over. "We like ta hire ya Canadians, cuz ya work hard for maybe a coupl'a weeks, aye? Till ya catch on, see?" *Wink, smirk.* It takes whiz-bones Billy and me a mere three days. We are rewarded with promotions, and separated.

Double shifts, sixteen hours on some days, a discordant routine regulated according to the insomniac psycho-mill. My new position sounds ominous: Utility-Pulp. Yet it's an easy, clean enough gig at the end of the pulp-making process. I push buttons and pull levers on gigantic machines. A small manufacturer's nameplate reads: Made in New Westminster, BC, Canada, a mere five miles from my home.

Every day, rattled by the mechanical depravity of the soulless mill, I wander over to Kawerau's river like a demented old pilgrim, who long ago forgot why he ever goes wherever it is he always ends up. And I dangle my feet, and I watch and listen.

MY FOREMAN IS a wily half-man, half-wolfman who takes an immediate dislike to me. Not sure what sparks his animosity, maybe the oil-and-water of our personalities, hard for him to stomach for some reason related to his top-dog position. *Methinks.* Quite larger than me, it takes Mr. Schmulk only two days to work himself into a saliva-spurting rage, with me, the subject of his bile stream, standing only inches distant. My eyes are narrowed, as much by the flying drool as the requisite posturing. The rest of me is poised with a calculated coolness that (strangely enough) seems to deliver an unexpected, manly kind of effect. Seeing that his hot spew has not reduced me to his slavish minion, he swaps faces in an instant and becomes sweet and friendly, inviting me to join him on a wild pig hunt the next weekend.

You wanna what? In five minutes we get through our first skirmish, and he promptly casts us as buddies in hog-killing fields. I barely get a word in. He whips a chair over and charges into a rant with great gusto, going into detail describing "the chase" through thorny jungle, perhaps catching a large one by a hind leg and being dragged over rocks and roots before pulling himself forward with every ounce of strength—to murder it with his only weapon, an oversized, Bowie-like knife.

The guy is fucking daft. Mr. Schnarzan has no idea I can finger-ape James Taylor and pluck a mean love song, and that I've just finished reading books by Hermann Hesse and Albert Camus. A sinister glint flashes through his wide-eyed swoon now and then, his voice dropping in pitch and speed during tender moments as he describes the chase, and especially, the knife. When he speaks his eyes spread a little too far, suggesting a loose connection with the brainy region. Worse, at the end of his spiel, he forgets he's been talking. I say nothing. His body's gone slack, and he's all doped up on his story, eyes slopped sideways into a hazy near-distance. Putting aside the paranoid thought that the murder in his eye might hold a special place just for me, I interrupt with a loose word. He leaves in a flash, dashing away without looking at me, as if he's crazy-hungry all of a sudden. I haven't yet heard of bi-polar, but that's what I'd be thinking if I had.

I avoid him after that (and he me), the dream of bonding over hog-killing gladly forgotten.

BACK AT THE barracks, we are befriended by four lads from the city. We, the fine young cocks of far-flung lands—could be New Zealand, *mate*, or Canada, *eh*—mingle like hairy reeds in a rising stream. They finished high school, hopped in a van, and drove down the windswept coast. Avid surfers, they travel the shoreline in search of waves like some mythical freedom that's been haunting humans from the get-go. The feeling is familiar. They're hunting for whatever living is all about, just like me, only they don't seem to use up as much think-juice as I do. And here we are, together at the Tasman Mill, this diabolical zone where that freedom must wilt a wee bit each day on a first job away from home. My own working-class angst can barely wrap its head around the fact that this cyclopean factory isn't interested in our minds or *who* we are. It's the body it craves and would gladly digest, along with our dreams of special glory. A grim awakening, as I suffered back home on construction sites and the odd factory job in the two years after high school. Alas, somewhere under a fat Pygmy moon, the Forest People dance and sing.[2] I lament.

We're quite different, Billy and I, but in an odd, unexpected way we fit together well. I sense in him a deep strength and honesty that I could rely on. Yet we are birds of a different feather found in the same nest. We sit apart, we sit together, and already we've known some brotherly places in this land of new choices. Yet the Canadian similarities are, I think, superficial. The occasional Kiwi comments, "You two are so different. How is it you're, uh, traveling together?"

"Well, circumstance, same hometown, mutual friends, timing," we mutter, wondering about it ourselves.

Billy wanders Kawerau's streets with a few of the local lads. They head out, tense and expectant, hot on the trail of a sweet-most scent. I imagine them fool driven on the drunken chemistry of lust, darting like hornets into the willing limbs of New Zealand's precious young daughters. From my room I watch them leave, and surely, it *is* my imagination. I don't know what they do nor where they go, and I don't ask, for I have no desire to join them. I stay back with my guitar, my books, and my letters of longing to and from my girl, Danna, who will soon join me after saving more money at her shitty job in Vancouver. I fill Billy and his buddies with my own lovelorn solitude, serving up a self-serving story, one that feeds the mystique of longing and ecstasy in my and Danna's letters of swollen, bittersweet love. Clearly, I've fool-found my own, and it's a hot, beautiful thing.

Never mind the 11,000-plus miles of deep cold sea between us.

God, how I miss her willing limbs.

A JOURNEY? HOW *did* a squirmy dude like me set his sights, tighten his nuts, and arrive one sunny spring day in New Zealand with one gutsy, short-on-cash Billy?

---

2   refers to Colin Turnbull's *The Forest People* and my own tendency to romanticize "the simple life."

Well, when high school ended I made my choice: a *non*-choice. *Not going to university.* At least not right away, although it was all planned and provided for. *I so wanted to please you, Dad… sorry for the wrench my punk-ass self threw into the works at the eleventh hour.* For I would fly the coop on a tailwind bound for some faraway locale. In my mind's workshop I drew up a flashy poster: "A Paddle Down the Amazon of Inner." Or maybe, "Drifting Fool down the Nile of Cool." The boat's all mine, the crew handpicked from a small life of heady dreams and lofty ideals: Socrates, Jesus, Honest Abe, John and Paul and Bob, Popeye—my whole team's up on deck. Let's hope the good, brave captain, the one in charge of maps and that trusty moral compass, will creep outta the cabin and show his face. *Little chickenshit nerd.*

A few others had found a hole in the fence and slipped away. A couple of guys from high school hopped a freighter bound for Australia. Like them, I would not go the way of the crowds. I'd cross the Big Ocean to New Zealand, Down Under—smaller, less jazzy than big bro Oz. A full-on ride into the wild blue, a good jump into the horizon clear across a bridge that would span six months, maybe a year. I *had* to go. In my restlessness and discontent I would forsake the predictable life chosen for me, slashing madly with my imaginary machete at the tendrils of expectation that would wrap around my tender yearnings and strangle my ability to choose something—anything else. I would rather one minute of the raw energy in my solitary angst than walk tall and benumbed in obeisance to those expectations. All I knew was that I was hungry for something *un*predictable, something I could not yet imagine.

That's about how it went, about how I imagined it all from my easy chair in the Church of Psychedelic Youth (save for the *chickenshit* bit.)

So it would be no "holiday" but a departure, a grand flight fuelled by emotion and a mere sliver of vision, one I hadn't the perspective to wrap my plain words around just yet. Though it is obvious—as it was even to me back then, at least in brief flashes—that I was running.

And that is how I ran, with my new friend Billy, straight into the pleasures of warm, generous Kiwiland, Down Under.

River Deep, Mountain High

As days turn to weeks, I feel I've been prematurely fast-tracked to hell's local greeting hall, further tidying up the picture of Satan's secret hideout tucked away right next to Paradise. Each day I log miles of neatly mapped streets that pass dull and hard under my tender feet. Always I come and go from my sweet river that runs like a lucid dream of whispering ghosts through the flickering movie of my life.

More and more as I sit on the river's bank, I feel it: a gnawing funk looming just below, where ruthless power hides and eyes don't care to go. Yet I keep coming back. I'm lonely for my girl, my home—so hard to admit. The river, my life, so silky and cool on the surface, yet underneath it's a muffled abyss of voices too remote to remember, never mind comprehend. The voice I conjure is the one that animates the water into a living current. Like an oracle of olden times, the river knows certain truths about me. I hear, when I listen well, the voice of a stranger. Yet somehow, it's familiar.

The mirror in the water, the mirror of the world—it all looks different. The view is harsher and brighter, and maybe a little clearer, as if some great kaleidoscope just shifted. Privately I pine for Danna, spending my rainy days writing her fat letters of sweet longing.

And so it is that early in our ocean-wide, words-of-love jet stream, we decide to make our trip together happen sooner rather than later.

For me, Kawerau's best features are: (a) the river that moves like a silent wraith but always stays put and (b) a certain dark mountain that looms over the town, doing an excellent job of appearing *not* to move (for now, bets are off.) An ominous black rock most of a thousand meters high, I often let its charcoal roughness capture my gaze.

Billy and I talk about scaling it. One of the four Auckland mates—the ruddier, darker one who claims a Māori[3] connection a ways back—warns us in grave tones (between draws on a Buddha-stick joint, mind you) that the summit is a sacred place. He infers, his eyes all googly and

---

3   The Māori ceremonial masks, dugout canoes, and totem poles seem to bear a resemblance to those of the faraway Pacific Northwest nations back home, as if "the ocean is the message." *Aotearoa (ah-oh-tee-ah-roa)*—"Land of the Long White Cloud"—is their name for these twin island jewels set in the remote southwestern Pacific.

dense, that the demons and spirits of ancestral Māori nether regions will not look kindly upon their holy spot being desecrated by mere mortals walking all over it just for fun—especially the non-believing kind with weird accents. *Respect.* To me it's a mountain, a little scary and rough looking, but it's just a mountain. *Could be wrong, eh.*

We don't climb it. It remains a symbol of the unexplored (and the poorly explained?), a prescient encounter at the beginning of what is to become a longer-than-expected journey.

Jona and the Open Road

One fine morning Billy and I are greeted by a smiling and tanned Jona, Danna's brother. He started his New Zealand "working holiday" six months before us. Of course I knew that Jona was in New Zealand when I decided to travel, and our ponderings might have followed similar loops and zags in choosing where to begin. Although he is my girl's older brother, I've known him only as that tall, weird guy in the larger hometown group (wait a minute, I'm sleeping with his bodacious little sister!) and had no specific plan to meet up. I reckon that, independent of each other, we caught the current of an alternate stream running opposite the bigger waves bound for Grandpa Europe.

And wouldn't you know it, Jona's tracked us down. Six months of travel in a congenial, sub-tropical island country seems to have brought warmth and confidence to his manner. In joining him I would leave that purgatory of industry, so I promptly—gladly—quit work. Billy needs money, so he stays on at Tasman's psychotic mill. Danna will arrive soon anyway; brother Jona is my early ticket out. We'll head toward the north cape for a refreshing two-week jaunt before she arrives.

With no expectations to point a direction, and a mere pinprick of guilt in leaving Billy on his own, I'm swept along into Jona's wander-struck ways.

IT IS A land of smiling farmers and the greenest of green hills, a land where 3 million people manage 60 million sheep and 20 million cows. A land, it is boasted (although it seems that never would a Kiwi boast), that grows the best grass in the world.

We hike along narrow country roads that wind throughout the luscious landscape, eager to discover what lies around the next bend. Rides are so plentiful that putting out our thumbs is moot. We are often brought miles out of our driver's way. The superb hospitality of New Zealanders rouses the inevitable comparison: how would a Kiwi be received in *my* homeland? We Canadians are not oafs. No, we're not so bad. But these Kiwis are freakin' *good*.

When we do ride it seems a loss to move so fast. Every gentle hillock and steaming pile of cow shit possesses wondrous luminosity. We cross numerous one-lane bridges over tinkling creek beds. Along drainage ditches and in moist depressions in lush fields, wild growths of sub-tropical plants with giant leaves could pass for gardens planted with love by stoned pasture elves. Old wooden shacks and clean, well-kept homesteads are spaced equitably over the land. After the desensitizing hiss of the mill our aimless walking, with each step, acts like an eraser on the past.

But there's always something ahead. We stride like young tykes, our backs to the traffic, oblivious to the hitchhiking or to where we'll end up. Jona, more traveled and already tempered into the unstuck ways of the quasi-mystical highway of the mind, describes how he finds whatever he needs, when he needs it: "No kidding. I think, 'Hey, I need a comb,' then—there's a comb right there, man. And next day it's, 'Hey, y' know, I think I need some sunglasses.' Wow! There, *right there,* sunglasses! Then I think, 'Gee, I need a pen,' and I look over and…" Yeah. Jona's path meanders wondrously through his land of plenty where the in and out do a suggestive tango. The nature of personal reality is hidden in plain sight within the spell of consciousness, whatever its truth, wherever it might lead.

And however one chooses—even, it appears, unknowingly.

HARRY IS A blond, bearded beekeeper in his thirties who decides to pick us up and offer his home for the night. We drive to a white wooden house nestled in a cozy cleft on a hillside covered in a variegated carpet of handsome shrubs, long grasses with wildflowers, and the odd clump of small trees. Covers of children's books try to look this good.

Harry bears the serious demeanor of a seeker of truth, or at least of a decent alternative to the mainstream variety. He tells us about the vital properties of bee pollen and natural honey, from which he makes an adequate living with his hives. Bee pollen: the seed of flowers. Flowers: a colorful life form with male and female parts, they say, but no penis/vagina setup. Could be called "flower pollen" or simply "pollen." *I'll have some of that there pollen stuff, sir beekeeper dude.*

His large (also blond) and energetic dog seems merely to suffer my presence. It seems also, from his appraising, sidelong glances, that Harry is inclined to trust the dog. Who can deny the intuition of a dumb animal? I'm judged by inscrutable powers of nature, which, in turn, nourishes the long-suffering hunch that I am indeed a being of questionable content. I ponder the dog's view, his apparent distaste for my very essence. Eventually, I wind up sympathizing with him and Harry. Ever since I first heard of him in grade school, Socrates has been one of my heroes. I would name that dog Socrates.

We leave the next morning after a delicious breakfast of muesli topped with little balls of flower sperm. The dog lies in a corner staring at me as if he's had some weird dreams and I was in them.

WE ENJOY A glorious interlude standing next to a lighthouse on the top of the hill at Cape Reinga, at New Zealand's northern tip. Here two seas meet in a turbulent boil of great power. Their distinct currents, one darker than the other, chop and converge in a frothy soup. Hundreds of gulls and crows and other feathered friends squawk and shift in the crosswinds. Jona jumps like Carefree Batman down the bank toward the crash and spray of sea upon stone. I'm held fast on the hilltop by the cackle and howl of the wind's latest song, its mere whisper bending trees as it whistles past my ears. It's a moment of great power and simplicity that cradles (and could destroy, in an afternoon) our small and messy human world. *My* world, where the visible path is overgrown with the mystery of love and adventure, of attachment and loneliness. The trusty boundaries of self also show up here in this grand pocket of wind, land, and sea as I stand dumb and high on this hilltop... even the medium-sized baboon (with no mate and no meat) pauses off to the side of the pack to turn his face to the sky and hoot triumphantly. I've seen it on *Wild Kingdom.*[4] Coming from a pack of sorts, I know its unlikely gift.

JONA AND I ramble down the northern reach of the North Island, stopping here and there along a small length of New Zealand's stunning, almost 7,000 miles of pristine coastline.

We stop also at the home of a young woman to fan their continuing flame. I am chaste, for Danna will soon arrive. Late at night while Jona lies with his babe I sit alone in the living room, companion to the fire's dying embers. Questions load up my mood and challenge me to find the relevance of this whipped-out trip. I relish the odd, solitary moment, as I did my visits to the river in Kawerau. In this there's a measure of peace, and presumed clarity. And I have been (as I still am) grateful for the companionship of first Billy, then Jona.

In parks and along the seashore, young travelers gather to sing, tell stories, and get high in circles around the magnet of fire. Most travelers are from New Zealand and Australia. A few are from Canada, the States, England, Scotland, Ireland. English speakers, mostly.

The past two weeks on the road with Jona have quickened my senses. He seems to drift among tanned limbs and smiling faces that swim in his wide, ready eyes. I too am happily absorbed in this cradle-of-life setting in the subtropical reaches of northern New Kiwi, my first taste of the wayward life across the big sea.

Danna

Danna and her willing limbs arrive on schedule. Jona flies off to Oz after a brief but intense reunion with his little sis.

For us lovebirds, nine weeks anticipating the return of our private delight has brought its reward. Her perfect match to my BC-made, down-filled bag—*zip!*—becomes our mobile master bed. Over the next eight months we crisscross the two islands of Kiwi. Our path turns and climbs as we come to know the sweet and the bitter of rookie love cast adrift—its past, its imagined future, and most curious of all, its slippery present.

---

4   *Wild Kingdom,* a popular wildlife TV show that aired from 1963–1987.

MANY AND VARIED are the youth hostels of New Zealand. On capes and on mountains, overlooking the ocean or in forests, many are secluded and await our arrival.

On the north coast of the Coromandel Peninsula, an old wooden mansion with tall rooms is surrounded by ancient deciduous trees through which shots of the nearby ocean tease our view. A marshy wetland teems with all kinds of fantastically noisy birds. Ahh, these birds of New Zealand, with their whistles, beeps, and cloings, their buzzing, chirping, pinging, and howling. We look up into the leaves seeking the source of the complex and tantalizing sounds. Clocks spring apart and broken bells ring mysteriously. One of the local varieties is called a bell-bird. This has to be a bird watcher's—and listener's—paradise. It is said that there were no land animals on the islands before humans arrived, only a few small lizards and birds, some, like the humble kiwi himself, flightless and docile.[5] Perhaps news of this Eden of Birdland traveled far and wide throughout avian havens, and New Zealand became a favorite home and holiday spot for all sorts of feathered folk. Maybe Kiwi liked it so much he lost track of where he came from, got comfy near bushes and twigs, and forgot how to fly.

One bird performs an aural parade, a smash-hit medley of songs strung two-by-two and without pause. Every call is radically different from the last, and always they are doubled. A tuneful montage of springs, boings, clanks, gongs, and quick little ditties fills the woods as we listen, spellbound. It is the melody of earth in bird-land, a roll call for a good five minutes, a holy musical heralding the first sailing of the Ark. We are witness to a genius songstress gracing the forest friends with a view of all her lands, of fickle breezes and ruffled wing.

In this hostel guys and gals are separated. I lie in a narrow bunk, the top one, a good ten or twelve feet off the floor. *Do not roll over.* Maybe it's the weirdo birds, or maybe it's the fear of falling. I must have read about it somewhere, but in my private shadow of mind, I listen. I listen to the wind whispering through trees. I listen to the house creaking under its own weight as it creeps toward the marshland. To my breath,

---

5   The now-extinct moa, the world's biggest bird, hailed from these parts. Ten feet tall and weighing over 600 pounds, it would have dwarfed the ostrich of today.

to the other guys breathing and farting below me, to the twitching in my brain. I feel the pulse in my chest, the buzzing of my hot feet, the hum of my organs and flesh as they perform their faithful services. The moisture on my eyeballs, slightly burning. *So much goin' on.*

Don't think I ever really noticed before. *Very relaxing.* Big.

ON THE SOUTH Island we save some money working in a Christchurch clothing factory. Even though Danna and I work across from each other cutting out football jersey patterns for the same overseas orders, she is paid considerably less because she's a *she*. Such unabashed chauvinism surprises us, so we talk about it with our coworkers. But this elicits nothing more than a resigned admission that, yes, it does seem rather unfair. As if the thought had never occurred before. Ultimately, our pinko-commie talk goes largely unnoticed.

What *I* notice is that our little corner of this sprawling textile enterprise is populated with accomplished musicians. I count nine out of fourteen or fifteen workers, as if my musical past has predisposed me to find a harmonic cluster in the seniority list of a New Zealand football jersey factory. A thirty-five-year-old Māori, Paul, plays guitar and sings. *Have ya met a Māori who doesn't?* Tiri, a lady of about fifty, plays guitar, banjo, and mandolin. Les, about forty, has been playing guitar for ten years and now teaches it. Superintendent Rick, thirty-five and also Māori, has done guitar work in recording studios in Australia. He also sings and plays trumpet and trombone. Lynn, twenty-six, has worked with a folk group. Marylin, thirty-five, plays piano. Don, eighteen, plays piano and organ. Reiss, also eighteen, plays bass. And a visiting Canuck... is by now doing a better job of noticing quirky patterns than performing music.

OUR MOST RELAXED Kiwi times are spent at the well-ordered homestead of Jona and Danna's Uncle Keith. He acquired the land for next to nothing after World War II. Like other Kiwis he was the beneficiary of a government program of colonial nation building and wealth distribution. *Pinko-Commies.*

In the southeastern region of the North Island, in the open spaces of his rolling paddocks, I look square into the blank face of sheephood, get a fix. Once the threshold of interspecies boundaries is breached, the chase begins. Like a skinny jackal I'm in for the slow ones. I get pretty good at cornering them, but unlike the jackal I'm not lured by the stink of hot flesh. Instead I'm driven to see just one more desperate pop of the "bleat-spring"—trapped among his brethren and with no wiggle room, the humble, wooly being is capable of surprisingly potent, straight-up leaps, as if spring-loaded. Seems an unholy disregard for Newton and his cocksure *Principia* law.[6] At times I see Danna and Keith standing on a distant ridge, the poise in their silhouette indicating they're watching me, or concerned, or both. Soon I return, all normal-like. What's cool is… no questions asked. So genteel, so WASP-y. My Italia folks would've yelled a dozen brash questions by the time I was barely in earshot: "Hey, whadda-the-hella-ya do a-there jumpa-like a crazy a-feesh a-stupid-a dinga-donga onna da land?" Something like that.

We come to know the true story of our carnivorous ways without the camouflage of conveniently isolated slaughterhouses and neat supermarket packaging. The reality of killing is gruesome, but at least it's experienced honestly here. On the farm, eating meat is a transparent, responsible affair. We see exactly what it means. Not to mention the fresher, better taste.

Keith kills and butchers one for a meal. As he cuts up the bloody carcass I'm intrigued by the calm aura of this hospitable and admirably reticent man. His ruddy face is relaxed and set with a barely perceivable grin, the fleshy imprint of many such rituals performed over a lifetime. One hears of the therapeutic benefit butchers enjoy on the sly. *Weirdos.*

Danna and I meander our way to Keith's farm several times, drawn as we are like pilgrims to his sanctuary of rolling pastures, and to his guileless warmth.

We have no plans. We drift along roads that remain, for us, nameless. We don't know where or how far we'll go. Gradually, as the months pass, we taste the bittersweet sprouts of change that, as so easily happens on the road, arise within and between even good lovers. Our highway of love winds and climbs and falls, and is often rough. Occasionally, we coast along easily. As each stretch of our connection is felt and faced there comes, unexpected and with grace, a corresponding expansion of experience.

6   Isaac Newton's seminal work on gravity, *Principia Naturalis*

AND YET, LIKE a couple of fresh-hatched turtles we are compulsive, half blind, and stumbling. Like them we seem to chase the sun on some undeclared faith in "the chase" itself.

What little I can admit to knowing these days includes the fact we've just crossed the widest of oceans. I know also that it is July, and Down Under this means that these lush rains are winter rains.

I'll have a look at this past year, a snappy one indeed, maybe shake down some of the comings and doings of us triumphant monkey-folk in these modern times. I like to yank my head up once in a while, have a look-see at the ongoing storylines.

But if facts and figures aren't your thing, go ahead and skip past the fine print.

The World, 1974

3.782 billion humans crowd together here and there, increasingly soiling many of its finest locales.

Some rather optimistic scientists beam a three-minute radio greeting from our largest radio dish into the cosmos, translated into binary pulses depicting the numbers one to ten, the hydrogen atom, DNA, our solar system, and male/female human stick figures. A subsequent outcry over revealing Earth's whereabouts to superior and perhaps carnivorous species results in radio astronomers agreeing to never expose us to this risk again. (*But never mind, because all our inane TV shenanigans and radio claptrap are also continuously and forever travel-ing outward from our dear blue marble, easily locatable with elementary extrapolations by any race of aliens with the techno-equivalent of the opposing thumb.*)

With a new theory on black holes and a fraternal salute to Albert E. (from *his* shoulder,) the brash young Stephen Hawking states, "God not only plays dice, but also throws them where they cannot be seen."

With uncharacteristic fear and distrust of the unknown, scientists self-impose a moratorium on gene splicing (lasts two years.)

The USSR lands a space probe on Mars. *Mariner 10* sends some nice shots from Venus and Mercury.

The CAT scan is developed.

Seven years after incorrectly stating that LSD causes chromosomal damage, US scientists announce that cannabis causes brain damage.

The hominid fossil "Lucy" is found in Ethiopia. The much later, 40,000-year-old Mungo Man skeleton is unearthed in New South Wales, Australia, supporting the "everyone comes from Africa" model.

Fritz-Albert Popp proves the existence of biophotons, tiny "particles" of light emitted from all living tissue.

Baron Von Reding Biberegg becomes the first known Westerner to be eaten by a Komodo dragon.

POLITICAL LEADERS ARE invited to the Davos Congress Center in Switzerland for the first time. They join business leaders in discussing economic and social issues.

Surprisingly, the Watergate scandal surprises the American conscience.

"Moonie" boss Sun Myung Moon supports (Watergate principal) President Richard Milhous Nixon, who publicly thanks Moon and then officially receives him.

After the political demise of Richard Nixon, Gerald Ford signs Public Law 93-373, which restores the right of US citizens to own gold, erasing Roosevelt's prohibition, the Gold Act of 1933.

The *New York Times* alleges that the CIA conducted illegal experiments on US citizens during the 1960s, one year after CIA director Richard Helms ordered all MKUltra files destroyed.

In the Middle East, Henry Kissinger does some of his finest kissing.

OPEC becomes a gang. The "energy crisis" grips the West while Big Oil drools over a 93 percent increase in net profits. *Yo, capitalism!*

India detonates a nuclear bomb made from "peaceful" materials.

The Kurds seize some Iraqi land. Turkey invades Cyprus.

Hundreds of thousands die in the Bangladeshi famine. Hundreds of thousands die in the Ethiopian famine.

In the USSR, Solzhenitsyn is exiled.

Twenty-nine years after the end of WWII, a Japanese soldier emerges from a Filipino jungle with hundreds of rounds of ammo and hand grenades. His direct superior, now a city bookseller, is tracked down to release him from duty.

IN PHILADELPHIA, THE city of brotherly love, Episcopal priests break the rules and ordain eleven women into their ranks.

In Canada, the RCMP hires female officers for the first time.

The APA nixes homosexuality from its list of mental disorders.

Patty Hearst disappears; the word "brainwash" trickles through the gray matter of millions (immediately, ruts form.)

The movies *The Towering Inferno, Blazing Saddles,* and *Young Frankenstein* are released.

First mainstream soft porn film: *Emmanuelle.*

The books *Zen and the Art of Motorcycle Maintenance, Helter Skelter* and *The Diary of Anais Nin* are published.

The game Dungeons and Dragons hits the shelves.

The Bermuda Triangle enters the public imagination.

The albums *Before the Flood, Born to Run, Pretzel Logic,* and *Court and*

Spark are released.

"Streaking" takes America by its great white ass.

A ten-pack of chewing gum is the first product to be sold with a barcode.

IN BRITISH COLUMBIA, the NDP is defeated, ending, as *Newsweek* put it, "the most significant rule yet of a socialist party in North America."

Auckland, New Zealand, enjoys zero unemployment.

2. Oz

It's Alright, Ma[7]

Rendezvous

Heading north out of Sydney we're off again into the cool unknown. The train makes many stops and eventually, as the city thins into eucalyptus wilds, a northbound highway flashes through the intermittent green. We spot a good stretch, pull the cord and step off.

Within minutes of thumbing a car pulls over, and—holy-moly— Jona is in the passenger seat. The last time we saw him was in Kawerau eight or nine months ago. Hitchhiking as well, he told his driver, probably in a panic, to pull over. Danna knew he was somewhere in the eastern half of Australia, and he must have known we weren't far behind from Kiwi way. Yet it seems a wonderful synchrony that our paths should converge so precisely, if only considering our serendipitous choice of when to pull that cord.

We burst into a chatter fest that must sound to the poor Aussie like chipmunks high on some good bud going down that first hill on a roller coaster. Our madcap racket gradually subsides into a tenderness that reaches back as only a brother and sister, who share things beyond memory itself, can reach. I sit next to them, but I might as well be in a car going the other way. Their renewed bond creates a self-contained field of safety and love that I can only witness.

When the highway cozies up to a golden beach we say goodbye to our frazzled driver. We'll stretch our legs and catch up in the spray of wild surf, for we have no reason to do anything in particular on this fine gift of a day.

---

7   From the song "It's Alright, Ma (I'm Only Bleeding)" by Bob Dylan.

The beach is brilliant and wide and all ours, an alabaster coastline far beyond any horizon we gazed into as kids. Not a straggler in sight. Danna and Jona plop themselves down, fully engaged, hungry for evidence. *Are you okay? Does the world change us? What about our "fixed" past? Where will you go? Will we see each other again?* I put my own words into their eyes as I watch them, bouncing questions off the bubble of their excitement and wonder. They could use some time alone.

Down the shore I feel content and hopeful. I look back at them now and then, as if getting a clearer look at my own singularity. What *is* my place? Here we are—me, my girl, her brother/my bro—on the surface of a lonely but brilliant marble spinning away, one day in a thousand.

Yes, my singularity! Alone did I decide to travel!

Before starting this trip, after Danna and I parted ways, I accepted the loss of her beauty, kindness, and intelligence. After a brief turn in the murky shadow of lost-love I came up free and hungry. I went to the student union office at Simon Fraser University and scammed myself a phony student card. I used it to buy a discounted plane ticket to Auckland, New Zealand, that was to leave from Seattle. A foreboding that something amazing, something perhaps even unimaginable might *not* happen, drove me to the ticket counter.

Then Danna and I met up again, serendipitously, in the company of friends. And we dove back in. Deep. It became *our* hungry change. But... watch out, little Danna, little Johnny. What is it, exactly, that you wish for? For a certain eventuality, as if from a singularity in *my* psyche, had already sprouted its vigorous little germ. Danna's coming on this journey turned out to be... I have to say it, at least to myself: an afterthought. Yikes. *Fuck!*

Just before leaving, an ex-girlfriend asked me *why* I was going. *Good question.* All I could come up with was, "Well, not for, umm... a holiday." I was hesitant and unsure what I meant, or had just said. But she seemed to understand. And so maybe am I beginning to, just now. If words had been snappier, I'd have waxed on about removing myself from home to better see my "real" self, corny as it would have sounded even then. I was haunted by the hunch that much of what we think of as our personality is a conditional form, an attractively arranged bundle of emotional idiosyncrasies, self-conscious projections, and second-hand impressions.[8] Some are artfully done, and with great power and flare. Others are fractured and buckling under the stresses of poor construction. *But I love my friends.* I'd have said that we're moved like puppets by underlying, mostly unconscious beliefs, feelings, and group-spawned agreements… that we are, arguably, convincing works of fiction steering flesh and blood through day and night, sharing what joy and honesty we can muster, but also passing along our pain and biases. *But I love my family.* And that we hardly think on our own, never mind in any original way. *Ouch.* A strange lot, we humans, building mutual ghosts in physical mirage, doing our best to dodge life's arrows, creating bonds with what love we know how to hold and give, and frequently (most of the time, actually) retreating into the bittersweet privacy of separateness. *Hard gig, this EarthTime.* I'd have rambled on about the wider world's web of images and mutually recreated images, about its unstoppable systems, its long memory, and its short attention span. *But I love my Earth.* Even its best feature, the love of family and friends, shared in that web—I would leave that behind, too. Somehow, weirdly, it is the love for my home, for my family and friends, and the security I feel… that has enabled me to leave it all behind. Something is driving me, on the slimmest of hopes, across an ocean of ignorance.

That's what I would have said to my old flame if I'd known how. No, I didn't have the words on my tongue back then but I felt every one, felt their depth and their aim.[9] It's uncanny, especially regarding early

8   The Latin word *persona* means "mask," from the Etruscans, and comes to English
     as "person."

9   We can look back at a situation, at key moments in life, and remember how we
     felt, and that the perception of the situation was complex, or maybe, in a way,
     "complete." And we might not have been able then to put any of it into words. Or,
     more astonishing, words were not yet developed in the child-brain. But the
     character and meaning of the situation were there. Long after this idea
     ("understanding" a situation *before* the development of language) continued to
     intrigue me, some clarity on the matter came by way of R. A. Masters' *Darkness
     Shining Wild.* In Ch. 6, reference is made to the development of the amygdala,
     which is associated with emotional memory, and precedes the development of the
     hippocampus, associated with cognitive memory.

memories before speech has found its "pivots on the tongue."[10]

But it was my gut that had the last word: *Travel, boy, and you'll get a better look at the whole shebang.* So I listened, restless and hungry as I was like so many children of cosmic love and psychedelic freedom. But I was not confused, at least not as an experience of confusion. *What you're looking for... is what is looking.* That's what St. Francis said. Maybe I'd be going about it in a roundabout way, but my hunch was that ducking into the unknown would provide a better view of *whoever is looking.*

Mulling over these matters on this most glorious beach ever, I suppose I've stumbled, slipped off the conveyor. I'm sure I must look dumbfounded, staring down as I am at the licking waves as if they are speaking in a special tongue just for me. I straighten my spine and saunter back up the beach.

I rejoin them just as Jona is giving Danna a stone he picked from the sand, a small one with a white vein shaped in a "D." *Sweet, ubiquitous love.* Her eyes shine tender and insecure. Her gleaming black hair flips and sails in the breeze, all but obscuring her smiling face. She's wearing a flimsy skirt, and her voluptuous charms all but overcome me. *I would have every inch of her.* It is a hunger I am rarely free of, something that feels beyond my choosing.

Just before my departure we'd experienced a renaissance of tenderness. I loved her body, her kindness, her sharp mind. And her fears, her insights. She was gentle, and I was a bit of a feel-good boor. At least with her I let myself be that free. When I spoke too quickly, a tad foolish or perhaps echoing something we'd heard before, she'd say, "Yes, but what do *you* think, Johnny?" And I wondered, *Yeah, what the freakin' jazz do I think?* She was unaccountably curious about me. Or maybe it was a deliberate, delicate probing. In the healing balm of her attentions, something inside winked awake.

But now something else burns inside, another desire altogether.

Psychofats

Parting ways with Jona again, Danna and I continue up the coast toward Cairns, a thousand miles away in the tropics. We've heard about

10   From Walt Whitman: "My tongue is ineffectual on its pivots... I become a dumb man."

hothead Queensland, the Texas of Oz. *Somepin' in d' heat make d' folk go a lil' wacky.*

Immediately after crossing the border it appears that all highway signs are peppered with bullet holes, as if a certain clutch and gear in the brain gets to slipping upon crossing a conceptual line and a social mania is turned loose across the land. Thumbs out, we head into the ancient emptiness of outback Australia.

A trucker pulls over. Pink faced and slack eyed, his look taps a prejudice labeled "redneck." But he seems jolly enough. We climb in and he offers a drink. I'm grateful and guzzle mine in one go. *Whew! Hot.* Finishing his, he flings the empty out the window—*plink*—adding to the endless glass shard shoulder. Barreling down the highway, a strobe fest of little rainbows whips up from the ground in parabolic splendor parallel to the moving eye. Our stolid benefactor notices *(shit!)* that I'm holding my empty between my thighs.

"Throw it out," he says.

"Naw, it's okay. I'll just wait'll we get to a town and dump it in a bin," I offer.

"Naw, throw it out," he says a little louder. Danna fidgets.

"No, really, I don't mind holding it."

"Throw it out!" *Bye-bye, chit-chat.* Sitting in the crossfire, Danna pokes me.

"Really man, I mean it, it's no problem!" My vapid sincerity is all I've got.

"THROW IT OUT!" Freakin' flipped out nuts and breathing for three, he strangles the steering wheel in two places. I look at the razor-edged twinkle drops on the side of the road, at the barren earth that surrounds and will digest us in an afternoon. The impact I'll have on this sweating turd of a man, much less on this timeworn land, is nonexistent.

I hurl my empty out the window. The beast relaxes, steering wheel A-OK. Danna is relieved as well, because now we won't have to *die.* Within a few more awkward miles we come upon a town and guess what? It's exactly where we're headed. *Thanks for the ride, Mr. Psychofats.*

We walk along the main street. It's a sunny midmorning but no one is out. There's a face in a window, an old gray-haired woman peeking out between sheer curtains. Another face attached to a tall, plump, squinty-eyed man (nice breasts) peers out at us, bolder than the woman. Looks like Psychofats' older cousin. The more we look, the more stiff-faced apparitions of modernity appear lurking within this popular mirage of civilization. We move along our brief tour of Dante's *Il Purgatorio di Whitey*, preternaturally bound toward a more heavenly place (so we hope.)

Within minutes a cop pulls up. "You'll have to come with me." *Redneck town, psycho-conservative hellhole.* Phone call from one of the window cells back on Main Street? Danna is nervous, but I feel my dignity's being hauled in for a spanking. I can get mouthy when pushed.

At the station the cop is polite, if one can call the stolid silences that follow my cocky questions and jabs polite. Perhaps our foreign accents provide a measure of grace. And perhaps he's beginning to wonder if I'm not a bit of a Canucklehead pain-in-the-ass. His self-control as he performs his so-called peacekeeping is impressive. He looks at our passports and scribbles this and that as I study the tightly wound muscles in his turkey-pink face and neck. *Harsh sun Down Under.* Time and again I protest that our basic rights are being trammelled in the muck of this sorely wasted time.

He turns and leaves at once. We exit the station, and hey, there's the highway.

We've been formally introduced to Queensland.

Wild Jack Pentax

You won't get far in Oz without hearing about a certain seventy-mile stretch of highway. Devoid of settlement and thickly wooded, it's where a number of young travelers have been killed over the years. The stranglings, shootings, gorings—and just over a week ago, a decapitation—have earned this road a grisly name lost in the fog of memory. Hitchhiking farther up the coast, closing in on this zone of mayhem, a couple of our drivers are positively delighted in relating details of a few bloody incidents.

We're tense as we enter the infamous stretch in the car of our most zealous raconteur, an excitable middle-aged guy all wrapped in the local narrative. Given the lack of settlements, I figure he'll take us to the next town, safely beyond. But smack in the middle of the stretch of death there's a turnoff to the coast, just where our jolly bloke "must drop you kids off." His buoyant smirk as he pulls over indicates that he's pleased with his performance. I'd bet the jerk is staging a strategic U-route back to the highway, doing his bit to promote the region's reputation.

Danna and I stand at the unmarked intersection. The sound of the motor fades into the surrounding silence, a muffled limbo like some lurking menace that holds us still. In every direction, dense eucalyptus forest disappears into a flatland of haze. There is no traffic. Then a car passes, only one. It's the main route north, but this is the freakin' "wild" in wilderness.

From within the forest we hear twigs snapping at a crawling, predatory pace. Danna and I stand close together. Fifteen meters ahead a young man emerges from the thicket and creeps toward us. He's wearing a straw hat and red backpack. With a few more steps, a glint of metal: a long machete hangs by his side in a clenched hand. His pink cheeks glisten from tears that drip from his chin. He's less than ten meters away; we are dead still. The time for words is... *not now, not yet.* Even from this distance it's clear that his eyes are intense and red. *Overfilled inner tube, pipes hissing...* Maybe he's on a bad psychedelic trip. *Maybe he's crazy.* Danna's arm trembles against mine. All I feel is curiosity and a tinge of compassion; I'm aware that fear would only mess things up. The guy is a walking contradiction: vulnerable in a grasping-a-machete-with-tears-running-down kind of way. And he has just emerged from a nameless thicket. Yet I just don't feel danger. Call me a fool.

He stops, looks down at his machete, then at us—sobbing gently—then down at his machete again, then up at us... and in one motion he raises it, turns, and flings it back into the bush with all his strength. Emotions flood his body. His head slumps, and his shoulders bob as he weeps. *How did this torrent of emotion begin? Why does he cry in our presence?*

I walk over, Danna close behind, and I embrace him. He mutters in choked-up phrases that he's going through a breakdown or catharsis, and that *we* are "good." He keeps telling us how nice, how *good* we are. We've done nothing. Maybe that's what he needs. And means.

Carefully, I ask questions.

"Wellington, New Zealand. Jack."

We offer our company hitchhiking to the next town. Even with three large backpacks and little traffic, a car stops in minutes. The next town is Mackay.

BY EVENING WE'VE found a pleasant campground overlooking a slow river. At dusk the colorful decor of the streets and dry warmth has me relaxing on a Mediterranean coast, knowing little and wanting less. After pitching our tents I find Jack sitting on a log bouncing a Pentax camera and a couple of lenses in his hands. He gazes into the dark river some forty feet below. I park myself beside him.

"I should throw 'em in." His face is still flushed in the aftermath of high feelings. The day's late rays shine on his skin, highlighting thin red lines that trace tiny river systems over his puffy cheeks and tawny splotches that spread over his neck. "Gonna throw 'em in."

"Don't do that. Just give 'em to me," I caw, edging closer to the shiny objects. I am flippant and hopeful, yet I assume he has no real intention of throwing away his fine camera gear.

But when I say, "Give 'em to me," his eyes dash into mine, opening fully and then squinting, like I've just hit upon the perfect ruse. He declares that if I don't take the stuff right now, he'll throw it all in. He opens the back of the camera and removes—ruins—the film. Befuddled, grateful, and amazed, I take the loot and fly.

The next morning, Jack seems relaxed. I reckon we've witnessed a convulsive crisis, one day in the life. He's psychologically tender, vulnerable. The night's rest seems to have brought out in him kind and receptive, childlike qualities. But his levity is overcome by a brief pall when his eyes fall on the camera that hangs proud from my neck. In the comings and doings of morning camp activities, I put it away. Between his oddball anxiety and my acquisitive delight it seems the prudent thing to do. His energy feels tense yet appreciative as he aims nervous smiles our way.

Now that our psycho storm has passed, I venture a question: "Hey, man, have you taken anything to get high in the past week?" When curious, I often enjoy a glorious lack of subtlety and get right to the point (thx Mom and Dad.) From his raw openness, I'm thinking he's coasting in the tailwind of some high-dose psychedelic trauma. He hasn't spoken much since the river and camera incident.

"No," he says, his voice dropping low for a moment, as if to close the subject. *Okay, bud.*

Late morning we put our packs on and wave goodbye. I don't expect to see him again. I could offer to return the camera, but... *hmm.* Never has a lens hung so long and steady. *What handsome girth has this fine tunnel of glass.* I'm a stooge to its cocky throb as I walk.

The next day there's a town party. The main street is clear of cars and teeming with festive townsfolk. We meet again, crossing the main road in different directions. Looking up and away—he might as well be walking backwards—Jack bumps straight into me. When he sees us, he is momentarily disoriented. I assumed he'd left town after we parted, and perhaps he'd made the same assumption about us. His face falls into shadow.

Immediately, and brimming with noble conscience, I hold up the camera. "Here, take it. You must regret giving it away." I'm talking about a Pentax pro camera setup with assorted lenses and filters. He's startled to see me—and positively desperate when his eyes fall on the camera.

"No!" Like a man obsessed, he disappears into the crowd, hunched over and walking backward, hands outstretched, his eyes fixed maniacally on the camera. *Goodbye, Jack dude.*

Under today's strange and auspicious Aussie sky, I accept the camera as fully mine.

SO WHAT HAPPENED immediately prior to our weird meeting on that empty highway? What was it called... Murder Row? We'd heard the news: a decapitation over a week ago. *Machete?*

After he hurled the machete into the bush and broke into uncontrollable sobbing, I felt the good work of healing spark alive. *Don't kick at the wound,* I told myself, *See the spark of light in his eyes, see that he recognizes something "good" in us.* I reckon we have a natural, self-preserving sense, Danna and I, one that precludes poking around below the surface looking for madness and such. In these trauma-jacked moments we might take things at face value just to survive.

Camera? Film?

Later on, Danna told me that when I was away for a few minutes back at the campsite the next morning, Jack said he had something to tell her. Danna, being one of the bodacious feminine elite, took him to mean he was smitten with her. Can't blame her, and maybe she was right. If not, perhaps we're lucky she made the wrong assumption and diverted the conversation.

Folks speak of evil, they certainly do. But all I see is pain and its contorting effects. Perhaps in fearing darkness—or in resisting it, as The Nazarene famously said long ago—we engage and even build it. And when we don't, when we "love our enemies," it might just pass us by.

APPROACHING CAIRNS WE are on the road again, thumbs out.

We've heard one too many stories about psychopaths and death. Perhaps our time with Wild Jack has roused some surreal activity below the surface of things. Danna and I have a little chat and agree that when the next car pulls over, if the driver appears even remotely "off," we will make an excuse and refuse the ride.

That car is a dented-up station wagon. We walk up and look inside. The young man behind the wheel looks like he went mad about a week ago and has found comfort in his brand new prison. He slouches in his seat and looks like he hasn't bathed in weeks. Portraits of lizards and snakes flit through my mind. I see him springing forth at any moment in the reptilian gulp leap, with me the gulpee and Danna some fine-ass dessert. His eyes are slack and dopey, and his face seems to hang desensitized from the bone. He speaks with the drawling cadence of an illiterate. I look down the empty highway, at the beautifully sunlit but lethal countryside. Deadly snakes with a rare, mad delight in chasing and killing people... mortally venomous spiders that jump ten, twelve feet... rabid, toddler-snatching dingoes. Danna and I glance at each other with the initiative of caged rabbits. We gulp down our clever pep talk and climb in like zombies over their buried will.

Turns out our young driver is an affable enough bloke, although I'm nearer the mark on the simpleton part. Says he grew up on an outback station. A few sentences in and it's clear the fella is oblivious to the world beyond his isolated speck on the map.

"Gee, it must be great living in the tropics," I offer, making small talk. I am delighted he doesn't seem at all like the serial killer type.

"Wot's that?" he drawls.

"You mean 'tropics'? That's the hot places near the equator, around the middle of the Earth most directly facing the sun," I natter, absently tossing a family of whacked-out concepts into his low-lying fog. I'm feeling relaxed and talkative, grooving on the big-scale imagery and enjoying the "conversation." He nods flaccidly, apparently recognizing stuff. Encouraged, I tell him I'm thinking of making the trip over the narrow sea to Asia. His station is near the city of Darwin, which faces the Indonesian archipelago, so I figure he's heard of Asia.

"Ayshja? Wa... wot's Ayshja?"

In a peculiar way we soon feel safe with him and, I guess, he with us. Perhaps he too had a crazy idea, wondering if he'd stopped for a couple of vampires posing as wholesome young foreigners.

Near the end of our ride with him I mention, during my buoyant monologue, that it's not such a bad old car. With a kind of dazed wonder he perks up, shifts in his seat and turns to me. "You want I should give you my car? You want the car? Take the car." *What? Why?*

Remembering Jack's camera I feel odd, flattered, and self-conscious, in a trickster-Gaia-having-me-on kind of way. Intelligent and fond of practical jokes, maybe she's been onto us lately. And perhaps, like Wild Jack, this guy's starting to like us cuz we're good.

"Naw, you better keep it."

He drops us off on the outskirts of Cairns.

One Bubble

For the past year on these austral roads I've been privately toying with an adventure through Asia. I refer to it indirectly in conversation with Danna a few times, skirting the issue of commitment to our almost-three-year relationship. *Right, like the time it slipped into conversation with the simple guy in the wagon.* The intimations of a cross-Asia trip are awkward reminders of a dream come true: my initial, solitary one. Danna has known all along. She came traveling to follow our dream together, the dream that began so tender and true after we split and reunited. That was just before I was to leave, my plans already made. But I suspect she wanted to get away from her boring home life too. The real thing is, my vagabond dream has eaten away at our connection.

When I stumble into the awkward subject of my fascination with Asia she doesn't say much, gives a cool reaction. Given her intuitive clarity she's probably known for some time that we're done. I can only guess at how she's grown weary with the ongoing discontent in our partnership and with my vague, intermittent references to a singular journey. If there's a psychic glue that holds couples together I'd bet that something in the traveling life tends to act as a rapid solvent. Especially if the arrangement is open ended, without explicit commitment to each other as in marriage or raising children. For over a year we've drifted among smiling strangers in the stimulating milieu of new lands. A blooming of mental activity, as natural for the traveler as fresh green after rain, has quickened in us both, each in our own way. Even a couple as compatible as Danna and I can become unmoored and directionless when so far from home.[11]

Somewhere along the way, as we cruise the roads Down Under, our story has come to the question of when, and not if we will part company. *Sad.* We're held together by a fading dream, the unfamiliar surroundings of a foreign country, and the always magnetic libido. But we must move on, like getting up and walking after sitting too long. From age thirteen I've pretty much always had a female partner. When we were nineteen Danna became my sixth girlfriend. Just sayin'.

Might be time for a break.

WE HEAD SOUTH to Canberra, capital of Oz.

The more I look at my way of loving Danna, the more it is emotional addiction, plain and true. It's no different than high school with that girl, or *that* girl. I didn't go broadcasting it, but each separation felt like high-anxiety abandonment. And now losing her lands me in the bleak unknown, drifting on a foreign horizon. Though this new solitary

---

11 Later in my travels, other couples I'd meet would be ungluing as well; at times, on a hunch that my presence might facilitate the action of the traveling solvent, I'd beat a hasty exit.

path has me scared crapless, I won't interfere with her desire to carry on without me. Self-respect alone demands it.

Back in New Zealand, traveling with Jona for a few weeks, I noticed and became curious about the differences in our attitudes toward involvement with women. I tend to jump in and "fall in love" while Jona seemed to exert some kind of control, as though detaching himself, to run a course of measured desire according to plan. I wondered: *Is it so easy to choose? This way or that?* And I made up a story: *If he can detach himself so easily, maybe he prevents himself from attaching, or "feeling it" as I do.*

Yes, of course. *But really.* Am I always the better? Maybe his is a wider understanding, and it's not Jona's but my own pet drama I meant, and mean, to address. I can admit now that I'm driven toward this or that beauty, something I replay and will become deeply attached to whenever falling in love is easy to imagine. Some kind of primal promise of heaven in the love of a woman, a union that would solve the riddle of separate existence with its antidote: sweet, romantic "oneness." And it will arrive as she finds me irresistible—and when her beauty suits *me*, of course.

I eventually conceded that it's possible to feel love strongly *and* to let go of it. Somehow, compared with my own compulsions, this seemed a bit more "sane". I climbed down from my spindly perch to admire Jona anew.

Yet I'm not so sure there is a "better" and a "worse" version of loving, not as can be compared, one person to another.

I determine to be free of my attachment to Danna's kindly *(check)*, intelligent *(check)*, and curvaceous *(check)* attributes. These matters of love, fear of its loss, and of being alone... For the sake of dignity alone there is but one choice: I will let her go.

Alas. We are two bubbles, our surfaces barely touching, coming unstuck in the caprices of a foreign wind. *So it goes.*

But we never lose our natural affection. Even as we part, I feel love and a sibling bond with Danna, whatever her path.

And compassion for all in our fleeting joy, and through our dark nights.

FIRST BILLY, THEN Jona, then Danna. Only now, after ten months in New Zealand and a few in Oz, am I alone. When two lovebirds split and fly solo it's "freedom", ready or not.

Not so ready, I move into a downtown room to lick my wounds in private. Two long, single-story row flats sit run down and dwarfed behind the modern concrete blocks of downtown Canberra. These are the green-and-white wooden structures of Reid House, a magnet for squatters of all kinds. One building has electricity and plumbing; here the units are rented. The other one is unserviced, abandoned.

I'm lucky to find an empty room boarded up at the hallway and window. I buy a latch and lock and break in, taking up temporary residence alongside dozens of homeless in the local hobo/hippie/junkie scene. Outside in overgrown grass amidst dumped debris I find a car seat and a broken table. With proper propping and placement these become my new furniture. Standing in the doorway I behold my new home: a dank room in near ruin. Abject, squalid, a tad ugly. *Good reflection.*

I withdraw from view into my dingy cell in surrender to an uncertain season of solitude. I want to hide away—I'm aghast at the prospect of suffering in public. The loss of my dear girl, even though it was my own doing... *For how long?* The question cannot be asked, for the heaviness of present misery far outweighs the luxury of digressions like pondering the future. I have no defence against the gloom I feel.

But the upside is, an experiential lid is blown wide. My personal and social cues are missing. No family, no friends. No one to say I should or should not be experiencing this, or be like that. Loneliness, melancholia, hold little tolerance for the masks we tend to wear "in public." I am the child I once was. The pages of the book of my life turn in the merciless breeze of an invisible storm. Pages, chapters, days, weeks, years... scenes and clues are released from some buried cell of being, clues as to how and why I feel what I feel, heartsick in the here and now. My strength, my buoyancy, have left me. The pain is plain—so ordinary, but dizzying. I'm the dust on the side of the road; the caravans on their ways to and fro into the grand vistas of life do not bother to notice.

Strings of early memories march along as if an irreverent St. Pete chucked the rules to torment me with an early preview, while he and his holy buddy saints enjoy a good guffaw. I could laugh too, but I'm not in the audience. The flashing scenes in this dark circus of time go on in repeating cycles for the better part of a week: an infant's head thrashing for a tit, being teased for this or that need, or catching shit for something I believed would earn praise and love, even adulation. Hiding in corners. The bully looms over the brood. The world is a huge, threatening, and terrifying place. The fighting, the yelling, the hitting and slapping; I can't tear away my eyes. The toddler screams... trucks and trains—what are these monstrous abominations? *Get me outta here!* These and untold, half-formed others spring into the spotlight from some buried store of records. It's all there, every moment of life recorded in the deep gray goo! *How?*

And yet all love me; not one reaches to personally abuse me. *How can this be?*

Clearly, my separation from Danna has triggered a tempest. I always have a book on the go; on the testimony of John Lennon from a magazine interview, I picked up *The Primal Scream.*[12] Primed as I am by what I am reading, these memories and drive-by scenes become precious clues on a zany path toward... sanity? Not that I can think such hopeful words as yet. Some would call this deep a funk a breakdown of the nervous kind. But what actually seems to be breaking down is the odd programmed behavior or emotional defence. And contrary to how it feels, this seems like a good thing. Occasional insights tighten the job, jolting the personality into realignment. It is painful, baffling, wondrous to behold—all of the above. *I am naked, and no one sees!* And though this big heart-fuck is the shittiest anguish of my adult life so far, surely it must be for the better. A complementary adjustment by some almighty chiropractor of the soul. Yeoww! *Billy, where are you now, buddy?*

I see what I didn't see before: reactions and sorely crafted stories, fictions of difficulty, of suffering arising from conditions set up long ago. In a way, these are illusions of difficulty, of suffering. Evidently, illusions are felt as real. Perhaps so much of what is normally experienced as real is, in fact, illusion. *Yet it is real.*

---

12 By Arthur Janov, the book is about uncovering underlying emotional bases, created in early trauma, for pain, suffering and neuroses experienced later in life.

And so the personality is altered, recalibrated. Yet I am still here. *How is this so? Is the personality not me?* For it is, evidently, inconstant and malleable.

Again, there is a sense of "knowing" these perceptions without the clear words to describe them.

Being alone in a foreign country is key. No one here shares my history, no one to hold me to anything they might see or imagine about me. And so I am granted (or I grant myself) virtual permission to take as long as I need to pass through whatever funk or purgatory I'm in. I stay in my room. Mostly, I lie and weep. I do not howl, for that would surely rob me of my privacy. Set against the sunny Aussie summer, my separation from the outside world is disorienting. There's too damned much to think about, and to feel. Thinking is exciting, but wow, it's a burden, too.

Back home I couldn't take this risk. Family and friends would claim to forever love me dearly, but they wouldn't forget. I'd be walking down the street in midlife, and people would see "that guy, JD, you know, he flipped out that time way back," heads turning slowly in quiet judgment, make-believe understanding, and pseudo-compassion.

AFTER A NUMBER of days I emerge to walk the streets of Canberra, looking and feeling, unwilling or perhaps unable to close my eyes. Things look remarkably different than they did a few days ago. It's all so raw and crappy and creepy. Residual anguish and unfulfilled, unconscious needs carve up the faces and rack the bodies of men and women. It is a pitiable condition, one that I (and I presume most others) truly and often unconsciously live out. The older the person, the more stark and ingrained the evidence. Every buckled brow, every tense and barricaded pair of eyes, downturned mouth, stooped shoulder, and scuffing heel—these howl and echo in the aching cavern of what I take to be my soul. It's horrible to behold, but I won't turn away. Only young children are awake—it's in their eyes. Although already, their little faces tighten and squirm in adapting to the "cruel world." A gradient of sensitivity and numbness, all stages of intervening years, can be read like a book in the people, these people on the streets of Canberra.

This plain view of the human condition, as I later come to believe, comes courtesy of a kind of inverted culture shock: one triggered by internal changes and not by the classic, external ones. I haven't gone anywhere, but I've covered some inner ground. I'm feeling the naked emanations of the modern, acculturated human, Western variety. For I've grown from the same soil, the same fields of thought and behavior. Normally unconscious and unseen, today it wallops. Whatever psychic mill I've just emerged from, and for whatever reasons, today it's *because* I share the same social conditioning that I feel it so strongly.

I remember a few tortured souls from home. Were they really weak, as per popular notion? At least they had the integrity to pass through whatever subterranean tunnel, not like me who waited for the convenience of anonymity in a foreign country. Is this what I sought when I first heeded the siren song of wanderlust?

When I was fourteen, maybe fifteen, and beginning to feel the angst of straining against the dark ways of the adult world, I thought to myself, *If I ever get so fucked up that I can't handle things anymore, I will travel to a place where people are suffering more than me (starvation, disease) and volunteer my help.* I must have reasoned, or assumed, that helping others would lift me out of myself, even enable healing.

Seems my dark night in Canberra hasn't been as bad as all that. A weeklong misery of deepened sight, of tears and isolation. A few pounds of tissue paper, fifty bucks or so. Got off pretty easy.

BREAKDOWN, PARANOIA. OR conversion, transformation. *Metanoia*[13] means "to repent and be forgiven." It is the act of turning away from something (falsehood, delusion, sin) and turning toward something else (truth or God.) I faced some old pain and subsequently made an about-face without knowing what I was turning toward except, perhaps, the truth of my condition. *And be forgiven.* In a foreign place, just a face in the crowd; there is no one of personal consequence to deny me forgiveness.

So, I forgive myself. I walk, and the walking is good. I see, and I'm grateful for the seeing. As it is, I've had the good fortune of passing

---

13   From the Bible: redemption, atonement, or a life change resulting from penitence or spiritual conversion.

through a personal wormhole without getting stuck in there, and without getting locked up *out* there.

For now, the tears have stopped. I find that I can once again feel the splendor of the brilliant Aussie sun. I'm twenty-one. I feel ancient, I feel newly made. And I'm tired of hiding.

Three things cannot be long hidden: the sun, the moon, and the truth —Buddha

Reid House

Curiosity about my new surroundings increasingly interrupts my solitary gloom. I come to appreciate the sub-society I've stumbled upon: the colorful tribe of misfits who inhabit the two row buildings called Reid House in downtown Canberra.

I meet assorted stragglers. A young beauty of sixteen or seventeen, with a clear, earnest face, comes often into my room to talk. Generous soul, she wants to help, to soothe me. She's had no real home, her parents perennially transient. Almost ready to move on her own, she is attracted to drifters like me. Her face is luminous, her body as fragrant a magnet as I've ever been drawn to. I'm a hapless sailor pulled into her protective lagoon, into her warm, glistening pool, along her alabaster dunes.

But I stop. I won't drop the curtain on my pinhole of clarity. I've been addicted to the bewitching balm of Danna's mind and body, and now, in the presence of this next heavenly beauty, I'm desperate to remain awake. *Go kiss her, Johnny!* But I must not jump back in, not now. I want to find another way out of this prison of pleasures. If I'm to emerge from this psychic funk without repeating the routine of using a woman's beauty for dope... *For how long, this sentence?* This is my bleak moment of honesty, my singularity the one thing I hold on to. Normally, the sexual pull aligns and overpowers all. I avoid explaining any of this to her; the authenticity and openness would surely invite a leap into intimacy and bliss.

And, despite the broad permissions of biology's imperative, she is a little young.

And so she leaves.

A psychotic clown of a woman sits rocking and babbling in a corner of the common area. As others come and go she singles me out, showing me to her room. She introduces me to her family, one by one. Along the head of her bed she has lined up a little crowd of rag dolls, an audience to her strange isolation. An orange-haired, middle-aged woman, she appears silly and childish as she talks to the lifeless faces, one after another. But how different are they from the living puppets languishing in this place? Like us the dolls are named and compliant, each one unique. A few days later, during a provocative group conversation when I steer the topic toward neurosis (mine?) and its desperate cousin, psychosis, my red-haired avant-clown abruptly stops her rambling to listen. A few vivid seconds later, she resumes her chatter but more slowly, as if in retreat. Perhaps with sufficient will and insight, her hollow ramblings might reveal much about her and the psychic zone she inhabits.

A demented scholar lives at the far end of the building. He is tall, with a gaunt face and stooped shoulders. His room is full of textbooks. He's a walking textbook himself, his binding slack and frayed. When we talk his face twitches and his eyes dash about defensively, although his conversation is not defensive. Ideas whip through his mind causing it to leap about like a nervous gazelle. The information he carries could fill shelves in a library; the disconnect between eye and word could send a psychiatrist's kid to college. His labored shuffle along the stained hall is stiff and weak, his burden heavy in the flesh. He mutters as he walks, his mind too full to hold back the random spurt of meaning escaping into an indifferent world.

Reid House is often dominated by the presence of a gloomy junkie whose eyes are decidedly goat-like. He lords over several slack-eyed flunkies. A pubescent harem of local girls hovers around him, drawn by some shadow male force, I must assume. He is not handsome, and he acquires a distinct and vile hatred for me and another guy. We two are often cheerful and bright eyed, and you know what? Gals like *that* too. The whole smiling and kindness thing seems to have skipped past Goat Eyes altogether. In a moment that serves as climax for an unlikely meeting of worlds, he stands and snarls at me (not sure why), crooked finger pointed and eyes glazed over with corrupted animosity. I look straight at him, no fear, no anger, nothing. He turns away. I then feel a weird chill, as if we are a species apart. The warmth and focus that are typical of humans are missing in Goat Eyes' eyes.

Across the way in the electric flats I find an old round dog of a man, the caretaker. His corpulence all but bursts through his thin shirt, a few threads holding buttons in place as he repeatedly blasts his dripping sinuses into a wrinkled gray rag. His room is stuffed (he can barely open the door) with pornographic magazines and books and all sorts of household junk. The one time I visit him he makes a woeful admission that his craving for collecting things is a "sickness." He's tried to get rid of it all before but—*snort, honk*—he just can't do it. His mom was like that, and now he, too, is hooked. His face is red and splotchy from drinking the hard stuff and his flesh a pasty pink, as though he never ventures into the intense Aussie sun.

A couple down the hall gnash their teeth in the grim process of what I suspect is the speeding up of the decay of civilization as we know it. In one day their small girl is transformed from a happy, confident toddler into a frozen mannequin. As her parents explode into all-out war, her spirit plummets from the high intelligence of an uninhibited three-year-old to sucking her thumb passively like a caged macaque. Naked, in a tight fetal position on the floor, she rocks back and forth to a rhythm no one hears. Her once-sparkling eyes are deadened by an already hidden pain. My own lonesome turmoil is magnified in her mute torture. When the mother snaps and falls into a screeching panic, my wounds are reopened. Mom and Dad, locked in a zone of anguish and desire, neglect the girl as they pass on their most crippling pain. Is this how it happens? How the fucking infernal world reproduces its shitty self? Such is the jurisdictional whim of nature: the beautiful zebra foal becomes a midmorning snack for a few edgy hyenas while Mom and Dad disappear in a cloud of dust.

But the bigger picture offers no solace, so I turn away. I can't save her, nor can I stay to witness this corrupting of a human life, to watch *her* become *me*. Seeing her raw torment makes my own pain feel small. In the child's experience, I stare awestruck at the inception of a thousand and more ways we kill our freedom and suffer life.

There is a long, wispy blonde lassie with a vacant look about her. I never hear her speak, and she's usually half-naked. Her eyes look sedated, but when they meet mine they spark alive and I get a jolt.

There's a self-described schizophrenic, tall with long, stringy black hair, mild-mannered and with a look of cultivated terror in his eyes; others call him Moses. And a fifteen-year-old blond kid who plays the blues on an old box guitar with the speed and finesse of a prodigy. He tells me he's been playing for only six months. I'm astonished. "Just love the blues man, can't get 'nuff of it."

And there are others. They are the nomadic young and old, in for a few days and then out again, living the vagabond dream, or nightmare.

AFTER TWO WEEKS of that murky urban scene I throw on my backpack. For reasons known or unknown, fortunate or not, I've been swept into a psycho-emotional storm, my small, dark room its purgatorial eye. But as all storms do it subsides, and time moves me along. I take to the road, hitchhiking around the southeast region of the continent, drifting like a seed in a fickle current.

In some way and in some measure, I have been remade. A snake sheds its skin, and some bugs do a cocoon thing. I have no understanding of what has happened. I can only say that everything feels different. Even the light and the air are not as they were. My eyes, my skin, have moved.

Tender and feeling every pebble, I walk with my own feet for the first time.

Spiders and Dreams

It is a land of farms, rivers, beaches, and attractive towns scattered throughout. Rather like rolling parts of BC or New Zealand, what you might not expect to find in Oz. I sleep in shacks, under bridges, or wherever a day of walking on a country road might lead. When darkness approaches I look around, one eye on a good night's sleep, the other on other eyes that might be aimed my way.

Walking a rural highway in a drier part of western New South Wales I feel at ease in the world. I'm drifting, and nothing pushes. That curious pause between day and night, when the wind has stopped and birds fall silent... the low sun sends long auburn rays across the flat, open country, lifting pale greens and cool yellows from drying pastures. The stillness and silence amplify my footsteps to those of a carefree giant.

A few homesteads are visible up ahead within a mile or so. I spot an old shack next to the highway, a good distance from a nearby house. Its twisted structure and broken windows indicate, even from a quarter-mile away, that it is abandoned. I spent last night sleeping clean and comfortable on a padded bench inside a jockey's building on the edge of a racetrack. Sure, I had to hop a fence to get into the racing grounds, and yeah, the back slider to the lounge area wasn't locked. True, I woke to the sound of keys at 4:45 a.m. and beat a swift exit. When walking about, you take whatever unoccupied roof you find. Tonight, that decrepit old shack up ahead could be mine.

It is dusk when I enter. The wallboards have disintegrated, and broken glass litters the floor. This shack is not so much "all mine." A community of spiders occupies the two biggest walls, west and north, perhaps the two that are still warm so late in the day. *I could turn and leave.* Never have I seen so many large spiders in one place, not on a nature show and not in movies. Forty or fifty humungous ones stretch across the better part of three inches each, with several times that many smaller ones between. All are still, gathered like a great crowd. *Hundreds! Aren't they standing a little too close to each other? Are they planning something?* You can't tell with spiders. *Are they sleeping? Ready to dance?* This is Oz, land of uber-poisonous crawly things that can *jump twelve feet.* Why so many spiders crowded in one place?

A stained and torn mattress leans against the wall closest to me, which seems to suggest a sleeping spot for the night. Eyeing the big guys, I step slow and nimble. Gingerly, I un-lean the mattress. *That's good*—no spiders behind it. I drag it to the center of the small room. Though I don't bother with the specific thought just now, my head will be within easy jumping range of the hairy eight-leggers. I spread my sleeping bag.

Getting dark. Immediately after lying down, I tell myself, and anyone who might hear: *I come in peace. Surely, you spiders (and any snakes around here) have no interest in me, for I respect your home, and I have no intention of disrupting your living space or culture or what have you. (Think prime directive, Johnny.) In case any of you venomous friends wish to pass through "my" space, I will take care not to roll over while sleeping.* (In silence, I declare that this will be so.) I peek up and behind me; there they all are, about five feet from my head. As a teen I got comfortable with spiders walking across my naked back or chest on hot summer nights in my basement den, half waking to the tickling rhythm of their feet. For whatever reason, I have not acquired much of the widespread fear surrounding spiders. Sure, I avoid them, but we go way back; we have some history. Like snakes, they tend to eat critters that bring illness to humans. *Bio-buddies.*

But here in this shack, with a good thimbleful of spider venom in store, the earlier ease of my teen years… well, I admit, it ain't quite so easy on this crystal-black Aussie night.

I lie listening to the odd lone dog and my giant's breath, which must sound to these spiders like an angry valley wind. This twilit room of broken glass and not-so-right angles, this city of spiders, the surrounding bugs that scream as if they've already crawled inside my head… as I lie at the center of this cyclone of sound-craft insanities, memories of early childhood nightmares come to mind. For reasons related to my present situation, for sure, and maybe due in part to my recent emotional tsunami in Canberra, I make an earnest attempt to remember the actual feeling of those nightmares. *Why not? What harm?* Feeling curious—about fear itself, perhaps—I turn toward this fear and invite the feeling of the nightmares. I remember them, draw them back. Seems easier than it should be.

After less than a minute of concentration a raw crisis boils up. It is the smell of a terror that dwarfs all mental workings, the screams of a thousand dying souls inside my very small head. The effect is so powerful that I immediately abort. I am terrified. *Is this primal horror always so bloody near? Does a hurricane inhale? Does Mother Teresa have a dark side?* It is far, *far* too much to bear. No, I *cannot.* I remind myself of peace and love and Mom and Dad, and throw in some holy-dancing Jesus for good measure. *Don Juan, Socrates, can you hear me?* I follow my breath and I follow them all down a trusty tunnel into blessed sleep.

But sleep is restless. Keeping a promise, my body lies as still as a corpse. Periodic visits back to the straight spine on a beat-up mattress in a twisted shack are signalled by the bellows of my lonely breath and the concert of nighttime bugs. *Too dark to see…* I shift in and out of vivid dream worlds featuring God, Lucifer, me, Jesus, Zeus, Aphrodite and me, Gollum, and a few singer-songwriters: Bobby, Joni, Paul, James, Neil, John... *sorry, buds.* Setting and mood come courtesy of those horrible Bosch paintings and some of Dante's scenes. Pain, sorrow, debauchery, cosmic guilt, emptiness. There is desolation of soul and utter lack of beauty and love. I'm held frozen by the pressure of an embryonic scream, like Fellini and David Lynch working together, taking Lennon/Ono's "Revolution 9" and jacking it perfectly to hellish visuals, then pumping in the stench of rotting flesh... *worst art ever.*

I wake from this most horrible part in a panic, with an urge to cry out as never before. Eyes opened to blackness, crickets screeching, blood pounding my heart out loud. In an instant I remember where I am, the home nearby, the loudness of the potential scream, the resulting confusion that I and these residents of a peaceful rural habitat would have to suffer on this weird dark night, and... *the spiders!* I swallow hard. I do not wake the neighbors. Part of me is disgusted with my aptitude for such life-numbing self-control: *catharsis interruptus.*

The collage of dream images is a merciless reminder that although waking Johnny can and does think all kinds of things, something else might be going on below the surface without his permission. Until my interlude in Canberra, I thought myself emotionally stable, at least since early childhood. Now I face a different prospect: this apparent calm is a veneer that barely masks, with my complicit ignorance, a cauldron of passions. *Yikes! I bet the whole civilized hullaballoo is no better!* In this unholy cauldron float grand symbols, perhaps not of my making. I believed I'd left behind the last traces of church dogma a long time ago with creepo Father Gordo when I was eleven.[14] *Ugh.*

When I wake early the next morning, the spiders are gone. *Gone!* I'd love to have seen their exit routes. I imagine their discussion in the middle of the night.

"What the...? What is this, a fuckin' meat-giant made himself all comfy in our chalet? The blind arrogance of these stupid, gangly beasts! We should kill him!"

---

14   I was an altar boy (I did it for my mom) for almost a year until the local priest showed me his goodies. I ran home and quit the Church, then joined the new credo of atheism until age seventeen.

"Kill him and drain him of his useless blood!"

"Nah, look at him. He's writhing in fear as he sleeps. Leave him be. He's already fucked, poor schmoe. We're outta here!"

At first light, all is quiet, the neighborhood still. As a rooster crows I continue along the highway. It's a cool dawn with bright warm rays on my skin. *Man, do I feel refreshed.*

My first ride on the road to Adelaide is with a young Christian couple, with nothing but good news to share. There's talk of Adelaide a slippin' into the sea (à la California) the very next day. *And yes*—smile, pant—*we're heading there ourselves, golly gee.* They're bloody manic with excitement, talking about beautiful Jesus and leaping straight through tectonic hell into rapturous heaven.

So that's how it is. We'll drive to the end of the world together. *Okie-dokie.* Unaccountably, I feel relieved of a great trial. I feel good, whole, awake.

For a couple of hours riding with my shining Christian benefactors I'm immersed in one of those best of times, when every detail of living is a grand surprise, and nothing need be understood beyond the plainness of it. The strong light of day reveals a world a phase removed, hinting at some esoteric alternate hidden behind the norms of the human movie. My very skin seems happy to be holding me together. *Good job, bud.* No earthquake could shake me off this cloud.

Nor be near as exciting as last night.

Dominelli Ford

Breezing through Sydney for what feels like the last time, I take a phone book and head straight for the D's to see if I'm in there. I'm not disappointed. I find myself in boldface letters, followed by "Ford." Dominelli Ford is one of Sydney's big auto dealers. A receptionist diverts me to a man who almost hangs up when I tell him I'm a Dominelli, maybe a relative, from Canada. A prankster, he reckons. "Get *atta* hea! Whaddya wont, eye?"

"No, no, listen. I'm serious, my name is…" After a minute of listening to a foreign accent, he gets rid of me by giving me his aging father's phone number. *Nice, thoughtful son.*

The next day, a Sunday, toward the southwest reach of the metropolis in the vicinity of Liverpool, I sit at a dinner table marveling at the same smells and dishes I enjoyed every Sunday of my short sweet life in my parents' home. The patriarch is a warm, generous man with white hair and vivid blue eyes. He is energetic and hospitable, just like my folks. He and his grandchildren serve me a dinner of green salad, spaghetti and meatballs, and red wine, eerily identical in detail and flavor to those at home. And, as if subordinate to some fateful psycho-genetic stream (sly old cosmos), his name is Bruno, like my father, and his deceased wife's was Maria, my mother's name. They'd emigrated from Italy thirty years ago while my family made the move just over twenty years past. *Fifty years ain't nothing to spaghetti sauce this good.*

Perhaps the sons—the Dominelli Ford sons and, I presume, their wives—were too busy to make it over for Sunday dinner.

I'M MULLING OVER the idea of returning to North America via California. *Maybe I'll stop for a visit at Janov's Primal Institute.* Still smarting from my emotional nosedive, I've lost the yearning for the self-indulgent romance I've been calling "traveling". I'm more of a cultural refugee. Back home I reckoned I should be able to keep one small step ahead if I smiled a bit, nodded, and didn't say a whole lot. *Poor, bourgeois schmuck.* Since high school I've kept it going on a wish and a smile. On the road it's easier: passport, some cash. Closest thing to a magic carpet.

I don't have a plan. I know I've been given much in this life, but I'm not sure how to give back. Lately, the best I've come up with is, *buddy, at least do not add to the mess of this sufferin' ship.* Not much, but it's all I've got.

On the way back to Canberra, in a semitrailer truck rolling down the highway, I feel I want nothing. *Nothing.* And that anything can happen. *Anything.* All anxiety has left me since parting with Danna and my several weeks of roaming. And especially since my recent, quirky fart-string of madhouse theater: the crooked shed on a lonely country highway on an eerie, silent night, with spiders and dreams and a scream that wouldn't; the next morning's gushing, Christianesque surrender at *The End of the World;* and before that, convulsions in my personal psyche ward in Canberra. No surprise that in just a few weeks a gnawing malaise has transformed into quasi-euphoric detachment. As the humming, rumbling truck serves my and the trucker's respective insanities on this one in a thousand days, a decision appears, already made.

And it is this: I will travel through Asia. My newfound clarity is the still screen needed to receive a pre-existing signal. Within a week I'm heading for Perth, from where I will fly to Southeast Asia.

And so it goes, that my overseas adventure has been altered in an essential way. For with this new arrow, I have no idea, exactly, where I'm going.

Or for how long.

3. Java

all the diamonds in this world[15]

Jakarta

I look out from the airplane as the world rolls to a stop. A big sky/
wavering green disappears into a great curve of horizon. Grass huts poke
through like early morning mushrooms. The sky has been ripped to a
deep metal-blue. It is midday, Jakarta Airport.

The psychedelic ruse continues as I walk down the portable steps. A
sweet tropical breath rolls up my pant legs, swallowing up pockets of
cool, dry air carried from inside the plane. Around the airport buildings, small dark soldiers with bayonets march in perfect unison, jerky
and stiff like platoons of Alice the Goon, like cheap mechanical dolls.
I've entered an alternate human realm. The hidden kaleidoscope has
shifted and suddenly, the world I came from has a name: the West. I had
to leave its self-defining thrall in order to become aware of its boundaries, or that it had any. And so now, with a mere shred of evidence, I will
go in the faith that this new strangeness is a tantalizing harbinger of
stranger things to come.

Up ahead sits a bus. Its sharp tilt and acid-dream paint job—*wait, is
that really a bus?* There's a windshield, but that's it for glass. At twenty
paces "Born to be Wild"[16] fires up and blasts through the square holes.
Good timing. It's a bus alright, and ticket guy with the great 'fro looks
like he just smoked a jumbo doobie. *Lookin' for adventure,* I take a seat, *a
true nature child,* amidst a load of smiling, bopping Indonesians. Love's

15   From the song "All the Diamonds in This World" by Bruce Cockburn.
16   "Born To Be Wild" by Steppenwolf, written by M. Bonfire.

patchwork of rainbows and doves has moved a few longitudes and years and latitudes down the road. The young are decked out in occidental sixties style, straight off the rack, complete with counterculture vibe, 1975. The look is convincing, and it's pulling my strings. Unguarded faces *head out on the highway* and *take the world in a love embrace.* The fare is pennies, the value-for-money knob cranked. *Explode into space.* I'm new at this traveling game, ziggin' as I zag, *runnin' with the wind.* Language I do not share with these kindred Javans, but we move together like leaves of grass in a merry wind.

It's very cool, even surrealistically reassuring, that a Canadian rock band has been kind enough to do the soundtrack for my humble arrival into this new land of untapped desire.

But chatter-head, that spry and faithless chump who's always ready to trade sweet wonder for something more calculable, steps in and hijacks the scene. Now lost in the pragmatic and the mundane, I fall for his ruse as I step off the bus in the inner city. As I busy myself with the business of finding a room for the night, I pull out my copy of *Southeast Asia On a Shoestring.*[17] I turn to a fresh-faced, barefoot waif who has appeared before me. The little guy offers to carry my pack, sell me something or other, and lead me to a hotel.

All for the price of a small banana.

JAVA IS ONE crowded chunk of real estate, and the big city sizzles. Turn your head—barefoot businessmen pull handmade shops, meals-on-wheels, tinkers and merchants, ringing bells, calling for customers. Look the other way—black-faced coal shovelers feed hungry fires in the belly of an iron horse.

Yet as I walk through these alien city lands of simple means and rank, wild-spice smells, I feel something familiar. Could it be mammonism? The possession of possession? It always shows itself proud, and here

17 Tony Wheeler's *Southeast Asia On A Shoestring* was Lonely Planet's first publication. Many of us on the road carried one and often arrived at the same hotels and restaurants. I soon grew disenchanted with the predictable "herding" aspect of it and came to relish the charms of the unexpected, and consequently, of going unprepared. I still have the original, tattered 1975 edition in my library.

in old-world Asia, its hypnotic spell of acquisitiveness seems to have swept the land with its introductory merry-go-round of hopeful ambition and promised pleasures. Mammonism—who even notices or takes the word seriously anymore? Cut loose from the tendrils of my own familiar media, it's easier to catch sight of certain things that were once taken for granted. I admit that I paint my own dim view of it, imagining how its modern form has crept into these parts and taken hold like an ambitious mold. Or maybe it was always here, cuz people are just people wherever you go, and the productivity-crazy, consumerist, profit-favoring modern system simply enables and amps up the game.

This is Jakarta, Indonesia's megacity capital, nine million human neurons of modern Indonesia's brain. Word on the street, spat absently to the side like a spent wad of betel nut mash: 90 percent of the country's money and power is focused here, in this dense coagulation of human brilliance and madness.

The ostentation of the despot state is high-strut, commanding. In the center of the city a vainglorious statue towers over the streets, a gigantic spiritual *faux pas* if ever I saw one. The political "art" of *tyrannosaurus tyrant* is big, dumb, and tawdry. It casts a long, dark shadow, a towering gift from mammonism's latest top dog—what the barefoot waifs have little choice but to look up to.

Yuji

At my hotel I meet Yuji, a courteous and formally mannered chap from Tokyo. His English is labored but easily outdoes my Japanese, which is nonexistent. Yuji's rudimentary handling of my native tongue is suitable for some enjoyable exchanges, and enables a good connection between us. Tokyo is as big as cities get, yet Yuji seems to possess the pleasant disposition of a country lad. After a few minutes I see that his Japanese culture so contrasts with mine that my take on urban and rural types is moot. Indeed, our differences reveal my ready images as mere stereotypes.

Having agreed to check out Jakarta together, Yuji tells me, with rising anticipation, about Pisar Ikan, the "fish market." I do for the first time what I will do many times: aimless and reflective, I ride in the wake of a fellow traveler's focused interest, be it to a nondescript village or to a world heritage site. I feel detached, without motive, and so I am easily absorbed into a plenitude of details along any which way. Perhaps I take the easy road. In this case I'm favorably drawn by Yuji's excitement and my own preconceptions of the activity and human buzz we will become immersed in at Pisar Ikan.

A bus takes us through miles of city squalor. We get off when we spot the rigs of a vast sea of ships. Single and double-masted fishing boats with hand-worked, solid teak hulls and huge sails in the colors of clouds crowd a vast harbor as far as the eye can see. Largest marina ever, with small dark men climbing like bonobos over decks and rigging.

Drawn by earnest, bright faces we hop aboard. A half dozen deck-hands—missing teeth, rags around foreheads—are up the main mast holding on with coiling legs, tying sails and tossing laughter around like punk demigods on a beer rush. Without the tangle of words we get that these fishermen are inviting us out to sea. Only three days in the East... *I wonder if Yuji'd go if I was willing.* I'm not so trusting as to brave equatorial waters alongside pirate-looking strangers I can't even talk to... not yet. A sketchy scene dances a drunken jig in my genteel brain. I come from an early batch of TV babies, watched a lot of Popeye and Looney Tunes. Wimpy, always seeking comfort in a hamburger (a green and cautious traveler), passes up a unique opportunity.

We walk past hundreds of boats. Boys rush over, sit us down, and trace our obvious facial differences with dirty, calloused fingers, chattering and giggling like chipmunks on good bud. Yuji and I, we are East and West, a novel delight. Yuji and I, us and the boys—it is this contrast in type, in culture, that (at least in part) drew us here, and together.

The most abject dwelling holes line dirt roads that wind around piers, warehouses, and the market. Every open space is infested with garbage, its deep stink, and a great community of rats. A few sheets of corrugated metal and slabs of discarded wood, in many cases just leaning against each other, form homes for entire families. Naked, laughing children scamper in and out. No electricity or running water or the mere thought of a tricycle or red rubber ball. In this corner of the world, the TV has not yet arrived. We walk along the bare earth peering into dark spaces at the humble expressions of toothless old ones, circles of wrinkled light, smiling, loving. Their equanimity begs the questions: What is happiness? How can I get some? Isn't that what I want? Shouldn't I? And how did these poor folk get so much when those with home theaters and summer cabins seem rather short on supply? Happiness: its presence, its pursuit. The prisms of personal and cultural expectation. It all seems so simple—and so bloody complicated.

The folks here have community, enough to eat, and a roof to sleep under. But barely.

When you realize there is nothing lacking, the whole world belongs to you... peace comes from within; do not seek it without... the way is not in the sky; it is in the heart.[18]

BACK AT OUR hotel room with two Aussies, Bianca and Mary, Yuji talks about growing up in Japan. He speaks about how, by age two, a child will already have been trained to bow when greeting a parent, indulging in little touching and playful contact. I've never heard this before, and I wonder if he is speaking of a peculiar family system of behaviors and forces or of a wider cultural norm. In any case my inner toddler grows twitchy; I feel a tantrum coming on.

He tells us of his travels to India in years past and says he wants to return. Yuji strikes me as a person on the trail of some kind of soul scent, one that evokes a yearning for "liberation." *What does this mean?* Having left behind his old world on the trail of that singular curiosity, he is at least questioning the ways and expectations of ancestral race and heritage. A Zen Buddhist, he feels drawn to the places Siddhartha Gautama walked on his path to enlightenment: Lumbini, Bodh Gaya, Sarnath. I like the sound of these names. I want to hear more.

He says he recently toured Oz, which piques Bianca's and Mary's interest. Yuji then says, "Australian women, they are *not* humble."

Ouch. Well, who is these days, right, babes?

Bianca and Mary shift in their seats. I imagine Yuji in Oz seeking to learn about a foreign land with humility rare among travelers, and

---

18 Trusty Buddha bits given from his spirit of plenitude and equally, I suspect, from his so-called "emptiness."

being treated to racist jabs along the way. I'd bet that racism is alive and kicking in any little hamlet around the globe.

How would it be if I visited Japan?

I was stung with the poison of racism when I was five, playing across the street with a new playmate. At once he stopped, shot me an evil eye, and declared with disgust, "Yeewch! You look like an Indian!" Less than five minutes into our play he spat at my feet, convicting me of a crime I'd never heard of. One of my buddies, who lived three houses down from this racist shit-fest, was "native Indian" and his mom and dad were proud of it, like mine were of *Italia bella*. In white, working-class PoCo, my immigrant-Italian family was a shade darker. But up to that moment I had no reason to know it, nor to notice that apart from my mate Sonny and his folks, and me and mine, everyone was creamy pale-pink. When the kid spat at my feet a sweet innocence blinked out and heavy knowledge moved in. My look—something I couldn't change, something that was just "me"—earned me a guilty verdict planted by someone holding an unaccountable wad of hatred. Foul in taste, its violence dehumanizing, I was struck as if by a physical force. My spirit staggered under its corrupting weight. I would not, *could* not, forget it.

Fifteen years later, a mere three months ago, an old white gal, looking all prim and ready for a lawn bowling gig, scowled at me in a grocery store lineup in a posh part of Sydney. I looked around to see what the trouble was. It was my apparent ethnicity. Too many Greeks in *her* neighborhood. I'd just had my hair cropped short for my Asian journey, so I suppose my new look fit her image of "wog." I remembered my childhood sting. Looking at the woman in starched whites I felt barely a twinge. It remained a bizarre novelty, for in the years between "the spit" and the old gal in Oz, there were no other such incidents. I shuddered under the imagined weight of a lifetime of such "minor," mind-warping incidents.

In Yuji's reactionary comment to Bianca and Mary I look towards grace, and an ancient lesson reminds: it's easy to look past the beam in your own eye to focus on the sliver in another's.[19] I am only modestly familiar with the racism Yuji speaks of.

19 Matthew 7:5, paraphrased

And I hope that for him it will also remain a minor glitch in a prosperous and beautiful life.

Jogja

Leaving Jakarta, we take buses and trains toward the south and the east. Although Java is intensely crowded, its people are good natured and healthy. The land is so lush and productive as to support a population that appears, from my traveling window, as one vast, continuous village. Human activity bristles and seethes along our path. Rice paddies and vegetable gardens heave ever present in the streaming, sunlit background. Java is said to be the most densely populated landmass of its size, the epitome of the "overcrowded poor country." It is as crowded as any suburban area yet extends for many hundreds of miles. No tractors, pipes, (and presumably) marketing boards, or test tubes... or pollution. And *way* more smiles. Of course technology can offer some awesome advantages, but I wonder if there's a measure of "technocentric vanity" that has many in the West assuming that those who function without the use of modern ideas and gadgets... always need our help.

We arrive in Yogyakarta, a.k.a. "Jogja," locus of Javanese culture and a city of extraordinary artistic activity. The people are possessed of an energetic and creative spirit, and produce a profusion of fine arts and crafts in a wild variety of mediums: batik (Indonesian word) and oil painting, stone and wood sculpture, silverware, leather goods, dance and puppet shows, and mobile orchestras. All this and more than I know fills the streets and floods the merry senses. I have never beheld so much laughter in city streets.

This is the land of ancient riches that first provided the lure for the Age of Exploration and of colonization. All those fortune-seeking dreamers and opportunists in sailing ships from Europe were looking for a shortcut to the spices of India and these East Indies. Over 20,000 islands, some of the world's largest, are scattered over more than two million square miles of ocean. Still one of the least explored areas of the globe, its geographical complexity guards a wild profusion of tropical plant and animal life that eludes discovery. Even today, few foreign travelers venture beyond the main routes. As a map-gazing enthusiast in my primary school years (a traveler of sorts, I reckon) I was drawn to this most wondrous mess of islands, coastlines, and equatorial seas in my *Canadian Social Studies Atlas*. Years later I would heap on more intrigue, indulging a more esoteric fancy and curiosity that reaches back to the last ice age and possible vanished civilizations on the mostly submerged subcontinent of Sundaland.

I now walk the actual dirt of the wildly arranged islands I visited and revisited as a boy in my bent old school atlas. I smell cloves in the air and taste it in the ubiquitous, delicious tea. Even the hand-rolled cigarettes snap and pop as they burn, spiked as they are with the aromatic buds. The smokers look festive, their personal fireworks displays all a part of the plan. Though always a non-smoker, I sit in tea shops and succumb to the flair. I smoke a few myself for the good taste while observing the mad swirl of life all around. Even the sugar bowl is alive with numerous tiny ants that crawl frenetically throughout the yellowy granules, lost in their inebriating maze. After several cups from which I skim flotillas of dead ants, I learn to take my tea bland.

The city's backstreets are dark and quieter, revealing a more intimate side of Javanese life. Wrinkled, twinkle-eyed old women come by offering massages. Small, mobile *gamelan* orchestras make evening rounds along the narrow alleyways. Their home-crafted, eerie-sounding string, wind, and percussion instruments use scales that provoke my Western, evenly measured musical sense. They drift along like benign apparitions, old and young alike, busking in their delighted and gentle way for a few rupiahs, if listeners will spare them willingly. For they won't ask outright.

The modest, family-run traveler's lodgings are called *losmen*. Off a narrow walkway adjacent to a main road I must bend over to enter one, which is run by a large, healthy-looking mother, her teenage daughter, and her adolescent son. The boy and girl have a guitar that someone left behind. Spotting me picking a lick one afternoon, they pester me for chords and songs with an earnestness that is any teacher's pleasure. A small group of travelers gather nightly in the low, dark common room, strumming and singing. We pass the guitar around, the boy and girl watching and listening from a shadowy corner.

In these mid-1970s the trickle of low-budget foreign travelers has already become a steady brook. On the second night of my stay a lanky, dark-haired young man dressed in a white suit of sorts, and carrying a jumbo American acoustic, enters the cave-like common room. He unbuckles the case and carefully removes a great-looking blonde ax. By his poise and the deliberation in his every move, his entrance appears rehearsed. He says nothing, and by his aura of "the entertainer" it's clear that I must put down the scrawny instrument I'm holding. He plucks and sings, captivating us for almost an hour. A good audience, we applaud between songs. He offers no banter between numbers, just adjusts his capo or simply segues into another song. The music evokes a sensibility where old jazz standards meet hillbilly Appalachia. But the voice is his dominant instrument: low, booming, and articulate. When the set is over, he calmly puts away his guitar and leaves, as though having rehearsed for a concert or testing the waters for an upcoming album. He comes again the next evening at the same time, like it's a scheduled gig. Once again, he doesn't say a word.

One morning I'm sitting in the central opening of the losmen mending a tear in my backpack with a sewing needle and thread. The mother sits preparing some food not far from me. Her eyes catch an intermittent flash and come back again and again to the thin, shiny object I hold between my fingers. She seems self-conscious of being so interested in it, noticing me noticing her. When I finish I walk over and hold it out, offering it to her. Modestly, she takes it, merely nodding as if to say, "I thank you so kindly for what means so little to you but so much to me." And it's true. In that moment the needle is also a symbol of the glaring material disparity in our lives.

I'm also learning that I love giving things away.

ONE SECTOR OF town is a residential marketplace for various kinds of artists. On our way there Bianca, Mary and I (Yuji is off somewhere on a quest) are greeted by an exuberant youth who offers a tour of the area. Won over by his earnest and hospitable energy we agree to walk with him. I become suspicious of his motives, however, when he bypasses most shops and leads us directly to a chosen few after shooting ahead to talk quietly with the artist-proprietor. *Duh.* The kid has never heard of "subtle." He is either unaware or unconcerned that he's become a hindrance to our natural meanderings. After several such scouting episodes I interrupt his venal banter.

"You get a commission if we buy things." Of course, I don't pause to consider my own momentous lack of subtlety. But at least I'm careful to speak without anger or disdain, for I am not without fear of trouble with punks in a foreign country. Just the same, I have implied that he is using us for his own profit, offers no real service, and likely inflates the price in the process.

I might as well have stuck him with a knife. His eyes shrink to slits oozing malice and fear. He spits curses and insults to the effect that my grandfather is a weakling. I turn my head in an effort to suppress the urge to burst out laughing. He raises his voice, speaking my doom. "You be *very* sorry, mister! You will have the evil spells by my uncles in Solo. They will hates you! You be *very sorry!*" I remember an American girl who claimed stones were thrown at her in nearby Solosurakarta. She had a feeling her red hair had something to do with it, something about the local take on witches.

There are tangible reasons to take this young street entrepreneur seriously. But all in all I think, *what a phony.* Even if it does exist I go in faith that I am not subject to the power of evil magic. Arrogant or not, or befooled by the self-righteous confidence of unaccountably high self-esteem, this is my conviction. But his curses do concern me, right here, right now. Bianca and Mary urge me to apologize, whispering that they've heard about dark, spiritualistic goings-on, witchcraft and the like, in Solo. Honest but naïve, I feel my words are justified and tell them his reaction is really about his own guilt. "And don't worry about 'black magic,' for it has no power over an honest heart." *Yup.* I say this, true or not, as if I know anything about it, acting nonplussed for my two female companions. But my mask is pretty thin, and I'm sure it fools no one. Slightly shaken but buoyed by a vague feeling of integrity, I look back at him. "You be *very* sorry!" he hisses as we walk away.

Really, I'm like Goof "B," slightly less daft, perhaps, than Goof "A," each of us standing stupidly across our own lousy moat from each other, with two gorgeous Australian damsels looking on.

The next day we three are in the same area. It's the best artists' market ever, and despite yesterday's tawdry theater we seem to like each other.

And there he is, standing in a defiant pose on the other side of the crazy-busy street. He peers at me like a cornered cat, his eyes steady, as if the passersby and the traffic between us are nothing. *The guy's hurting.* And really, I don't want any trouble. *Me and my mouth.*

I ask Bianca and Mary to wait. I walk over and apologize for disparaging his sense of honor, and especially for doing so in front of others (but not for what I said.) He says nothing, but his eyes relax a wee bit. I walk back to my two Aussie gals. "It's all good," I tell them. "I made good with him."

Bianca and Mary purchase some wildly colored batik shirts. The only thing I buy is a small black-and-white batik I spotted just after the spirits were called off. Unlike any other I've seen, it depicts a traumatic childbirth, the anguish of the mother, and some kind of spirit—benign or sinister, I can't tell—lurking like an animated shadow behind them. The gals look at the cloth, then at me with mild discomfort.

Odd little batik that it is, I fancy it a talisman for a safe journey through Java.

Parantritis

While in Jogja, Yuji tells us about some nearby temples that are over a thousand years old. He speaks of the Hindu Prambanan, which we admire and then irreverently climb all over like happy toddlers. He describes the immense Buddhist Borobudur with reverence, but also with disappointment. His head slightly fallen and his voice soft, he tells us that alas, we cannot visit, for a restoration is in progress. Perhaps these historical sites have survived modern Muslim times by their sheer size and majesty.

But it's the more nondescript side trips I enjoy most: places chosen by simply looking at a map and following a whim. This is the lazy (although I prefer the term detached) way of *my* choosing. I show them my map and suggest following "this here thin black line" to the nearest coast at "this here dot called Parantritis" about thirty miles away, directly south. No historical monuments, just one of those intriguing coastline squiggles with a spot name on it. My traveling friends—Yuji, Bianca, Mary, and Holger, a tall Dutchman—seem receptive on this fine day to the peculiar value of the random and the unexpected as presented by *moi.* We will rent bicycles first thing tomorrow.

Finding a rental place is easy. I hold up my arms like I'm riding a bike and follow the smiling faces and pointing fingers. The bikes in these parts are large, old contraptions with a thick, curvy design, "beast-cycles" with balloon tires, circa 1940–1950ish. Very heavy.

In no time we're pedaling through luminous country. Firestorm greens, auburns and ochers, and deep violets and blues are splashed through my retinas with an intensity that triggers flashbacks of a child-hood amnesia fetish. The edge of the city is transformed into a festive rural parade. For that's what it is to me, marching along in majestic form, never mind that it's us moving along. People are everywhere. I say again, Java is the most densely populated landmass of its size. Within a few miles of the city, children run toward the road from rice fields, shouting and laughing, waving and singing. They spot us from 200 meters away, their small brown bodies moving across the shimmering green like a wild herd stricken with unnatural joy. Bianca, with her fair skin and whipping blonde hair, is the likely visual lure, even from a distance. *Bianca*: Italian-feminine for "white." She is a strikingly fair and bonnie Italo-Aussie lassie.

Twenty or so kids crowd in tight, forcing us off our bikes. They lead us from the road to a shady patch between some empty buildings, giddy and chattering among themselves. Smiling and eager to please, they crack open fresh coconuts and offer them. We sit under the trees and drink the delicious milk while they study our faces, our clothes, and especially, Bianca's white skin and bright hair. Several boys' eyes trace the sensuous shape of her breasts, more snugly clothed as they are than those of the local women, for this is Muslim Java. Their trust is disarming, offered openly and in abundance like the sustenance pro-vided by these generous fields. They touch our bodies, amazed by the hair on our arms and legs. Soon our bellies are full, and we can't offer ourselves for further inspection without some weird embarrassment. We say goodbye amidst a flurry of small brown hands and ride off like reluctant, shabby superstars.

Down the road we encounter an antiquated blacktop machine. A squad of men are making repairs to the uneven, over-patched road. The hand-drawn machine is the size of an ice-cream merchant's rig and rolls on wobbly wheels. The men dig buckets full of soft asphalt from the hot, smelly contraption with small toy shovels. One by one they dump their buckets on the road. Instead of a steamroller, the locals come out and pat the hot tar with bare hands, wincing and gasping. This is how they fix this road and why it's as lumpy as the bare earth beneath it.

Halfway to the coast we come to a river large enough to employ a small ferry serving foot traffic. The ferryman asks what seems an inflated price for this part of the world. The clever Holger and I, having locked into a mutual zone of logic-smitten pride, separate from the rest with an air of manly cunning.

Off we two blunderbusses go, wading across the river carrying our Beastcycles above our heads. In yet another sorry spasm of reason I tied my passport/money belt to the frame to keep them dry. We're not sure how deep the river is but I figure we can turn back anytime. A third of the way across, the water is up to my chest and the current is strong. *If I'm gonna turn back, this is it.* Holger is taller and isn't feeling it like I am. An urge propels me onward, unexamined and tense as urges are. As in many boyhood adventures, I suspect it's related to sharing the experience with other jacked-up doofuses, not to mention today's little audience. A few more precarious steps and the current washes my armpits and splashes my face. The river's force scares me, but to turn back now would be like the cat, the headlights, and the center of the road. It is an extremely heavy bike, never mind the psycho gravity of my precious papers perched stupidly on the spokes. For a few seconds I stand barely holding my balance, vacillating, looking back and forth, the dumbest cat in the 'hood. One wrong move…

We drag ourselves onto the opposite bank and lie panting in the gravel. No words. In the one sore glance we afford each other, Holger looks spent, woefully dumb, and as embarrassed as a self-absorbed twit can muster. I'm sure I look the same. The bemused looks of villagers waiting for the ferry, which gurgles without effort across the river, with our dry friends aboard… sigh. We will pay the sixty or seventy cents worth of rupiahs on the way back.

Ahh, sexy, gentle Bianca and lovely, smiling Mary. I have a hunch our foolish caper, our stingy vibe, our lack of trust and selfish endeavor, has brought us to a fork in that most popular of roads. *Sigh.*

A short ride, Holger and I lagging behind. Soon we spot the blasting white of a mini-range of wind-sculpted sand hills through a grove of shade trees. As we move closer, a blue sliver of choppy ocean cuts through. We park our bikes on the beach. An old woman walks down from some buildings and offers us tea and a snack. The ocean looks all agitated and frothy.

Yuji says he's heard about magic mushrooms growing in the area.

"The locals believe water demons hide in the ocean," Bianca says, "ready to snatch away anyone foolish enough to go in."

"Nonsense!" Holger says.

"But haven't you noticed that Asians rarely, if ever, go swimming?" Mary asks. "They account for the ocean's power with stories of ominous god creatures lurking in there."

"They're just fairy tales, that's all." Holger again.

"Maybe it's about weird currents and great waves. Maybe they speak a vital truth with their monster stories." This is me, remembering the frightening power of the river and my stupid challenge.

None of us go in for a swim.

4. Bali
take these sunken eyes and learn to see[20]

Isle of Light

As I hovered over a map back in Perth, I perused the different routes I might take through Asia. That's when I first spotted a certain small, roughly triangular island. The huge reputation came later.

As I approach Bali heading east across Java I hear stories: jewel of island jewels, fruit basket of Earth, Isle of the Gods, Morning of the World. Indonesians call it the Island of Light. Such imagery and intrigue leads me to a large old ferry at Java's eastern end.

For once, the rumors fit. Eden's garden is placed way yonder west between two rivers made great by history. Or we might hear snippets of its whereabouts along more esoteric paths in the eastern Himalayas, beyond an impenetrable wilderness of mountains, gorges, poisonous beasts, and a reality out of phase, where only a still mind and clear heart can go.[21]

Yet with its mist-blown paradise of translucent green fire, Bali fits the part. The Balinese move across sculpted rice fields as if locked in the island's own grace and rhythms. It is said that the spirits exist not only in stories and symbols, but are alive in the winds that caress every hillock and rice stalk. Here gods and demons move alongside all creatures and breathe with plants, the whole shebang a mere "reflection of an unseen

---

20   The voice of Paul McCartney in the song "Blackbird" by the Beatles, written by Lennon/McCartney.

21   Referring to the "eastern Garden of Eden" somewhere in the vicinity of the "Hidden Lands" and not necessarily exclusive of the mythical Shambhala, from *Heart of the World* by Ian Baker.

fabric of energy which majestically moves beyond time."[22]

Although just a small island, it is one of the rare lands apart from the Indian subcontinent that is currently dominated by Hinduism. Bali is its own distinct culture in the vast archipelago of Islamic Indonesia. The name Bali is from the demon king of three worlds, nemesis of Vamana, who is Vishnu's fifth incarnation in Hinduism. Vamana defeated Bali, who then was banished to rule part of Patala, *one* of Hinduism's hells. Thus "Bali" might conjure images of heaven or hell, *your choice, mister.* Never mind the island's preponderance of demon statues, masks, and paintings.

Like many travelers I find myself smitten by the otherness of Eastern lands and myths. Bali, like any place of imagination, and real footsteps, provides unexpected gates of experience that, contrary to plain logic, one simply cannot turn and go back through.

I HOP UP the steps of an overcrowded bus and shuffle to the back. My backpack is bulky and so am I. I drop to the floor and lean against the last seat with my pack as a cushion. A bunch of roosters appear in the clearing dust, hanging upside down a foot from my face. Their legs are tied together and held in the grasp of a Balinese man. Looking both shocked and vacant, a dozen pinhead eyes stare and blink in random flickers. Heads jerk about spastically with their suspicious gurgling sounds, a cluck here and there, the vagaries of human culture and chicken stylings providing small details in a continuum of morphogenic spectrums that spin my head in a matter of seconds. The bus clanks and bounces through the hills, maintaining the ambient dust level to a light fog. I can relate to the roosters' feelings of vulnerability. I imagine that I see in them something akin to what we call feelings, so I send a soothing vibe into the crew of beady eyes that hang mere inches from mine in an attempt to penetrate and probe *their* morphogenic spectrum. I tune up my effort with empathy, visualizing a great spread of happy, golden wings for a good minute. Nothing.

Besides the roosters it's all legs and torsos in my immediate hemisphere of vision. Straight ahead, as the dust cloud shifts, I am blasted

---

22   From the book *Ring of Fire* by Lawrence Blair with Lorne Blair, page 23.

by a perfect scene of catholic heaven. A teenage woman sits against the back wall nursing a baby. Her smooth, generously filled breasts immediately double in value with my keen attention. Noticing my stare (it would require an effort to look elsewhere in my cramped position,) she smiles a most demure smile, a half-naked, nursing Mona Lisa. Warmed is she, I presume, by my earnest appreciation of her.

Engrossed as I am in this permanent vision of mother and child I haven't noticed that a smiling old hag is perched energetically on her haunches, to my right and smack between me and the young mother. Her long, wrinkled breasts sway on the bus's heaves, her nipples nearly sweeping the floor. She squats forward, grinning and focusing, her torso aligned directly toward me, just as I am on Hot Little Mama. The triadic absurdity of our dumb human stage is so plain that even the roosters pipe up and make a racket, an upside-down gallery of fools applauding the nonsense of our doomed pleasures.

As soon as I notice her the crone starts yakking at me in Balinese. Her rant is muffled (toothless) yet authoritative. *Is she grandma, accompanying young mama on an inter-village trip?* Her ragged voice has a soothing quality. Her face and body lingo indicate she is referring to the nursing mother, who now blushes (erotically, as I fancy.) A ridiculous, wishful delusion on my part maybe, but it seems the grandma is offering the young woman, motioning to her breasts, clearly nudging and smirking. *Is the old crone mocking my Western prudishness, sparking wild ideas she knows will paralyze me? Is she the young woman's madam? A silly old bat on the verge of senility?* I'm downright sheepish. Moses, Paul, Augustine... thanks for nothing.

I nod and offer a limp smile. I take some fruit, a salak and some lychees, from my bag. I peel and eat them rapidly, offering some to the women in a gesture of generosity aimed on a whim of great cultural and social fusion. But really, I'm just embarrassed and trying to change the subject.

The wrinkled one declines with a brief hand flutter, looking away toward a window and muttering a few last words to herself. The nursing mother smiles. The roosters sing. Dimly aware, I'm more like that baby than I care to admit.

ON A BUS not so crowded as the last, I sit comfy and curious in my own seat.

I look around and marvel. Even though a dozen fellow passengers are staring at me, the only foreigner on board, I'm not uncomfortable. Coming from a large, darkish immigrant family with notorious older brothers in an average-white Canadian town, it's nothing; this Bali bus ride is a downhill glide. In villages, crowds of youngsters often follow in amazement. *Can I bask in the flawed glory of this princely flavored treatment and still heed the lofty humilities of Buddha and Jesus? What is ego for, anyway?* Already I've encountered the blockhead-guru delusion[23].

So, how *do* these pleasant, brownish, Far-Easterners see me? Clues come in the turn of an occasional nod, the fall of an intrigued, self-conscious smile, or the wild twinkle of a furtive eye. It is my position at the center, the hub of many lines of sight, that best defines my view and situation. With my tanned olive skin and black hair I could pass for a bearded, newbie Indian swami to these fervently Hindu Balinese.

A refreshing insight awakens me from my less-than-awakened musings: I'm already on stage, of a sort. I'm from an alien world and not a whole lot unlike a madman to them. *Punk god.* I'm feeling bemused, sort of comically smug, and—*ping*—a novel opportunity pops up. *Why, I can do a "crazy wisdom" routine with impunity—have some fun, get somethin' done.* Practice me' sorry acting skills.

Dry my wet laundry.

It's in my backpack, washed this morning and folded in a hurry. I take out a shirt and hang it on the frame of my seat. I look up: a nod, a smirk, a twinkle. I take my wet clothes and walk down the aisle of the moving bus. Like a time-lapse film of a garden bursting into bloom, big smiles flash throughout the bus as I spread my laundry up the aisle at elfin speed.

Thirty minutes later I spot some roadside shacks and a small crowd milling about up ahead. I fly up the aisle, gather my clothes, and hop off the bus. I saunter over and stand in the crowd. The only other foreigner is a twenty/thirty-something gal from New Zealand. She's been living

---

23   Its dumb lure draws the occasional wayfarer, here in Bali and later in my travels, into a sorry staging of "holy one," the role worn like an oversized coat that doesn't fit the scrawny figure beneath. I felt embarrassed for the poor blokes.

here with her Balinese husband for seven years. She's here, I'm there, and together we gaze off the edge of a cliff across the vast bowl of a gigantic collapsed volcano. Looks to be a good several miles across. In the center a much younger offspring has risen through lush greenery. More than a third of the world's active volcanoes are said to be located in Indonesia, with an average of three earthquakes a day measuring at least 5 on the Richter scale.[24]

Bali must be sitting over a powerful magma plume, a river of fire shooting up from Earth's mantle. Perhaps the Balinese have unwittingly fashioned this great gush of geothermal power into a steady outpouring of art forms, like so many vents from a seething underworld into the daylight of village and field. Thousands of demon-bearing temples dot the island, grim and grotesque yet ethereally beautiful. In yards through ornate gateways, on the sides of roads, in townsites, their stony presence is hard evidence of a culture seething with rare vitality.

As we stand on the ancient volcano's timeworn edge I wonder at its vastness and age. At the much smaller central cone, red-brown rubble flows into the verdant growth of its lower slopes. A little farther—as far as possible—a few huts poke through the dense green at the bottom of the steep wall of the vast old crater. Do they sing about demons and fountains of destruction? Deny it altogether? This Kiwi lassie has crossed a sea of changes to raise her children here in their lush homeland of dreams and genes.

I climb aboard a local minibus, a *bemo*. A small, converted pickup truck, it is crammed with passengers facing each other, yet not facing each other on opposing bench seats. On this rocking, bent old bemo I've been eyeing, as subtle as I can manage, an attractive local woman directly across. After stepping off she pauses in front of her hut, tilts a hip, raises a leg. Steaming gold trickles from her foot, visible at the bottom of her batik sarong. The last few drops jerk free, and she disappears into the hut. *A devi just released from her stony prison, heedless of the local decorum...*

I set down at Ubud, an artist's town in the island's interior. Home after home is open, offering the works and hospitality of painters, sculptors, jewelers, and woodcarvers. At a hostel there's talk about a nearby sacred monkey forest with psilocybin mushrooms growing on its lush floor.

24   From *Ring Of Fire* by Lawrence Blair with Lorne Blair.

Not far along a track, monkeys high up in trees squawk and yell as I pass by below. In the moist soil where cattle saunter about, I find a few gray-white, blue-tinged mushrooms. Probably *Panaeolus cyanescens*.

Kuta Beach

With an international airport, Denpasar is Bali's hub city. Boomtown, mid-1970s Southeast Asia is an ant crawl of smoky cars and noisy scooters. It's an economy hyped on a transition of scale and kind where one often sees the odd twist of mixed-up ways: from a bus window I spot human lawnmowers going at it on the half-acre lawn of a corporate hotel, one man squatting in each corner with hand scissors.

At the notorious Kuta Beach, hippie traveler plays alongside jet-setter wannabe. Giant sea tongues roll and heave and curl in the equatorial waters. Firm, tanned, half-cooked noodle folk slide happily over and under; I notice only a twenty-minute lull in the wave action in over a week. Frisbees, surfboard or no board, local entrepreneurs hawking trinkets, smoke, food, dope, and the warm sea breeze heavy with love-smack in a pseudo-happy-land milieu. The sheer force of ripe pheromones permits all persuasions, including the not-too-uncommon sight of inter-cultural bliss enjoyed between Western gals and their dumbstruck, young Balinese lads (I see no evidence of the implied reversal.) All of this or none of the above, in your own custom-fit dream.

The weather is utopian. The dense green that blankets the island bears evidence of an extravagance of rain. For my two-week stay, torrential downpours pound the island but only at night, the intensity of which I've witnessed only rarely back home in lush Lotusland. Rainwater pours off roofs in sheets and every village path becomes a gushing stream. I shower at night by standing outside, the balm of paradise ruling out the chills. When morning comes the clouds are gone, the land bathed only in bright equatorial sunlight that glistens in the rapidly evaporating moisture. Colors and textures are accentuated to a surreal luminosity, with wisps of living mist animating every nook. Soft brown cows appear vibrant with beauty and momentary relevance. Even the noisy, smoky scooters reveal sharp, ugly details whose clarity, at least, appeals to the senses.

Away from the tourist glitz toward grass huts and kerosene lamps, young Balinese are hungry for the popular sounds of the West. Guitars and boomboxes have already arrived. Walking the trails among homes and tiny shops, words in the latest pop songs seem to acknowledge my nascent mythical curiosity... images of demons and desires, of moving among shadows, among travelers and the Balinese themselves through a continuum of darkness and light, however we show up in this phantasmagoria of a world.[25]

With the music already here, of course they want the rest of it too: cars, TVs, dishwashers. It isn't easy explaining the cost of runaway consumerism to folks who are looking forward to indoor plumbing and refrigeration. No, they don't want to hear what I, who already have these things, am saying: "We'll make our own mistakes, thank you." Custom-fit paradise blinders—who can resist a pair? They're just leaving, and I've just returned. How easy it is, coming from the suburban West, to romanticize the "simple life."

Yet there are disapproving looks from elders. They watch their oddly clothed grandchildren bop to strange new music and talk in an unknown tongue to uninvited foreigners. In those of older ways I have unlikely and unwitting allies. And *I am* the problem. The old Balinese, with their ancient stories, ethereal music, and visceral dances, look on with discontent. Change doesn't come waltzing along in ruby slippers. It reminds of my own parents' uprooting from southern Italy to find a home in the modern world. And my father, with *his* disapproving looks.

WALKING ALONG A path I hear a brief splash of dramatic shouting. I steal closer and spy through some bushes a crowd gathered on make-shift bleachers for a show. It is the Barong Dance, one of Bali's celebrated traditions. A dozen men prance about nimbly, some wearing demon masks depicting a scene from a Hindu saga. Now and again the dancers step aside for a drink. Over the next hour the men's faces become increasingly trance-like (drunk? high?), and in the show's weird, almost frenzied climax, they appear to stab themselves in the chest with pointed

25 Imagery taken from the song, "One of These Nights" by the Eagles, written by
     Don Henley and Glenn Frey

daggers. At times they drag the point of the blade across their skin (how sharp, these knives?), but never do they draw blood. Several men collapse and are carried away by ready-to-go man helpers on the sidelines.

From my hidden spot on the other side of a shrub, both the actors and those watching are on stage. A few tourists are in the audience, perhaps having paid to attend. But with the greater number of Balinese present, the spectacle carries an air of authenticity. An old man is sitting in the front row; in his serene countenance shines the reflection of many such scenes and, as I imagine it, those of his ancestors looking on. And in the frightened toddler who stands wrapped in his arms I see myself staring at scenes of hell and purgatory, in the graphically illustrated *Cattolico* prints on my mom's rosary altar.

A Psilly Cosmology

Perhaps the following psilocybin mushroom stories will be challenging, provocative, or even objectionable to some. I could omit them, deferring to a broader social decorum. But I'd be leaving out a key juncture in my travels, never mind copping out to perceived nay-sayers in order to play it safe. In speaking of these controversial forays into altered consciousness, perhaps I expose a vulnerable side of my psyche, one that might appear, at times, unstable or grandiose. I take my turn in the telling of what has become a cultural stereotype, sensational in its fringe and caricatured depictions over decades. In doing so I must speak on the dissolution of the normal self, the one named and trained, the one who must play by the rules of the tribe. The one, perhaps, for whom those rules play so fundamental a role as to remain unseen by many. I wish to believe that you, dear reader, are, in some way, a part of my tribe.

What follows is my wordy rendering, as lean as I can manage, of an unprecedented cerebral and visceral experience. It is an attempt to describe, as objectively as possible, a seminal experience that must remain subjective.

ONE DOESN'T VISIT Kuta Beach without hearing about the Blue Meanie omelet stand. Borrowed from the villains in the Beatles' *Yellow Submarine* animation, Blue Meanie is the street name of the slender, grayish-white psilocybin mushrooms that grow on the island. For four or five times the twenty-five cent cost of a regular omelet, a clever restaurateur has cashed in on the subterranean curiosity of travelers, even advertising the goods unabashedly with a large BLUE MEANIE sign on the beach. Children are sent early in the morning to moist cow fields to collect the little buds of rare, phantasmagoric delight.

An odd feeling of psychic hunger has drawn me in. I stand before the Blue Meanie omelet hut one brilliant Kuta morning, the tireless surf crashing behind me. Since leaving Oz it's been a merry-go-round of culture-swapping and their attendant bouts of self-inquiry. Now, with this opportunity for descent into realms hidden by, and from, culture at large, it seems that the over- and underworlds of creation have beckoned. I'm a naïve stooge in the presence of the Blue Meanie sign, for it stands before me as a token of my curiosity, what courage I've mustered, a measure of what many call faith, and a good bit of blind credulity. And the waves here at this beach of pleasures are giant-sized, warm, and constant.

Yes, I will sample an omelet extraordinaire.

My day is borne on a mild psychedelic euphoria as I, a deliriously wounded seabird, flap about in the surf. A half-hour smile gets stuck and that's it: wacko smile for the day. The sea bobs with brilliant, heaving Aphrodites and bucking Apollos, all hungry for ecstasy and slithering like happy dragons in a creation-fire soup. Now and then I dip into the old memory bag for my logbook and map to remind myself that these splendid beings are generic humans just like me, swimming in a tropical ocean on a familiar planet, at a beach called Kuta.

Not long after the psilocybin peak I'm greeted in the waist-high water by a congenial Balinese lad. He invites me home for a meal. Feeling giddy and grateful, I leave the slippery fizz of the sea like it's the first and only womb I've had the pleasure of getting lost in. My skin tightens up in the drying air. The ride is extra lumpy on the back of his screaming, desperate, rather psychotic motorbike. A generous madness of snap-crackle-ping and odd shots of hiss-flash-moan are both inside me and echo, with aching immediacy, across the impersonal sky.

We arrive at a spacious split-level home, solid upper-middle-class by any standard. Two exposed stairways line opposite sides of a large central area, big plants in pots, dangly ones hanging, the walls the color of raw milk with highlights of fresh custard. It's a third-world country, but this kid's place is well beyond my family's working-class digs in suburban Vancouver. I'm still high on the shrooms, so these classist details are momentarily noted and discarded. I do feel a bit odd about the whole affair. I hear a whisper: *I'm already beyond their "crazy"*. My faith: my foreign looks and manner will ring kindly bells in their credulous minds.

Inside, several guys my age walk about, distracted or busy or both. A mere glance, no greeting. *Mom, Dad?* My host issues a terse knot of words to one of them, presumably to announce I'll be staying for dinner. *Cold, hard.* He explains that he shares this fancy place with fellow art students. Monkey brain takes notes: *Modern digs. Folks must be loaded.*

He leads me to his room and offers a massage while we wait. The whispering continues: *probably gay*. I'm a wayward vessel whose charmed fictions were ordained way back in the crucible of creation. The small self born and raised on a wild Canadian coast is a mere speck in a vast continuum; the past and the future blink like drunken fireflies on the tip of my psychedelic wand. That he might be gay is unimportant, and the info has already departed, off to catch one of those empty helter-skelter trains where thoughts like to crowd into. Like the topic of class and money, it's not worth a scratch of concern. If ever I carried a trace of homophobia, it is here dissolved in a wash of impersonal ethos and logos.

I listen again to the running tale of soft words, and now it's my body that speaks: *Yes, a massage will be good.* I lie on my stomach. Balinese Art Dude does a great job, especially on *beauteous maximus*. "Turn over," he tells me, a barely audible snort. His hands are ravenous. My flesh would gladly give itself. *I'm cool.* Spiraling hands zero in, closer, his resistance now swollen to the edge point of bursting. *Now the picture changes…* one of those pesky, testy gates is before me: a choice will be made.

Thoughts ricochet at the speed of insight: *If I keep my eyes closed and imagine the soft hands and willing limbs of smiling, singing Joni… well, yes. And I could stay for dinner.* I'm a psilocybin scout, a psychedelic rookie toying with intent and pure happenstance. Or is it, maybe, the inevitable turn of a deeply probabilistic stream I must find the skill to navigate? Social and sexual rules have dissolved in wispy strands of what

I have habitually referred to as memory… as the psilo-chemistry continues its wondrous, personal-yet-impersonal dance.

Then a familiar voice speaks up, like a gentle call to arms, a casual alert to the wider realm of collective wisdom, or folly: *Presently, you are a savant-fool on a shitload of shrooms, and Johnny, you already know: the ephemeral pleasure—Joni or no Joni—is not the issue, for it is everywhere, anytime, pretty much. The real value of this alleged experience, whether you let it happen or not, is already yours. Soooo… would you like to own this? How will it sit as memory in that illusory slipstream of fore and aft that you will soon reenter? Hmm…*

Alas, my trusty alchemy will await consummation by more conventional yin/yang plumbing, at a later date. Who knows? Maybe my heeding "the voice" is as much a matter of timing, or dosage.

I sit up gently, smiling. "Sorry, guy, I'm just not gay."

"Oh, really? Come on, are you sure?" he asks, famished and twitching.

"Yeah, sure I'm sure." *Smile.* "Say, would you mind giving me a ride back to the beach?" He grumbles and jerks himself straight, then walks stiffly out of the room.

I'll admit I've been pretty naïve about "gay." Didn't even hear about it until I was twelve or so. Even after my priest tried to grope me when I was eleven and I ran home and quit the church, I believed I'd dodged some dark and unsavory man-boy altar duty business (that I knew Jesus wouldn't approve of), with the priest as the unholy chief of some fallen-angel rite. Yeah, and I'm embarrassed to admit, this interlude in Bali marks the dawn of my realization that "gay" is not culture specific (early 1976.)

I walk out to his motorcycle. The poor guy follows in silence. I've forgotten about dinner, and I need a ride. Don't know where I am, but it looks like a nice part of town. Clouds and mountains are running gauntlets through time-loops back into the yawn of Creation. And so on. It's that kind of day, though no one seems to notice.

The ride back to the beach is noticeably quicker, jerkier.

THE PSILOCYBIN TRIP that resulted in the awkward rendezvous at the art student's pad turned out to be a mere yummy appetizer. So far, foreign cultures have served as a looking glass into my own as I carry it, and

as it shifts before and behind my gaze. The resulting jostle of worldviews—and the Blue Meanie omelet stand—present an opportunity. I
would overthrow the tyranny of my own culture's chosen sanity and
laugh about it, with little or no public involvement. So goes my faith.
So goes my heroic ignorance.

In regard to the psilocybin mushrooms and the full-course meal I
anticipate, the need to care for my body should be minimal in the body-
warm sea, providing a measure of safety and freedom. And nobody who
knows who I am knows *where* I am. I'm as free as I'm ever gonna be. Good
guesses (for one's "freedom" back then was not encumbered by the likes
of mobile phones or the internet.) *No matter how far I go, within blunt
reason, they won't haul me away.* This is my belief and my faith. *Already
beyond their crazy.* Thousands travel through here but I'm guessing, by the
refreshing reaction of the locals, that I'm in one of the first large waves of
budget travelers. We are still a new and interesting species to them.

I return to the Blue Meanie stand two days later. Inside my raw little
brain I imagine a direct flight through some unnamed, unseen barrier
to a personal celebration of the unveiling of Truth and Freedom, no less.
I'm beginning to see how I took only what I wanted from the religious
milieu of my early years... how Jesus's "kingdom of heaven" business
got deep into me, although I rejected, at the same time, any notion of
"saved and damned." *Just the good news for me, thanks.*

I walk past the female server straight to the kitchen. The cook/pro-
prietor can't speak English, and neither can the young boy—probably
this morning's picker—who follows me in. Spotting a large pile of fresh
mushrooms on a broad wooden table, I walk over to it. The man is at
my side at once. I brashly pick out most of the bigger ones and set them
aside. Altruistically, I turf the first of a few wispier brown ones that
don't match the others. The cook snorts. His entrepreneurial hard-on
could probably sire a chain of restaurants in different circumstances.
He continues to make disapproving noises as the number of nice big
ones passes twenty and continues to grow. That is, until I flash him
a corresponding handful of cash. All quiet now, he watches me finish
counting. Sixty large ones are about three times the normal dose. *Goin'
on a hunch.* I watch him put the mushrooms into three eggs and cook it.

I take my high-octane Blue Meanie *omeletto mysterioso* out to a table and eat it, slowly and with great relish. It's still morning, and I'm the only customer in the open-palm restaurant

I will do my best to report on my next six hours or so. I will aim not to dramatize (but I will), nor to overreach, in an attempt to describe the irrepressible energies and dimensions of mind given access by ingesting these sacred flowers of the soil. But I will.

It is an experience for which the word ecstasy was surely coined. A continuum of ecstasy, or the Kingdom of Ecstasy, one that contains our universally celebrated sexual variety and augments its reach into realms beyond that of body and mind, yet still remains within the insatiable hunger of *anima/animus*. And it all happens right here, in me—it doesn't have to make sense, but maybe it does. There is no ego in this, for it is a democratic deal where everyone qualifies for starring role. I am Everyman, neither above nor below, and all of the above/below. I know it, I "am" it, and it is my every breath, in and out, out and in. I am a vortex of mental storms and emotional tsunamis, yet I am *not*. Rather, I am a small but excellent hologram of all that is, whatever that is. In the turbulent wonderland of all-that-whatever-is, psychic dams are wiped out in the great purge of a small life of hidden tensions and illusions. Personality gets a good wash and tune-up (as I am to learn later, as days turn to weeks and months... and years.) And it can't be undone, no more than you can unscramble an omelet.

The ecstasy is physical/sensual. I slosh and tumble in the giant, benevolent hands of the ocean, body-surfing and flipping head over heel, four-in-a-row. It is psychological, emotional. Looking on in wonder, bits or layers of my self-image fly off in bizarre, poetic symbols, in a conceptual salad of words that, despite their seeming incoherence, ring instantly each to their origin, linking back through years to a source that possesses the most profound meaning—yet in the end is irrelevant and hilarious. A deluge of illusions, a bloody great show.

The ecstasy brings me into a realm beyond the merely sensual. A larger... identity (?) that includes stuff-out-there is revealed, and I am It. That I am housed in this body and defined by its mind become ludicrous, then very intriguing ideas. My skin is a porous sheath, both me and not-me. That I've experienced this limitation as reality is a gut-splitting revelation. I breathe with the trees, and my flesh heaves with the ocean. I sense a pulse in the air and the movement of mountains; indeed, my movement *is* their movement. Laughter is a cellular bio-gizmo that riddles the flesh in syncopated rhythms, strengthening the body-temple and protecting it from sharks and errant currents. And healing someone downwind to boot, the lack of mechanical specifics notwithstanding.

Swimmers and wayfarers begin to stare. They smile a sweet tide of toothy smiles at a young man babbling incoherencies, laughing with wild abandon, flipping in the waves like a dying salmon. Privacy beckons, so I swim way, way out, a quarter if not a half mile. I stop and look back.

In the far distance I behold shimmering twin white lines and a thin band of green just beyond. The white strips are the giant surf breaking, and the sunlit sand. The green is the world remembered, teeming with crowds and noises both chaotic and songlike, held together with stories and agreements, now a thin line in the intangible distance. I remember the news: five swimmers have gone missing in the past three months due to aberrant undertows or sharks, or both. *Meh.*

All the while a cornucopia of verbiage spews like a latter-day vent still farting along a tailwind from the Big Bang. A glorious tower of babble piles away from flipping mind and flapping lip. I've eaten from the Fungus of Knowledge, and guess what, folks? Nothing to do with good and/or evil! Stories are translucent; truth stands clear. Personality dissolves, and "psychosis" is lovingly cradled, then playfully discarded. For it is found simply to be another possibility or attribute of self. Just another version, another passing mythology.

The verbiage keeps coming. The content of the word salad consists of references to personal details taken on like programs or building blocks, mostly from my father and two older brothers. As I revel in the revelations, it strikes me as outrageous and comical because here "I am," apart from any imprinting or programming of others' qualities, layered as they were, like veils onto me. Until now I assumed the veils *were* me. Clearly, this has been a powerful and perennial misconception. Off they fly in layers made of word symbols. This has made a sham of that diaphanous beast: personality. A recalibration. A work of fiction, reworked. It seems that whoever I am is not to be found in the applied fictions of boyhood or even of the social mind. *When I let go of what I am, I become what I might be.*[26] Ha!

Occasionally, my head bobs up and looks across the soupy water toward the open sea. I always look in the same direction, as though receiving a signal: "Hello, India?" I ask. The words, like all the others, surprise me, but this greeting is on some kind of loop. Each time, I go down in a convection current of seawater-crazy laughs. It's as though some great wise one has heard my unrelenting guffaws and reaches across centuries and an ocean, from his land, saying, *When you realize how perfect everything is, you will tilt your head back and laugh at the sky.*[27] I don't know where India is, other than it being the biggest and maybe the weirdest country on the overland-to-Europe route. I've hardly given India a thought. (Later, referring to a map, I see that I kept looking WNW, direction spot on.)

I remember my camera, money, and passport, which I, reluctant to leave them in my non-secure room, brought along and left on the sand in a bright blue nylon day bag. When I walked away from it, as the psilo ally began its mind work, I looked back at the little blue sack and smiled. It sits on the beach for six or so hours, an unguarded flaming blue dot among tourists and locals who continually walk past it. I told no one of today's excursion into the realm of psilocybin, for I'm flying solo these days. From time to time, I scan the beach with my extra-hued vision and locate my significant spot of peacock-blue with great joy, first directly toward the beach, then over to the left a hundred or so meters. Then way, *way* over to the right. And then I spot it from even farther away, from a different angle. Some curly and ravenous currents must be looping me around, pulling at these shores. My day bag remains untouched all day on a busy beach in a "poor" country.

A preposterous yet "natural" visual phenomenon prickles my fancy: I see in curves, riding eye beams through space along a ribbon of time on the Einstein Express. With naked vision I peer around clouds that hang against the mountain in the distance by moving my head back and

26   Lao Tzu.
27   Buddha.

forth or up and down just a wee bit, as if it is subject to a great shifting curtain of magnetic essence, as if my vision employs the faculties of an immense, ethereal head that stretches for thousands of meters in every direction, whipping my perspective into mad distances on some linkaged, laser-optic mechanism. And the palm trees… they undulate seductively, exactly, *because, you see,* they dance within the bloom of creation in the same sexy rhythms we human volcanoes of love enjoy but on a smaller, time-cramped scale.

This revelation in imagination, this whoever-I-am, doesn't buy the standard explanation as a chemically induced hallucination.[28] The word implies falsity, and the psilocybin experience is suffused with the conviction that "reality unclothed" has been revealed. Normal reality—*normalady*—is an arbitrary standard, mostly cultural in form and harnessed emotionally and sensually by us group nerds. Social thresholds (silent nerd agreements) act as gates to perception, gates that must click tight and be maintained daily, whose significance must be both hidden and observed by each nerd in the group. That is why human activity varies so radically: "human A" is content to sit for weeks on end staring at a flickering screen, eating donuts and drinking soda pop in a windowless cell, seeking a code to tap into some abstract, numbered system to strike it rich, while "human B" will sniff suspiciously at the morning breeze before heading up some unexplored river valley in search of the hunting trails his uncle mapped out in a dream during the last full moon.

28 Discovery of endorphins, key/keyhole analogy: perhaps some developments in modern biology support this vision. About the same time as my stay in Bali, it was discovered in the US that certain chemicals or drugs register their effects on the nervous system because their molecular shape mimics that of naturally occurring neurotransmitters in the brain. These neurotransmitters—and corresponding drugs—fit, because of their mechanical shape, certain receptors in the brain like a key into a keyhole, as it is often described, giving us subjectively felt moods and feelings. This can be seen to infer that certain drugs, with their attendant experiences, have their effects because the nervous system permits it, by way of the receptors that are "designed" to receive them. Thus, in what I hope is not too much of a conjectural leap, the drug experience is not simply a function of the drug, but primarily of our brain's—rather, the human entity's—pre-wired potential and capacity for these experiences. Feed the same shrooms to a crocodile's more rudimentary system, and would the croc dance? I'm guessing, no.

The normally-real is now seen to be an arbitrary simulacrum of the amplified presence of whatever-I-am on this glorious fucking day. *Amen.*

AFTER FIVE OR six hours, I look toward the shore. Wading relaxedly, and with the occasional *laissez-faire* flapping of my rather excellent limbs, I let the surf carry me back into the world.

A silent soliloquy continues… *My feet touch the sand, and I walk into a new world; indeed, I walk into a new body. Floating in the equatorial womb all day, the liberating psychedelic experience has simulated an exquisite bodiless and egoless interlude. The ends of my fingers are white and look like ten little squirrel brains. I rediscover my allies in gravity and fellow humans, dislodged as I've been from my normal planetary role. I walk on two legs automatically. I look down a great distance along two muscular trunks to another ten wrinkled knobs like I'm peering into a deep chasm… a bit of vertigo. I'm awestruck that my conscious self is housed improbably in this head, in this sack of flesh and bones, looking through these eyes, employing some wacky perpendicular form of biped locomotion and remaining upright effortlessly, without falling. An exquisite balance is continually effected as first one leg, then the other, raises itself to propel the inertia of my bulk against the falling motion of each leg, magnetically bound to the land in a forward bouncing rhythm. My feet are intelligently supple, molding to the earth in a springy cohesion that tells me they're made precisely for the job they perform so adeptly, so beautifully… kudos to superb design and workmanship!*

I walk with ease, steady and automatic, assuming a natural grace. I am an upright, sentient creature topped with conscious love and a thick coat of wavy black hair. As the ocean sounds fade, the symphonies of land systems increase. Birds, insects, motorcycles—I hear their raw textures for the first time "again." The wind rustles palm leaves in delicate concert with a tickle in my head. This is first union, and I am the child-lover. I enter a luxuriant, breathing forest.

Alas, I enter what only an hour ago was "me." Now there is separation. Within minutes the new body's strangeness has faded, just as the earlier ecstasy in the ocean has. My familiar orientation returns to flesh and mind, gentle and firm, in a graceful crystallization of identity. Where there once was wild freedom, I settle into a form that restrains and defines but is also comfortably familiar. I feel unaccountably good and whole for a thing that must stand and walk and breathe on its own.

And so, Mr. Ego Patrol is back to work after a satisfying leave.

YOU'D THINK THAT after such a psycho-sensory orgy I'd want to repeat it, like any kid in a candy store. Instead I feel cleansed and filled with wonder. I've returned from a grand tour, enriched beyond my understanding of it. A period of rest, restraint, and reflection is in order. It's as though I discovered from the air an unknown sea dotted with a thousand islands, and the information with which to draw a map is at hand. It is time to go down and take measurements. To continue exulting in the feeling of discovery by flying over the archipelago in endless loops would preclude drawing a map; I might burn away vital interest in making sense of what I've seen, or run out of gas. More psychedelic omelets now would make me a swine hoarding pearls. It's unthinkable. I must integrate and seek understanding on this most amazing thing. I will examine those islands up close, day by day.

It will be a year before I consider taking mushrooms again, and still I won't. Years later I'm still measuring, and a clear map is... *hmmm*. I remain reluctant to say more, for map making is best left to others.

IT ALL SOUNDS amazing and mind bending, and it is. But if I inspire inappropriate or hasty willingness to experiment with psychedelics, I offer another view and a prudent word. One could refer to information available from the time, before 1966, when researchers were free from legal restraint (as well, new research is being done.) For example, much has been written regarding the importance of "set" and setting. Setting is easy to determine: it is the world out-there at any given time, one's immediate environment for the next six or so hours. It was, in part, my recognition of the benign social milieu at Kuta Beach, and the near absence of bodily concerns in the tepid surf, that prompted me to risk going further than I normally would by taking as many mushrooms as I did.

But set, or mindset, is not so easy to comprehend. One's beliefs, fears, and expectations, all highly personal yet formed and maintained socially, often remain unconscious or hidden. It has been said that the most potent of these are, specifically, the unknown ones. And in the psychedelic trip the unconscious rules. All the hidden stuff of one's intellect and emotions, in the form of myths both personal and collective, spews from some core place, molten and at your disposal. You are a volcano of humanness, and perhaps more. For this reason the most profound respect and caution is essential. Is one willing to face the sublime range—or horrific turmoil—of the world that heaves beneath the comfortable boundary of the conscious and consensus one we share? The only one many of us are aware of and talk about our whole lives? Is one willing to tear away the veil of culture and personal conditioning? One is advised to think hard on these deeply provocative questions.

Perhaps things were just right for me on that beach; I was lucky, or my timing was spot on. But a dive into the unknown without a trusted guide (and one *is* prescribed along with the taking of any psychedelic in most references) might not result in happy swimming for all. For certain it does not. It's clear there are many who would be advised never to smoke pot nor drink a beer, never mind ingest powerful medicines like psilocybin mushrooms. In these personal capacities, or on any given day, it appears that nature is wide-ranging, and uneven.

HOW BORROWED MIGHT the visionary experience be? Like the cloaks of personality acquired from my father and brothers that came loose and flew away, might one shed more nonessentials? Some reliable cross-cultural references have been available long before my trip-in-the-surf: the Huichol Amerindian culture of the deer (peyote) hunt, Mesoamerican shamanic psilocybin use, iboga cults in tropical Africa, and ayahuasca journeys in the Amazon.[29] Each of these bears a traditional worldview perhaps not in conflict with modern psychedelic visions.

My own mindset was aligned and tempered over the years by the writings of several psychedelic pioneers: Huxley, Lilly, Watts, Leary, Grof, Weil, and Castaneda.[30] Each writer contributed to a cosmological

---

29   *Hallucinogens and Culture* by Peter T. Furst; *Marriage of the Sun and Moon* by Andrew Weil.

30   *Doors of Perception/Heaven and Hell* by Aldous Huxley; *Center of the Cyclone* by John C. Lilly; *A Joyous Cosmology* by Alan Watts; *The Politics of Ecstasy* by Timothy Leary; *Realms of the Human Unconscious* by Stanislav Grof; *The Natural Mind* by Andrew Weil; *A Separate Reality* by Carlos Castaneda.

model of my own synthesis, realigned, as it was, on my own splashing trip. (I wonder what sources influenced *their* mindsets.)

I'd like to believe there is "truth" in the experience of non-duality, of ecstasy. Carl Jung's theories on the collective unconscious and "synchronicity", and Rupert Sheldrake's "morphogenetic fields", suggest that some recent cracks have formed in our simplistic model of cause and effect: what is called mechanistic reductionism.[31] Epitomizing this presumed shift are the mind-stretching horizons of subatomic physics, where the border between subject and object has been reported to be dancing a peculiar dance, one that sashays in rhythm alongside many an ancient tune, as the physicist Fritjof Capra puts forth in his seminal book.[32]

A favorite, and perhaps more playful alternate is Terence McKenna's suggestion that psilocybin is an "intelligent organism", an "elder life form" that is basically here to help us mature as a species, just as we are "on the brink of flight to the stars." In McKenna's vision, the spores of the psilocybin "body" traverse space, seeding innumerable planets that have resulted, over millions of years, in "mycelial networks in the galaxy... in hyperlight communication across space and time." But his is not simply a suggestion or a vision, for the mushroom itself speaks in its own voice, directly to the subject "in the cool night of the mind."[33]

I consider, with respect, the words of the "marvelously weird" Terence McKenna, and those of all the above esteemed writers, for they help to make my little excursion into the ocean at Kuta—with a little help from a few wild blue meanies—appear to be not so psilly after all.

WHILE SOME STORIES are told and retold flaunting overexposure, others grasp for words as they slip through gaps in our collective attention. About the time I entered Indonesia, its military was entering East Timor. As I indulged my desire for adventure and explored fantasies that bled real, some real bleeding was going down in a tragedy that bears the tears of the East Timorese.

31 *Synchronicity* by Carl Jung; *A New Science of Life* by Rupert Sheldrake.
32 *The Tao of Physics* by Fritjof Capra.
33 *True Hallucinations* by Terence McKenna, P 209, 210.

It's hard to say why this genocide didn't hit the world's newsstands. We on the road in those parts, at least some of us, did hear about it. I've since learned that the hands of my people in the West helped weave the moneyed blankets that smothered their cries so that they couldn't be heard from the other side of the globe, in darkness we in the brightness of day couldn't see, and sleeping, wouldn't waken to.

It's hard to say why some suffering goes unseen and why some receives proper attention. The sins of power, of its hoarding by an emotionally diseased few who "gnash their teeth" on the flesh of the shell shocked, are the same everywhere.

5. A City-State, a Peninsula, a Kingdom

throw out your gold teeth and see how they roll[34]

The World, 1975

Roll over, Galileo: Pope Paul VI honors Stephen Hawking for his work on the Big Bang, placing the two scientists at opposite ends of a 300-year-long lightning rod of papal tolerance. (Stevie himself stated he felt a certain connection to ol' Galli.)

US and Soviet spacecrafts couple like lovestruck, interplanetary bugs.

Earthquakes destroy the 1,000-year-old Great Temples of Pagan in Burma.

As if Medusa herself once took a holiday in the Far East and couldn't resist an exotic shenanigan, a life-sized clay army of at least 8,000 unique individuals is unearthed in China.

A skull of *Homo erectus* is found by Richard Leakey on the eastern shore of Kenya's Lake Turkana.

Natural principles of pleasure, endorphins, are discovered in the human nervous system.

Auras are "measured" at UCLA.

---

34   From the song "Your Gold Teeth II" by Steely Dan, written by Becker/Fagen.

Newsweek, April 28: "scientists are almost unanimous" that global *cooling* is happening.

The Tao of Physics by Fritjof Capra provokes the comfy paradigm of the new kid on the block, scientific materialism, by exploring the parallels between modern subatomic physics and ancient Eastern mysticism.

FIVE CENTURIES AFTER becoming the first Europeans to colonize, Portugal gets the empire blues; its planet-wide domain folds as a Marxist revolution unfolds at home.

The UN declares Zionism a form of racism.

A helicopter escapes from the roof of the US embassy in Saigon carrying the last Americans from South Vietnam; Vietnam is united under Communist rule.

Gerald Ford replaces, then pardons, Richard (Tricky Dicky) Nixon.

The elected government of Australia is dismissed by the governor-general.

Found guilty of electoral corruption, Indira Gandhi declares a state of emergency and arrests her opponents.

Saudi King Faisal is shot and killed by his nephew.

In Ethiopia, Haile Selassie dies in prison a year after being deposed by a military coup.

The Khmer Rouge takes over; a horrific stench rises over Cambodia's "killing fields."

East Timor declares independence from Portugal. Quietly and ruthlessly, Indonesia invades.

Beirut explodes. Jimmy Hoffa goes missing. Francisco Franco dies.

ON JUNE 27, two months after leaving a pier in Vancouver, the *Phyllis Cormack*, a.k.a. *Greenpeace V* (the original *Greenpeace* that protested the Amchitka nuclear test in 1971), confronts Russian whaling ships over the Mendocino Ridge off the coast of California. Captured on film is the harpooning of a sperm whale; a new course is set for Greenpeace and the world's environmental movement.[35]

The Rockefeller Commission Report reveals to the public for the first time that the CIA and the Department of Defense conducted experiments on both unwitting and cognizant human subjects in order to explore mind-control behavior with LSD, psilocybin, and mescaline.

New York Times article: "Are We a Nation of Mystics?" Forty percent of Americans report having a powerful mystical experience.

West Germany decriminalizes hardcore porn.

Canada's Anglican Church ordains women into the priesthood.

L. Ron Hubbard, founder of the Church of Scientology, returns to dry land after years sailing the seas with his "Commodore's Messengers," a group of young and largely female acolytes.

The specter of Y2K first appears with the issuing of twenty-five-year mortgages.

"Crop circles" begin to appear in farmers' fields (and in newspapers) around the world.

The arrival of personal computers, then Microsoft.

HBO, the first satellite distribution network.

Disposable razors.

THE ALBUMS *Blood on the Tracks, Still Crazy after all These Years, Katy Lied, Wish You Were Here, Venus and Mars, One of These Nights*, and *A*

---

35 *Greenpeace* by Rex Weyler

Night at the Opera are released.

The movies *Jaws, Monty Python's The Holy Grail, One Flew Over the Cuckoo's Nest, The Rocky Horror Picture Show,* and *Return of the Pink Panther* are released.

The books *Life After Life, Shogun, The Invisible Landscape,* and *The Tao of Physics* are published.

New York City, bankrupt financially but ever prosperous artistically, gives birth to non-identical twins punk and disco, and to *Saturday Night Live.*

Pet Rocks bow-wow across America.

About this time, Balinese and Javan tigers become extinct.

Sick and Tired

Few countries are as varied and captivating as Indonesia, the one I'm set to leave. I visited just two of its 17,000 islands. If it wasn't for the measly one-month visa restriction I would surely linger. And so the path of least resistance, a.k.a. "just happen," has me scheduled for an 8:30 a.m. flight bound for Singapore.

I pulled into Jakarta the night before, checking in from a weeklong ramble in consciousness in Bali. My state of mind, both emotional and cerebral, could be described as a bursting packet of monkey-work delight, pliable and willing, having recently been spun, bounced, and flushed inward by way of rarely utilized circuitry. I hold on, as we all do, to the mere evidence of one's continuing existence, while affording the odd, nonchalant smile for passersby. *Man, the postcards I cannot un-send.*

My flight to Singapore leaves in three hours or so. On this dreary early morning I lie, all groggy and hot, in a vermin-infested, sticky scrap of a hotel. All through the night I was hit a hundred times by mosquitoes, little kamikaze punks sting bombing me like fighter jets at groggy Gulliver. As long as the ceiling fans stayed on, they couldn't navigate the high winds. But the electricity was intermittent all night, over and over, until my instinct for self-preservation lapsed and I got careless about covering my face with the flap of my cloth sleeping bag. The continuing drama of dreams, the interruptions, the mad attacks—like I was strapped to the inside of some Freudian kaleidoscope wired to the delirium of a madman.

At least I've been taking my anti-malaria tablets daily... *uhhh, oops.* I missed the last two days. *Fuck.* That explains why I'm hot and cold and shivering in the heat, with a headache like a cold blade sunk way in deep. I'm pounding out a great tide of sweat while a vicious brew pushes at the back end. Some fellow travelers help me with my pack from wherever this stinking hotel is in Jakarta's vast urban sprawl (*no idea*) to the airport miles away (*huh?*). I have no clue on direction, so I tag along in good faith, airplane ticket tucked away somewhere. A kind French gal sidles up beside me and helps me stagger along the tarmac to the airplane, her arm supporting my flagging waist. She smells like a bouquet of carnations crushed into a bowl of hot lemon butter.

By the time I slump in my seat, my mind is a sad swirl of limp thoughts: *Insect pricks—I hate them! Pukey seasick stomach... gravity gonna pop my head... too high!* Singapore is just far enough from Jakarta for a nice big jet arc, reaching a maximum elevation, whatever that is, before immediately descending. Up and up we go! *Me skull's gonna blow!*

Going down never felt so good. By the time we land, I'm fine. Healed. Down the tarmac I prance, *a dervish imp all over your dweeby doubts, my weird-smelling friends!*

An hour later we find a hotel and I'm doubting alright, shaking and cuddling the blankies. Four hours on, delirious and trembling, four off, all clear. All week. My mates, even the aromatic French lassie, keep their distance. *I'm cool.* Trading places, I doubt I'd be eager to cozy up to this kind of funk either. I write some letters home. They turn out to be curiously objective, though a little off kilter socially. Regrettable, irreversible, like the postcards. Like the whole lonesome week.

My illness seems odd, especially the on-off, four-hour bit. I locate a Chinese doctor who (much too readily) gives me a prescription for chloroquine. He isn't clear about whether I have malaria or dengue fever or what. A real dingbat doc, straight from the toon-bot calendar. My joints ache like a malevolent spirit crept into them and died. The diarrhea is volcanic. Add cramps, nausea, migraine, and the shakes. In the good four hours (all normal, a little lightheaded), I go out for food, look around, and return in time for *delirio diabolico*. The four-hour thing is pretty faithful, like one of those geysers.

DURING A FUN spell, I take my old Yashica to a store to explore the prospects of an upgrade, Singapore being a free port and all. After explaining my intention to the shopkeeper I unsnap the camera case. As I flip open the cover, a nice fat joint pops up as if spring-loaded and flies end over end across our field of vision, tracing a wide, impudent parabola. Up and across it shoots, slows, then down it floats, landing on the tiles in the middle of the store. Bounces and slides a few inches. Sound is muffled, light glare extra white. Our focused attention has pulled our little timeline into a big fat *kairos* slo-mo moment. The few customers in the store stand with shocked faces, in a frozen panic that might rightfully be felt in the presence of a hissing grenade. Several point, and all are gaping dumb. A fountain of adrenaline erupts from some hidden gland and I dash forth, swoop down, grab it, and *fly*.

But bursting from a store and racing down a main street, *uhh,* in a city-state that punishes littering and even spitting with stiff fines, not to mention beatings, jail, and rumored executions for drug offenses… *joint in hand!* A few more steps and around a corner, I pull back midstride to a casual stroll. I do not look around, I simply deposit a small item of refuse in a garbage can. All nonchalant. No one notices. *Gotta get back before the shakes…*

A brief explanation. Left to my own preferences, I don't bother much with the weed anymore, thanks in part to the wholesome effect of my three-year association with the agreeably sober Danna. But lately (and I'm not sure why) I'm often given joints and lumps of hash by fellow travelers, storing them somewhere and forgetting. When I walked into the camera store, indeed, when I crossed Singapore customs I was, to my knowledge, free of contraband. *You'd better be,* for Singapore (as well as Iran) has a reputation as "most hostile to smuggling, especially drugs." After the camera incident, I acquire the habit of frisking myself thoroughly before crossing any border.[36]

Kuala Lumpur

I walk past numerous roadside food stalls, little tinkers and tailors and shoe menders and artisans and you name it sitting hunched on the concrete, hawking and stitching, prying and carving. I stop at a Chinese temple where hundreds of sticks of incense, some as large as trees, are stacked and leaning on a wall. A few burn in great clouds of gray smoke while people offer prayers. Just a few feet away, someone is selling holy cloth, and right beside him on the sidewalk something's getting fixed with a hammer and chisel. Splayed here and there in the sun are the bent forms of old men and women, settled and comfortable on the hot concrete. And the traffic is helter-skelter; careful now, as you step... no, not off the sidewalk, because more often than not you move along *with* the cars, braiding your way within this functioning urban chaos. Whoever said the pace of Western cities is fast?

I think of my home, *Oh Canada*. Cushy cars, big TVs, and fancy stereos flit across my inner screen. I look around. Whole families live on roadsides in makeshift shelters like "neat forts" built and discarded after a few days with childhood friends in the woods. I remember my record collection and books, how I locked them away. I remember that devious former self and marvel at how detached I've become. I feel lighter, larger, freer. The things of life, while providing pleasure and security, also exert a dubious pull by one's attachment, a force augmented and made insidious by its often unseen nature. With each day, new things crowd in on the horizon of expectation to entice and claim a new charge on one's attention and energy. Yes, hindsight is ever clear as I walk, unhindered and carefree on these abject streets. I fancy myself a fleshy wand of mind-stuff riding whim upon moment in a loose-fitting, physical realm.

Yet I feel conspicuous walking the streets of these "poor" countries

---

36 But alas (skip ahead a few months), while digging in my money belt for a traveler's check—in an Iranian bank, of all places—I discover a suspicious lump. It's a sample of black hash that some generous fellow had given me back in India. Evidently, smuggling is easy-breezy when you are utterly ignorant of the deed.

of Asia with my bright-green backpack. It sits high and cocky on its aluminum frame, a look that I suspect approximates a human peacock. Soon I'll enter India, where I imagine large, longing eyes staring at me, mistrusting, as though I'd betrayed or cheated them of... *green nylon, aluminum.* This brash backpack is "giving me the shits," as some of those affable young Kiwis were fond of saying.

But all this talk of detachment, poverty, and conscience; the truth of it is, the most condensed value in what I carry is my passport and traveler's checks. These things are surely seen yet not visible, not exactly. And they connect and tether me to a favored reality of great flourish and power, one that affords me a magic-carpet-like pass to wherever my roving desire fancies. Without them... *big trouble.*

I walk along a narrow side street lined with all kinds of small-scale industry. My eyes fix on an old Chinese man in the shadow of his street stall, his calm eyes glistening, as if aimed from a greater distance than the usual. In them I imagine his many years and especially, his grounding in this very moment.

In front of his shop sit several khaki-colored canvas backpacks. They litter the sidewalk so that passersby must veer around them, an attention-grabbing device that ensnares the rabbit brain I am today. I bend down to scrutinize (first mistake) one of the shoddy-looking packs. It is squat and rotund, its frame made from two semi-circles of iron-rod frame (!) welded together at a right angle. This back and shelf supports a great bulk of heavy cloth that is fitted with thin, flimsy shoulder straps. And no weight-bearing hip belt. The size of this grotesque monster could easily accommodate eighty pounds. I shouldn't have gone near it. Squatting for further inspection... I trade my sleek, light, Canada-made one for this travesty of logic and taste.

Uh, yeah. It's not long before I learn that the shape and color of my backpack will not absolve me of the immutable fact that I'm an alien, a money-dispensing Westerner. This crude fact seems to trump all other matters encountered along any fair-weather stroll in a third-world foreign land. The reality of those large, longing eyes having anything to do with flashy nylon was in my imagining it.

I carry this hulk of a pack halfway around the world, walking like an ostrich. It sticks out too far, pulling on my shoulders and making me stoop to counter its mass. A hulking blob on a metal frame, it presses smack against the small of my back. I have to shove my ass out to support it, accentuating my lumbar curve.

And so there's no doubt that an old Chinese purveyor of the crappiest backpacks in the East was indeed enjoying an acute appreciation of the moment at hand... the morning his glistening eye fell on my gullible face and bright green accessory.

BROWSING A NARROW street I notice the preoccupied look of a young Indian man, whose head and upper torso have emerged from behind a door on the crowded sidewalk. He looks up and down the city block several times—he's in a hurry. Across the road and down a couple of stores, our eyes meet. He motions me over with agitated enthusiasm, then urges me to follow him through the narrow doorway and dark hall. And guess what? Like a drone on cue to final enslavement, I'm in.

We enter a large open area where a celebration is underway. I'm quite sure it's a wedding. In a long row at the head of the room, Indians dressed in white or deep colors sit cross-legged on the floor. I am shown to a spot in the center of the second row directly facing a handsome young couple, clearly the focus of these festivities. They beam smiles so pure that I am momentarily refined by some ethereal force emanating from within their blissful contagion. My first taste of India is in the welcoming intensity of this beautiful couple. *Young Shiva and Shakti come down in sweet rainbows, bleeding highest love upon me!* Servers bring us strange, aromatic foods placed on fresh banana leaves. I eat with gusto these new culinary wonders in a ceremony I know nothing about. These brown people, who look like darker versions of me, Mom, and my little sister, are kinder than I'm used to. That I'm invited in and received with such respect, even to be given a seat of honor... I must be the lucky passerby in an orderly ritual.

I ask no questions and offer only appreciative gestures and enthusiastic gulping. By their calm aura, frequent smiles and (presumably affirmative) head wobbling, they ask for nothing more.

Penang Den

Shortly after arriving in this Chinese island city I ask some youths if they know where to find an opium den. I've heard about such places and want a firsthand look, maybe sample the goods. The punks lead my buddy and me a block off the main drag down a back alley to a short wooden door. They ask for money; I refuse. This pisses them off, of course. We go inside.

My traveling companion, a cheery lad from Calgary with curly red hair, is kind enough to escort me through what must seem to him a foolhardy tour of dark curiosities in the inner recesses of a foreign city. He is more conservative than me in his taste for adventure and has no such interest; he offered to come along only for my safety. We met several days ago and discovered an odd, mutual fondness that wouldn't be lost on our contrasting types. A couple years older than me, he's more cautious, polite, and "straight." Yet he's confident, strong, and surprisingly open. In the den he sits by, more wary than involved, while I indulge my desire. (In retrospect I should fly to Calgary to hunt down the sturdy bloke and thank him for watching over me that night. Days earlier he'd given me some advice. Observing my shy handling of an opportune moment with a cute traveling gal, he'd said, "Hey, man, when you see a chick you like, just be nice. That's all you have to do." Wow, it seemed so simple when he said it, his eyes big and earnest. Then, his focus dropping slightly while gently poking at the scrawny mess I'm cultivating on my neck, he advised me to "Trim it a bit; the ladies don't like it.")

A wispy, emaciated man motions me over to one of four raised bays arranged in an arc against a wall. Several spidery old addicts lie in the body-sized smoking stalls, taking deep draws from tall pipes. Their milky eyes are windows on a remote and private realm. I can barely detect their breathing. The owner motions toward the only empty stall. I lie on my side and rest my cheek on a small wooden table about six inches high, its top cocked at an appropriate angle. My host shows me the nominal amount of opium, indicates the price, then lights the pipe. The black goo bubbles and sizzles like a tiny tar pit inches from my face while I inhale. I finish it, and then order another half for a full-on trip. The old man raises his eyebrows, takes my money. My friend, with his striped shirt, shorts, and fuzzy-pink giant's legs, looks like he just beamed over from a middle school sock-hop in wheat country. He leans forward, fist within fist upon bouncing knee, ready to bolt on my last draw. His eyes are fixed on me, tense and concerned.

I stand. *Uhhh...* the world is on a tilt, and there's an increased viscosity in the air, or in my mind... really, it's impossible to say. I step out of the smoky den and grab a wall. My mind has lost its linear poise; it floats like oozing goo in a slow opium sea, spreads into shadows, then flies on the hyper trail of every wacky sound this Chinese city hurls at me. Entering the alley, we come face to face with the same band of punks who brought us here. They waited the forty-five minutes; they know the drill.

"Police, police!" they yell. "You trouble now. Police, come!"

"Yeah, yeah, sure," I manage to drawl. "Police." Like I'm the toughest punk east of Rangoon, I can't summon a moment's concern for their whiny yelping. There is no fear. I simply don't care.

Calgary bloke grabs my arm and pulls me up the lane into the chaos of the main drag. I stop on the center line, breaking free of his grasp. Rickshaws and ancient sedans stream past on both sides, enhancing the spinning sensation that is the natural motion of the new world I inhabit. Oriental faces whiz past on a flesh-and-noodle merry-go-round. The dome of night booms beyond the chaos of chirpy foreign voices. Chinese characters swirl in a sky-filling mobile of neon signs that tell me nothing, and I don't mind. It feels unreasonably good to scratch my neck. I relish the deep pleasure on my skin, in my blood. My body shudders. *Mmm, like cumming without a boner.* I have no idea where our hotel is. And I know I couldn't find it. The good news? I don't care. I stand swaying on the central nerve of downtown Penang as if I'm held in place by the *schwing* of the city's own kundalini. I've never known such pleasure in the simple act of scratching and not caring. Even so, embedded in this urban madness, way high on opium, a speck of me—a witness to the madness—knows, remembers... that I *want* to care, that caring about things normally brings meaning and connection in this whacked-out world. Of course, this jewel of cognition is merely intellectual, fleeting, and will not spoil the mood. I continue to scratch.

Out from the flux of warping faces and Chinese squiggles my red-haired chaperone reappears. His tense and very large eyes swoop in like wild holy sparks from the void. He grabs my arm. "Come with me." The words—soft, booming—blaze a linear intrusion into my indolent, loose sack of a mind. "Peripheral" is the only way to see and think and scratch. Staggering along an inner-city main drag in a foreign state not yet arrived from the political and flesh-and-blood squalor of the third world, in this condition, is close to my dumbest move ever. Fortunately, my buddy's words jog my dump-heap memory and he's able to lead. Like a drunken creature I follow, my babble an incoherent gush of half-wit remarks, though I imagine it to be a poetic force that somehow edifies my servile movement down the street. It occurs to me (not that I care) that I must look, led by my more upright partner, like a creature from some dark crevice caught unawares out in the open. *My precious.* Looking left and right while dodging traffic, my benefactor pulls me down this road and that lane. Mr. Calgary has become both the subject and audience of my deranged blabber. He ignores me and my nonsense until we arrive at our hotel.

I lie on the bed, giggling. Streams of outlandish thoughts are interrupted by pangs of nausea. If I lie absolutely still, the nausea abates. Throughout the night I jot down comical, nightmarish images, falling in and out of sleep. The name "Edgar Allen Poe"[37] and his opiate-inspired visions mean nothing to me. I clutch a flashlight in my teeth as I drool demented laughter and comedic snot on my notebook. I'm as quiet as I can be. *Don't wanna wake m' friend.* But I do, more than once.

Eventually, after spouting a page or so of colorful but insensible word strings, I'm reminded of the business of "not caring." Seems a curious thing. Why should not caring feel so damned good?

THE NEXT DAY, many questions and possibilities come to mind in the aftermath of my nibble at the forbidden fruit. I'm cast back to my teenaged years, when street drugs arrived one after another in our small suburban town

Somehow my friends and I walked an intuitive road. We sensed a threatening shadow and steered clear when the new kid on the block, heroin, pulled into town. We played with pot and psychedelics by way

---

37 It is believed that much of the inspiration for Edgar Allen Poe's surreal imagery was influenced by his fondness for opium.

of a creative intellectuality, hammering out wondrous reworkings of what is and what might yet be, as all kids do. We strummed and picked guitars, wailed on harmonicas, and sang songs. In those who were dabbling in the hard stuff we felt something quite different, like a numbing of the bristling energies of optimism, or a submergence (or lack) of the hope evoked in the firing of our own fledgling imaginations. At least that's how it looked and felt to me from a short and tender distance.

Now, after my day of opium, ideas and questions swim wild in my mind. *Why should not caring be pleasurable?*

And a question remains, an echo of the other: *This "not caring"—is it about pain?*

Following my own partiality, I reason that caring itself could hurt, as it might in one whose personal reality has grown unbearable. Personal trauma; parents pass it along in their outbursts, their stories and beliefs, their punishments and rewards. Parents who themselves dwell unconsciously in the hidden gravity of *their* jaded pain, who un-bury it only to press it like an imprint into the psyches of their children. *Into me.* And these are the average, normal families. For the person who carries a greater burden of suffering, the not-caring induced by opium might not only feel good but be near-impossible to resist repeating. I keep remembering how good it felt to not care.

Back in PoCo, Lotusland, as we strummed our guitars, heroin moved in like a dark shape under our radar. Eventually, a sizable population of junkies were hanging out in our Itchycoo Park.[38] I knew some of them.

----

38 "Itchycoo Park," officially called Lion's Park, was renamed by us "hip freaks" in the late 1960s after securing it as our main hangout in PoCo. It was eminently suitable for unrestrained toking, music making, and sexual rendezvous by its luxuriant privacy, bordered as it was by the railway, the Coquitlam River, and thick underbrush shielding it from the highway and the shopping center. I believe it was my buddy, Rick, who named it after the number one hit by the British band the Small Faces. Within a few years the local authorities "solved a problem" by radically thinning the surrounding jungle and transforming it into a family-fun park, eliminating the privacy that was integral to its existence as our beloved Itchycoo. In the last year before the captains of order reclaimed their territory, it had been overrun by the latest and darker aspect of the town's youthful explorers, the junkies of whom I speak. This likely bolstered the conviction in many a modestly informed mind that "pot leads to heroin." So, they could have the park; we'd already lost it to the junkies. *Sour grapes?*

More than a few died along the way; at least a dozen faces come to mind.

As I stood swaying on that busy Penang thoroughfare, when it felt so damned good *not* to care, was I able to remember how caring gave my life meaning *because* my own level of pain is relatively average, or maybe less than average? Could I have been conscious of this if my pain had been more burdensome?

And did my recent psycho realignment by psilocybin release me from a critical wad of it?—I have to ask, even if these questions and fancies are without logical foundation. *Sigh.* The psycho skins of my father and brothers—they blew away and only "I" was left. No one left to applaud, lay blame, or *to* blame. Perhaps something stirred, that "steady" observer beneath the cloaks of the personal drama, hard to pin down and so often skipped over, a state of awareness that eludes the common, the chatty, the worldly self. A sort of conscience/buddy/witness poking his head up for a look-see back there in the surf at Kuta.

What if Buddha was right: that we *all* have a whack load of suffering inside us? It's the human story. We're all sailing the same suffering sea. Yet some succumb to the opiate dream while others walk away with a simple "no thanks." Drawn on a few breaths into a wild carnival of simple pleasures, the opiate weaves its mystique into the flesh of life itself. Repeat, and repeat again. Great pain or little pain, I imagine that Opiate Spirit is not fussy. And, I presume, it will claim anyone who hangs around long enough for the poppy's wondrous yet insidious bio-chemistry to place itself. Some say this is not always so, and this poses more questions on the nature of mind and disease.[39]

Those few heroin users we might have been able to talk to back in PoCo didn't have much to say on the matter, submerged as they were in the addict's zone of misery, release, and need. One guy I knew rather well articulated his reasons for finding out for himself the nature of this new controversy, this buzz: for he would ignore the warnings and all

---

39 It is paradigm-popping to consider the possibility that the well-known but under-appreciated "placebo" and "nocebo" effects—powerful as they are in the individual—might also be expressed by way of culture or group influence. See *You Are The Placebo* by Joe Dispenza—and I apologize, Mr. J.D., for my rather permissive take on your profound ideas.

the fuss, and face this new bogey-man himself, the much-demonized heroin. I was overcome by a heavy foreboding when I heard him speak that way. Had this young man, whom I'd always admired for his courage and intelligence, fallen under a spell of pride? Had he imagined possessing some kind of special immunity from risk? Is pride simply a bolder face of pain?

I played a lucky game in Penang's under-belly lanes, and turned around in good time with Mr. Calgary's help. And likely, with my "brave" hometown guy's unknowing help as well. Given the emotional and conceptual complexities in our psyches, each one, there surely is much about pain, choosing, and addiction that still eludes our unsure grasp.

Yet both addiction and various spiritual disciplines seem to lead the individual toward dispelling the illusion of personal specialness; one by hijacking the brain's endorphin[40] system, the other with intention by means of solitude, fasting, meditation, or service. Both by the humbling of ego and invoking a discipline to transform one's "interior" self. For the one who passes through the fire of addiction and comes through "whole" again, transformation of some kind must occur. For all, humility is the hallmark of what remains after much has fallen away.

Without having traveled along either path in my own life, I have nonetheless come to the conviction that the specialness illusion is ego's best bait—*and* worst bargain. Which, I suspect, began and ultimately shows up again as the face of fear: the little mess inside each of us that cannot bear its own desolation in the prison of a separate self. The commonplace shit that got Buddha out of his palace, on the road, and into the history books.

Later on I return the favor shown me by the genial Calgarian, serving as chaperone for fellow travelers bent on "getting a firsthand look, maybe sampling the goods" in opium dens in Calcutta and in Bombay.

Phuket

There is a coastline of great geological drama along the southern leg of Thailand on the Malay Peninsula. A rock saga of some thousand million

40 "endorphin" from *endo*genous m*orphine*, see note 28.

years punctuates the sea in ghoulish form, creating convoluted waterways and nooks and crannies for all sorts of tropical birds and fish—and the odd high-roller film crew. Phuket is an island where travelers gather at several beaches along the ocean-wild coast. We leave our clothes and inhibitions in the sand to swim in the surf and, with any luck, into each other's fervid imaginations and willing limbs.

Traveling the vagabond trail has taken a stormy course of late. Upwind and not so long ago I was in Canberra running a psycho-emotional gauntlet. It rearranged what I hadn't expected to be subject to rearranging: my thoughts, feelings, foibles—my personality. Add another order of realignment in a reckless mind swim in the giant surf at Kuta Beach, dengue fever in Singapore, and the Penang opium reverie, and you get a three-month period in which the opportunity for personal stagnation is at an all-time low.

I arrive at Patong Beach in a subdued mood. I am by no means suffering, but I'm tired. I feel well enough and even blessed with good fortune. I look forward to an easy beachside rest of sorts, although I must look like I've been beaten by orcs and dragged through a fire swamp.

For the most part I keep to myself, swimming and overeating at the grass-hut restaurants. These simple lodgings, with no plumbing or electricity, are the only amenities. On this tropical shoreline of brilliant alabaster and azure deep, such primitive means pass as abundant luxury. The milieu of young, middle-wank Westerners gathered here feels like a shared dream. *If we dream, what might we wake up to?* Somehow, our "paradise" feels arrived at in haste. Perhaps we each carry our own private version, incognito and not far below the surface, along with the personal angst to fire it up.

My paradise, this time around, is one of quiet pleasures. Even the breeze can hold my attention for, well it's hard to say for how long. Perhaps my pensive state enables me to notice a certain reserve, a subtle malaise that stalks the locals. I suspect they're beginning to sense the double-edged nature of the tourist dollar bonanza that has recently come their way. Even so, they serve us faithfully and remain respectful. When I notice their take on these new modern ways—and it's often the elders, those with the years that afford perspective—I also notice how they notice my noticing *them*. Like the old ones in Bali. Reluctant and disapproving of change, these elders are an awkward link between times and cultures.

We hedonistic tourists, privileged by fortune of birthplace, maintain our pseudo-paradise by serving only our desires and curiosities, which appear to have much to do with nudity and the readily available Thai-stick: pot so strong that some of us reckon the local opium must be laced into it.

And we eat like ranging mutts with the part of the brain that registers "full-stomach" cauterized. After a period of overindulging, in which "hungry" has become a dim fiction, the rediscovery itself is delicious. Considering the real hunger in parts near and far, it is a shameful, self-absorbed reality. We are like spoiled aristocrat brats, really.

I BORROW A mask, fins, and snorkel and head toward the rocky outcrop at the end of our sandy bay for an undersea look-see.

As soon as I jump in I can't make anything out in the murky water. After a few seconds I realize it isn't silt or mud, but a concentration of fish life even more varied and lush than the subject of any of Jacques Cousteau's interludes of fine eloquence. Numerous schools of fish hover in multi-jeweled flashes just inches from my face and hands. Streams of sunlight blaze through moving constellations of beady eyes and hot electric blues, yellows, and neon reds and oranges. They flicker like small prismatic light-houses, drifting and shifting about. Through fiery streaks and diaphanous clusters of fluorescent color I catch a glimpse now and then of surrounding rocks. They appear to be made of lava and form complex undersea corridors. I've jumped in at a key intersection of great, cavernous fish ways along huge walls of rock. Like a bubble on a breeze I'm carried on swirls and eddies from a multitude of fins and tails that fan the seawater.

But I drift on more than the muscle power of fish. In a few minutes a strong current has taken me, engrossed as I am in the intense multiplicity of swarming fish clouds all around me. By the time I surface and notice this I'm a hundred meters from the cape and going out fast. I tell myself I will beat the current, and I *need* to believe this. A vile fear takes over and pumps my limbs to their utmost propelling power. These are very good fins and still, there is no progress. The current is an invisible river that could illuminate towns up and down the coast. When beating the current turns into swim-for-my-life, my arms and legs thwack and whip against the surface like a broken water toy. Minute after terrifying minute I swim while the gap between me and the beach remains. I'm losing strength. *Losing.* Then, with that last charge of energy at the end of all things—*Mom lifts Cadillac off bleeding son, etcetera*—I explode in a final, thrashing fit, reptilian in its simplicity and utter lack of humanity.

I pull myself ashore and lie on my back in the gently lapping surf for a good twenty minutes, bellow breathing. Gradually, I calm down. The deep texture of sky-blue is a balm; the sun has long fried the sea water from my skin. I'm in a numb state, not yet conscious in the classic sense. There is a feeling of safety, perhaps gratitude. *Numb.*

Slowly, thought returns. Once again, I have been careless. It seems plausible that had I let the current carry me, I might have been returned to shore up the coast. But would that be a mile, or hundreds away? Or would that current have preferred a direct route, say, to India or Africa?

Hilltribe Pigs

That great fickle ocean is oftentimes easygoing and predictable; for sure it's a reliable supplier of protein. But every once in awhile it is transformed into a destructive beast. For this reason, I presume, houses are built on stilts in low areas of the countryside. Metal sanitary pipes drop waste below where groups of ravenous pigs cluster. In the off hours you'll spot the odd lone hog whining, snout bleeding, the poor dim porker panting, its spirit broken from vain attempts to quell his hunger.

I've joined a tour of the Hill Tribe region of the Golden Triangle in northern Thailand. It is where the infamous poppy tycoon, Khun Sa, is said to be crafting an empire. This so-called evil genius publicly called certain Western leaders on their own game. He offered, on the condition of economic cooperation from the West for a clean start, to convert the lucrative opium operations into legal food crops in exchange for independence for his people, the Shan. He would provide the names of CIA operatives who were in on the contraband industry. "We don't negotiate with criminals" was the predictable response. In Khun Sa's own words: "They can arrest me anytime, but that will not be the end of opium. They can kill me—that also will not be the end of opium. It would just mean they would have to find a new Drug King." The real picture of our drug problem is more complex than portrayed by the media or imagined by Ma and Pa Suburb in the West.[41]

The area is populated with several Tibeto-Burmese tribal groups who speak different languages, often living only a mile or two apart. Colorful tribes; dirty, apathetic ones; happy clean ones; dirty, happy ones; this is what my unschooled eye takes in. Some are scattered and docile, and some more aggressive, like the ones who mark their hilltop territory with the open-jawed skull and hide of a large wolf-like animal. Stretched and fixed on primitive wooden poles and situated ominously at the entrance to their village, we pass under one on an inbound trail.

Some tribes are more organized and robust, like the Karen (Ka-*wren*), who have been fighting the Burmese military regime like a nation in their own right. It's said that they're armed with old Chinese weapons and use obsolete Indian rupees for currency.

Opium is the local brew. Older men are often splayed about with that faraway look, limbs flopped wherever. They love factory-made

41 From *Who is the Drug King of the Golden Triangle?* (Journeyman Pictures), *Khun Sa—Opium Warlord of the World* (You Tube). Khun Sa's Mong Thai Army was stationed in his city-fortress of Ho-Mong in southern Burma. In 1977 Khun Sa offered to halt opium production in exchange for an independent Mong Thai: the Shan land. In this way the civil war between the Hill Tribes and Burma would cease, and the Hill Tribe people could grow rice, tea, coffee, and mushrooms and produce traditional textiles and precious stones. In the dangerous war environment, by growing poppies for opium, the hill people would not risk travel to markets. Merchants, protected by Khun Sa's army for a fee, made the rounds to buy opium. The opium was then brought to plants on the Thai border (also protected by Khun Sa) to be refined into heroin. Most was produced in Burma. Khun Sa recruited, by force, boys and young men from villages for his army. He built schools and monasteries and provided for these same people. In his city of Ho Mong, opium was forbidden. In the view of Western powers, angering China (who backed Burma) was not worth solving the opium problem by supporting the Shan's drive toward independence. Yet to end production of two thirds of the world's heroin was quite the offer. Instead, America's DEA wanted to capture or kill Khun Sa like they did Pablo Escobar in Colombia. Many would argue that that was a good PR boost for the DEA but that nothing had changed. The DEA's offices and activities in Bangkok likely would have been similarly boosted, and justified, by Khun Sa's capture or death.

cigarettes, continually pestering us for them. Even the youngest children smoke them with ease; it seems that as soon as they can walk, they smoke. Great visuals for cigarette advertisers—or their ideological foes. *Your choice, mister.*

Along the jungle trails we come across gun-toting bandits who eye us in silence like lizards at rest as we pass. This is why it is advised to travel in a group led by Thai guides, who also carry weapons. Our two guides (only one, Jonny, speaks a choppy English) carry an automatic machine gun and several pistols. Of course, this detail can make you feel safe or paranoid. *Your choice, mister.*

As well, groups of carefree young hogs are often seen trotting along with purpose, as if on an organized tour themselves. *Sweet little fellas.*

We'll be spending a night with a tribe who, according to Jonny, is very proud and whose customs we, as visitors, must afford the utmost respect. "For example," he says, "they be *serious offend* if you refuse to the food." Having entered the village of the very proud tribe, we visitors, all eight of us foreigners, mill about with ease. They might be proud, but they're hospitable enough to allow us free movement around their homes. I don't feel we're being watched. By handing over a few dollars I've walked into their world, for no roads go there. I reckon the cash serves to appease the uppity spirits, or accommodate the dodgy business of bandits. I reckon we've purchased safe passage for a short spell with the lush moolah we've handed over to be part of this three-day jungle jaunt.

So, what do I do with this uncommon access to a remote people? I do what I suspect most of us would do. I bring my cloistered awareness into their forest world. Seems we both, me and these hill people, maintain our respective distance. Besides the significant language barrier, I'm sure we each have our reasons, acting on unspoken mutual agreements that have resulted in my being here on this day. It seems a benign enough social milieu, and in my capacity, I become the observer.

And I am entertained and informed by their pigs as well as by them. I stand at the edge of the pig pen, self-conscious of my involvement here. Not only do I feel separate from the tribespeople's world, I also feel little connection, in purpose or camaraderie, with the other seven in the tour group. I've been going solo lately, and I'm fine with that. My social context, my feelings of "Where do I fit in?" and "What am I doing here?" make no difference to the pigs.

This is the day I discover that pigs, too, are precious beings who want to have fun just like us monkeys. I've looked in on them several times, drawn by the lifestyle contrast with their smaller, freer brethren in the surrounding country. Making do with what they have, the bigger inmates run around athletically in the mud. They don't take any notice of me or of the tribesmen who frequently walk by.

But things are not so carefree when dinnertime approaches and it's time for slaughter. One of the older men makes a beeline for the pen. His slow, steady pace and fixed gaze foreshadow a grisly and serious game. The reaper is twenty paces away when one of the pigs, perhaps the most gifted of the bunch, raises a quivering snout. He has detected, from a distance, a most gruesome "hunt" in the tribesman's approach. Does he pick up on some subtle difference in the man's poise as he walks? Does he feel it in the wind, tuning in to a kind of porcine sixth sense? The simple wisdom of dumb beasts? Perhaps it's always the same guy, and the pig recognizes or smells him. I hate to think that maybe the reaper is one deranged nut ball and gave this particular porker the evil eye last time while dragging out his mom.

Cunning Pig sounds the alert with a cold shriek, one of those maximal screams of the primal kind. In an instant the pen is a muddy, screeching whirl. *They know.* The village is filled with horrific sounds of mayhem. The man casually follows them around and singles out his quarry. The One—it is he who screamed first—knows it's his turn in the morbid roulette round. He screeches louder and runs ever faster. But it is in vain. *Why does the reaper go after the very one who first noticed, who runs most crazy wild and is, therefore, hardest to catch?* The man, who is calm, as though the act of terrorizing and killing an animal is a therapeutic boon—indeed, his favorite mid-week kick—nabs the beast with the help of three henchmen who arrive at the peak of madness. I cannot tear my eyes from a sight I've never seen before. The pig's face is contorted into a very human expression of panic and dread, the eyes fear-stricken, the tense upper lip stretched into a wide, freaky curl. The four men drag him out by his hind legs up the hill, the screams getting fainter with each step.

That face—like Goya's *The Scream*. Perhaps pigs routinely feel a range of emotions that I have chauvinistically assumed are reserved only for us. Won't be long—a mutation here, a bit of continental drift there—till they're dancing around a fire chanting to some pig god about pig rain, and fashioning big curly wangs out of straw and mud.

SUPPER WILL SOON be served. I pretend to myself that it won't be the same pig, but you won't find any freezers around here.

Or toilets. I have time, so I go for a stroll in the woods to find a good spot.

A path winds along a creek on the edge of the settlement. I follow it, noticing that a half dozen or so of the smaller Pigs of Freedom have spotted me and are trotting close behind. *Must be going the same way.* I leave the trail and head up through a sparsely wooded hillside. Warm sunshine dapples the trees' translucent young leaves. A gentle breeze carries into my face the sweet vapors of their waxy afterbirth, a color-enhancing sheen on each fluttering surface. Ahh, nature's simple magic. *Bless this fuckin' planet.*

The pigs have followed me off the trail. *Friendly little fellas.* I feel some remorse that a large number of my kind love eating their flesh. Indulging the notion that they sense my newfound empathy, I turn to them, wondering. They stop, all of them, like Piglet's well-behaved cousins, and wait for me to continue. I shrug, carry on, and a minute later, I find my spot.

I pull out a joint that yet another generous wayfarer back in Chiang Mai laid on me, and I light it. The pigs have arranged themselves into an intelligent, evenly spaced semicircle about ten feet away. *Hail, oh ye pig folk of the world!* After a draw I could scream it across the rich emptiness of the woods. But the tribesmen might hear, and if they come running, well, the language gap... me squatting, toking, the pigs standing by in a perfect arc formation watching me... a cultural faux pas that could get me lynched, for all I know about these opium-loving, pig-eating folk. Ah, the bane of tourism and that niggling "prime directive" thing. Yet you'd have to have the skin and maybe the brain of a rhino to not notice that one's mere presence irrevocably alters their time stream.

Alas, I am still at the center of eight little piggies' attention. And like the resourceful inebriate that I am on this loose day of tainted heaven,

I wonder if they're offering crude homage for the compassion I felt for their penned-up brethren. *Ah, ridiculous.* I shake myself from my blathering thoughts, but under the circumstances, I can't let the matter rest. Poised expectantly and starting to show impatience, the pigs begin to grunt. If I wasn't so damned sure I'm still on planet Earth where humans dominate and are feared by almost every other creature, I'd say that these little piggies are about ready to mutiny.

The deep funk of my fumes creeps along the forest floor. The piglets shift about like they need to pee badly. *Hey, fellas, what? What?* A grunt here, a shuffle there. All the while sixteen beady eyes are fixed on me. I take my time, for supper won't be served for a half hour. And this twinkly chirpy forest… *it's beautiful, man.* One by one, they edge closer… *little guys, buddies, this is getting weird.*

Suddenly, I *see.* An insight bell clangs so loud that I nearly fall over. These earnest little dudes are not urging me to get up and continue leading them on our gay walk through the sun-dappled woods into the lands of baconless mirth. No, they're not.

They are here to compete *for what I leave behind.*

I am, *right now,* feeling rather transparent in a vulnerable, two-legged-with-my-pants-down kind of way. My latent dangle of love-fire is redefined as tender, succulent tissue. Evil hog-demons are poised for attack a mere six feet away, barely holding. Finally, I stand, and before my pants are up I must hop three times and grab for a sapling so I don't topple down the hill. I watch from a safe five feet away as they gulp it all down with leaves and dirt for trimmings, grunting and shoving. A feeding frenzy that I thought peculiar to piranhas. Nature's, uh… simple magic.

Back in the village I'm feeling kinda spry. A little lighter, a bit disoriented. Not to mention the wickedly potent Buddha-stick, as they called it back in Kiwiland. And hey, I have arrived just in time.

As dinner is passed around and I imagine chowing down… *oh, my.* The main course is a dish of barely cooked (or uncooked?) pork… for sure the hog whose screams are still moving air down the valley.

And we must not *seriously offend.*

The Asshole

It started with a humorless foursome of scholastic nerds I keep running into. Well, it would be difficult not to—run into them, that is—since they make up half the Hill Tribe tour group and we're surrounded by a jungle wilderness. These four Toronto university students are doing a study of some sort, taking notes every few seconds, I'd bet even on taking notes. They follow each other around, enacting quaint little displays of competitive one-upmanship. They are two gals and two guys. The guys are taller, a little twitchier, but all are on an even keel in their consistent nattering and nervous flitting about. One of the gals is shorter and much cuter, more demure. The taller one seems to dominate from time to time, which only gets the guys all wound up for the next round. One guy, the skinnier one, seems to frequently steer his insanities into a crazy spiral until he's buzzing away right next to me like an oversized gnat. A gnat bearing pen and pad.

I assume that we're supposed to be friends because we're Canadian. Or has my hirsute and ragged look, and my increasingly detached vibe, begun to cast that on-the-road charm? In any case, it seems they flaunt their collective neuroses in my presence, as though I'm part of the team. I move along, gaining some therapeutic distance. It's awkward, and I don't want to engage them. But there they are, beside me again, yakety-yakking at each other, pens in hand, with the odd furtive glance aimed my way. It's the closest I've come to feeling professorial, only I have no interest in them and offer no teaching. I'm what, two years older? I'm sure it's because of them that I toked up on the trail with the pigs and all; it's not like me to go off by myself and get high. If it wasn't for those weird pigs capturing my attention, I would have felt awkward about the whole thing, until I remembered why I was holding a joint, which had everything to do with the four from York University and the strange anxiety they seem to induce in me.

But alas, there's a half-hidden side to it. I pause and shuffle around my inner labyrinth, looking for clues. *Why do they shadow me?* In my shining school days I was a full-fledged nerd myself. *I* could be flitting about these parts with paper and pen had things gone the way they were supposed to, if the wishes of my adult benefactors had held more sway.

But I ditched that scene without understanding why; turned away as if avoiding a trap. I did well in school, but the rating system got to me over the years. Even though I didn't have the words or the courage to say it, I was revulsed by the whole thing—revulsed by the rewards as much as by the shame and guilt that seemed to oppress those who couldn't cut it. And the teachers—the glows of admiration, the vicarious pride—all this fostered a subtle malaise that I couldn't ignore, and surely did its part to steer me away from the game of further studies.

There's more to it, for sure, common enough stuff, mostly. That my childhood provided for a hazy identity, an exciting hybrid: let's call it BC/Mediterrania, born as I was into a dual world, immigrant crucible. Revealed (too early, perhaps) was the relative value of "master," whether anointed by church, state, or academia. Canada/Calabria, God/molecule. This nourished my discontent, which eventually added its own steam. The Jesus story, on Roman Catholic prime time, was somehow transfigured at an early age: the Only Savior Dude became Real Sane Human, a kind of loving Don Juan[42], and, *I must be one too, eh?* I was just a kid, but it all added to the store of psychic fuel that ultimately launched a traveling game. I sought a road of change, a road that could carry me along in a manner that would animate the backdrop—what is usually invisible by its constancy, yet would be made visible to me on this shifting road. I sought a way that would lift my senses away from the past, a past that, for anyone mired in the sins of complacency, would commit one's existence to that backdrop... whose familiarity and comfort would make heroic the task of imagining something else, never mind escaping it.

And now here I am, drifting along a jet stream of dreams without career plans. *Sigh.* I can only imagine in what ways or to what degree my life would be different had I not started this global trek when I was supposed to enter university. As much as the four from York are irritating the shit out of me, if I didn't go overseas when I did, there's a good chance I'd be right there with them. It's good to see another side of things, catch a peek into hidden potentialities. This gaggle of high-strung students reminds of a life that might have been.

42   I refer to Carlos Castaneda's Don Juan.

More to the here and now, it threatens to pop my euphoric bubble of most awesome creation in my brave new world of travel: a brash, holyish world where trees sway like a chorus of hoochie mamas, the past erupts in a volcanic release of tears and molten words, and continents whisper clear across the sea in a low, seductive voice. Notwithstanding these stiff challenges to the hegemony of reason and sanity, I feel as free as I ever have. I find myself curiously "unstuck" in the world, having left behind my home, my girl, and even my home world, the West. Not to mention parts of me along an emotional wormhole in Canberra and other flakey bits that came loose at Kuta Beach. I now wander this beaten path of travelers without conscious purpose, my fledgling sensibilities tickled by moments of direct power, ecstasy, and random but meaningful opportunity. *Flow, man.*

And so, at an oddball juncture on a young man's errant path, and with the fertilizer of four Canuck clucks newly added, the compost heap of my personal potential sprouts... The Asshole. Seems an unlikely turn perhaps, but there you go. It's tempting to think of it as a reality burp, a result of the psychic indigestion of many years. Perhaps over these past few months I have nibbled away and swallowed more than I can readily integrate, and now we're in for some high drama, shadow style. As my mother once said, nodding resignedly and peering askance at me after I indulged my penchant for nonsense one too many times, "When the donkey speaks in Latin, you *know* it's going to be a strange year." And so, by some dark, mild magic, the ass begins to sing.

In one explosive burst I meet the duskier side of Johnny-be-goodboy for the first time. Having remained silent in the students' vexing presence for two days—having cultivated such polite silence for most of my life—I erupt, issuing verbal spankings to all four, even the cute gal. One after another I slay them with profanities and wet snarls. Poor nerds, they leave me alone after that.

I don't pause to question the sudden zag in my behavior. I'm sure a few sessions with the meter ticking would reveal secrets hidden in the day to day of any life. *I'm onto that.* A good therapist would lead me to sniff out a cache of feelings, repressed or ignored, a hidden story perhaps, especially considering the immigrant Latin pressure cooker I was raised in. A season of rigorous self-inquiry might occasion a healing release within the tumult of psyche. A reprise, and more perhaps, of my stirrings in Canberra.

But since no such therapist shows up on my path, I'm left to my own graceless ways. Now unleashed, these energies will take a while to subside. My old costume is lying in a heap and this new one has me standing tall, a perpetual psychic boner fuelled by a certain "shadow" energy. In an unholy instant I seem to have earned a PhD in Dickness, with its attendant mastery of the performing art, and this is my time to shine. *Alter ego, giddy up!*

The Hill Tribe tour comes to an end. The Asshole moves on, not ready to come down. I'm a mouthy rascal—mean, unprincipled, obnoxious. A real gem, one in a million. I'm nosy, insulting, and worse, I don't care if I piss people off. Unlike at home, where I'd receive payback for months, maybe years, on the road I enjoy the gray-zone benefit of anonymity. You could be diminutive and humble one day, and on the next, a dancing devil. And on the *next*, no one will know of either or expect anything in particular. This behavioral latitude has become a reckless plaything.

But a minimal watchfulness remains. My conscience is on autopilot—but a tiny flame remains. For several more days I enjoy my mischief in-the-dark. The novelty of this new role is too good to put down.

Then, on day five or six of The Asshole, my depraved behavior, while clearing the room of most decent traveling folk, attracts a kind of buddy energy from a weird little French dude. He's like a follower, a devotee. He smiles, stays close, and says little. He offers uncritical support, readily accepting me and my jerkiness. Even pipes up a few times, backing me up with grunts and the odd snarl. This in turn casts a self-aimed spotlight on my own uncharacteristic and outrageous behavior.

My side-kick's vibe feels "good" and unchallenging, like he's savvy to some superscript that transcends these days of smallish ways. Almost like he's come along to witness things, to offer a mirror. *That subtle grin, his taciturn demeanor*... seems like a chill dude, a humble guy. I suppose the one humble thing about me is my owning up (at least in private) to being an arrogant prick of socially awkward proportions.

With the French dude's unexpected support I am both judge and on the witness stand—somehow I wake up. My sleeping conscience becomes conscious. All those folks I harassed and insulted, offended unjustly, and disdained stupidly. I'll probably never run into any of them again. *Sigh.* I count my blessings for coming through without getting sucker punched, and coast down the rest of the way. I am "free."

French guy seems to get my transition, nods and leaves. I'd swear it was a knowing nod, with a fleeting grin from one who was in on the game (even if I wasn't... quite.) *Goodbye and thanks, little French dude.*

However, as is often the case, along with freedom comes responsibility. Now that I've let the Asshole out, I must guard against his annoying return. (I'm sure that some in my daily life, years later, would nod in agreement.) *Why did I let him out? Did I have a choice? Did it "just happen"?* You could say I've had much to draw from during my childhood, never mind the murderous Biffs who've been running the show since rocks and spears and precious fire launched us into this hot-headed, planetary dream. Foisting responsibility upon my family once more (and bless their good love and great song), it's as though I learned the aggressive play in the very roots of this flesh and life, but never dared to indulge. For whatever reasons, I've not expressed these emotions till now. Perhaps I simply didn't possess the gumption.

That human conduct is habit forming is plain to see. I wonder if it reaches further, in another order altogether, like in that renegade theory of modern biology: perhaps *morphogenetic fields*[43] of behavior are as real as personal habits, like rivers of psychic ooze flowing this way and that, powerful and easy to get caught in. The 101st monkey—in this case the quiet, curious one—takes a sudden zag, jumps streams, and rocks the punk. No doubt he has his reasons.

And then, of course, come the reasonable doubts. What about going back, retracing my steps? Never really happens, *amen.* Forcing the genie back into the bottle? *Nope.* You might as well try folding up the future and stuffing it back into a special little monkey's DNA. *Unscramble a psychedelic omelet.*

---

43   "morphic resonance" from *A new Science of Life* by Rupert Sheldrake. My apologies for such a loose and irreverent handling of a very intriguing theory.

With any luck, he—the Asshole, genie, monkey #101—will do something worthwhile like tell a good story, or invent a time-saving gadget. A juggler, a song-and-dance man.

Something to help keep the inmates lighthearted along the cold, dark trails.

THE DAY I leave Thailand happens to be the deadline set by some uppity students for the complete evacuation of all American military. The Vietnam War has gone on long enough—too long for the students. *Too long for me.* The American presence has no doubt altered the region, especially Bangkok. Has the steady supply of GIs on leave—and their American dollars, or French francs before that—something to do with peasant girls flocking to the city and shedding their clothes for the ever elusive baht? The thriving red-light district, world-renowned scam print production plants: *You want doctor paper? University your choice, special price for you, mister.*

But the Thais are proud of their home and not about to give it away. Thailand, an ancient land, is one of few countries that can boast (but probably wouldn't) of never having been conquered.

I have all this to ponder as I head for a bus stop. In yesterday's newscast students threatened to shoot any Americans seen walking the streets, starting today. I recall other recent news in which two travelers, held at gunpoint and refusing to part with their belongings, wound up parting with their lives.

As I walk with my backpack on this Saturday morning, along streets that shouldn't be so quiet, I wonder how American (to an eye glazed over with political angst) I might appear. *But surely they mean soldiers,* I assure myself, repeating it like a mantra. In my fear and ignorance I'm anxious to skip forward to sitting safely, unseen, on a bus.

I stand at a bus stop with a small crowd of Thai citizens. A drunken sot drains his bottle and flings it off to the side. He sways for a few seconds, gaining focus on his surroundings, then staggers straight toward me. He demands, in grand form before his Thai audience, some money for another mickey of Mekong, the popular hootch of the region. Perhaps his courage has been bolstered by the recent student rantings. I

look down at this morning's abuse of good monkey flesh and say, "No."
I say it without bother, for he is a small man and in no condition to be
getting tough with anyone. He looks dumbfounded, sees that I don't
cower, then becomes warm and fuzzy, almost fawning toward me. *What
an asshole.* I know the routine.

Speaking broken English (not so common in these parts) and now
evidently "at my service," he asks where I'm headed. "Bus no come.
One, two hour." He steps into the street and flags down a motorcycle
taxi-cart. I'm impressed with the guy's intent and focus for someone
who's pissed out of his gonads.

He approaches the driver and talks to him in Thai. I think, *Hey, the
guy's not so bad.*

I get in. When I turn to thank him, he socks me hard in the jaw.
The next instant the driver's rig lurches forward and we speed off. All
without *this* asshole curling a lip.

Perhaps this is the effect of cause: karma, not quite instant, but gittin'
me soon enough.

My jaw aches for weeks. I should've had it fixed in money-magical
Bangkok when I had the chance. But I didn't know then how badly that
boozed-up chump had deranged my temporo-mandibular joint.

Years later my face has remained asymmetrical at the jawline.[44]

---

44 More years later, during a lowbrow scuffle with a brother during which he socks
me on the opposite side that the Bangkok drunk had so many years earlier, I find
that my jaw is more or less corrected after many years of clicking, creaking, and
general discomfort. However, the asymmetrical jawline remains.

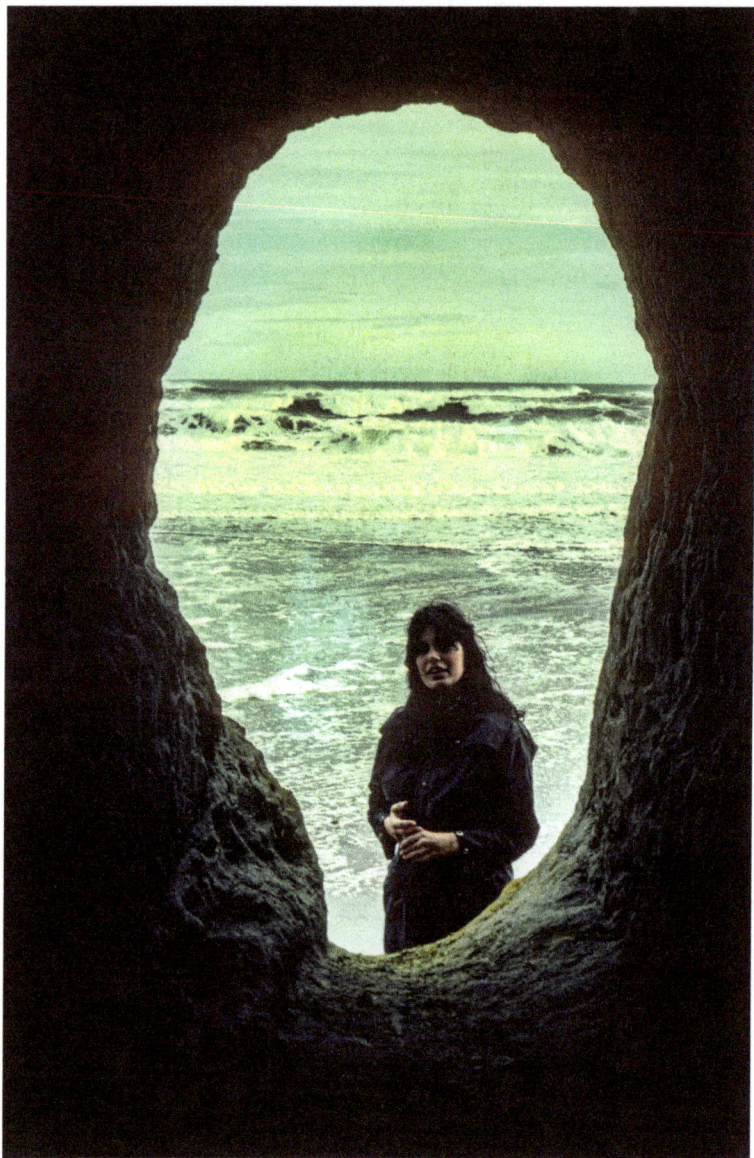

From a cave at the southern tip of the South Island

Danna and I early on

At Uncle Keith's farm

Danna and Jona after first meeting up in Oz

Hitchhiking in N.Z.

Naked Danna, Bay of Islands

The family who ran a losmen in Jogjakarta

Giant incense on a Penang street

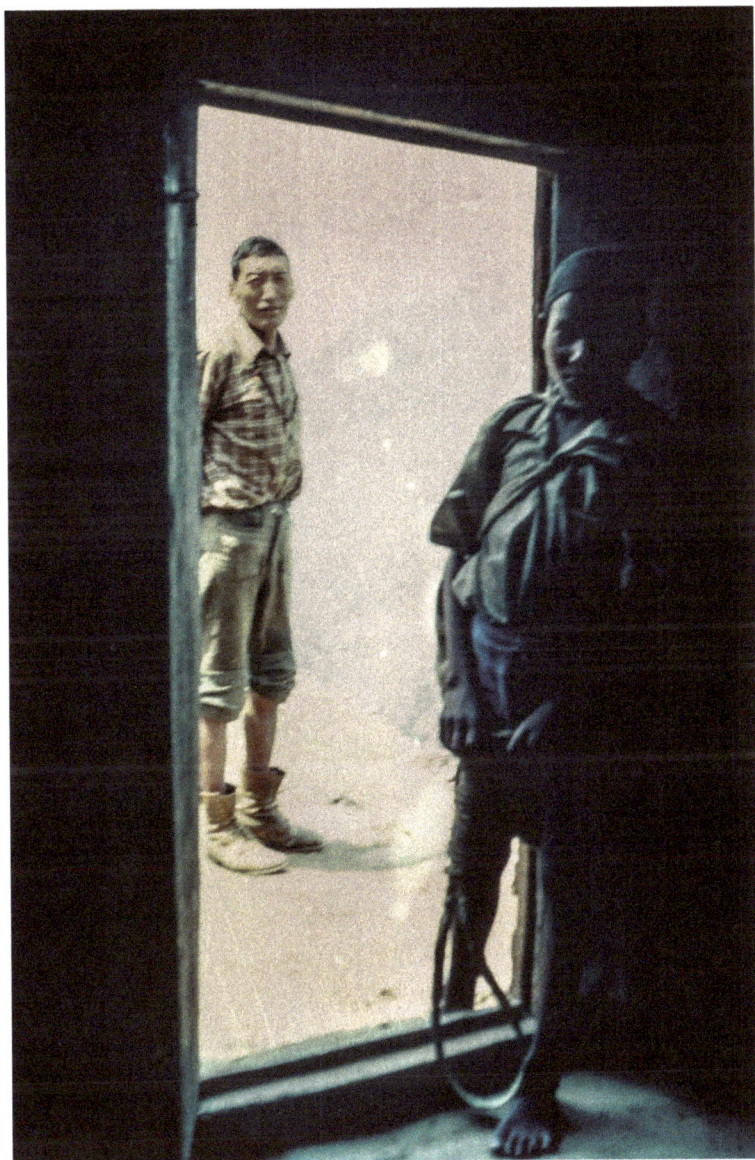

Boy with noose in the Himalayas

Fishermen at Pisar Ikan, Jakarta

Yuji and the friendly fishermen

Hill tribe boys, Golden Triangle

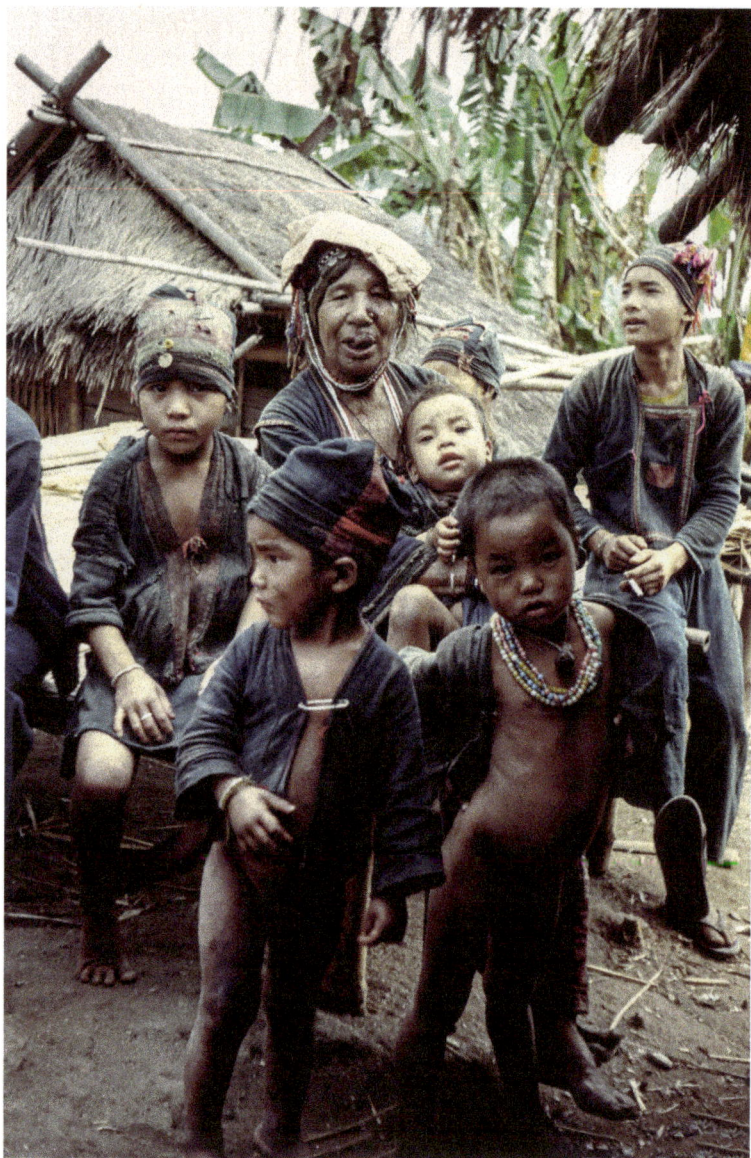

Hill tribe family, Golden Triangle

Children from my first train in India

Karen girls in the Golden Triangle

Shut-eye on Sutter St., Calcutta

Man meets Ox in Himalaya

The Annapurna massif from Pokhara

Snake charmer in Delhi

Tibetan children in Darjeeling

The 'King of the Dead's veranda in Benares

Boatman on the Ganges, early morning

Men transfixed by the Swedish lassie's red braid

Peshawar street scene, overheated film

Rishikesh street scene

Family at the Benares ghats, overheated film

Katmandu virtuoso

PART 2

India and Back and India and Back

6. Calcutta

If I had ever been here before on another time around the wheel…[45]

Catching the Horizon

Dum Dum Airport is pretty boring, even for an airport. A few plain boxes stuck together, windows. *Good name though.* It is Calcutta's, and it offers no clue on the peculiar madness that soon will follow.

In the taxi to the city, I sit pressed against the glass like three-year-old me at Stedman's, the local five-and-dime. I stare spellbound at a parade of creaking bullock carts, ragged, barefoot figures, and the unordered weavings of ancient cars, bent trucks and nimble rickshaws. Rows upon blocks of decrepit shop buildings waver behind glittering streams of sunlit dust. I sense a sedated madness in the streets; I imagine some sweeping spell of shallow comfort cast in the absence of hope, for my own hypnotic fixation on the new scene before me is far from impartial. Each frame conjured by auto glass and my mind's fitful movement is a world come and gone in a flash, created and disappeared. A carnival of oily, dark-brown faces phases in and out. Into their eyes and those of their beasts of burden do mine occasionally plummet, teasing me along through a brilliant movie of brief but bottomless little fires. I feel small, a wayward speck bearing witness to and engulfed within a strange but familiar cosmos. For something inside me has been ignited by this grimy city's onslaught of sights, sounds, and smells—a grand explosion of countless mini-explosions.

That something "inside me" is, I think, *familiarity.* An eerie familiarity, the scene before me playing off an amplified and prolonged déjà

---

45 From the song "Déjà Vu" by Crosby Stills Nash and Young, written by David Crosby.

vu. What is it about this city's hum, its moving parts, its citizens' social agreements scribed into every weather-worn face? Perhaps it is something new, perhaps not. In these first minutes I get to catch sight of it all as a massive sensation flooding the senses. All-engrossing. *Unexamined.*

It feels (dare I say it?) that I've come back to a land upon which these feet have never fallen. A strange tranquility suffuses the madness, the pace of time. The very light and air. I can't put into words this hugely unreasonable feeling. No, I can't make the words, for what they say does not make sense. In this way, without realizing it, thinking is held away. For if I dare to think I'll have to say, *Oh shit! I feel like I've just returned to this place!* The thought itself offends my current conventions of thought. I am twenty-two, and the concept of reincarnation, although I know about it, has not yet gained entry into my great room of pet "reasonables."

I hankered after amnesia in my early childhood, fancying some liberated feeling of wonderment. Distilled from cartoon depictions, I must have come up with a near-holy state of obliviousness as the reward for a good bonk to the head. Here at my first arrival in India, something reminds of that vivid newness born of forgetting, of erasing the past.

But the sweet innocence of childhood cannot play here. To look at me, a passerby would see yet another unhinged foreigner casting about in mild shock. The sensation of "alogical familiarity" is at the same time out-there and in-here. It feels as if my eyes have been washed of gunk, a haze lifted and clarity restored.

I remember my time with Danna Down Under. Now I understand. Within days of arriving at a place I'd urge us on, map in hand. I often felt like leaving as soon as we'd arrived. *Let's just see what's beyond that ridge—c'mon, baby, look!* She complained that I was rushing, that we didn't stay long enough to *feel* the place and our time together. *Duh.* Her reasonable protests questioned my motivation, and in her questioning I began to question myself. But only barely, until the next worm in my brain twitched along.

Now, in this city of abject beauty and for the first time, looking out the cab's window like a hitchhiking alien caught in some unfortunate time-loop, the urge to keep moving is gone. And this, only this—that the urge is gone—is why I am able to recognize its previous and continuous hold on me.

It's natural to surmise that I've been carrying preconceptions about India that came to fruition upon arriving there. But I don't think so, although I can't say for certain, since I have no fixed vantage point, no reliable data. This is because, well, *I am* the data. I have no memory of such preconceptions, but this means little, for (I don't know about you, but) my mind/brain is nothing if not diabolic *and* divine in its capacity to mystify, preconceive, hide evidence, lead me on, etcetera. Other than the psilocybin-induced *Hello, India* word beacons at Kuta Beach, and noting the subcontinent's lumpy expanse in the middle of my planned journey to Europe, I've hardly given India a fancy thought. Sure, I heard about poverty and health risks on the long roads through Asia, but that's about it.[46]

In any case, my unprecedented reaction upon first entering the streets of Calcutta remains mysterious to me. For now, I'll walk farther into a strange land that seems to know me. Down long, squalid, chaotic streets I'll go, anonymous, like untold millions.

JUST A FEW hundred British years old, Calcutta, West Bengal, is perhaps the youngest among many ancient Indian cities. It is also the largest and said to be India's most important cultural hub, its intellectual nerve center. Word on her streets: what Bengal thinks today, India thinks tomorrow. Perhaps it is Calcutta's youth that permits and promotes new thought.

I hire a running-man rickshaw to find a hotel. Barely able, he pulls me, another traveler (a big dude), and our backpacks down old lanes lined with crumbling brick buildings. He insists on hauling us both for the extra cash. It feels vaguely elitist, and maybe degrading somehow

---

46 Unlike many on the road at that time, I held no "mystical" attraction to India. Yet preconception and anticipation can prime one's expectations to "season" experience, in a brew of thought and feeling often influenced by other travelers. As well, some have a low defence against unexpected (or expected) change, while others resist with great flare. Or fear might play a bigger hand. When on the road, and perhaps especially in a foreign land, inner experiences and changes are more readily triggered. Some transmit at a more subtle, less featured level, and can take time to register consciously.

for the poor cabbie *wallah*. But it's probably my own projection, and I wouldn't venture to guess at his mindset. It's the visual get-up that gnaws at my conscience. The slap-slap-slapping of his bare, callus-caked, archless feet punctuates the rhythm of the bouncing rickshaw that carries us like the self-important Brits who built this city. Our man of burden is thin and middle aged, and after a few blocks he stops to catch his breath. Bent over and wheezing, he's a giant, honking bellows and it looks like he's about to keel over for good. A hearty sprout of guilt nudges us off his rig. We pay him well, but he doesn't seem to notice. He remains stooped over, gasping and hacking as we walk away.

A great stench of urine permeates the air. So vast and heavy is its power that the sheer dimensional absurdity suggests the image of a loaded, festering diaper the size of a corner store left somewhere nearby, some flying toddler god having dropped it a few days ago and now everyone's avoiding the risky unknown of divine/human protocol. Cows sit chewing in the middle of the busiest intersections of this megacity as cars, trucks, buses, rickshaws, and motorbikes curve around them in teetering streams. Bare, shitting asses perch on inner-city curbs, middle of the day, *whatever*. Whole families live on sidewalks under tied-up tarps. The street is home: bed, kitchen, toilet. Evidently, a pale, custard-like diarrhea is going around.

In the city center we climb aboard a bent-up bus with a sharp tilt, so crowded that my companion and I are separated in the shuffle. Once the bus starts moving I must deflect a continuous flurry of hands that grab at my pockets while all around, only inches from mine, hover a half dozen blank faces. *Lying with his eyes while his hands are busy working overtime.*[47] The separation of dull face and frenzied hand is impressive. Later, my friend describes the same bewildering pantomime.

The next bus lunges away before I have a chance to get my second leg up. I and two others jump away. Every possible space is jammed with bodies—inside, on top, off the back. My traveling friend is on board, so before the bus gets away I jump and grab a hold of the bars on the outside of a window. I hang, backpack on and knees tucked up, staring stupidly

---

47   The voice of John Lennon in the song "Happiness is a Warm Gun" by the Beatles, written by Lennon/McCartney.

at three blank faces on the inside. They look at me as if nothing unusual is going on here in this glorious modern world, limping along as we are in this cage on wheels upon the greater wheel, the greater cage of karma. I don't think they'd be much surprised if the bus were to suddenly sprout wings and fly off into the oblivion of Vishnu's hissing arms.

SPEAKING OF HISSING arms, the city was named after Kali, the wild and grisly mama goddess who is one of Shiva's consorts, the one who seems to make the Great One himself go a little wild. Always is Calcutta's ferocious gal, Kali, depicted wearing a necklace of freshly severed male heads, with several of her many hands brandishing a selection of murder weapons. Admittedly (hopefully) some subtle facets of meaning elude me here. I get the sense that Hindus like to dazzle with their prolific use of symbolism, layered together in different combinations (like their spices) and always on display in a continuing parade. Other mate goddesses like Parvati represent a more placid feminine aspect and serve to calm ol' Shiva down. Some say Kali (or Durga) and Parvati (or Shakti) are one and the same. Or am I confusing things with Vishnu? Such is the head-wobbling complexity of Hinduism.

Perhaps, as Hindus say, nothing of this world exists as it appears. Everything is *maya*, illusion. Here we speak in the language of Vedanta, from the Vedas, India's essential and oldest religious texts. Somehow, a disappearing act is alluded to in the symbols. The disappearance of the universe itself, the great serpent consuming itself by its tail. What is left? *Why, only what is real, of course, a morsel of God-being inside every one of us!* But mine are admittedly piecemeal and motley impressions, with little "proper" understanding of an ancient and awesome culture.

Alas, for what it is worth, I report what I see and hear. I've heard of a Himalayan Buddhist sect that has its adherents awaken at 4:00 a.m. each morning to laugh heartily for half an hour, then return to sleep. What better way to unhinge oneself from the attachments of ego and "world"? Or maybe not, as Hindus seem to warn of the ego's tenacious, team-of-wild-horses ways. Dalai Lama #14 said, "Doesn't matter if you *believe* in God. What matters is how you act, how you *are* in this life." Not sure when and where, but I can still see the impish delight in his face.

And this also I see: that Shiva is one of the big three, Brahma-Vishnu-Shiva, often seen as three faces sprouting from the same luxuriant neck. This, the Hindu Trimurti, represents three aspects of the "one God" of Hinduism: Creator, Preserver, Destroyer. Or G-O-D: *generator, operator, destructor.* In this way, some sects assert, Hinduism is essentially mono-theistic, and all the great and small god forms are merely symbols created by, or for, those with more of a penchant for the storied abundance of tradition and ritual than for direct understanding or perception.

One hears many things in this multifaceted land, even the idea of God as conceptual soap for washing away the illusions of this world, of *maya.* God as concept, God as mental floss, the soul's best detergent. I've just entered India and already I've heard each of the Big Three referred to as Creator in some capacity. And Brahm*an*, not Brahma, is the impersonal godhood residing within each person. A Brahm*in* is a member of the top caste. Not to mention brahma, the Indian breed of humped cattle.

Below the Trimurti a multitude of lesser rank fills out a cast of mil-lions. There are many faces, even those of non-verbal critters. We have monkey man Hanuman, elephant boy Ganesh, SomeOne riding a golden goose, anOther dancing on a rat. There's Kali's ferocious tiger, not to mention the omnipresent holy cow. And let's not forget snaky-armed Vishnu, whose first incarnation was the fish Matsya, his second the tortoise, Kurma; his third Varaha, the boar; his fourth the chimerical man-lion, Narasimha; then a succession of increasingly lovely humans. This phantasmagoria of creation unfolds along a great rolling of tempo-ral cycles (yugas) of twenty-six-ish thousand years (corresponding, curi-ously, to astronomy's "precession of the equinox", the mystery of Earth's "wobble",)[48] mere pinpricks of time in the great billion-year "breath of Brahma." Seems someone came up with this stuff long before young Charlie Darwin started collecting bugs out in fields, or Galileo cast his curious eye into the heavens.

"Someone" so old and so clever that young upstarts History, Mythology, and Science all might rightly agree they've forgotten

---

48   For a fascinating look at these ancient cycles, which encompass Hinduism's Golden and Dark Ages of civilization as related to the Earth's wobble and what causes it, see *Lost Star Of Myth And Time* by Walter Cruttenden.

something bloody important and should maybe consider seeking group therapy, patch things up.

Three Dweebs in Howrah

I stand in front of my hotel on the popular drag for budget travelers, a sultry lane called Sudder Street. I meet a German and a Dutchman in a chai shop, and guess what? We all want to see the "real slums". We reason that, naturally, while in Calcutta, one should see what it's known for. In recent times Calcutta has been described, in some worldly magazine like *Time* or *Newsweek*, as the most impoverished city with the most sprawling slums *in the world*.

The young woman in the tourist bureau is exceptionally bright eyed, wearing a hot-pink sari and extra makeup, including the ubiquitous red dot on the spiritual "third eye" between the other two. She is almost breathlessly cheerful.

But when she hears our callous request on the whereabouts of the slums, our tourism belle is visibly offended. With curt brevity she directs us to Howrah Bridge. She's turned cold. I'm hit by one of those uninvited, short-lived pangs of guilt. But it is soon overcome by the boyish steam I'm busy brewing with the other two spiritual dullards I've just joined forces with.

We set out. That memorable bridge spans the Howrah River, one of the watery fingers of a vast delta system where two great rivers, the Ganges and the Brahmaputra, converge in India's northeast lowlands. Multitudes cross the Howrah Bridge daily, mostly on foot. Cars, trucks, donkeys, goats, dogs, chickens, and surly cats and rats crowd its old metal. The circus of life makes a symbolic journey of transition from one world to another, with the very waters of change flowing beneath. This is how it strikes me, and this is just the sort of cliché you'll hear within hours of entering India. From the bridge, the random sprawl of greater Calcutta stretches like a great purgatorial underworld, as far as the soul would dare to wander. A reasonable likeness, I fancy, of one of several included in the prolific Hindu myths.

We reach the other side and take a hard turn down into ramshackle buildings. Children and women scurry away upon seeing us, then peer out from shadows, huddled together, like we've stumbled into some morally crippled realm of fear and pain. Up ahead, three or four men work outside a shop. When they spot us they turn, drop their tools, and stand firm, scowling with raw menace. Quickly and meekly we creep past like despicable scoundrels hoping to get away before the stones start flying. I understand now why my partners, when we started out, were surprised I was bringing my bag. But I won't be snapping any pictures here. After one or two more such hostile encounters, with women and children staring from shadowy doorways, we make a sharp loop back up toward the bridge. We've walked a mere three or four blocks in our vainglorious tour of the slums.

We don't say a word as we sneak away; guilt and shame take their due. Our little bust has given my ethical parts a timely tune-up, for I'm flushed in a sudden rush of hot and honest blood. *Am I a moral cripple to have assumed that these people, in their abject conditions, are a sight to be seen, a special kind of exhibit? Go ahead, get some engaging close-ups—nice little trophies to pass around the living room.*

Maybe if I walked alone, with no camera bag...

Now the bridge looks crowded with thin, barefoot bodies clamoring for a break in the everlasting toil of living. The begging, the dull eyes, the open sores. My own eyes are dull with the sudden blow of a reawakened conscience. We walk the bridge and I stare disillusioned at an off-kilter world. Minutes ago I beheld, in this same scene, a celebration of the plurality of life. Now I'm oppressed by its suffering, and that suffering is inside me. *How?* Nothing out there has changed.

There! In the middle of the bridge sits a white-blonde, pink-skinned toddler. Alone and crying, she looks desperately all around. I didn't see her the first time across. *Did someone just plonk her down?* She has pink eyes. *Albino? Abandoned?* I walk by her like I've lost my soul and I'm walking past my own bleeding mother. The shell I wake in every morning has cracked, and a harsh light cuts in and blinds me. Time itself is in geologic contractions that crush my honor, my dignity in ruins. I keep walking like a drone without free will.

I get a sudden, sweeping view that whatever I do—by intervening or not—pulls into alignment a future peculiar to that choice. Heavy doors swing shut. I know I won't go back. Various unknown machineries start up, rattling my production lines of destiny and intent. I could have stopped back there. *My so-called heart and soul.*

But this is India. It's pointless. So much misery at every turn. There—a legless leper drags himself along the feces-littered road, groaning and begging, looking up at me with beseeching eyes, *oh, most generous foreign sahib.* But I am no generous bloody *sahib.* That pink baby sitting alone on the bridge, looking at me, crying... this Shiva-the-Destroyer guy has taken my doofus head and is destroying bits of it willy-nilly, probably having a good laugh at my puny emotions.

But never mind moral trauma, *baba.* For the subtle glow of paradox emerges like a lotus blossom from a pond of deepest shit. As this saga of worldly travel unfolds, events, even mundane ones, roll onward and fall sensibly, uncannily into place. A grand drama yields its mysteries when it chooses, and if I look. I know, I know, it's me choosing and "it" looking, or appearing... or it's *me* doing and creating. That's just a wee peek at what some of the spiritual lore (or propaganda) I'm hearing on the road these days, says. But I do not see it this way—nor any way. I will not dignify—nor suffer—the pretense of a definition. Not today.

The ways of my culture, as I carry them within the field of another, are losing ground. An unrelenting pull plays Twister on my habits of thought and behavior. Gradually, my own are as if subsumed in those of the surrounding multitudes. In this old world which is so new to me, I cannot be sure anymore of even the plainest things. That every mind is part of a greater integrated field—as in Huxley's "mind at large," Jung's "collective unconscious" and "synchronicity," quantum theory's "entanglement," or Sheldrake's "morphogenetic fields"—is, right now, as believable to me as the performance of my own legs.[49] The Hindu scriptures assert that the mind is the consummate trickster. *I have no perceptual anchor, for I am the data.*

The picture keeps moving. The pink baby on my path, and how I react, conjures a myriad of gates. The universe is full of surprises and has a great sense of humor, or tragedy. *Your choice, mister.* And it is, perhaps, an omnipotent, omniscient, and omnipresent one in the grand

49 *Doors of Perception/Heaven and Hell* by Aldous Huxley; *Synchronicity* by Carl Jung; *A New Science of Life* by Rupert Sheldrake.

old fashion; call it God, Allah, or Brahma; the early Jews dared not name a name then provided us, it seems, with several. I get it.

Now it's up to me: will I pass through the gate? Is my mind clear enough, my heart really beating? On what side am I standing? Which way am I facing?

ON THE OTHER side of the bridge, we three sensation-seeking nits separate with a nod and a grunt, fitting remarks for the pathetic abortion our cocksure adventure ends as. I never see them again. Except for the final *I'm outta here* look on their faces as we scramble away and apart from each other after recrossing the bridge, I don't remember anything about them. One of them had curly hair; a pair of glasses were involved. The short loop we physically walked in the "Calcutta slums" belies the dead end it in fact was.

A little later when I hear about Mother Teresa I think about the albino child and I imagine, against unknown forces and odds, how they might be brought together.

7. Himalaya

'scuse me, while I kiss the sky[50]

The World, 1976

On Jan. 31, on the second full moon after the winter solstice, the year of the fire dragon begins.

Two years after scientists in California begin to wonder what happens to the remarkably stable principles in refrigeration gasses and spray cans, it is determined that something is metabolizing the ozone layer, and that CFCs, the aforementioned principles, are the likely culprits.

A synthetic bacteria gene is created at MIT.

A deadly virus is discovered near the Ebola River in the Democratic Republic of Congo.

The Bronze Age is reassigned back to 3,600 bc, Thailand.

Almost a million die in earthquakes around the world, including 200,000 in Tangshan, China, the deadliest in the twentieth century.

The first space shuttle, *Enterprise*, is unveiled in the US. The *Viking* spacecraft lands on Mars; from a locale we've named Cydonia, "the Face" stares up through Earth's finest optics.

---

50   From the song "Purple Haze" by Jimi Hendrix.

According to certain unequivocal principles of biophysics, a certainty comes to pass: the body of the German Werner Heisenberg expires.

PORTUGAL IS THE first country to include the right to a healthy environment in its constitution.

Habitat 1, the first United Nations summit on the future of our human world on this blue and dizzy planet, is hosted in Vancouver, BC, birthplace of Greenpeace.

Venezuela nationalizes its oil industry.

Canada abolishes the death penalty. Holland de-penalizes cannabis possession.

Vietnam is reunited; Saigon becomes Ho Chi Minh City.

Mao Tse-tung and Chou En-Lai die; the "Gang of Four" go to jail.

In Soweto, South Africa, protesting school children are fired upon and killed by police.

In Northern Ireland, militants continue to bomb and kill each other over issues demarcated by the Roman Catholic and Protestant groups, the two chief sects of Christianity.

The Rhodesian government agrees to allow blacks to participate equally in politics. Four years later the country gains independence from Britain and is renamed Zimbabwe.

Military coup in Argentina; Isabel Peron deposed.

In Poland, "solidarity" is born.

The US turns 200. Jimmy Carter becomes president.

The Parti Québécois, a "sovereigntist political party" that advocates separation from the rest of Canada, wins. Results in many Montrealer anglophones migrating to Toronto, which takes over (from Montreal) as Canada's largest city.

THE ORIENT EXPRESS comes to a full stop. The first trips on transatlantic Concorde flights are booked.

Females enroll at US military academies.

The *Hite Report on Female Sexuality* introduces a new verb: "to orgasm." A new group-sex club, Plato's Retreat, opens its doors in New York.

The *New York Times* finds the courage to print the word "penis."

VHS and Betamax are launched. A new porn industry booms.

Fax machines proliferate successfully around the world; IBM presents the ink-jet printer.

The Apple Computer Company is launched.

FROM OZ: *A dingo ate my baby!*

Vicious or rotten or both, someone in the Sex Pistols swears on prime-time television in Britain.

The Muppet Show debuts.

Hotel California, Songs in the Key of Life, The Royal Scam, Rastaman Vibration, Wings Over America, Dreamboat Annie, and *Hejira* are released. (Thx, Joni, for bringing to life my own "refuge of the road" every time I listen and reflect on our contemporaneous travels.)

Taxi Driver, Rocky, Carrie, and *The Man Who Fell to Earth* are released.

A Course in Miracles is published.

So long, Rick buddy.

I ARRIVE AT the fabled Himalayas, a photogenic pile of geological rubble that towers over a third of humankind. The abode of Tantric gods both Hindu and Buddhist, it is the setting for fantastic stories of magical men, restless demons, even paradise—Buddhism's Pure Lands and even the Garden of Eden.[51] The yeti—part man, part beast—is known in these parts as "demon of the snow."

I, a single unit of flesh and bones, thought and feeling, arrive on a current of countless personal pilgrimages. Over continental divides and through millennia, we never stop doing it. The truth is, you don't always know why you do what you do. Arriving in India, my sack of knowledge is lighter, my pouch of charms (and bag of snakes) nowhere to be seen. *Nice.* Of course, you lose sight of one thing, something else pops up. The rigid standard of attributing captaincy to the conscious processes is starting to soften and bend, the old mind works going on a sputter here, a stall there... I suspect I'm drifting sideways and even backward on reason's trusty old road.

But given the complexity of all things, the seen and unseen forces surrounding and moving even the tiniest bit, even plain logic would suggest that it's not exactly logical to rely on logic alone.

> *The intuitive mind is a sacred gift and the rational*
> *mind a faithful servant. We have created a society that*
> *honors the servant and has forgotten the gift.*
> *Not everything that counts can be counted, and not*
> *everything that can be counted counts.*[52]

FAMOUS FOR ITS delicious tea, Darjeeling is a good-looking Indian town built on a fair Himalayan slope. Many expat Tibetans walk the zigs and zags of its cobblestone streets and paths. On the vertical stone steps connecting them, the exchange rate of smiles is way up. From this 7,000-foot height, and on a clear day, the highest point on surface Earth is visible in the distance. Mt. Everest is, to the Tibetans, *Chomolungma,*

---

51 Garden of Eden myth from *The Heart of the World* by Ian Baker, p. 237–238.

52 Two quotes from A. Einstein. "Not everything..." was on a sign hanging in his Princeton office.

"Mother Goddess of the Universe." The Indians call it *Sagarmatha,* "Churning Stick in the Sea of Existence" or "Summit of Heaven. "

I pull out my 1974 Bartholomew World Travel Map. From Darjeeling in northern Bengal, a road heads downhill and westward into Nepal. It's a sketchy dotted line that draws my eye away from the heavier, solid ones.

The map also shows what appear to be two small Himalayan states in the vicinity, Bhutan and Sikkim. The autonomous Buddhist kingdom of Bhutan is not granting visitor's visas. So isolated from the rest of the world is Bhutan that a mere ten years ago the use of money was not yet widespread. *Honey, we could use a bit of shoe leather; let's take some of that extra yak butter over to Gompo the butcher first thing tomorrow.*

Sikkim has only this year abolished its own monarchy to become an Indian state (so it is written in India.) Acquiring a visitor's visa is possible, but the wait will be several weeks. Only a certain number of visitors are allowed at a time, and a visa costs dang near a month's traveling dollars. And getting one is not a sure thing in any case. *Meh.*

Clearly, I'm bound for the dot at the end of that dotted line: Katmandu, Nepal.

I TAKE A bus down the mountain and a taxi to the border. I'm unaware we've crossed it until a man runs after us, yelling and flapping his arms. He is the border guard, and he must've sniffed out something as our crowded cab chugged by his shack on the side of the road. Something, maybe the outline of my backpack through the glass, provided the signal to interrupt his billions of humdrum head farts, with another five seconds to complete the journey to brain-spaz central. Few foreigners come this way, so the locals pass freely back and forth. No doubt the taxi driver was hoping to avoid the hassle of stopping to make my entry into Nepal official. I might have driven into a country without knowing, leaving later by another route. *Hmm...*

The shack we passed, more like a ramshackle ticket booth, is the federal building that handles all passport and bank business, and for both countries, oddly enough. My passport is stamped and money exchanged from the same drawer behind a wicket that resembles an opening through which you'd expect to buy merry-go-round tickets.

I poke my head into the side door. Running Man pokes around the drawer looking for the right bills and coins from a random pile that includes both currencies and several visa stamps. He pauses to look up at me, tilting his head like one of those clever mutts upon catching an odd note in the wind. I smile and turn away. The deal could extend into an all-day drama if I get too nosey. Not that I'm in a hurry, but there are others to consider.

I look around. This is as technologically oblivious a place as I'm ever likely to encounter. In the distance stand the giant mountains that dominate these parts. *Himalaya.* Their rugged band of snowy white stretches across the horizon; otherwise, the land is dry and dusty. A few gnarled trees, their leaves trembling in the vision-bending heat. A scattering of water buffalo chew away, flicking flies and staring into emptiness. Could be a lazy, mammalian stupor or that lofty *Emptiness,* for all I know. Men hang around here and there, chewing, staring. I wonder about holy cattle, about mindfulness and mindlessness, about morpho-pan-genetic-bloody resonance and the similar look of the men and the buffalo.

The taxi takes us to Biratnagar, the first Nepali town on this eastern road. Between some buildings on one of the town's side streets grows a thick grove of cannabis. I walk into the green and am immediately joined by two earnest, smiling boys, one of whom carries a cluster of roosters by their tied feet. I wave my hand at the plants, many of which reach as high as ten feet, as if to say, "Hey, fellas, how 'bout all this crazy free stuff?" The boys smile with excitement but do not seem to appreciate the significance of my theater. I have one of them take a picture of me standing dwarfed and mostly obscured among the plants. They walk with me for a stretch while the roosters converse.

The road to Biratnagar was quite bumpy and dusty, and there are at least 200 miles between this small town and Katmandu. I recall the great volumes of dust inhaled crossing the Nullarbor plain along Australia's southern rim, and my long week of histamine misery in Perth. I was immobilized, alone and dripping in an overstuffed chair, separated from compelling, itinerant travelers by a blurry, dopey barrier. What comes to mind is a trio of vivacious Irish lassies who teased my hopeful, illogical self with frequent warm smiles and random chatter in that beguiling and mellifluous accent.

Coming in low on the western sky is an airplane heading for a landing. I hurry in the direction of its projected path. Within an hour I'm sitting inside one.

The flight is spectacular, a front-row seat to a streaming panorama of the most muscular peaks on the planet, the king of all ranges. Mostly dry, braided alluvial flows trace every little tree of the massive drainage system into the northern Indian plain during monsoon. Like a root system or a complex of nerve endings, or lightning, the artwork of water on earth reveals that nature is both sublime and lazy. Her fractal form is blown wide across this vista from up high, tossed back in elemental light through my retinas, repeating the design on its way into my brain as I imagine, and again with every synaptic firing. Rivers are mere trickles among the shifting washes of color in the floodplain sands. Great herds of water buffalo and shimmering flocks of birds bring it all to life in movements that from this altitude appear orchestrated by a single mind, a great big one with a sudden blaze of blood to its vast, merry head.

Our pilot—let's call him Amphetamine Ali—flies the plane like it's an MGB on a rolling shire road.

"A Day" in Katmandu

The city lies in a cozy green valley nestled within a cluster of foothills, mountains themselves, pushed up against the sunny side of the Himalayas. It's a setting that fits popular images that go with the territory: hidden kingdoms in remote valleys, learned ones who possess esoteric power and wisdom, erotic mysticism, giant tigers terrorizing the natives, and the elusive yeti. It's easy to be drawn along these well-worn mind trails, especially when imagination is quickened in the knowledge that no one who knows you has any clue as to where you are.

A tall, pyramid-shaped wooden temple, said to have been built from the wood of a single tree in 1596, stands in the center of town at Durbar Square. It is the hub where several streets converge, and a natural meeting place and vantage point from which to view the surrounding street life. The city is named for this structure, Katmandu meaning "wooden temple" and referring to the heart of the city where sadhus and beggars are welcome to stay. At its top a massive roof and spire provide shade and shelter, its eaves carved in erotic relief sculptures. I pay more than my share of attention to these. Nepalis sit nearby, at ease with and paying no special attention to this communal tribute to human pleasure, nor to my enhanced appreciation of it. Children play on the steps, oblivious to the "pornography" above. Along the bottom couple of steps and on the plaza floor, merchants from the mountains, many of them refugee Tibetans, display their colorful clothing, trinkets, and jewelry. Some of the goods appear worn and authentic while others flaunt the crappy sheen of manufactured "artifacts" provided for us tourists.

Across the square in what looks like an abandoned building in partial ruin, I spot a panther prowling the upper floor. The huge black cat pauses to look down at the crowd below, muscles tense, tail twitching. A half block away, an old cow walks in circles in the middle of the street. I hop down the temple steps and walk over. Passersby come to touch the pitiable beast, uttering perhaps a word of prayer, empathy and compassion set in their faces. A couple of blocks along, an old tree grows atop an even older temple like a spidery crown. Two patriarchal billy goats sit perched like sphinxes at the entrance, chewing slowly in unison. To my left and right, children frolic in dusty lanes among human and animal droppings.

In the 1970s, Katmandu is no large city. Within minutes of walking from Durbar Square the city thins into patches of green. On a narrow footbridge I meet a young entrepreneur who, for a small price, plays with fingernails and a bow a violin-like instrument that looks like a wooden shoe, his ease and articulation that of a budding virtuoso. Reminded of the music I once shared with friends, and of the trance-like joy that overcomes the normal mind when carried in its flow in its creation, I tip the boy generously. Below us, women whip clothes on rocks after washing them in the slime of the nearly dry river. I cross the bridge.

A friendly young farmer, thirty-ish, walks toward me from his field. Speaking good English, he invites me in for tea and a massage. Remembering the gay Balinese art student, I decline his offer with common courtesy. He bows his head with respect, but not before a telling spark escapes his eye.

Along a dirt track the pluck and drone of a sitar can be heard coming from an old building in a meadow. A few more steps and the holy bathing ghats of a small temple come into view, greasy smoke rising from a single pyre. Farther along, a team of women sits in the shade of a Bamiyan tree. Grimacing, with no eye protection, they produce gravel from boulders with ball-peen hammers.

I loop back around. Distant eyes at the top of a hill watch over Katmandu, painted on two sides of the flag-adorned golden stupa of a large temple. I begin the climb, drawn by the meditative gaze in those (what I take to be Buddhist) eyes. At the top I find young Nepali families squatting on the temple site, ungoverned and comfortable in their squalor, washing clothes on large flat stones. A few monkeys prowl about, inspecting the laundry and lifting sundry objects for a sniff. It is now dusk and a cool whip of breeze beckons me back toward town.

On the edge of the city a Tibetan refugee camp spills over with the exiled homeless. Back in the city proper, soldiers stand guard with polished bayonets at the door of every bank. Word on the street: the ever-present neighborhood toughs—USA, USSR, and China—have cast hopeful nets on political territory, each with their own propaganda library here in quaint but strategic little Katmandu.

Then it's back to my end of the cultural rainbow, reluctant as I am to admit it: jam-packed, Western-style pie shops cater to the inflamed palates of budget-tourist hash smokers. I cringe at the look and vibe of the group that best represents me today, my fellow travelers. When gathered we often appear stoned and indulgent, and at least dabbling in the illusion of entitlement. I regret the thought: like spoiled royal brats dressed in colorful rags. Yet I'd probably delight in interacting with any one of them. It's when we get into groups that things seem to get wooly.

Curious, I walk into the lobby of a semi-spiffy-looking, but small hotel. There is a desk with a clerk behind it. Though no five-star (or even three-star) hotel, this is sure evidence it's a tad spiffier than the budget variety I'm used to. Across from the clerk a set of wooden cubicles hangs on the wall, each one labeled with the room number and the name of the current occupant. In all the cheap hotels I've stayed at in the East I've never seen such an arrangement, whereby things are organized to the point that one can see who's staying in what room at a glance. The moment I step inside my eyes fall first upon a cubicle bearing the name of a J. Taylor. At the same time I hear, coming from upstairs, the superb and soothing tones of a familiar voice and distinct guitar-picking style, one whose influence I know well from my own musical emulations. I listen good and hard but can't tell whether it's a recording or is being performed live. (Ol' James baby is *that* good.) Who knows? I've never heard the tune before. Credulity in two-step with mere coincidence? Repeating a pattern of behavior that has become an idiosyncrasy of mine, one I'm not yet inclined to examine, I turn and leave, as if back into the sweet unknown. *Is this free will, mama?*

Within a few blocks my sweet unknown morphs into three large hogs in a dark lane, their snouts probing the debris-laden ground. The night is warm and clear, the air dead still; the sounds of people and vehicles are muffled and slow. A low rumble, a truck creeps along the road. With a loud grunt one of the hogs stiffens and listens intently. Let's not forget that pig folk, if not endowed with cinematic grace and beauty, are indeed shrewd and sensitive creatures of the Piercing Light. In a lightning flash of recognition, three flesh-and-bone missiles bolt away down the alley. Three men jump out and sprint after them in a vain attempt to capture a ton of meat. For sure they'll get away, free for another day. Meat-eating Hindus? Or a hit squad of a different bent operating at night so as to avoid offending the life-worshipping sensibilities of the majority? *Ah, freedom,* I sigh, as I walk back to my hotel feeling on this charcoal splinter of night a kinship more with the four-legged.

Before I reach my bed a kind Tibetan family invites me into their home for a few rice beers. The woman of the house, a big buxom mama of three or four soiled but healthy-looking kids, motions me in. Standing in her doorway she is jovial, generous, and interested in my ethnicity. "Italian stock," she leans forward and declares, "is *very* good." Her gaze is rather steady, but what the hey? I'm thirsty. We drink the rice ale, and I talk (probably too much.) She talks—energetic, dramatic, passionate. Almost hungry.

What appears to be an old embroidered shoulder bag sits on a table in the dim light. In the other dim light of my liquored buzz I offer to buy it, remembering the flashier junk back at Durbar Square. In a moment she whips from flush-faced belly laugh to sitting forward with a hard, cold stare. Her kids seem to take this as an urgent signal to disappear. She inflates the price, sells me the bag, then whips halfway back to prowling leopard charm, all sweet talkin', tail a-flickin'. *Oh, mama.*

Gopi Krishna

I spend much of my time at the top of the temple steps in the roof's shade captivated by the shifting scenes below. A few itinerant sadhus, beggars, and orphans sleep here. No other travelers. I meet a six-year-old boy who hopped a train from Kerala, 2,000 kilometers away in the deep south. A brother and sister, seven or eight years old, live near the square in adjacent streets and alleys. When I first meet them, the boy, the younger one, offers in hushed tones, "Hashish? Woman? Smack? Change money? Buy, sell something?" Rat-tat-tat go his connections, and the only English I hear him speak.

A Muslim introduces himself by asking, "What is your religion?" I tell him I have none. He turns to his companions, and after some discussion he looks at me quizzically. "Are you a dervish?" I imagine spinning tops and swaying cobras. "No." Cultural poseur maybe, a real lean bean for some mystic babe, I do hope. But dervish? More discussion, more excited this time, then, "Are you a holy man, a fakir?" Thanks, uh, but, "No, I am not a faake, fuck-err… faakk-ear. I just have no religion." The men argue, their passion rising. The convergence of cultures, the struggle with language, meaning. As though God himself, having seen on numerous occasions how a happenstance meeting of worlds can degenerate into centuries of wailing and gnashing, imparts a tiny breath of clarity into my foggy swamp of a mind.

Interrupting them I say, "Oh, uh… I'm, I guess… Christian." Immediately, the Muslim's face relaxes, and he offers his hand. He nods and smiles. I nod and smile. We… feeling *good.* They aren't interested in my version of personal choice. To these three—Muslim, Hindu, and Parsee (Zoroastrian)—religion is, perhaps, a matter beyond personal choosing. Soon I see that the circumstances of ethnicity and geography have allowed for my service as emissary of the Christian world to these three of a world-come-together. Though I long ago extracted a god-awful tangle of Christian dogma from my once tender mind, I am from the Christian world. Indeed, I carry it within me and bear its unsung fruit: my habits of thought and behavior, for yea and for nay. Even as I bypass its defining doctrines, the religion's sensibility—its hopes and its fears—has informed my so-called personal ones. I didn't see this before, but it's all over me like each of theirs is all over him. And whether they have the words for it or not, this, I believe, is what they ask. *Thanks, God. Thanks for saving all those babies.* Humans. *You dumb fucks.*

And so I befriend this strawberry-chocolate-vanilla trio, and several others who show up at the temple every day: an Iranian student in exile from the oppressive rule of the Shah and his SAVAK's hounds; a middle-aged local Nepali man; an important-looking Indian Muslim; and a highly respected Indian sadhu from Cochin, Kerala, called Gopi Krishna. He looks tall (but is not) and has a handsome face with probing, compassionate eyes. He speaks perhaps a few dozen words of English, but by his discriminating placement and subtle emphasis—and by the respect paid to him by those clustered around as he speaks in his own tongue—it's clear that he's an intelligent and magnetic person. He's illiterate.

I ask him about his inordinately tall turban. I start with the preconception that it signifies a degree of spirituality or prestige in his sect of Hinduism. Perhaps it's the label that draws others to him in deferential groups; as usual, I'm along for the ride. Blurring my eyes and giving my head a wee tilt, the tall turban speaks with the same authority as, say, a three-piece Italian suit or a large rock in a ring does a few doors over in Europe.

I hang out at the temple for more than two weeks. A small group shows up daily to smoke *chillums* and to be near Gopi Krishna. Of course, I can't understand a single tongue flap, but there are times when we fumble along amiably in mine. A simple affection is with us.

After some pointed probing on my part Gopi tells me, with remarkable clarity in his rock-bottom English, that when he was six his family was butchered by Muslims: convert to Islam or die. He alone was spared. The surviving villagers and local clergy took this as a sign that he was divinely favored. Taken in by local Hindu priests, he began a religious life. Years later he took to the wandering road as a *sadhu*, a holy man. He describes droughts when food was scarce and he kept moving, begging, on the edge of life.

A few times I feel the urge to launch into the nature vs. nurture debate, but… *a-no-a-spiek ingleese*. A picture of our different lives. Mine: a superfluous ration of coddling love, a private, separate home and bed, red tricycle, TV, books (so much information I doubt the authority of any particular school), babes galore, rock star dreams, too much candy, and a perhaps precocious (or overwrought) fascination with transformational, buddha-on-the-road mythologies. His: family gets butchered during boyhood, raised by priests, subsequent repeated risk of starvation into early adulthood, never learned to read, born into and embedded in a Hindu worldview and attendant caste system. Owns no clock or mirror or keys, never mind a bed. Our two worlds: Nurture a Go-Go. Apart from these circumstantial psycho-bombs, who are we, really?

Yet we are "in sync," "cut from the same cloth," "in alignment." *Nature?*[53]

I ask him what he owns. A few words, a few gestures. Smart man, he knows what I ask. He looks at me for a steady moment, then around at the faces that surround us and await his response. Then it's back to his turban. He unravels it as his three-foot dreads fall over his shoulders and skinny frame. One hand remains on his head, cradling a small cloth bundle. He brings it down from its usual place hidden among the dreads atop his noggin, and unwraps a gold ring and several gold and silver coins, very old and by their rare look, no longer in circulation. These, and his cup, staff, sandals, and dhoti are his possessions.

Travelers from all over find their way to Durbar Square. A fellow Canuck joins us at the top of the temple, bearing a guitar in a case and a thoughtful demeanor. Upon learning he's Canadian, Gopi looks at

---

53   More recently, the nature vs. nurture debate is increasingly seen as a "specious dichotomy." In *A Hunter-Gatherer's Guide to the 21st Century* by Heather Heying and Bret Weinstein, the authors suggest that our perceived hard-wiring and influences from environment are "inextricably linked." In *The Biology Of Belief* Bruce H. Lipton describes the cellular mechanisms by which environment can determine genetic expression.

him for a few seconds, then at me, then up a bit into nowhere. From that nowhere, and after a deep draw on the chillum he's holding, he says, "Canada people, *discipline* people." I don't always discern whether someone is Canadian or American in these foreign lands where we can appear so similar next to others. But I respect Gopi's take, whether by discipline he actually means discipline, or means to say reserved or serious or self-deprecating, or polite and nerdy. Or something else.

Gopi, like any sadhu, smokes copious amounts of *charis* or hashish. This is done as frequently as a Catholic priest would make the sign of the cross while living inside a cathedral. The world is Gopi's cathedral. Every sadhu I've come across in the land of Hindus smokes hash with reverence for what is experienced as a sacrament. In the Roman Catholic Church, priests gulp down swigs of wine—the blood of Jesus—several times during mass. Here at the top of Chillum Temple, Gopi answers my inquisitive expression with "good *pranayama*." He holds in a deep draw from the chillum, savoring a holy moment. This "pranayama" is the breath of Shiva, a wee gust in the storm of creation.

And Shiva's breath is fogging up the place. From my elevated position I see several groups focused on a burning chillum. Some enjoy their euphoric sacrament next to a couple of policemen standing on the plaza floor at the foot of the temple steps. For this is how it is: people smoke hash out in the open, broad daylight, in the center of Katmandu, capital of Nepal. It is said there are one or two hash parlors in the city, but, *meh*.

After a week of hacking my throat learns to accept the large volume of resinous smoke that a typical chillum will channel. Sit with a sadhu long enough, and you'll sure enough learn to smoke like one. The dainty puffs I prefer are gone in great clouds. One or two grams are mixed with a bit of tobacco to produce a hot ember almost an inch in diameter. Perhaps there is a little male bravado bonding in this subculture of the chillum, barely recognizable in a society seemingly devoid of the macho-flavored ways of the West. This is a gentle land; half the population is vegetarian. On mosquito coil packages, the directions say to close the doors, fill the room with smoke, then open them to allow the mosquitoes escape. No, not macho.

Yet I do feel included when I'm finally able to inhale with a free-flowing, maximum-lung draw (even though it's probably a sparrow-snuffing

volume of smoke.) Knowing glances and the body language of acceptance further draw me in. It could be mugs of ale in an English pub, it
might feel the same.

Sharing notes, and also for amusement, I demonstrate the hash-
smoking method of my youth. I borrow a cigarette and place a tiny
piece on the burning ember and suck madly at the wispy smoke trail.
It looks absurd here where the quantities we handle are of a different
order. Gopi giggles.

Walking the streets of Katmandu it's remarkable to witness the respect
shown by strangers for this man who lives like a pauper and walks like
a king. At my urging and courtesy, we sit for tea and perhaps a bowl of
dhal. At one makeshift street stall, not much bigger than an outhouse, my
tea comes with an extra: a fly floating belly up, hidden until I've drunk
half the glass. The glasses are dull and stained from poor cleaning. By
his fidgeting and displeasured inspection of his own cup, Gopi isn't crazy
about the lack of attention to hygiene either. As we sit, the young man
does his cleaning with a half pail of murky water and a handkerchief-sized
gray rag that is gossamer thin from overuse, it needing more of a wash
than the grimy glasses that might as well have been dug from the dirt. The
rag rests on the lad's shoulder and doubles as a sweat cloth with which he
frequently wipes the filth from his brow and neck. After the third wipe, I
give a disapproving look, but he has no idea. He stops and tilts his head,
his eyes spreading ever so slightly in consternation.

Gopi handles his food with both hands. One of the first things
learned upon entering India is the right hand/left hand rule: you eat
with the right, wash sphincter with left. Using toilet paper is considered
grossly unclean, as well as costly. (Why pay to merely smear and wipe
when you can wash away all traces with water?) Upon my arrival in
Calcutta, I was reminded of the rule by the reprimanding look of a
white-haired old man from across a restaurant while using both hands,
ignorant of the hygiene code. I ask Gopi about his apparent lapse. He
curtly refers to the practice of washing hands and knowing whether
you're about to eat or shit.

One afternoon, close to the end of my stay in Katmandu, Gopi
suggests we take to the road together. There's something of the older/

younger brother dynamic in our *sympatico* friendship. I don't respond directly; his words go the way of so many comments made and received graciously in passing. I'm inhibited in part by my inclination to travel alone, but more by what I see as unassailable inequities in our lives. Money seems a solid ugly that will grind and stall the blending of our worlds. I'm not comfortable with this prospect even if *he* doesn't mind. Perhaps Gopi takes these concerns into account, and he's wise enough not to let it bog us down. Maybe it's just me, caught in an imagined web.

Do I, in my complicated folly, turn away once again into my sweet unknown, to pass by a rare gate in negligent haste?

Parade

I'm sitting at the top of the temple steps at Durbar Square one morning when a parade marches by. A few old men stomp along in front banging pots and pans. Others blow on whacked-out horn instruments. Children follow, laughing and yelling and running about. Merchants along the street pause, smile, then continue their business. About an hour later the same parade comes by but from a different direction. Then again from another. And another. A whole day is spent making joyous noise throughout the town, like yesterday, like tomorrow. No drinking in sight, but some fine hash is going around.

The parades happen daily, at least during my several weeks in Katmandu. Maybe this is their norm, or I've happened along during a season of heightened festivity. As it turns out, I'm lucky to be in town during a truly epic parade.

On this extra-brilliant day the streets are jammed with thousands of revelers. All have come to witness the passage of a thirty-foot-high monster buggy contraption, its wheels taller than men. Primitive and elaborately adorned, this rickety coach carries a chosen virgin goddess. I can't see her, for she is hidden behind god-embossed panels inside a cage-like room about twelve feet up in the midsection. A man walks around a narrow veranda that circles the cage of gold. Looks like he's snuck up there, all smug at getting away with it, but doesn't know what to do now that he's up there. The long, narrow spire of this sketch case of a holy rig extends another fifteen feet, twice as high as the little room, and is shrouded in fresh evergreen branches, with a crowning tuft of green at the top, the sprout of life itself.

The monster buggy is pulled with ropes by scores of townsfolk, young and old alike. Anyone can join in. Progress is slow; the massive, seven- or eight-foot diameter wooden wheels squeal and crack and moan. The axle-to-hub integrity seems, *uh*, not so well integrated. The wheels each lean at a different angle. A couple of times the contraption teeters on the edge of collapse, barely holding, cranked so far that I'm sure it's going to snap and crash. The crowd moves in waves and peaks of running—always away from imminent calamity, oohing, gasping, and yelling. The virgin gal must be freaked out but good. When it's clear that mayhem and ruin have not befallen the citizenry, everyone crowds in again in blissful madness, pulling on the ropes, singing, drumming, and tooting many horns. The sun is the central blast furnace of the universe, aimed right on this parade.

The virgin goddess for a day is shrouded within the colorful orna-mentation of a Trojan-horse-sized carriage, a golden buggy that crawls by in careening fits and jerking starts. Poor thing is said to be unmarriable after becoming so honored a symbol of virginal purity, a cryptic reversal of her good fortune in being chosen for the role. As is often the case, the wider significance and meaning of the ritual eludes me. I'm honored and grateful to be a visitor on this occasion, just one of so many splendid sights on these serendipitous Asian roads. Indeed, I'm thrilled to witness the bittersweet spectacle with a naïve clarity, uncluttered by knowledge.

Trek

Apart from walking or pedaling a bike, in mountainous areas a traveler must risk the sporadic, poorly maintained and often perilous road vehi-cles. They are buses usually, but it could be atop cargo in a freight truck clutching canvas and rope, or in the dusty buggy of a cart drawn by a donkey or a horse. More often than not, motor vehicles leave behind dense clouds of noxious blue exhaust. Given the scarce pleasures of cash in these parts, I get it: who would consider (or even imagine) repairing a motor that still runs?

On a jaunt toward Pokhara, my bus stops for a short break. Figuring on ten, fifteen minutes tops, I hurry over to a tea hut and order a tasty, nutritious meal on the go: an omelet wrapped in a chapati. I must be the last person back to the bus. As I walk across the gravel lot, I see that each window frames a dark-skinned face or two that stare at me with a lazy curiosity. As the only foreigner on board I will be watched without respite, no matter what trivial thing I do. Their looks aren't appraising ones, more like numb stares.

Still twenty paces away, I bring my steaming meal up for a first bite. A large hawk swoops down and plucks it from my hand, brushing my face with a wing. Before the bird flies ten feet the greasy omelet slips from the rolled chapati and falls into the dust. Immediately, as if having bet on the likelihood of this quirky event unfolding exactly as it has, a large mangy dog dashes forth and chomps it down. He bolts on a sharp angle into an empty field. Clever mutt, that's why he's so large.

Each face in each window of the bus smiles and nods, a dead eye here, a missing tooth there. *On with the show.* This particular skit could be called "The Zen Omelet" or "The Dog, the Hawk, and the Egghead." Or maybe, "Fast Food."

THE MOST MASSIVE mountains on planet Earth. Spectacular beauty, legendary remoteness. Innumerable, untold crevasses. A society or two of lofty beings hidden from view, pulling invisible strings. *Shambhala.*

Himalaya: Sanskrit for "abode of snow." A glance at a topographical map of the world will show that no other region compares. As large as India or Western Europe, this great, jagged expanse stretches from Afghanistan to Southeast Asia's back door, and includes well beyond a hundred of the world's highest peaks. A dozen or so major river systems begin here. So vast is this immense frozen sea called The Roof of the World—the Himalaya-Tibetan cordillera—that it will draw the mind and shred it into a million stories. Pretty much how the mind is anyway, if one heeds the old Vedic wisdom.

A trek is in order, yes: an invigorating crawl along the Roof's eaves. I turn toward the valley and town of Pokhara, a short bus ride going west from Katmandu. From Pokhara we will hike along foothills adjacent to Mt. Annapurna, one of ten Himalayan peaks over 8,000 meters. In the distance across the valley from the town, another more dramatic-looking peak dominates the skyline. A slightly twisted pyramid is placed atop an already towering, major chunk of rock in the middle of a muscular massif that stretches for forty, fifty, sixty miles? Its name is Machapuchre.

To me it's the Lost Pyramid of Lobsang Rampa, after the Tibetan-American pop author and my memory of first hearing, at age twelve, about "Eastern mysticism." That was in my buddy Rick's bedroom on the day he showed me his pile of Rampa paperbacks.[54] Rick spoke of mental powers, a "third eye," flesh-eating plants, and lost civilizations, all within a couple of minutes. The colorful, hokey covers of those Rampa books sat on his table at the very edge of my comfy world, like the first draw of a brand-new sense. Till then I thought "otherworldly" was the interior of my own home, where the skin tone was a shade darker and the ranting a notch higher. It was the gloomy trio, omniscient/omnipotent/omnipresent, that the Catholic Church reaches so thoroughly in emulating from their own telling of the nature of God, and that unblinking eye in the triangle in the illustrations they peddled. It was when I discovered Jesus wasn't Italian, but Jewish. At Rick's house my eyes fell upon something new, a peek beyond a cultural veil. Yet it was a veil behind a veil, since my family's immigrant experience had already provided me with the suspicion we all live in a house of smoke and mirrors.

Rick heaped on more intrigue, informing me that with his intention and "mental vibe" he was able to influence the growth of a row of potted plants that sat innocent and defenceless on his window sill. He was on fire. While he spoke I could see Lobsang's eye on a sly tilt right there on the coffee table, staring solemnly, out of the corner of my own. *Turn off your mind, relax, and float downstream,*[55] becomes my internal auto-Muzak program, cranked on to provide the faint drone of a soundtrack.

Of course, Rick could communicate directly with his dog, Sandy. Both skittish and devoted in the extreme, her intelligence was surprisingly quick. I all but believed him as he sent the eager mutt scampering around the house obeying various instructions, delivering a mop, a broom, various footwear, an umbrella, and other household paraphernalia. That hypnotic third eye (three eyes/triangle eye—yikes!) staring

54 *The Third Eye* and other titles, by Lobsang Rampa.
55 Voice of John Lennon in "Tomorrow Never Knows" by the Beatles.

up from the table seemed to agree, as if it was using Rick's persuasive crazy-talk to harness Sandy's clever obedience—and my own credulity.

It is now ten years after that first visit to Rick's place. As I look across the Pokhara Valley to Machapuchre and prepare for the Annapurna trek, it seems I've all but forgotten about third eyes and eye triangles. I'm now far and away from my and Rick's comfy old world, but not so far from Lobsang's, as it turns out.

SEVERAL SMALL GROUPS of foreign travelers walk across a wide plain, a beginning. Some have paid for a local Nepali guide; a few strays like me weave our way randomly along. We cross a hot, dry valley that stretches for a mile or so toward a dense crevice in the distance. Our beeline toward it is the only straight and level hiking we will encounter in a week. An hour later we're climbing.

During this first ascent I distribute my entire cache of bandages to other travelers who have already developed blisters on their feet. They're all wearing snazzy hiking boots. I didn't much think on that; my runners are cheap and soft. Lucky for me, they remain comfy and give me no grief the whole trip.

Our path winds among massive foothills. We pass women carrying loads of straw, wood, and even slabs of flagstone in sacks on their backs, their loads supported by straps that wrap around their foreheads. Happy, frolicking children (some obviously diseased) and smiling men and women welcome us at many turns on the trail. In huts along the way, and for the price of a candy bar, the foreign trekker is offered a meal and a place to bed down for the night. Tea is always brewing. Meals consist of bread, rice, potatoes, a green-brown blob of overcooked veggies, and perhaps an egg, if you ask. Which I do at every hut (my *lookin' for Mr. Protein* phobia is in full bloom.)

Few roads are cut into this high country and none past the main towns near Katmandu. Pom-pom-adorned freight trains with a hundred legs chug along carrying supplies, stopping in tiny settlements. We hear them coming up the trail by the pleasant tinkling of numerous bells. These donkey caravans own the path; we stand aside as their human leaders keep them moving.

The foothills, large mountains themselves, are in many places shaped into vast terraces. The brilliant sun backlights the lush, long grasses, Earth's own trusty therapy, vital fuel for any journey. Getting from one mountain to another involves a steep descent of several thousand feet, then up again as far on wide stone steps.

At one such gorge, a village built on a mountain's edge is partially visible through moving cloud wisps across a short distance. It appears and disappears—very close. *Too* close, like a floaty, misty illusion. Tapping fantastical tales hidden in the deep of years I stand on the edge, wavering, a mere breath away from this city-in-the-clouds apparition. A different kind of flight lifts my belly and spins a tale behind these eyes, a vertigo that wobbles my legs and is the messenger of gravity in alternate forms: physical, psychical, and imagined. Alas, the mist clears at the wave of a giant hand, and my fancy is gone. That ghostly mirage is solid-real, and the better part of a day's climb away. Down, down, down, and all the way back up.

Arriving in the mini-town I'm impressed with the indomitable vitality of these mountain dwellers, surviving so well as they do on the hard edge of things thousands of feet up. The village's squat, primitive buildings are all attached; there is limited space on this rarefied, miniature plateau. I wander through the middle of it along narrow, haphazardly interwoven stone paths. I imagine a private space behind every wall. I feel (a bit) that I intrude, but I walk alone, and the Tibetans, or Nepali, are kind to me. The smiles are subtle, but more, they have a look of genuine respect. The men and women I encounter are not threatened, nor do they make any special fuss. It's as if they accept, as a common occurrence, a stranger from afar passing through their tiny, indeed, their intimate town. I hear only the sounds of men and women working, children playing, and the comments of goats and chickens, sights and sounds that probably haven't changed since the last ice age.

After a good meal of tea, eggs, and rice, I continue. An hour past the tiny town I'm walking alone in the vast wilds. The longer legs of a lanky Greco-Australian catch up to me, so we walk together for a stretch. We share a certain undeclared Mediterraneo-Anglo complex that steps up naturally, allowing us to volley back and forth in easy conversation. Our dear identities, the ones we claim and imagine, will serve well our personal alignment. How vast and fast these brains, these "selves." *Good old times.*

A great yearning pulls us up the trail. At 11,000 feet the forest, with its moss-covered trees and trickling streams, differs little from the woods back home at sea level in my west coast marine wonderland. Huge, blooming rhododendron bushes are interspersed throughout. Snow-capped peaks are visible now and then through mist and vines. The occasional wordless question falls, asked or unasked, heard or unheard. This is a great wilderness, large enough to contain a great many things, not to mention the Buddhist void it might have inspired and presently occupies. A vastness equal, perhaps, to imagination *and* emptiness.

The trail is not always clear. At one point we decide to wait until someone with a local guide comes along. It takes a little over an hour. We follow until the trail emerges again, then lag behind, losing them to better enjoy the stillness of our forest walk.

On a quiet stretch, when we haven't spoken for a good while, I hear a gentle swooshing overhead. I look up; three eagles fly a tight circle twenty feet directly above, their spiraling flight following along. Without a sound and without stopping I nudge my companion. Eagle #1 is locked in and staring. The bird's eye reaches far into mine with a focus that overcomes my own foggy effort. Up we stare like dumbstruck turkeys. A few more circles and Three Wise Eagles fly off. Maybe we're too large, or we've just crossed paths with those mysterious adepts of the winds and sky, *travelito incognito.* The last vestiges of disbelief have been long discarded.[56]

Out of the mountains, we're back at the start. We've walked a one-hundred-mile loop that took over a week to complete. I followed no map, just kept walking.

A Good Day to Die [57]

It's time to cross the foothills that divide the Katmandu valley from the plains of Ganga.

---

56 The traditional belief that the ability to fly over vast distances and the highest mountains was developed in Tibet and Mongolia. See *A Story Waiting To Pierce You* by Peter Kingsley, pp. 24–26.

57 "a good day to die," the voice of actor Chief Dan George in the movie *Little Big Man.*

As is the norm, our bus is in poor condition. Its sharp tilt attests to years of mechanical neglect and abuse. We're in for thousands of meters of steep ups and downs (mostly downs) with hairpin corners on mountain roads with no safety railings. I look at the bus heap from twenty paces, then consider the Hindus' view of corporeal existence as a temporary prison. I wonder whether our driver is a good Hindu, unattached to this particular life of illusion. At the point of surrendering control over my safety, which happens often enough in this part of the world, I feel a nagging, freaky suspicion that maybe this time I shouldn't. Yet I climb into the bus, locked into some fateful dream that I have evidently bought into. I look around at the surrounding mountains. Control over the whos and whys regarding a public carrier isn't what a traveler in India is likely to hope for or even think about, so futile is the prospect. Yet that is where my sorry thoughts keep running to.

I climb aboard with three Swedes, two blond guys and a red-haired gal. Ascending the mountain is easy; we chug slowly. *A-okay.* But the descent shifts focus, like it or not. Evidently, the driver is cast from equal measures of docile and insane. This is *not* Burnaby, not Goteborg. *Job application back at the station. Docile? Check. Insane? Check.*

Within ten minutes of peering timorously into the great chasm immediately outside my window, we're interrupted by a big thud. We go skidding along the gravel shoulder and slide to a stop a foot or so from plunging over the edge.

When thought returns I rummage through my trash bin of logic looking for a scrap to justify hope. *Walk out of these mountains?* It might take days to reach a village. *Tigers?* The story goes that over centuries they've acquired a taste for human meat—dozens per year, they say. *Force the driver and his cronies aside and take the wheel? I can DO it.* But within minutes, as if overcome by some hypnotic force of the group mind, my sensibilities merge with those around me and I surrender the reins of my survival. A rusty box, a bent chassis, four wheels I'll bet are out of round or at least unbalanced; this is the magical wagon of today's traveling, super-dream. And let's not forget the "big thud" at the front end that sent us skidding. And that the whole mess is driven by a fanatic from a Hindu horror-comedy. *Best opportunity for learning the detachment, baba*. Hinduism is a vast complex of the human theater, and I'm just learning the ropes, which oftentimes feel like slippery snakes.

Everyone gets off the bus while four men, including the driver, climb underneath. Except for us queasy Westerners (so attached to living,) everyone seems calm. I find their resigned serenity strange and bewildering; they behave as though this critical situation on a steep mountainside is the most natural, easy thing. The crowd stands on this edge of rock and dust, a gentle breeze ruffling their clothes. They appear relaxed, patient.

The four begin to argue with gusto, the general fanfare below punctuated now and then by a disturbing, almost rhythmic thud/crack. I look around. No reaction from the Indians, indicating that all is well. The Swedish chick is visibly shaken and asks, "Will someone *please* find out what they're *doing*?"

I ask a swank-dressed gentleman whether he thinks the men under the truck know what they're doing. He stands straight, hands clasped behind his back, and looks across to the next mountain. There is a strange sort of distance in his gaze. He speaks calmly and with confidence: "Oh, yes—gualavide meg-anigs." He seems serene, and perhaps compassionate toward our anxious, Western ways.

Squinting past my own fear and ignorance I get down to see what these "qualified mechanics" are doing. The argument has mightily risen, and so has the frequency of the banging, now a steady *whack-whack-whack*. The driver blindly wings a hefty boulder into one of the steering parts, more engaged in arguing than in focusing, mentally or visually, on where the boulder happens to be striking.

I get up, barely thinking. Or not thinking. *I think.* There's nothing useful to say to the Swedish lass, *but I think I'll say something.* This shit-fest of human competence has turned the afternoon into a stupid fantasy. I go back to my seat and tell her not to worry.

I stare into the deep valley at the road's edge. I think about dying, about souls, about worms and meat. About the singularity called the person. About my own childhood's end back in the Catholic Church, their tales of heaven, hell, and purgatory disappearing within a child's mere whim of curiosity. About the cycles of civilization, black holes, the play of mind and matter. The four-billion-year-long Day of Brahma. I think about God thinking, about Him breathing... *dark matter in, big bang out*. And *my* breath. *Precious*. Mom and Dad... *is it true? Will I see you again?* So much can fill the mind, yet so little one knows.

I'm afraid, but I don't want to show it. Don't want to make it worse for the Swedes. I'm a few years younger, but they look to me cuz I'm quick to ask, ready to hop down and *look*. I want to inspire calm, as if I'm their protector.

All at once we hear the sounds of appeasement, their voices down a notch. The four men clamber out with a conciliatory air. Everyone climbs back in for the long descent. The incident appears to have seasoned the driver's mood, for now he is careful. And, well, this *is* a narrow track overlooking a good facsimile of the Crack of Doom from the Cliffs of Insanity.[58] But after ten minutes, his confidence reinflated, he resumes his insane gallop down the mountain's flank.

My senses and emotions have passed beyond my previous beyond. In my private recreation, something shifts. It's as though this whole bus ride is one great rubber moment, and its tension is released slowly as we roll all the way down. The immense flatland of India's northern plain seizes my focus. Hazy Ganga has gripped my continuous gaze, as if there exists a hypnotic realm that will direct the situation toward some order of peace, safety, and sanity. I am intent on drawing us into it on the slightest chance that it exists. That big rubberiness has made us all one and the same, and there is nothing else. My head is painted across the sky. The world has expanded into a subtle phase just to the left of itself; the usual whitecaps of mind are gone in a sudden expansion of "All this." All this is still; emotion, gone.

The four doofuses are back at it, crowded into the driver like teenagers at a pinball machine. With any luck someone's driving the bus by some unseen system of ethereal linkage. *Aha! New kind of free will, baba—make the bus fly like Vishnu, baba!* India can do that to you, allow you—encourage you—to think you've joined the holy ranks of unseen power and that, for a brief spell, you've got your hands on some bloody huge levers.

---

58 "Crack of Doom" from *The Lord of the Rings* by J. R. R. Tolkien; "Cliffs of Insanity" from *The Princess Bride* by William Goldman.

In this vagabond world where an eagle's eye or abandoned baby will serve up a fresh order of humble pie, it could be that the crazed wing-nuts crowded into the front of this bus are the benefactors of the peculiar detached state I enjoy. On this and other bus rides in mountainous Asia, I come to accept whatever might come of the question, "Will I die today?" Along this edge where life and death teeter, one can look either way. Not only toward life or death in the so-called "for real" but also to the qualitative, to *how* one might live. It might be a good, prosperous and joyous time, or one that is more like hell. Barreling down the mountainside in this careening mechanical crapshoot I am a calm, joyous fool, perfectly satisfied with all the danger and risk heaped my way, knowing so very little that every detail is a surprising jewel. *He who ain't busy bein' born*[59] ... exactly this, baba.

I gaze through the rattling window into a vast depth as our driver skids and honks our supple lives along the snaking route toward his next paycheck. May sweet serenity follow me down this mountain's gaping side! May this hyper-conscious ape never forget the unequivocal acceptance of dying, of leaving behind whatever this life is, offered, as it is, a sacrifice on the altar of experience.

Odd twist it is though, that when I let it go—really give it away—I am suddenly immersed in its most impassioned presence, moment by moment, for as long as it lasts.

> *The world is but a show, glittering and empty.*
> *It is, and yet is not... Only the onlooker is real.*
> *To the Self the world is but a colorful show which he enjoys*
> *as long as it lasts, and forgets when it's over.*
> *Whatever happens on the stage makes him shudder in terror*
> *or roll with laughter, yet all the time he is aware it is but a show.*
> *Without desire or fear he enjoys it, as it happens.*[60]

---

59   "He who ain't busy bein' born is busy dyin'" from the song "It's Alright, Ma (I'm Only Bleeding)" by Bob Dylan.
60   Nisargadatta Maharaj.

8. Benares/Ganga

I am he as you are he.[61]

COMING DOWN THAT MOUNTAIN HAS BEEN BOTH A TRIAL AND A CEL-
ebration of existential persuasions. Accepting the prospect of dying
seems to bear an unexpected boon—or great illusion, if that's all it is.
Either way, I feel deeply rested.

Leaving the hills, our bus takes us to the last outpost near the Nepal/
India border. We climb aboard the only available wheels, a horse-drawn
carriage, and clomp along for forty-five minutes till we reach customs.
On the Indian side we graduate to rickshaws, one of which swoops over
and whips us ten minutes along to the train terminal. This border region,
like others in Asia, cuts up transportation links and leaves them hanging.
"Country" seems to end at what began, presumably, as an imaginary line.

A massive civilization lies ahead as we approach its edge from the wild
side on its northern fringe. We've come from the direction of the highest
and most vast mountain wilderness, a barrier to the other massive Asian
civilization a couple thousand miles over in China. Spreading away
from the feet of the Himalayas is the land of Ganga. It is a continuity of
geography and of culture, a broad, rich river land that is the dominant
region of India. Here lie the metropolises of Calcutta and Delhi, along
with a dozen or more million-plussers. Throw in a few venerated hot
spots like Benares, Hardwar, Amritsar, and Allahabad, and you get a
scale of human folly matched only in China and in Europe.

The three Swedes and I will continue together for a stretch, or until

61 Voice of John Lennon in "I Am the Walrus" by the Beatles, written
by Lennon/McCartney.

one irritates the shit out of another. I'm not sure what their relations are, only that they're from Sweden. The guys seem congenial and compliant, perhaps having developed the art of gentleness to a surreal degree. They barely speak, but the lassie is vivacious and assertive. Everywhere we go their fair skin, but particularly her red hair, attracts hypnotic fixations of attention. On my own there is no such ballyhoo, for I blend in fairly well, a look and vibe that could be described as spunky-hippie-sadhu wannabe cruisin' on some pretty groovy waves of *maya*. I suspect it serves me well.

This is my introduction to Indian trains. It is the daytime journey of many frequent stops from Raxaul near the Nepali border to the holiest of Hindu cities, Benares. It is my second super-dense populated stretch; the first was Java. Our window becomes a movie screen featuring a whizzing kaleidoscope of urban and rural India.

The train stops at the first city, Muzaffarpur. Within seconds a crowd snaps into place like a heap of iron filings concentered on our window. They gape and gawk, all as one, in a singular trance. There is no glass but it's barred, otherwise chaos surely would erupt and leap in. The Swedes are nervous and begin to complain. Even the gentle dudes mutter curses. The lassie aggressively (but vainly) shoos away the big, dumb crowd. I look from face to face; not one appears available to connect with us as real people. There is no indication they're aware we're involved in an experience together. They are deeply absorbed in *their* nifty movie showing on the side of a train. *Who's on whose TV?* The profound barrier "reduces" us to these images, but we're also exalted as symbols of something strange and vast, with great suggestive power. And this portal between alternate mythologies, or realities—the illusion itself—goes both ways.

Meanwhile, anxiety continues to rise in my fair companions. They resort to cussing and swearing at *our* little TV. Naturally, as TVs go, there is no response. Acting on a hunch, that a reversal of signals might stir things up, I grab my camera. One, two, three, four; each shutter click is a little hand slapping faces one by one, interrupting the collective stupor. Instead of joining the cursing Swedes, I've pulled out a magic remote. The jig is up; the audience blushes as TV land pops and disappears. Numerous awkward smiles move this way and that like random fog wisps before vanishing.

LIKE MECCA AND Jerusalem, Benares is one of those rare cities called holy by millions. It is believed to be one of the oldest, where learning and the arts have had numerous centuries to grow.[62] A veritable spiritual cauldron, the city smolders vigorously and occasionally spawns a prophet or *avatar:* a holy Big One. Buddha had his start under a bo tree down the road in Bodh Gaya and began his teachings in nearby Sarnath. A couple of Jain prophets hail from this town. But its stature as the holiest for Hindus—Shiva's hometown, specifically—is what makes it the champ.

The city, also called Varanasi, sits on the left bank of the Ganges as the water flows, along what is said to be its best river frontage. It is one of the only spots this great river of over 2,500 kilometers takes a bend and heads south to north; and so from its western shore the city has a front row seat to the rising Sun, planets, and constellations.

The famous ghats, a great expanse of stone steps, descend and disappear into the Ganges's murky depths along the city's length, about four river miles. In the dry season the long descent of the ghats is visible, but when the river is high only a few steps remain above the waterline. Many ornate temples, and up higher a steep wall of city buildings, overlook the ghats and the river. More ancient ones are hidden away submerged in mud, great blocks of stone drawn inexorably into the forces of gravity and flow over untold centuries, as evidenced by one temple that leans hard toward the moving waters.

Hindus believe it auspicious to die in holy Benares—one might dang well leap straight into godhood! Multitudes make the pilgrimage in their later years. The plan, when the time comes to "shuck off the material form," is to be cremated and have one's ashes dissolved in the blessed river. Many beg for their sustenance and to buy the firewood for their own funeral pyres. Intermediate Care, Hindu-style. Scores of old beggars form gauntlets of beseeching faces and outstretched hands at the ends of streets that lead toward and down the ghats to the river. Having come from all over India to die, it's no wonder Benares has earned the nickname City of Death, although City of Light is the official tag. It is Hindu macabre:

---

62 In *My Music My Life* Ravi Shankar mentions that his home town, Benares, is reputed to be 10,000 years old. Seems it has become near-conventional for Western historians and archeologists to dismiss India's telling of its own history.

dark but burning bright and lively, like all of Hindustan squeezed into a writhing multiplicity of heaven, hell, and places between.

The serious business of what is deemed most sacred unleashes an intensity that is tangible and captivating. There are many travelers here, but our presence is barely felt, engulfed as we are in the city's freely reverberating emotion. Thousands trickle down the ghats at dawn to wash and pray, washing as much for matters religious as hygienic. Thin cotton clings transparent as the reverent, the atoning, and the enraptured dunk themselves repeatedly. Not specifically hidden nor openly leered at, pendulous breasts and puffed schlongs are minor details in the engrossing spectacle.

The Ganges is said to be infused with a holiness that makes it unpollutable.[63] Hence, the bodies of the diseased are thrown into its sacred and feculent brew to be purified while the healthy dead are burned at the water's edge. But as well, the bodies of young children and holy men are also thrown in. *There is much I do not comprehend, sahib.* Sewer pipes dump a green-amber-brown slime that drips unchecked over the ghats while just a few feet away men and women wash themselves in transcendent devotion, faces cocked heavenward. Hawks and monkeys sit in trees, as captive as an audience ever was.

Or is it Shiva himself, hanging around the old digs, watching over his temples and the ever-turning wheel? I watch the monkeys watch the crowd, and surely, someone watches me.

A BAD BARBECUE blows on a balmy breeze.

My nose and I go walking for a closer whiff of what promises to be provocative, sensational, and grisly. Veering toward the riverfront area I stop on a short, bridge-like walkway twenty feet above four infernos. Each oversized bonfire unleashes a terrible heat, sending greasy streams of charcoal smoke into the already heavy air. The few men tending them continually poke long poles into the burning masses to achieve steady consumption. Just visible between layers of firewood, the flesh and eyeballs of a head melt and pop in the flames. In a minute it's a charred black skull. Dozens of

---

63   It is claimed that the waters of Ganga retain high amounts of dissolved oxygen, and that bacteriophages, the viruses that eat bacteria, are also present.

carnivorous crows flit about, squawking like hungry game hawkers on the first day at the midway. A dozen or so dogs hang around, darting here and there, desperate for chunks that drip from the pyres.

An arm springs from one of the blazes. A reckless mutt dashes to within inches of juicy, rare-cooked meat, only to be clubbed by a cussing fire-keeper. Yelping, cursing; keeping it burning, controlling the scavengers. Someone's weird round on the turning wheel.

Boatman

From the dense bustle of the city, my gaze is often drawn across the river and over the green and spacious landscape toward the hazy horizon. Early one morning I seek out a boat to take me there.

The sun's first rays have not yet touched the thick mist that blankets the river when I walk down to find a boatman. A few rupees will buy many things. Within minutes I'm sitting in a hand-carved wooden boat, rowed along the shore by a quiet old man.

We cut across the open water through cool mist. The clear, gentle sound of water trickling off the oars seems to reach in and tickle my brain. In these foreign lands that do not speak your name never mind demand something of you, a mild euphoria is often and easily educed. I have no fixed goal. For a few cents an old man heartily rows me wherever. He'll take me miles upstream if I choose. Any working-class modern kid knows the Aladdin story. This morning, on a whim, as many lie defenceless in their beds, I've fumbled into your-wish-is-my-command, India style. As incongruous as it appears, we're both easy with it. He wants my cash, and I want… whatever I want. Today it is passage across the River Ganga.

The boatman wears a woollen shawl this cool morning. When we reach the opposite shore he jumps into the chilly water and pulls the boat up. Looking back toward Benares I behold the ghostly image of a medieval city floating on mist over a silky river. The long wall of city buildings is dotted with glowing amber lights. Inside, people start their day. High above, the deep-blue tint of sky slowly brightens. It is 5:45 a.m. Doing nothing more, it still would be a rare jewel of a day.

The boatman speaks no English, but from his unwavering gaze it's evident he's willing to wait by the riverbank while I go a-wandering, or *whatever it is that you are doing, sahib.* It's a great gig for him, earning several days' pay for one morning trip.

The grain is tall, over my head. Throughout the green fields a network of shady paths is lined occasionally with tall palms. Here and there the tracks widen into coconut groves. These vast rural acres of quiet could be a hundred miles from the streets of Benares. Yet mere minutes away, the crowded, filthy city sits like a cold sore between the moist and the dry. How often does a Western traveler come here? By the brief glances of the occasional passing Indian through the grass, it's hard to say. It seems they hardly notice me, but of course they do.

Now and again brown earthen jugs catch my eye, attached somehow next to coconuts way up high. The heat of the sun is climbing to its usual oppressive level, and I'm thirsty. Safe drinking water is not available in Asia, so travelers tend to rely on green tea, chai, or Coke or Fanta. In this savanna wonderland across the water, no such choices have popped up in more than an hour of walking.

Through some shrubs I spot a small group of men and boys chatting quietly in a shady clearing. I walk over and greet them. I point to the jugs and make a drinking motion. I'm thinking coconut milk or sweet, crazy-water, anything. The oldest man nods. One of the boys climbs thirty feet up the palm, hand after foot as quickly as a monkey, detaches a jug, and brings it down. The old one takes it from the boy and hands it to me. They are silent as they watch me upend the jug and swig back whatever nectar is inside. It's alcoholic, like beer or young wine, but no matter. Not yet 8:00 a.m., I haven't seen booze for a while, and what the hey, it's tasty. I drink and I guzzle. Impressed or dumbfounded, they all stand quietly and watchful as I down half the jug on a hot morning, probably not a good move. I thank them, holding out a handful of change, something I wouldn't do in the city. Or if I hadn't just guzzled more than a liter of strong, fresh coconut beer on an empty stomach. The man pokes through the coins in my palm and takes a fair price and no more.

I continue my pleasurable stroll through the sweet, buzzing fields. Soon I find that the buzzing is not so much in the fields as in my head, which moves about as if it's especially heavy today and is connected to my body with a good-quality steel coil. Recalling the fizz of the brown jug I turn toward the river, trading adventure in the tall green for a chance to lay in that cozy old boat. *Damn the booze.*

When I reach the shore I play-fall into the cool river, eliciting no more than a slight raising of the boatman's brow. My momentary relief is not like the devout dunkings at the ghats. *A saucy, impudent little snot desecrating the holiest of holies.* It's in his face. *Shiva will have him later.* Or maybe he's Muslim and frowns upon drunkenness. Ignoring me and looking back at the city, he pushes the boat out. *Or maybe Kali will take her due.* No, he must be Hindu. He seems impatient, perhaps remembering that bloodthirsty goddess's bounty and the lingering ghosts of the *thuggee* movement in centuries past.[64]

The boatman's sudden terse mood (and moves) demand a few quick moves of my own if I'm going to get back to Benares as planned. Rising to the need, a soggy lump pulls itself aboard as the boat moves over deeper waters. I sprawl face up. The hot sun fries the moisture off my face, further deepening an already deep tan toward the average look of the Indians themselves.

Brahma's Boons

As summer monsoon season approaches, the heat of Ganga is intense, especially in the city. I've arrived in hell unexpectedly early, and it's really fucking sunny. When the sun has risen a small distance into the sky, at about 8:00 a.m., many retreat into shade to collapse on cushions and chairs. But Benares is now wide awake.

In the central town area, tucked in close to the ghats, rickshaws are the wheels and the streets are jammed. It's a slow-motion river of crazy-painted rigs and bullock carts. The drivers might be uptight, but

---

64 My morbid whimsy recalls that the English word "thug" is derived from "thuggee," the name of a group of assassins devoted to Kali, a movement that is said to have persisted for more than a millennium until the Brits stamped them out in the nineteenth century. Thuggee assassins did their death-cult thing in northern and central India, on the Ganges posing as boatmen or on the road by befriending travelers and pilgrims, then robbing and killing them. The preferred method of sacrifice was by garroting, a practice the thuggees claimed was taught to them by Kali herself. In subsequent rituals she was paid her due with one third of the robbery proceeds, the body, and to sweeten the deal, a bit of sugar. *Is so logical, baba. No?*

instead of blaring horns and belching motors I hear only the gay tinkle of a thousand bicycle bells, a kind of alternate, freaky-nice rush hour. Happily stranded in one such traffic jam, I'm wonderstruck at the relative safety and altered consciousness of these streets (from my view, of course.) If a toddler or a drunk were to step out into traffic, they'd likely only suffer a bruising, a broken nose, or a bad cut, much less likely the serious maiming or death where cars run free. Ironically, one becomes conscious of the constant danger only with its disappearance. Few large cities anywhere still enjoy this kind of pre-auto levity. Is the apparent docility of the Benareans explained in part by the absence of this peril? How chill would the skittish wildebeest become in a freaky-nice savanna where Mr. Lion lacks fangs?

Today I'll be getting my fill of rickshaws, bullock carts, and crowded pavements in the searing sun. I must crisscross the city to update my smallpox shot and to purchase a train ticket. Since this will likely take most of the day, I hire a rickshaw for an all-day price, at my suggestion. The driver seems to like the idea. *Duh.* We agree on a figure, a sweet deal for him, judging by his (rare) immediate assent. But since he'll be working harder than I probably ever have or will, and is twice my age but looks ready for retirement, I'm happy with our arrangement.

There's a prevalent attitude, a near code of ethic among budget travelers: one must strive *not* to inflate local rates lest the place be "ruined" for later visitors. And I dig, I truly do. Might even sympathize with their disapproval of the daft, rare one who offers the extravagantly ballooned price equivalent of back-home rates. But that our relative wealth would gradually spill over to those with poorer nutrition and limited opportunity seems acceptable, perhaps just, and likely, inevitable. Eventually, I reckon that everyone learns the other's game and the field becomes more common to all.

But once we settle on a price, always a good one for the local server, I insist on sticking to our agreement. In this case I must endure the persistent weasel's continual whining for *more money, more money* for the duration of our verbal contract.

Six hours later, after receiving an infected arm from the nurse's dirty needle ("Oh yes, see? needle clean, nice, yes?"—splash with alcohol, smile, grin) and having to go several places miles apart for the disparate forms that—*presto*—produce my train ticket, we pull into a rickshaw depot near the ghats. It's supper time, and my driver doesn't stop his exceptional nagging until his rig comes to a full and final stop. A fleet of rickshaws sits idle under mature shade trees, their sweaty drivers enjoying a well-earned rest after hours of pedaling dead weight around in the infernal humidity. Here my driver is transformed into a reasonable and amicable man, as though it is standard practice to harass the foreigner for one more rupee right to the last pedal of breath. I endured his pestering all day, holding firm to our agreement.

Perhaps my driver respects my obstinate resolve, for now *he* offers a treat. He motions me over to a government *ganja* and opium stall. For some reason *charis* (hashish), the much finer product, is illegal, but one can purchase three grades of weed, opium, and a fresh cannabis substance called *bhang*—moist, potent little green balls intended to be mixed into a milk or yogurt shake. He buys a small bag of high-grade ganja and invites me over to sit at the top of the ghats. He stuffs a chillum and starts smoking, a pleasant turn after the day's lowbrow theater.

I'm about to take my first draw, smoking chillum raised in both hands, when a pair of shiny, extra-large black shoes appear right next to me on the stone ghat. They belong to a tall policeman. I am one fat hen in a slew of skinny wolves. Sure, the driver bought the grass at a government ganja stall, but it could be a setup. Rampant corruption courses like high current through Asia's various circuits of organized insanity. Perhaps the sly old rickshaw driver will get his extra fee after all.

I look up—accused, nabbed, guilty and, *Okie-dokie, you got me.* In plain, well-articulated English the cop says, "Oh, don't worry. I want *only* to be watching you." *Only* indeed. He stands like a silly guard with big, happy eyes, taking in what must be a novel sight to him. Of course, the use of ganja is legal in Uttar Pradesh, India's most populous state, and today, I might even trust the cops on the matter.

The driver and I drift away, gazing past the chattering tangle of human folly before us toward the shimmering waters of the Ganga and beyond. The tall policeman watches me, smiling and rocking back and forth in his glossy black shoes, one hand fidgeting with his billy stick.

AH YES, THE infected arm. Within days an odd, reddish line climbs up my arm from point zero. At about the time it passes over armpit territory a fellow traveler, bearing a kind of pioneering, hip/neo-Buddhist demeanor, points at it and admonishes, "Hey, buddy, ya gonna take care of that thing, or have ya had enuffa this go 'round already?" Ten minutes later I'm in a pharmacy.

I ask the pharmacist for penicillin. He glances up from his papers, head drops back down, points to a shelf. The level of professional apathy in this guy is masterly. I check out the medicine and do a little impromptu research, drawing on faded doctor memories. I give our business relationship another shot by presenting what looks about right regarding dosage and number of days. His head wobbles indifferently, looking up for a mere split moment. I buy it, take it for a week, it works. The red line disappears, and now I'm writing you a book.

AH YES, THE "head wobble." It is a peculiar motion I see all over India. Maybe I'm daft, but it seems the wobble could mean *not sure/yes/I guess so/I dunno/who cares/go ask Vishnu, or Whoever it is that you are worshipping*. It is a motion both up and down and back and forth, combined into a kind of drunken "S" or figure eight. Perhaps this is why it seems to mean anything and nothing—the wobbling head traces what would become of an infinity symbol after some good *charis*. Often I'll ask a question and get the wobble in response, then watch as the person walks away indifferently. *Interesting.* Occasionally, after being taken for a local myself, and as someone prattles away in Hindi asking me a question or two, I offer the wobble for an answer. *Why not?* Oddly, they seem to understand and leave satisfied, heading off in a certain direction that I'd bet my *just so* wobble has permitted or verified.

THE TANGLED ALLEYS of old Benares draw me into their beguiling patterns time and again. So labyrinthine and random are these paths that I seldom know where I'm going. At times I come to a dead end where someone looks up quizzically as if to say, "So, why have you come to this here place, exactly?"

One fine day I'm befriended by a cute, friendly boy while admiring a baby sitar in a merchants' stall. He speaks decent English and helps me get good deals on some Benarasi silks, a pair of oil paintings, necklaces made from heavy black thread tied into series of attractive knots and loops, and two cloth-spun hanging lanterns done in the colors of soil, red to browns to black. He accompanies me for several hours. When the shopping is done he invites me to his home on one of the musky lanes not far from the bathing ghats.

In the presence of his father, who is as many years my senior as I am to the boy, he asks me some questions. Sexual ones, if my hearing and senses aren't flipping on me. The father is calm and nonchalant, reading a 'zine and whittling a bone or something. Thinking I must have misunderstood the kid, I say, "What? What?" Dumbfounded, I turn to the father. With a weary, lazy smile and a calm, kind of I-don't-mind-if-you-wanna-fuck-my-boy tone, he says, "He is desiring the intimacy with you." His head doesn't wobble, but he offers a single tilt, a "wob," if you will. His eyes go lazy and narrow a bit, perhaps offering a nod to the vast panorama of our cultures' arbitrary insanities, and to my great, gaping ignorance. Never mind, for with his apparent neutrality, the father has permitted the boy to have sexual relations under his roof with a strange adult man. Since this really is Daddy talking... well, polite and befuddled, I turn down the offer. This is more mind curdling than the Balinese art student; at least he was my age, I was high on mushrooms, and no parents were involved.

I say goodbye and leave, if not abruptly then with the polite finality of suddenly remembering an appointment... an appointment with my own comfy sensibilities.

Would our little exchange have been different if Mom or sis were present?

WITH THE HELP of the oddly smitten little playboy I bought that baby sitar for eighteen bucks. My habit of collecting things nudged the sleeping musician in me till I imagined its droning sound blending with the guitars, mandolins, and harmonicas of my teenage years. *I will bring this little sitar home to my smiling musical friends.*

I've carried it for weeks swathed in an orange-and-black swastika cloth, making a few Germans I've run into wince some mighty entertaining winces, despite their recent birth years. I purchased the cloth as a souvenir of the curious fact that swastikas are ancient Aryan good luck symbols, displayed all over India with festive flair. Interesting cloth, and maybe I'll freak out a few more Germans (the full-on Asshole has mellowed to brief, impish efforts.)

Then, thinking again of the lovestruck boy and his dad, I swoop in on a socio-philosophical pendulum. I'm a guest in a strange land, caught between facing up to my own (perhaps acquired and undeclared) morality, and a reluctance to judge the ways of that strange land. Social convention, freedom, depravity, love… my understanding or sense of these—what they are and how their edges might blur, one into another—is now questioned, or at least a bit shaken.

Back into the mess of alleys, I'm aware of how sensitive to an outsider's gaze these Benareans are. My bungled joy jaunt in Calcutta's slums sidelined that shallow, self-absorbed mode called sightseeing. I'm a respectful visitor, grateful for the privilege of meeting others in their homeland and, with any luck, succeeding on my end of the bargain, which is in keeping my eyes and my heart open.

With all this to churn the inner machineries, a tubby, bright-eyed Aussie bloke enters my frame from an adjacent side lane, like a giant orange quail popped into the neighborhood. A comedic boon sent from Brahma to keep me company, maybe lift my spirits. This guy's a bouncing, hyped-up windbag, a plump, bizarro Tigger, a boorish blowhard much too loud for these tranquil lanes and my pensive mood. Uninvited, he has become my walking mate, a wisecracking asshole right at my side. Within a minute his self-confidence balloons and he's flicking "pennies" around as if to mock the Benareans' poverty. He'd have been beaten to a pulp back in Howrah.

"What the hell?" I deliver a scowling *malocchio*,[65] very *Italiano*, right here in Hindu Land. But it's no match for his hot wind. *I'll lose the buffoon at the next turn.* This I do with uncommon agility, his bloated guffaws subsiding around the corner well after I've ducked down a side lane.

Brahma's boon turns out to be a riddle, or a swift boot in the self-conscious ass.

---

65 In Italian, literally "bad eye," "evil eye."

King of the Dead

Walking along a lane I glance into a half-open door. I catch a glimpse of a life-sized tiger sculpture against the pale-blue sky and double back for another look. The German guy I met only an hour ago follows. The brightly colored cat is positioned mid-stride atop a veranda railing. Several women scurry by, hiding their faces. A man of humble demeanor beckons us with a curious hospitality.

He speaks in earnest about his master, the King of the Dead. He will be "back *too* soon, and most *glad* to meet your acquaintance." Like I'm wearing one of those important British uniforms, I stride across the open area of this choice Benares flat, straight to the tiger veranda. I look out over the ghats and the river of ancients. It really is a king's perch, taking in the panorama of the city's long arc along the Ganges and the countryside beyond. A good view, a spot to build on. Almost directly below is the central cremating area, several fires sending up constant streams of dark smoke. Across the river toward the eastern horizon the northern plains disappear in a gray haze. The German stands beside me, having followed me over to the veranda. The word sounds Italian, or (in fact *is*) Hindi.

The man points to a framed photograph hanging on a prominent wall of the central open area of the spacious residence. It is the King in portrait: a puffed-up man with drunken eyes and a loose smile. I look at my companion's expressionless face, wondering at his reaction. A pretty, self-effacing woman brings us tea and biscuits. She and the view are like drops of water in a weird desert.

'And aren't we lucky?' the manservant oozes with every affectation of his body lingo when, a few minutes later, the King walks in. His every jerk and sway is anticipated by the skittish groveling of his servants. *Like slaves.* There's a flurry of activity in the adjoining rooms as women, men, and children are roused by the wave. Servile homage is enacted in myriad movements to flatter the master, who slops it all back. I cringe and turn away. That anyone should have such autocratic authority over his people is deeply unpalatable. Feudalism is said to persist in India, and this small sample leaves a bitter taste on my plebeian tongue. The air of bloated decadence recalls Fellini's *Satyricon*.[66]

The King does not address us nor even acknowledge our presence. But he knows we're here of course, for after some whispering among his underlings it is announced there will be a performance for the guests. *Oh.* The women and children disappear behind doors *(doh!)*, and three men start dancing to the accompaniment of musicians. It isn't long before the King joins in with slitted eyes and slovenly sway. The tempo quickens, and the heat rises until crotches and thighs grind together in their own awkward rhythms. *What happened to all the women? What? Why?*

I suppose I've shown exceptional naïveté, oblivious as I've been, for example, to the reality of same-sex flourishing and the more inclusive appetite of the bisexual. *Think, Johnny, think. For instance, the little playboy and his dad just the other day; the Nepali farmer; the art student in Bali… that weird episode in the Melbourne public toilet.* And so, a little slow on the uptake maybe, I've come to understand and accept that occasionally, men like men and women like women. *Okay.*

On the dance floor the King slobbers and pants, almost keeling over once or twice. As much for stability, I'm guessing, he humps a dancer's thigh with extra gusto. The whole scene is, for me, quite obnoxious. A good strong leg fuck, the King's outstanding, swinging drool tendril… *I'm outta here.* I will not patronize this very bad performing art. I know, here I go again. I'm supposed to respect the ways of my hosts; shouldn't judge by my own culture's biases (or my emotions'.) I ought to defer to the ways of a people I likely don't know enough about. *The bigger picture.*

Instead, I'm seized by full-on loathing. The slobber, the mock fucking, the lording over, I feel like I'm smack in the middle of a drunken fiefdom. With a long, wide tongue I stand and sneer at the King in mock gagging, my hands outspread, like one of those tough Māori warriors. I don't hiss or shake my head, but I'm not bad. Never mind that

---

66 Refers to the Italian movie maker Federico Fellini's 1969 film *Satyricon*, which depicts debauchery and impersonal sensuality, a film that had piqued my suspicion that no real satisfaction, no increase in happiness, can come of it. The desperate hunger for sensation, deadened feelings fuelled in the hidden furnace of buried trauma, all too common in the human drama… *Is this not so, baba?*

he's twice as big as me and has a small battalion at his command. I walk out, and the music stops. The German follows.

"Boy, you sure had some strong feelings in there," he remarks as we reenter the alley. Maybe *I'm* the real wingnut. Yeah, maybe. *Probably.* But boy, does this German guy seem dull.

Later, by mentioning King of the Dead here and there, I'm able to piece together a common enough story. The King is the owner of the land where the bodies are cremated, a considerable chunk of riverfront that (presumably) extends uphill to include his spacious palatial residence with the tiger veranda. That alone would make him a rich man in any city. He earns a tax each time a body is cremated, so he really *is* a rich and influential prick. Thus his title and lordly influence. Never mind India's reputation as a persistent bog of feudalism.

Monkeyland

Alas, the land that perhaps carries the most benign cultural bias toward all creatures is also the biggest source of monkeys traded for scientific use. Here in India they are as free as microbes, and they abound in city trees and at railway stations.

I sit in the shade of a teahouse lamenting the sight of a smallish monkey chained up in the hot sun's burning dust. He has draped a sheet of errant newsprint over his head for shade. Suffering his sunny hell he lashes out, snapping at anyone passing by close enough. I can't blame him for raging against the bigger, clothed ones who smell like evil fruit and know how to make things like chains. *Bastard pricks.*

Well, on this fine day of good *charis* and interspecies compassion, I overcome the barrier of mistrust that normally separates me and any simian cousin. I get up, walk over (with courage I wish I could channel at will), and unhook the chain that tethers him to a metal post. As soon as I'm in range, when I squat to fiddle with the chain, he jumps onto my head. In a holy instant he sees that I've come as his emancipator. In the time it takes to unhook the chain and stand up, the little devil decides that instead of scratching out my eyes it's a good time to poke through my hair and look for the sweet grub. With Kid Monkey riding my shoulders grooming me, I walk to a shady spot and fasten the chain.

The incriminatory click transforms my little buddy back into a hissing demon. I leap away, just out of range, perfect time.

WITH SUCH CHARM and grace as little buddy's, how can I resist a visit to the renowned Monkey Temple in Benares?

I visited a snake temple in Malaysia. As soon as I entered, a man draped three large green snakes all over me—neck, arms, crotch. I stood still and surrendered to the oddly appealing, writhing massage of their cold crawlings. *Opportune moment to ponder the attachment to fear, baba.* Glad I didn't get a boner.

I hear there's a rat temple in south India. *Rat temple? Why?* Why anything, I suppose.

I'm familiar with the unpredictable behavior of monkeys, having been assaulted on several occasions. When I first arrived in India, I spotted a cute little one with a humanlike face close by in a branch. I pointed it out, amused and all chatty, to my companions. When I turned back, whoops! That cutesy little thing had darted down the branch, teeth gnashing and slashing at me, inches away. What a performance; the little bastard sprayed slobber on me. Later I heard that staring into the eyes of any primate is taken as an aggressive act. I suppose I should know this. It's a useful lesson now, one that comes in handy, especially in dark crevices of inner cities.

For sure, monkeys have had me on edge. But today I will walk straight into their holy lair.

The Monkey Temple in Benares is a common enough looking temple set in a shady grove. But the instant I enter I'm a vulnerable guest in a deviant society of smelly, filthy thugs. Hundreds of monkeys of all sizes crowd the temple, giving it the look of a vermin-infested mansion in a ghost town. The great chamber of the temple circles a stem-like mantle in the middle of the structure. Monkeys stand on several tiers of ledges lining all the walls, including the massive centerpiece. A few diminutive women walk gently along, supplying seeds and bananas and doing the thankless, disgusting task of dealing with the endless production of monkey shit.

On the widest ledge a few feet above my head I spot several brutes doing the Hollywood, leaning on a wall with a shoulder. Their constantly darting eyes follow me intermittently as I slink by like a scoundrel. Within seconds they pepper me with seed husks, and with good aim. There will be no second chance. I must speak humbly with every whisper of body language. I don't dare allow my eyes to rest more than a moment upon those of any monkey (but I can't resist looking: quick glances are permitted.) I keep moving, slow and steady through the mess of grain, fruit, and shit.

Slow walk, no stop. Seconds later I emerge into the breezy outdoors.

Hocus focus

What is it about fortune tellers and the East? *My cash, maybe?*

I admit that the first time, in Penang, I invited Fortuna's frigging by walking straight up to the wrinkled crone and offering my outstretched palm. Sitting hunched on the sidewalk, she'd casually assessed several lives (and been paid for it) in a few minutes, then pulled me in with her twinkle-eye, toothless smile, and two short come-hither flutters of her bony fingers. After feigning *(but jeepers, maybe she really means it)* mild shock at so unusual a palm as mine, she managed to lob several messages in small yet effective dollops of English-ese: "Don't wake up late." "You think *too* much." "You have fine mind and life of prince." "You will suffer deep, very deep, then good, very good life." (*Still back there on fine mind and prince, ma'am.*) Although the messages were given life by my idle self-indulgence, they immediately vexed me. *Do I want to hear about the future? Is that cool? Would I believe it? Would I pretend to—or not to? Isn't that a little like a violation? Of timeline, a kind of personal prime directive?*

The next place I ran into a fortune teller was in the middle of a Katmandu intersection. A plump, middle-aged man who looked remarkably like a turbaned Professor Marvel noticed me as I noticed him from halfway across the road. We kept looking at each other until our paths crossed. Magic was in the air, tourist dollars were flying in on travelers' coattails as never before, and this guy was in business. He spoke a decent and rapid English. As soon as I heard "your future," I told him, "No, man, I don't even *want* to know," and held out my outstretched hand, this time palm down, to keep him away. But he grabbed and held it, turned it over, and gasped a most melodramatic gasp. He let go and gave me a prolonged, spooky look. We looked weirdly at each other, retreating, until the crowd engulfed us. Yeah, I was supposed to hunt down my specialness and enter into some kind of swami deal that would fill me with hope and wonder, and his pocket with cash. But there would be no magic and no tourist dollar that day.

This morning in New Delhi it's time for fortune teller number three. I sit reading in a plush armchair alongside a few other travelers in the shade of my hotel's porch, not far from Connaught Place. Across the yard on the side of the road, not five meters from me, an odd-looking Indian sits cross-legged and Y-eyed, with a carefully constructed pyramid of luscious mangoes right in front of him. He stares straight at us and says nothing. He's there every morning with mangoes and with the same vacant yet expectant look in his slightly diverging eyes. He knows that, eventually, one of us will walk over and buy one. Not a bad living for a simple guy, his modest mark-up saving us a five-minute walk to the market.

For the last ten minutes or so a tall, turbaned man has also been hanging out front, a bit farther away on the edge of the road. He tries to get my attention, beckoning me with come-hither eyes and hand flutters. *Oh, all right.* I get up and walk over.

"Future? Listen, man, I have no interest in fortune telling, and even if you *could* see the future, it's not part of the deal. I just don't wanna know, bud. Sorry."

"Okay, okay," he says, "if I make for you, yes, a *truly* surprise—for *you-ou*... thirty rupees, yes?"

Hmm, a "true" surprise. After all, *I'd* be the judge of that. For about $3.29. *Ah, fuck.* It's a fine morning, but how much finer would it be with an added "true surprise" at that price? *Damn the logic.*

"Okay, if you truly surprise me—I mean *truly surprise*—I'll give you thirty rupees. But no future talk, you hear?"

"Yes, *yes.* No."

I follow him around back. He says he'll guess the name and age of a girl I've been thinking about lately. "But do not tell her names." Standing in the lane he talks quickly, in English, in Hindi, all garbled and strung together—and to whom? The yakking sounds more and more like chanting as it takes on a steady rhythm and musicality. The flow is mellifluous, smooth and *ommm*-like. True surprise or not, the morning has taken on a new glow with this dubious magus wailing in the rubble, his eyes fluttering and cocked heavenward. Just looking at him makes my temples feel raw.

Then, shushing me (I've been as silent as a doorknob) he stops at once, pulls out a pad and pen, and writes slowly, deliberately. He concentrates hard and looks skyward once or twice, as if listening for something scheduled to arrive on a heavenly breeze, on about a sixty-degree angle straight out of the sun's ungodly glare. Finished writing, he crumples the paper into a nice even ball and places it in my hand, closing my fist over it. He tells me to hold tight and "do not let go." *Okay, weirdo.*

Another minute or more of chanting. Then he asks me to slowly and clearly spell out my girl's name and the number (her age.) He writes this down on a second piece of paper and folds it into a neat square, places it in my other palm: "Do not let go." He does a final chant, and this time his legs are involved. I'm flustered, but I have nothing on which to base any suspicion. There's a lump in each fist, one crumpled round, the other folded flat. I'm on the lookout for any hokey-pokey, gripping the papers so they don't morph or quantum swap within the slippery illusion of time and space, or what have you. I focus on their different feel in case any unscientific transformation might take place. *All the cryptic angles, I've got it covered.* Finally, he tells me—with brazen confidence, almost defiant—to open my fists and read the papers.

They each spell out, in awkward block letters and no attention to correct spacing, Danna's full name and her correct age. One strings the letters along one and a half lines, the other along four shorter ones, both otherwise identical, with the number at the end.

"Thirty rupees," he says, holding out a hand. His steady eye reads my sustained "true surprise" with no difficulty. *I am not so smart, no?*[67]

The last thing I want to admit at a time like this is that I am as dull as a raw yam.

---

67 Many years later, as I prepare for this book, I come across a similar report in *A Search in Secret India* by Paul Brunton, pg 37.

And so, standing once more on the Cliffs of Insanity, with a fog thickening down below... I imagine the guy tapping the time stream, somehow looking ahead when he was concentrating and writing on the first paper, to a couple minutes later when I slowly and clearly spelled Danna's name. *Sounds good.* And monkeybrain wants to access all relevant hearsay: What was that strange story I read in that snappy little paperback[68] about whole shiploads of sailors in calm seas observing, at close range, the violent tossing of a "ghost ship" in a storm? And don't the magi of physics infer that time itself is not some absolute phenomenon ticking away behind all things, that it is integral and bound to the expanding universe, which began with a bang? Examples of prophecy abound: the Bible, Lady Shipton,[69] Nostradamus. Not to mention "prescient" dreams as reported by many, me included. One does not need objective proof for direct experience. If you have even one dream that clearly describes an event that comes along a day or two later, you will know that something "non-fixed" permeates the essence of the mind/ universe, or at least of time as we know it.

Isn't it true, in this event-crammed, speedy world, that we strive to immerse ourselves in that powerful point of being we call "now"? We behave as if it is elusive, but it's all that we can rightfully say we can know. Yet we jump out of airplanes, hang from ropes over cliffs, race death machines, ingest all kinds of mind benders, and take up any manner of meditation technique—and the heavenly firings of sex, our dear favorite—to zero in on the elusive point of consciousness where we *are* most profoundly. All are experiences that forget or at least morph our sense of time. The ancient Greeks named a couple, at least: *chronos*, the linear, clock-friendly, hands-down winner in the modern West; and *kairos,* the experiential mode more popular in traditional societies, especially those attuned to the cycles of nature and the cosmos.

That slippery essence that can't be captured in words, the Zen moment, *satori, samadhi,* the "holy instant"... someone once said the

68   *Beyond the Time Barrier* by Andrew Tomas, 1974.
69   Ursula Shipton, commonly known as Mother Shipton, was a woman from Yorkshire in the 1500s, whose prophesies included descriptions that are eerily similar to many details in modern times.

instant does not exist in time; that time itself is contained within the instant.[70] Is this how "now" is *not* defined by past or future? "Now" as something wider?

But enough of wily talk, let's put away this lunacy of words—and return to Truly Surprise Guy. Perhaps I've been more than willing to cast a misty world from a grain of sand. Later, skeptic buddy Jona (long come down from his mystic Kiwi ways) suggests that this would-be wizard could've been snooping over my shoulder at the post office that morning when I picked up a letter from his sister. A good memory, a flair for drama, and an entrepreneurial spirit were all he needed to extract a bit of cash from wide-eyed travelers like me.

But if he did peek at my letter back at the post office, why bring up her age? It wasn't written anywhere.

Just before he leaves he sneaks in a wee fortune: "You *will* meet Mary. And soon to be receive very, *very* good news." Well I can tell you, I want to meet her, whoever this Mary is.

And sure, my whole life, its mere existence, has been nothing if not good news.

ON A DAY pure and strong in the unknown, I walk in loops and zags around Old Delhi. The parade of humanity, the spirit of multiplicity—the unity of sameness in one and all—is all the sightseeing I desire. The drab, continuous compression of city and filth, of human upon human, is as beautiful to me on this day as anything in this world. I slow-walk down the middle of a main street among rickshaws, bullock carts and motorcycles, past diseased beggars and big-eyed orphans. My stride is casual; the city can hardly be bothered to notice a wayfaring stranger like me.

Up ahead, about a block away, a commotion. It's a street fight between two gangs, twenty or thirty big young toughs. Up the main drag and smack into the melee I wander, then stop. I stand, as if invisible among them, as if I inhabit a queer bubble of safety. At close range I marvel at how tame their fighting appears. Their yells and punches lack the passion and venom I've come to expect from head bashing. Sure, I

70   This sparkling idea is, I believe, found somewhere in *A Course In Miracles*.

admit there's a dreamy perspective that overcomes the unattached trav-eler—and any objectivity he or she might dream of possessing. I stand motionless in the crossfire of spit and fists, an arm's length from a half dozen goons dancing all around me. One of them might notice and sock *me* in the snout. Instead, the overall fanfare feels muted, and they appear almost polite as they whack at each other, either ignoring or not seeing me.

Walking again, I emerge from the center of their brawl, past whiz-zing, fisted arms. Continuing down the street, I look back once or twice in quiet consternation.

Angry Vishnu

As soon as I wake up I know it's time to leave. I gather my stuff and head for the main rail station, Delhi Central I believe it is called.

In India getting a ticket and finding one's coach can involve a pro-tracted negotiation with chaos and madness. Up ahead a dense mass topped by flailing arms and bobbing heads is a sure sign of a ticket booth. Some try to force their way through like bulldozers at a dump. I glance at a fellow traveler, sharing a moment of disgust for this pointless waste of energy, so commonplace in this land. Lineup? I look on as a burly man pushes aside a small woman, mowing his way to the front. *That's it.*

As I'm slowly learning, many are the ways encountered in this extra-strange land, some fascinating, some comical, some perplexing, even disturbing. One often attributes the enigmatic (or downright weird) to the quirks of a culture that, upon closer examination, make sense on a different basis of thought. I often retreat toward the comfy perspective of anthropologist in the field. Maybe this human bulldozer is a force of Shiva, a divine plow setting new seed events in place, the fruits of which are beyond the puny scope of a mortal mind like mine. Didn't Krishna, in the holy Bhagavad-Gita, paint Arjuna's flesh-and-blood battlefield with a metaphorical brush, revealing a depth of meaning that made the mayhem seem more... serene? And didn't Castaneda's Don Juan thoughtfully thank Señor Lizard before nabbing and roasting him for dinner?[71] *I say.*

---

71   From *The Teachings of Don Juan* by Carlos Castaneda.

But here in this busy rail station—as with the King of the Dead and his drunken fiefdom—I fail to *see*. I do not arrive at a place of contemplation from which to appreciate a deeper meaning, nor manage any leap of context. I see only a selfish brute who just knocked down a petite woman.

Snap! Between a sense of justice, the thin edge of tolerance, and the will to act, I spring forth like one more fuckin' Napoleon on his brainsick gush for glory. The Asshole trying his hand at a good deed? I bark at my fellow traveler, a Frenchman, that we *will* make a line. Coursing through me is the sizzle of lightning, the dazzle of all Himalaya's rivers crashing into India. I yell at a policeman who's been standing by apathetically and *order* him to come over. I do not pause to reflect on the sudden and outrageous jag in my actions, which I'm sure any passing eye would see as clear evidence of a recent and spectacular launch into psychopathic brilliance. Usually, I seek no power over others; I'd rather slip away sensibly while the thugs work out the glory details. But today is different. The train station is *mine,* for I am Angry Vishnu.

"Line everyone up two by two!" I shout to the policeman. He obeys, aggressively ordering people into a neat line. A minute ago he was standing by idly in the face of chaos, as he likely always has. Now he moves with the urgency of obeying a command from on high. The cop, my "partner" and me, we waste no time pulling this and that person into place, pointing here and there with the might of overlords. The power I wield would better suit a nine-foot beast. Everyone submits, even Bulldozer the Dick.

Within minutes a transformation has overcome one of the busiest railway stations in India. It's a sight I've not seen at any other time or place in this land. Everyone stands in a neat line, and no one is shouting. They all look defeated, with that reluctant, dog-shakin'-paw kind of humiliated look.

When the best leader's work is done, the people say, "We did it ourselves."[72] Not so here; they're freakin' scared of me. The two-by-two line extends clear across the great hall of the station and out the door. Such is the strange beauty and hidden power of focused intent. And on *their* part,

72   Lao Tzu.

perhaps, a certain group placebo effect, Hindu style. I'd bet one or two of them witnessed lightning bolts flash from my eyes, and would later describe me as a nine-foot beast.

Will it catch on? Could there be a new god (what harm in adding one more to a cast of millions?) of orderly queues? Maybe Ganesh will take this one on. Seems like a chill godling with some influence.

Eh. Probably not during *this* Kali Yuga.

Watermelon Family

My job done, I'm off to catch a train. All heady and surreal and weirdly aroused, I exit the station.

I must find my coach. Fifteen cars stand along the platform, each one with a notebook-size sheet of paper tacked up with about thirty names printed on it. A small crowd of frantic ticket holders heaves and wiggles in front of each small white rectangle. Again, each person is shoving or yelling or both, as if panic-stricken in the presence of mortal danger. This time I submit. Luckily, I need to check only a half dozen before spotting my name. Many people are still running back and forth between cars and screaming as I enter my coach. My despotic performance back in the great hall was as potent as a one-beer piss against a monsoon. That new queue god: stillborn and dumped. Back at the station, they're probably clubbing each other from whacked-out brain signals. I wash my hands as the train snorts off indifferently.

Rail travel can conjure a mood highly conducive to inner reflection and a buzzy kind of calm. Having just left behind a rare blooming of group dementia, the contrast is keen. Even on a dull train day, the continuing stream of images warping past can be mentally purging. The flashing by of scenes is the dazzle of time and one's viewpoint, the omnipresent. Sensory gates are swung in a wild multiplicity of visual treats. Adding visceral pleasure to inspiration, there is neither the need nor the inclination to reflect upon any of it. *Time is the moving image of Eternity.*[73] That's what's going on, the whipping scenes a mere blur of *maya,* that most tenacious field. The phenomenal world of duality, with its heavy clouds of emotion and multiple kingdoms of narcissistic

---

73 Plato.

thought, cloaks the unity of Absolute Reality in this human realm: this is kindergarten Vedanta as I've come to understand it, in the bits and pieces coming from the thought kingdoms of fellow travelers. But if the cloak, the illusion, is blurred, what, exactly, is clear? And who, exactly, is looking? I suppose one is meant to keep asking.

I share a compartment with a family. I sit next to a window, my skinny frame aligned with the streaming light of the countryside, turned away from the steady stare of five pairs of large brown eyes. *I am man, I am alien.* Never has a window functioned so well as an inter-cultural soother.

As I shift in my seat my pen rolls off my lap and onto the floor. One of the children rushes to retrieve it with kindly deference, revealing politeness that was hidden behind a veil. Though they've been staring at me like owls at close range for a half hour, they are not, evidently, being rude.

The thin ice now gone, the father takes a watermelon from his bag and cuts it up. Without any exchange of words (*Can they speak English?*) we're all munching on the tasty melon, dripping and gulping the sweet juices on this hot afternoon. I look back at them bravely with *my* brown eyes.

The father speaks: "You know-o (*munch, gulp*) you can *only* get in India." He challenges me, peering straight into my eyes as he chews and drips.

I look at his smug face, at his mauled slice of fruit.

"You mean this? Actually, I've been eating them since I was a boy, and I'm from Canada."

Munching mightily, he looks at me for a few seconds, as if thinking about what I've just said. Then (head nodding in the affirmative, steady stare, chewing stepped up a pace,) "*Only* in India."

Over the next minute or so I assure him in one or more ways that I am no stranger to the delights of the princely watermelon. But his is the single-minded conviction of a trumpeter marching toward the enemy, and I am no match for his intent and poise. After all, he is the man with the watermelon that you can get *only* in India, and the wife and kids are watching.

THE DROPPED PEN that launched our little charade is the snazzy tool in my new project: I've been keeping a daily journal. Seems like the thing to do. I've seen others scribbling away with purpose. It's all very invigorating and strange, this thing about writing down what happens or how I feel or what I see or ponder in a day. That's a lot going on, a lot to think about.

But soon my musings become both contrived and flaccid, a poor combo, if you stop and think about it. A seed of pretentiousness has grown like a bad germ inside the luscious mango of my creativity. I foresee situations that could be good journal material, then as I experience new and interesting things I immediately spoil, thinking, *Ooh, that'll be good.* I *suck* at journaling.

On what has become a more lucid than usual train ride (thanks, watermelon family; thanks, Ganesh,) I ponder my demon of a diary and grow disgusted with my dullness. In a brilliant spasm, I toss my journal out the window. Watermelon Family looks mildly amused, or perhaps it is knowingly detached, while affording a minimal, perhaps condescending, effort at smiling. "Ahh, he is experiencing the Detachment; it is indeed *so new* to the Western boy." (Dad affords a single head wob.)

At once, and despite my low rung on the enlightenment ladder, I feel light and innocent, free of a ball and chain that I don't recall picking up.

Cop Thieves, Indian Train

Approaching the holy city of Allahabad the train stops, and all holy-isms aside, two policemen stomp into our coach. I'm sitting with a Brit and an Italian on their way to Goa. The cops look this way and that, then come right over. A mere glance, and they look past me. They order my two companions to empty their backpacks. They find and seize several pounds of Manali black hash and demand one hundred rupees (eleven US dollars) from each of them, immediately, in fines.

The cops read me well. Though I accompany the smugglers, they waste not a second on me, as if they *know*. No flute, but I'm wearing blue with a knotted black necklace, hairy and bearded and smiling as if some kinda' *kundalini* goodness got ahold on me, and has an eye on you, too. Really putting on a show here in these illusory fields of *maya*. The cops take the hash and the 200 rupees and flee like cop thieves on an Indian train. The Indians sitting near us accept the brash corruption with equanimity. The two fellas mutter that they'll have to return to the mountains for a new supply. Tourist season in Goa is coming up fast.

Field of Maya

Pouring south off the roof of the world—shooting straight out of Vishnu's toe and through Shiva's dreads go the story bits—the Ganges River takes a gentle curve toward the east for a long, lazy passage across the wide northern expanse of the Indian subcontinent. Its rich basin provides for one of the world's great flourishes of culture.

Rishikesh is a pleasant town made holy by its location, where Ganga leaves the Himalayas' foothills to enter the plains. The holiness of this wee city is said to bring mercy to all its animals. Pigs and chickens, goats and cows—*you all run free now, little children!* Never was liberty so sweeping or humility so infused into the very molecules of a town. The streets are quiet and, yes, humble. If Dr. Dolittle[74] got into our world and was cunning enough to establish a compassionate fiefdom, it would look like this.

But the gentle citizens of Rishikesh couldn't detach themselves from the usefulness of ponies, who alone remain in bondage, pulling carts and carriages throughout the town. Just one detail brings it all down from the good doctor's hopeful conspiracy; the stompin' jackboot of beastly burden is real enough for the ponies. Or maybe they're in on the deal, servers both humble and strong, balancing a bigger karmic load. No doubt they hold their heads high, and their human conductors treat them kindly enough.

I stand at the dock waiting for the small ferry to cross the river. Some townsfolk, a few sadhus, and a patient, downright regal-looking young cow wait with me, all of us quiet. I sense that as far as Ms. Cow is concerned, in regard to her dignity and rights, her place in the pecking order of universal values amounts approximately to mine, perhaps slightly higher. An astonishing number of succulent fish more than two feet long hang around in nonchalant clusters in the clear water in easy view, mere inches from the surface. No one's fishing, at least not here. *See, little baba? Even the fish, even they are all yogis—all relaxed, just soooo fine.*

Across the river from town, a sizable cluster of multicolored buildings nestles in a foothill cleft. It is why there is a dock and ferry. Walking in the crowd among the many ashrams I reckon there's nothing like

---

74   From the 1920 book, *The Story of Doctor Dolittle,* by Hugh Lofting.

this anywhere: a traditional community of independent religious sects, a functional part of the world whose purpose is, presumably, to bring the seeker out of it. Along the tiny streets one can sample from what appears to be a free enterprise marketplace of Hindu flavors. Each establishment casts a lure for the soul with brightly painted architecture and human advertisements outside. Numerous ascetics pepper the pavement fronting the ashrams, some chanting hypnotically, each with dharma on display, each doing their own pet penance on the road to enlightenment.

Without even listening for them, the traveler will hear miracle stories: walk on water, walk on fire, regenerate a severed limb, create a body double to do your bidding elsewhere, materialize objects at will. *Nice.* One hears of Svengali masters controlling others' wills, and even the ultimate miracle of resurrection. *Cool.* The stories[75] continue to entice multitudes, as surely they've done for millennia. With so many charismatic gurus fine-tuning their psycho magnets, the seeker might well be advised to fine-tune their own intention—and discernment.

A visitor might travel through Canada or Australia or even Europe without affording Christianity a thought. But to travel in India is to take a good look at the phantasmagoria of mysticism and organized life that is Hinduism. Engrossed in its ubiquitous melodrama, you might even overlook the fact that there are large and vocal Buddhist, Muslim, and Sikh minorities, not to mention potent sprigs of Jainism, Zoroastrianism, Judaism, and Christianity. Hinduism offers millions of colorful gods, numerous sects, gurus galore, and a caste system that is political and economic in its wider effects. Perhaps it is misleading to think of Hinduism simply as a religion, so complex and vast is its effect on this most long-lived of extant cultures. It is said that originally the Aryans, with their Indo-European and Indo-Aryan tongues, brought into India—to the peoples already there—the Vedic religion, Hinduism's main precursor.[76] The Rig

75 These are "miracle stories" gleaned from *Autobiography of a Yogi* by Paramahansa Yogananda. As well, similar reports have emerged regarding paranormal realities in the Eastern Orthodox tradition of Christianity as detailed in books by Kyriacos Markides: *The Magus of Strovolos*, *Homage to the Sun*, and *Fire in the Heart*.

76 Yet the theory of an "Aryan invasion" peopling the Indian subcontinent has been discredited, as explored in *Underworld* by Graham Hancock, p. 96–99, and in *Gods, Sages and Kings* by David Frawley.

Veda has been described as one of the most ancient of all writings. Most scholars today believe they are a mere few thousand years old, but some see the source of these writings reaching back into the misty unknowns of prehistory. At the least these notions speak of a superlative cultural mystique. And to borrow from the cosmology itself, a most tenacious field of *maya* has graced this land for millennia, in this human realm.

Back in Katmandu I commented to Gopi Krishna that there are many Hindus in number, yet they live almost entirely within one country. He paused, holding in a champion's toke, and looked up for a moment with the chillum smoking away in his hands. I'm sure he knows there are quite a few of what we call countries out there, and that India is one of them.

He looked at me, releasing the smoke on a long exhale. "Ahhhhh. *Every*body Hindu."

A BRIEF ZAG into Kashmir brings yet more opportunities for that rarefied and reflective awareness that one might be graced with on precipitous mountain roads. Once again our zany drivers are the benefactors of a strange peace, gained in the aftermath of facing down Death in chasm after chasm along hundreds of miles on our way to and from Srinagar. It might seem unlikely, even illogical or paradoxical, but one can get accustomed to the likelihood of "dying today." I've heard it a few times now: loaded bus flies off into the abyss.

In India, the valley of Kashmir is often described as Heaven on Earth, and the Kashmiris themselves will tell you so. Breathing in its temperate beauty, I am roused by memories of crisscrossing my own British Columbia's countless lush valleys by thumb in my teen years. The city of Srinagar cozies up to Dal Lake, a seemingly complex waterway dotted with the renowned neighborhoods of houseboats, many of which are available to rent for the traveler.

This land is more Central Asia than India; Muslim rather than Hindu. The look of the Kashmiris is a variegated mix of east Asia, India, and includes a resemblance to "Mediterrania." I fit in rather well. One even will see the odd red head. This surely is a great DNA crossroads, situated as it is in a sweet spot along the ancient Silk Road.

Eager for what lies ahead on my journey, I head back south toward my westward path.[77]

Postcard to Rick (Bless yer soul, buddy.)

It is early morning. I just got off an all-night bus from Kashmir and I'm sitting outside a train station near a Pakistan-India border town. A Sikh stronghold, I hear. All sorts of people movin' around in a movie—*my* movie, they say. A crazy-anxious stupor is all over the scene. Unreserved Indian train (*gasp.*) I hang around the station, and as the tension rises I look around for something familiar, for other travelers, who also spot me. Now we are six, three guys and three gals, and there's a notion goin' 'round that we'll take a coach for ourselves.

Hark! I hear a faint rumbling. It could be an earthquake, but in case it isn't I start moving around with the others in this crowd of hundreds who've just noticed the rumbling as well. Now it's all screaming and yelling and jerking about like headless chickens. As the train pulls up I hear the *thuds* and *fwaps* of bodies hurling themselves at the windows of the still moving train. *They're not barred; windows on these trains are usually barred!* Through a window I dive—*nice*—to sprawl across a seat. My new mates stand battle ready at the doors, snarling and holding off the hordes as the gals hurry on with our packs.

I feel alright; we got a whole compartment. There's guys and gals from Sweden and the States and Scotland and Switzerland and Spain to get acquainted with. Later I try to sleep, but I'm distracted by the interested glance of the petite Scottish lassie, her psychoactive feminine micro-parts having already penetrated the dust and oily sweat I wear. I would do it all over again just for this.

---

77 It was after leaving the region that I heard about a most curious and sensational claim: that the graves of Moses, Jesus, and Mary lie in Kashmir. See *Jesus Lived In India* by Holger Kersten, and *Jesus In Kashmir: The Lost Tomb* by Suzanne Olsson.

9. Through Islam with Hayla

a smile from a veil[78]

ON CITY STREETS FROM AUSTRALIA TO INDIA TO EUROPE, THERE'S A DIS-
tinct feel in the people, in their mental atmosphere. In passing faces,
in the eyes—*especially* the eyes—is this qualitative expression focused
and carried. In this way each person is its emissary and mirror. Again
and again, a shift in the character of this social vibe seems to coincide
with a crossover into an area dominated by a different religion. Cross
that mountain range, over the plain and down that river, from Shiva to
Allah, Siddhartha to Jesus, and something in the eyes changes in kind. I
didn't recognize this when first leaving the West from Australia, preoccupied as I was with the novel experience of having just left my home
culture. But crossing from Muslim Java to Hindu Bali provided a first
sensation of this flavor of faith. Then back to Muslim Java and Malaysia
and into Buddhist Thailand before belly-flopping onto the great Hindu
expanse of India.

Within India one encounters Muslim enclaves, most noticeable in
cities where eyes whizzing by seem now to take direct aim; the gentler feel
of a few blocks back has become more focused and intense. Goa is a small
Christian speck on a broad Hindu canvas, an illuminating taste of my
own tradition minus the glitzy trappings of technology and consumerism. Up north in the mountains where Tibetan refugees have made their
home, Buddha reigns, and smiles are easy and frequent.

Zigzagging across the vast southern rim of Eurasia I am drawn to notice
these shifts in qualitative feel. Like a prism, I reckon, does each faith cast

---

78   From the song "Wish You Were Here" by Pink Floyd, written by Waters/Gilmore.

its own palette of colors over our political, emotional, and perceptual lives.

Today, as I stand at an open window in my hotel in Lahore, Pakistan, the scent of unknown things wafts in on a musky breeze, a purging headwind upon the hidden preconceptions I carry westward.

On this follow-the-sun tour, in these vast lands of Allah, I feel that I have entered a zone that is a cultural step closer to the West. Yet it is a new world, like none I've encountered. Compared with the patchwork landscape of faiths I've just passed through, this new region is more a hegemony. Yet there is something in the clear-eyed and more aggressive look of the people, after having just crossed India, that feels more akin to my Latin roots. Something, perhaps, that is shared in a common history: the legacies of Abraham, Moses, and Jesus.

Having just crossed an imaginary (but real) line that divides the Punjab between India and Pakistan, Hindu and Muslim, I look in the direction I'm bound. I imagine mountains and valleys, rivers and cities on the paths ahead. Just as so many along the roads I've come have been left behind in the dust of mind.

Eli the Punk

My traveling buddy of two days, Eli, a cheery Jewish Brit, walks in with an extra bounce in his already bounced-up gait. He's brought along the hotel owner—tall, smartly dressed, thirty-five-ish. Three large older men flank him; they could be business partners or family, bodyguards or thugs. They're cordial enough and dressed in suits as well, but the young and dapper owner does all the talking. Eli asks questions and plays wheeler-dealer in some business proposal involving large shipments of hash smuggled through the mail. My ears perk up, as would those of anyone nearby. Neither Eli nor the owner make any attempt to be discreet. As she passes by our open door, a Nordic beauty in a long, peacock-blue dress casts her vivid blue eyes straight into mine. We meet in silence this way, a moment's notice by the scent of unknown things.

The deal takes a hard turn and the door is closed. It looks and feels foolhardy, even risky, and evidently, I've become part of it. The hotel owner presents one of his business ventures: "You see, I have factory with Bible and hole to cut in," he says with a chuckle, his eyes alive with mischief as he describes an example of his wares, "and making box for *so* much hashish. I have friendly in post office, no problems to you." He offers these gutted Bibles for several dollars, quite a sum. Of course, the symbolic ripping out of the heart of Islam's main rival is a sweet side effect for these rascally Pakistanis. If we buy these desecrated Bibles we also provide evidence of an inferior culture in moral decay. But all tribalism aside, why would we risk such a deed with gang-tough strangers when it would be easy, if we were to descend to their level of impudent disrespect, to carve out a Koran on our own?

Eli must be having similar thoughts, for his voice suddenly increases in volume and takes an arrogant turn. The deal, or whatever they had in mind, is clearly kiboshed. I stand to the side and say nothing. An insult is given or received, or both. One of the men grabs little Eli by the throat and lifts him up the wall like a rag doll. Uncle #2 turns on me. I feel an inexplicable (some might say foolish) strength in being nonviolent. A solid *no*, I remain dead calm with an outstretched hand raised to stop him. It works. We're in Muslim country; I won't play the stupid-odds game in daft bargains I didn't ask for. Avoiding the whacking of hard objects on the miraculous, supple temple of the body, refusing bloody agony and such, this is my offer, and it is accepted.

Eli breaks free, and the men retreat, their leader cursing and threatening like tough guys everywhere. *Yes, your Royal Flatulence, you are indeed the Great King of Dickness.*

THE SMELL OF fear and greed have done their bit to prod me along that westward path. Without bothering to wake Eli I'm up early the next morning and leaving the hotel. I hop a bus. Having sniffed out my move Eli hops along and follows. *Meh.*

Down the aisle my eye catches a fine sample of twofold otherness: a single flip of feminine blonde in an otherwise continuous pelt of male black. It's that Nordic chick and her dazzle-blue eyes. My stride is quickened by Eli's fool-passion ways on my heels. And the bio-magnet feels strong this morning; I go straight to her.

Can such a woman elude the attraction that will obsess most men? I feel unexpected compassion, locked as she must be in her uncommon beauty.

She looks at me and almost smiles. I say, "Hi, can I sit?" She speaks in an appealing, forthright voice, her eyes steady and sharp. She is subtle, but everything about her manner seems to accept my earnest presence. That is to say, she doesn't tell me to get lost. Her accent is German or Danish or Dutch; I'm not savvy on the northern subtleties. The roll and flow of her words feel clear and confident. After I sit, Eli stands in the aisle looking at us like a clown on quaaludes, his head tilted, mouth open, and eyes so dreamy they diverge a bit. *Dude, sit down.*

Her name is Hayla. We're bound for the North-West Frontier Province, the rugged land of the rugged Pathans. Before the bus leaves, as I settle in hopefully next to her, a cocksure young man walks over, stands in the aisle staring at us, and asks what country I'm from. It's a bold and aggressive move. Who knows? Maybe he's a little peeved that I slid into the empty seat next to the hot foreign chick just when he was about to. In any case, my fraternal yet undeniably foreign look often stirs the curiosity of local youths.

When he hears "Canada," his finger shoots up and fires a round of air stabs. He stands tall and accuses me, in a voice that includes the whole freakin' bus, of dealing nuclear spunk with India, Pakistan's neighbor/ nemesis. It was a year ago that India exploded its first nuclear device, the sixth nation to do so. And since it was only a few years before that that West Pakistan lost East Pakistan, with India fighting alongside the Bengali (soon to be Bangladeshi) rebels, he likely bears a mountain load of justifications for his anger.

But contrary to appearances, this little shit fest is not personal. The guy confronts a symbol with eyes, a human flag, an enemy soldier, nothing more. Yet I am one, "they" are forty. Getting personal is my best option.

I stand. My eye level now slightly above his, I speak forcefully but with respect. I tell him that I did *not* sell anything to anyone, that I'd rather we hadn't thoughtlessly yanked open the nuclear Pandora's Box. "I am *not* the government of Canada, and I don't like nuclear *shit*." Nothing like the nefarious Canada he had in mind, but a bit of a freakin' weirdo nonetheless. His hot air deflates before my own puffed-up talk, and he sits down. I glance at Hayla. Well I've impressed myself, but I'm not sure I know anything of what's going on inside *her.*

As well, I know little of what's going on in Pakistan. For instance, I know not that at this time a military coup is brewing, one that will soon overthrow the elder Bhutto. I've heard of bullets flying in this and that city; I met a couple of Aussie thrill nuts on the trail of those bullets. But with the ever-present bayonet boys stationed at every bank and government office since Down Under, I take it all in stride, assuming that those ugly, pointy things must be used from time to time or they wouldn't exist. We meet other travelers who, a day after us, spent a night in the same Lahore hotel as we had. They looked out the window, then dove to the floor as a spray of bullets rattled the building and the street. Snipers were sniping from the roof, and from shadows below.

Our bus lurches awake and crawls from the station. We drift carefree through a dangerous stretch, with Eli hanging in the wings. Not sure for how long, for such is the way of the traveling life. We carry on together, Hayla and I, drawing slowly on each other's otherness.

THE FEISTY ENGLISH Jew with a taste for misadventure continues to plow an awkward path parallel to mine. I'm with Hayla now, but Eli continues to sniff about in our periphery. I'm aware of him, but I'm not sure Hayla bothers to notice; he is one of likely many young cocks often flitting about her periphery.

Eli is bent on striking big cashola in Europe's underbelly market. I've met a few Brits, Frenchmen, and Italians who make this trip of thousands of miles with little cash. The desperate can be spotted by their hawkish demeanor, the bounce in their step perked up by random pokes from survival on the road. Eli seems to carry himself with the authority of his imperial countrymen; the British have made the journey to India for centuries and practically owned the place until recently. He walks around as if knowing he'll be recognized as a regular. He's a barber from London.

We arrive in Kabul. Before two days pass I'm with Eli on yet another dim caper. I'm naïve enough to get sucked along once more in the wake of his juvenile folly. His golly-gee bravado has me along as a rather detached accomplice on his continuing quest for mass quantities of the best-smelling hash in the world. There's little danger handling small chunks of the illegal stuff; but large, salable amounts presuppose bigger and darker probabilities.

It's not until we're standing in the dimly lit den of an Afghan supplier, staring at dozens of stacks of hash pancakes (and on several adjacent tables, piles of rolled-up shapes of the stuff) that I appreciate the possible consequences my idle curiosity has conjured. It's enough black to feed all of Europe for weeks, maybe months. The room is infused with the spicy scent of an ancient medicine. It is a mini-warehouse laden with the rich spunk of that most wondrous plant: cannabis, hemp, marijuana, *kif.* Eli has a knack for nosing in on the smack of things. This building has to be a mere arm of a powerful business. Men lurk in the shadows, true to my cliché imaginings. If the Hindus are right and one goes about aligning one's reality without necessarily being conscious of it, then… *why am I here, and what am I doing?*

Eli picks up a hash cake, feels and smells it. Then, as if frigging Fate herself, he tosses it down, rejecting it. The Afghan leader's poise tightens, his eyes harden. I detect movements in the shadows. This short, wiry English dude is toying with him, like he did with the Pakistanis back in Lahore.

Alright, that's it. I turn to leave. No one stops me, and I don't look back, making clear to myself and to Eli—as well as to the surly Afghans—my own predilection in these matters of contraband freight and macho pissing games. Eli doesn't follow me this time; I leave him to his *whatever* dream. It's the last time I see him.

I head back to the hotel, back to the room I share with a comely and intelligent Danish chick, the type fallen angels fall even farther for.

WE HEAD "JUST to the next town" together once, twice, three times. It's a game we play to keep ahead of any plan that might lead to an "arrangement."

In Afghanistan I walk the streets of two different worlds, whether I go alone or with Hayla. On my own I'm treated with respect and without fanfare, free to look around without drawing attention. With Hayla I'm assaulted on all fronts by the dagger-eyed appraisal of men, never mind what *she's* getting: *Are you married? You don't protect her; she walks ahead of you. She must be free for the taking. She is a slut. You are not a man; you are too weak to control her.* The prurient messages read bold in their artless faces. On a busy street a young man plants himself in front of us and proclaims, directly to me, "You are *not* married!" as proud and loud as if revealing a nefarious plan.

Hayla dresses modestly, with a looser fit of cloth, as do all female travelers in these parts and tender times. I'm surprised at the benefit I feel now that my attention has shifted focus. Where it was once compulsively drawn to the shape of thigh, breast, bum and hip, now it's more about her eyes, her face, her movement, the way she carries herself. Her intelligence, her personality; these are more "visible." It is a strange... freedom? It reminds of that Sufi saying, which is perhaps hard to hear in these modern times: "Freedom is the absence of choice."

The imagination thrives; it intervenes, extrapolates, and carries much sway, for I find that the power of sexual beauty is not diminished when wrapped in a bit of extra cloth. Our deep-running drive will not be dampened by such superficial measures. And perhaps my modest epiphany reveals that I am, in a way, too immature or "primitive" to handle such freedom with an even mind.

Following Hayla's artful sashay is no burden. As things go between fellow travelers, I walk ahead or drop behind her. I could pose as her husband, but it would require a contrived and sustained effort on both our parts. Given the social pressures here, I'd comply if that's what she wanted. But I reckon she's too independent for that. I watch with detachment, compassion, even amusement as she slaps away the rude fondling of passing hands. As she moves along the dirt path, her easy, pneumatic stride sends shock waves through the all-male crowd. Even my young globes get the odd passing stroke. *Hey, I won't be changing these guys anytime soon*, so I don't react. *Keep walking.* The Afghan men violate her comfort zone a good measure beyond how they ruffle mine, but she remains cool. She curses a bit but recovers fast, and doesn't seem to hold on to blame or resentment. She's been through these parts before and doesn't complain, and she never lays it on me. But it must be oppressive, even overwhelming at times.

Hayla knows she possesses an exceptional rear view, and she lets me know that *she* knows what an *uber*-magnet it is. Back in our room she perches on the edge of a chair, all but naked with her backside toward me, tracing its even curve with her fingers. Her eyes are deep into mine and she's saying something about her past, and about men. I sense a story that is not without suffering, one she's not telling me. By necessity, by sheer numbers, she keeps men at bay, like she did me when I first made a move on her. My hunger is plain and constant, and she knows, with that simple stroke, that she has me whenever she chooses. Yet the play of energies between us is more balanced than I make it sound.

I'm surprised, as if for the first time (for it's always the first time) by the "narcosis" of sexual attraction—of female beauty. The Bible mentions Watchers, fallen angels who could not resist the daughters of men.[79] *What chance do I have?* The power resides in what we see and in our craving, in the blood as it bucks and heaves, as it flashes a promise of grace in union... a promise of finding a place where we might know ecstasy and solve the riddle of aloneness, even patch in that missing place in our soul.[80] All this packaged within the pleasures of carnal hunger. I've been mulling this over, aware of my tendency to be drawn deeply into a great dream of romantic love with a beautiful woman ever since my emotional seclusion back in Canberra after splitting with Danna. I am, perhaps, none the wiser. Hayla surely notices my mixed bag, draws near, then retreats. Aloofness, heat.

And so our paths entwine and bounce along, with Hayla usually one step ahead.

Hash Man

On a bus from Kabul to Ghazni I smell the rich fragrance of fresh hash like on one of Eli's sketchy dream tours. *Eli, where are you now?* We're near the back of the bus, so it's easy to scan everyone: no one is smoking. I turn to Hayla but she's fallen asleep. We're the only foreigners. As the sweet pungency fills my lungs I meet the knowing eyes of a turbaned young man, thirtyish. He sits alone, grinning a mighty grin.

I go and sit next to him. As with most encounters with Afghans, there are no words. A large sack sits on the floor beneath him. Motioning to it, I reach over and pull open the course burlap to reveal a solid ball

---

79 From Genesis and Numbers in the Bible, and the apocryphal Books of Enoch. The mysterious giant beings called Nephilim were said to be the offspring of the Watchers—fallen angels—and the "daughters of men."

80 These are ideas beautifully explored in *We* by Robert A. Johnson.

of fine fresh black about a foot in diameter. I lift the sack with both hands: twenty, twenty-five pounds. He lets me do this even though it rests between his feet. Using a small knife he carves off about two grams, stuffs some into a pipe and lights it.

As we smoke, first the bus driver, then a few of the men, admonish my Afghan host. He deflects their outbursts with a coolness that allows me to feel safe. From the tone of his voice and the reactions of the others, it sounds like, "Ah, fuck off and mind your own pathetic business, you old turds." We keep toking. Hayla shifts around a bit but sleeps throughout. Soon our minds take a sharp turn into *euphoria gloria*, in this case done up in dry brown hill country under the great blue maw of heaven upon earth. The complaints and cussing of the all-male naysayers sound softer now. The young Afghan gives me the rest of the chunk.

While still dodging the spit-launch ranting of several of the men, he motions me aside and gets up, clutching his sack of black gold. He walks to the front, pushing past the old turds, and tells the driver to stop at a nondescript point along the highway. The bus lurches over. He ambles out into the afternoon's low sunshine, the argument heating up. He stands at the foot of the steps, delivers a final snarl, then swings the sack onto his back.

The bus groans forward. I turn to catch a last sight of him. Stooped over from the weight, a not so St. Nick of the Afghan desert walks across the parched earth. There is no visible path. He stops to wave, smiles, then angles off toward a cleft between some low brown hills.

Trom-blown

We stop briefly in Ghazni, stomping ground of the terrible emperor-warrior Mahmud of the eleventh century. Ruling an empire that stretched from Persia to the Ganges, he is said to have punished India every year for twenty-five years with severe pillaging, taking slaves, sacking temples, and stealing anything, including elephants to carry it all.

Walking along one of Ghazni's main roads we hear the excited yelps of children. We spot them, still a block away, laughing and hopping about in a moving swarm, at least twenty little kids of all sizes. The center of this cyclone of noise and joy is a shabby-looking man who marches along an erratic path. Perhaps he is free, but for sure he has departed from any sense of belonging to the normal human hum. *Is he a good soul? Love dancing for the kids? Crazy? In a state of grace?* Modernity, with its balmy institutions and obedient service employees, has avoided this hinterland of central Asia, even though it has been crisscrossed for millennia by invaders and caravans on the Silk Road to China and India.

The Fried Piper marches at a snapping pace, one arm shooting in and out in an impassioned air-trombone performance. He blows staccato notes far and wide through his clenched mouth, his cheeks puffing full/empty full/empty in mock (yet quite real) virtuosity. His eyes are at once wild and entranced, a psychedelic one-man parade love-dancing the heck out of our comfort zones.

The moment he spots Hayla and me from twenty paces away, he turns and marches straight toward us. He lands directly in front and gives us a special one-minute concert, his phantom trombone pummeling my nose in a tense pneumatic outburst. His eyes go slack in the wondrous climax of an especially hopeful flourish of note strings, then at once his wacky recital shifts gear. Leading with his eyeballs he stomps off, the children following like bouncing bonobos.

The occasional upturned mouth and odd eye twinkle breach the stoic expressions of the merchants, as the ruckus of laughter and *trom-blown* subside with the dust they kicked up.

Bamiyan

Apart from the allure of her feminine charm, I follow Hayla as I followed Yuji back in Java: for the ready-made tour. I'm not so much heading somewhere as I'm on the way to wherever (Italia) with Hayla moving in the foreground. I get to tag along to some sights I'd otherwise miss.

This time she's heading to a province called Bamiyan in Afghanistan's rugged lunar interior. Cupped in some craggy valleys lay several lakes called Band-i-Amir, fabled for their intense blue colors. As well, the town of Bamiyan is known for its sixth-century archaeological wonder: two giant Buddhas carved from sandstone in a cliff face laced with adjoining tunnels dug by enterprising monks.

The ride on the small bus is hot and dry. I've had intense allergic reactions twice already in the crosswinds of travel on dusty roads much like this one. I imagine riding in the fresh wind up top with the luggage. Partly in the hope of avoiding another round of histamine misery, and partly in response to my impish delight, I climb out the window on a straight stretch, grab hold of the roof racks, and haul myself up. *Ahh, clean air.*

Two Afghan men afford a brief nod as if my arrival from below, as we barrel along the bumpy track, is not only reasonable but expected. Sitting with them amongst the backpacks I'm rejuvenated by the hard wind and stark visuals, the edges of which evidently warp alongside Einstein's alchemy math. The jagged mountains stretch across and feature the subtle shift of a curtain of colors cut in against a deep and luminescent blue. Alexander, Genghis—going east, going west. Low, rudimentary buildings dot the land, irregularly formed, dusty brown mounds in a dusty brown world, like they were shaped on the spot by a giant hand in a hurry, and then humans came along like hermit crabs.

We slow down for a group of camel riders. We are eye level, me and the camels, their large lips quivering within spittin' distance. We look at each other with mistrust, unable to bond, me atop the bus and the camels on foot, in this ancient Central Asian wilderness.

Within another half hour the driver has discovered that one of the *touristas* is on the roof. He stops the bus and orders me down. I refuse. *C'mon, fella, your guys on the roof—I'm one of the gang already.* I sit, immobile and stubborn, imitating the cool, manly aloofness of the Afghans themselves, looking away into the barren distance as if the issue is settled. What's he gonna do? Pull out a sword?

But the prick won't move. He talks gibberish for three, maybe four minutes. He's *pissed,* and he gives no sign of relenting. Alas, I climb back inside before the casual entertainment turns into a great big pain in the ass for my fellow travelers. Hayla looks away, probably irritated in knowing that I press her buttons.

The first of the lakes comes into view as we round a corner. After miles of barren landscape the lake draws up the pure, sweetest poisons of our overwrought senses, its brew rained down from heaven's forgotten holy ponds of liquid-blue grace. The deepest ever of any blue, it is too bloody blue to be true. But so truest of blues is this deepest of hues... that the cloudless sky looks anemic.

The driver stops and we get out. A short, sweaty American dude promptly goes mad, unable to navigate the sensory leap with any restraint. Up and down, to and fro he jumps like Tarzan's ape, shouting, "Goddam, goddam, goddam!" His bouncing is erratic, and he's a bit tubby; I'm drawn in for a closer look at feet and inches and the gaping chasm before us, wondering how his inner compass might steer the leaping bulk along gravity's merciless arrow. A few hold a tactical view (*ugh*) on the chess pawns of reason. Bits of clever hearsay interrupt the muffled sounds of ecstasy: photo-ready biochemistry, mystery minerals, weird life forms, deep cold, and cool-blue goo, to name a few.

On this very ridge, not fifty feet away, a lone cyclist takes in the view with us. We are crossing paths. I walk over to where he stands gazing into the valley. Like a pilgrim on his way to a place unseen yet fixed, he keeps looking. He's from Switzerland. Riveted onto the bike frame is a panel of sheet metal on which a map of the world is painted in oil colors. A red line traces, in loops and meanders and switchbacks, the route he's come along. He's been on the road for sixteen years.

NOT FAR FROM the Band-i-Amir lakes is the town of Bamiyan. It was once a thriving center of trade and culture until ol' Genghis smashed it and every living thing in it to avenge his grandson's death. That is some deep pain. Now it's a quiet town in a green river valley, situated near the base of a high cliff face that stretches for a couple of miles.

Carved within this natural stone wall are two huge, faceless Buddhas. They are titanic in scale although not the same size, and in their time were adorned in multi-colored paint, glittering gems, and gleaming metals. A complex of caves and tunnels weaves throughout the cliff wall. Row upon crooked row of dark holes resemble the cross section of a giant termite hill from a distance. We climb the stairways that connect the many levels of this ghost plan of almost one thousand caves. Standing in a cavity next to a Buddha head, we each measure about one Buddha ear in length. The story goes that the faces were sliced off by iconoclastic Muslim marauders long ago. A measured vandalism committed, perhaps, with the conviction that a violated symbol is a more effective tool of subjugation than is a completely destroyed one.[81] Perhaps this imperially butchered wonder marks the westernmost of Buddhism's great monuments.

Up near the Buddha ear I gaze out across patches of green in an otherwise barren land. I am in awe of the demands of physical labor required of those monks in digging out these caves, tunnels and stairways, never mind the creation of the giant statues themselves. In contrast is the easy life of the wanderer I have become, as I stand here today, concerned only with what stimulates my curiosity, and Hayla's earthly charms. I watch her move along the stone that surrounds us. I'm still held in the effect of the deep indigo of the Band-i-Amir lakes, as if it has followed me along the valley floor and up these steps. I fancy its moving presence in the air, a translucent blue having infused Hayla's fair skin and permeating reality itself… right then I'm snapped back by the jarring voice of that same American yokel: "Goddam if that ain't the prettiest view of a godforsaken country. Goddam."

Back in the village, as the sun sets its impartial rays upon our smiling, dusty skin, we sit, Hayla and I, gazing at the distant wall of holes and maybe the biggest statues in the world. The Doors' *Riders on the Storm* wafts out from a teahouse in the warm evening breeze, reminding me, in a melancholy moment, of our remote position and the warm, beguiling sounds of my old wooden guitar.

Highway Hyenas

At the Iran-Turkey border Hayla suggests we hitchhike through Turkey and then on through Greece and Yugoslavia. She's full of ideas, this nineteen year-old Hayla chick

After passing through customs we walk the mountain highway into the desolate wilderness of eastern Turkey. It is the land of the Kurds, and it bears a reputation as one of the most dangerous places in Eurasia for hitchhiking. It's a gloomy panorama that I'd bet Tolkien passed through just before conceiving the barren evil of Mordor. Check a map. There's a town called Batman.

We've walked less than two miles when a Ford Pinto pulls up. A window rolls down and the sniggering faces of five local men appear.

---

81 If only the Taliban, centuries later, possessed such cunning.

This is how they greet us; there is no pretense of civility. The small car is jammed; all are dressed in the macho-gaudy style of the stereotypical pimp. They offer a ride, sardonic and lecherous and snide. They insult us twofold, for there isn't room for *one* more, even without a backpack. We continue walking, assuming they'll leave. But they follow along, pestering us with lewd, threatening remarks. They laugh wickedly and we begin to squirm. We talk back, aiming to repel them, and within five minutes our protests turn to shouts. Then curses. But they like it, our anxiety feeding their predatory delight. The more we react the more excited they become. I feel trapped; wilderness surrounds us. Looking back, the border is a smudge and a squiggle high on the horizon. Blonde and shapely, sweet-faced Hayla is a siren of sex to them and I, well, they might enjoy all kinds of things. And if they don't, *goodbye, Johnny*. In all my travels, carrying a weapon has never crossed my mind.

A semitrailer truck pulls over. We rejoice and climb in, uttering parting curses to the vile slob-men. But our buoyancy is short-lived. They put their car right in front, blocking us. The British driver backs up and pulls away, but little Pinto is more agile and zips into our path, again and again. Our driver joins in the snarling and yelling. The Pinto Pals laugh and snort throughout their malicious game. Our driver, exasperated, says politely, with excellent articulation, "Sorry, but I must be moving along. I cannot stay."

We get out and walk quickly, trying to ignore our brutish stalkers. We're too far from the border to turn back. A second truck stops, but again they block us three, four times. Closing in on panic, we want to run at them and attack, but we are not yet that stupid. The psychopathic pals smell blood, grunting at Hayla and slopping back our heavy despair like malevolent hogs. The second truck leaves.

Then a blanket of order rolls down the road toward us. A military man in a jeep has been watching from a distance. He approaches slowly, and we welcome him with a yell. Armed, he gets out of his truck and walks toward the Pinto. They argue, exchanging increasingly harsh and angry words. Another semi-truck driver, having assessed our situation from up the road, drops his speed just enough for us to burst into a sprint and run alongside. I hop onto the running board, fling my backpack through the open window, and hold on with one arm. Running as fast as she can, Hayla takes off hers and thrusts it up to me. I take it from her and throw it in, grab her bouncing arm and pull her up. The driver guns it as we climb in and sigh some long, deep sighs.

Our Bulgarian hero is going all the way to Trabzon on the Black Sea coast. He and Hayla are able to communicate in German. He's a jolly bloke, bleary-eyed, and smells like a mickey of vodka is already flowing in his thick-arm veins.

The Fuck Machine

A few hours later we're approaching a village in the Bulgarian's truck. Huts are scattered along the rough, winding road. Poppies and other wildflowers color the hillsides in vivid streaks and splotches. Against the background of green, and the blue sky with its mighty white cloud forms, the sunlight amplifies numerous spots of red, yellow, purple, and orange as if staging the best possible exhibition of terrestrial colors for visiting aliens.

As we round a corner a group of children comes into view, from toddlers to about age twelve. As soon as we appear they make their move. One of them releases a counterweight that pivots on a beam suspended atop two short log A-frames. This releases the main bulk of a large phallic contraption that swings lewdly from the torso of a boy no older than six. In fact he's riding it, and is dressed for the occasion with a cap and spiffy, baggy trousers, like a grown-up young stud from the 1930s. For the ten or so seconds of their special performance the child fucks the air with gusto, a big smile stretching his puffy face. The others stand around, boys and girls alike, some with mock smiles and a couple of the older ones—a taller girl especially—looking hard-faced like premature retirees from innocence, their toughness like scar tissue. The tall girl stands off to the side.

It seems the Fuck Machine is too elaborate to have been built by youngsters like them, but who knows? It's the middle of the day, and they're in plain view of several homes. It's not as if they can run and hide their toy. It's more of a stationary item, like a seesaw.

THE BULGARIAN DROPS us in Trabzon. We ferry hop along the Black Sea coast and cross the Bosporus, a narrow ribbon of sea that separates Asia from Europe. We arrive in a city of many names. Byzantium, Constantinople, Beyoglu, Stamboul, Islambul. Istanbul: a great city in the western hinterlands of Islam. Prayers are publicly broadcast through strategically placed PA systems five times a day, sung here as they are in Lahore or Herat with raw reverence, the intention being inclusion for every person in town. There is little room for dissidence and no separation between mosque and state in most Muslim-majority nations. Yet Turkey, a secular state, is an exception. We westerners believe that separating the two—faith and governance—is necessary in a democracy. But the view from Islam offers a different perspective, perhaps to ensure submission[82] to what is deemed most important in life: a people's spirituality and love of God.

Understandably, travelers are seen from a certain distance. I wander into the large mosque featured in many postcards of the city, where row upon row of men kneel on prayer mats facing the same direction. Within seconds I'm discovered—because I'm the only one standing, the only one wearing hippie clothes?—and hastily chased out. Apparently, non-Muslims are not welcome in *this* house of worship. I am immediately critical of the exclusivity, but my judgment is presumptuous. I am the visitor and unfamiliar with... just about everything in this or any corner of the world.

Yet my arrogant charm doesn't stop there. On a balmy evening, sitting at an outside patio in the central district among locals and travelers, Hayla and I share a drink with two young Turks. One of them asks where we're from. He seems pleased with Hayla's Denmark, pleased with Hayla, for sure. But when he hears my Canada, he goes off about America's deficiency of culture compared with his land's lush contributions over the many centuries. His point isn't made in the spirit of exchanging ideas but by way of aggressive, condescending jabs. No problem; the Asshole is ready.

"Culture? Yeah? So why are you all watching American movies and listening to their music, huh? Culture? Yeah, right! All you've got is a bunch of old buildings in ruin, just like your stagnant country!"

---

82   Islam: literally, submission (to God's will).

I've had a couple glasses of wine. They do not clobber me.
My sincerest apology.[83]

GREECE'S NORTHEAST FRONTIER lies ahead. We will leave tomorrow this land of Islam, and reenter the mesmerizing world of technological affluence, relative political freedom, and the unchallenged credo of capitalism. We will again be beckoned by the consumerist lures of personal freedom and material prosperity, perhaps invoking that peculiar American idolatry: the dream of achieving a life of a prince or princess, each one. All in all, a most potent and infectious bag of ideas and tricks now offered (for a price, of course) at the prayer mat of most world cultures.

We—Hayla the tall, blue-eyed Danish Amazon and I, a West Coast Canadian of southern Italian flesh and blood—will reenter the grounds of our home cultures.

It is where any religion is welcome, in principle at least.

And although it circles the globe, some call it the Christian West.

83 A good place to mention Turkey's impressive and intriguing evidence of ancient human activity: the 9,000-year-old city of Catalhoyuk; the multi-level subterranean city (among many others) of Derenkuyu, which lies beneath the fairy-chimney-land of Cappadocia; and the history-zapping Gobekli Tepi, now considered to be the oldest megaliths in the world.

10. The Old Country

Doctor, my eyes[84]

U-turn

Hayla and I walk through a small village on the Aegean island of Thassos. It's not one of the trendy islands; indeed, we are here by its plainness and easy access, for it lies close to the northern highway.

At a little store we pick up a cheap bottle of wine. Drawn toward the sea we walk to the end of a road and into a serene grove of evergreens next to a pebbly beach. With a word and a nod we spread our sleeping bags on the dry forest floor. It's early evening and the low sun sends golden warmth sparkling across the water. A sea breeze rustles the upper leaves of the tall trees, swaying branches. Gentle waves lap the shore in rhythms that appear to be random, washing pebbles ever smoother. It's easy; there's no tension, not in the sea and not in me. I open the bottle.

In India much is written about the grand illusion of duality. Around the world big songs sing it, brave ones speak it, and poet pipers dance along a hopeful path. And it's old news. Those lively, mysterious ones, mostly hidden behind the pomp of church, mosque, or temple, flash smiles in the dark—*take another look, love.* They delight in telling us: the divine *is* you. And so the word unity does not suffice, for it implies separate things put together; the term of choice is non-duality.

Yet our persistent experience as separate Hayla and Johnny beings is most vivid in our bodies, male and female. *The yum of yin, the yell of yang.* More subtle is the island of inner mind, thinking as if all by itself, holding to the ever-alone-and-private bargain. *We experience ourselves,*

---

84   From the song "Doctor My Eyes" by Jackson Browne.

our thoughts and feelings, as something separated from the rest... a kind of optical delusion of consciousness.[85]

Hayla and I lie in this forest, thinking whatever we think. Separate again do we appear from the wide Grecian sky, the clear face of a greater being the ancient ones in this very land called Gaia. Today she is seductive, showing up according to my whim and appetite on this sultry evening, her swaying branches and lapping waves a clever disguise, the very matrix of such pleasures. She spins the big blue yonder into a chorus of love calls with our little voices, crying and laughing in the grand drama of one and other as we lie on Her sumptuous grasses, sipping Her wine.

There seems to be a consistent message in mystical lore: we shroud the good truth in webs of thought, in the heavy emotion of our suffering world. But the truth of our nature is always there, unchanged. *Just remove the clouds, baba, the sun always shine, shine, shine.*[86] The constant perfection, the perfect constant. But we turn away, distracted, obsessed with survival, competition, sex. *Inter*-consciousness. The world, the cosmos—so beautiful, so terrible. By the sorcerous veil of division we self-propelled, polarized, timorous little bits are set loose in the heavenly hell of physicality, on the run and on the hunt in the planet's seductive thrall. Since leaving India the thoughts keep returning... Hayla and I lying together, yet apart; it is mere appearance. That big sky, its separation from us: *not so.* If separation is illusory, its deception informs all earthly sensations. Thinking, talking about it, it's all part of the illusion. Like a conversation in one of those "real" and fascinating dreams. But it's just a dream. *Thanks a bunch, India.*

For some time and a few hundred miles I've been mulling over my next move on this global trek. My plan-in-progress features a blurry line on a world map tacked up in the mind's grand hall of sights and fancies. A loop around the Mediterranean via Israel, Egypt, Cyprus, and Crete... Morocco, Tunisia, Malta, and Portugal. Why not? An NYC

---

85   Albert Einstein.

86   We are and always were complete, as mystics say. Just one example from the many I have come across: "The Overself is not a goal to be attained but a realization of what already is." From *The Short Path to Enlightenment*, by Paul Brunton, Pg 16.

Nadine I met back in Benares—pretty, smart, sincere—gave me her Manhattan address, a valuable thing, I'm told. New York City: a good port of entry, capital of the world, where multitudes have funnelled through from one life to another.

Or will I soon be back in Canada? I've been away for two years; my folks expect it. Sister Rita will be in Italy in a week. The last time I saw her was half a lifetime ago when I was eleven, when she moved back to Italy with her young family. I've not set foot in the country that is in my past, that's supposed to be in *me*.

Hayla and I have traveled together since Pakistan, but we share no plan. She'll head north at Venice to her native Denmark. I will find the village of Mosnigo di Moriago where Rita's in-laws live, not far from that great city of history and canals. Odd bits and strings—thoughts, pictures, fuzzy notions—litter the floor of that grand hall of plans. But they do not pester me. I lie still, pleasurably still, free from worry.

Then it hits me. *Bong!* One snaky path leaps from the floor straight onto my map. It shudders, choosing me as I choose it. *Ahoy! U-turn ahead!* I raced through India, but something hooked me. When I first laid rookie eyes on Calcutta's streets of dust and dung I was overcome by alogical familiarity, then mild shock: *why do I feel I've "returned"?* Today, on this Greek isle, an enticing scent has jumped from memory onto an eastbound breeze and from this moment, I will follow it for thousands of miles... the fragrance of cumin in *chana*, a bowl of dahl.

Or maybe I've caught the current of previous untold pilgrims who, having heard of yogis and jewels, hit the road with secrets in mind and hunger in their eyes. These days it's stragglers, dreamers and junkies from Britain, France, Italy and Germany. I'll join them on a path that's been beaten for centuries, and I'll blend in just fine. The first time, traveling west, I stumbled through on a vague fancy of circling the globe. It was casual, laissez-faire. This time I'm drawn into a stream so ancient that the term Indo-European is as much a mystery as it is a defined term.

So it is: my compass is flipped, and from this moment I am, in truth, on my way east again. Italy, a few more miles west, is no longer my destination but a side trip and turnabout point. *Those weird spices...* I recently snagged a copy of *Journey to the East*[87] in a spirit of tribute to the wandering impulse in pilgrims everywhere, and perhaps anticipating today's change of plans. Maybe old Hermann will keep me bouncing on my moral arches, as he's done before. I turn to Hayla's graceful profile in the twilight and thank the old horn bag Gaia for my good fortune on this young lassie's manifest charms.

That wine. I'm buzzing, and who's complaining?

But it would go down better mixed with olive oil and sprinkled over some greens.

AS WE MAKE our way west and south toward Athens a memory is roused as if by geographical proximity. We are passing by an "underdeveloped," relatively inaccessible peninsula shaped like a three-fingered paw that juts southeast into the Aegean. It is on the northeastern-most of those fingers, in the approach to and on the slopes of a "holy mountain," that a tradition of monasticism, available only to males, is said to survive from earlier days of the Christian world. Twenty monasteries are scattered around the mini-peninsula, among them Bulgarian, Serbian, and Russian. The region's 1,800-year Christian presence, and the cultural significance of its monasteries, must account for its autonomous status (maintained as it is by special arrangement with the Greek and European governments.) It has been spared direct attack during Europe's many periods of strife. It is a world heritage site, a storehouse of rare historical books, documents, art, and artifacts. Surrounded by dangerous seas, its name is Mount Athos, the Holy Mountain, the Mountain of Silence[88].

What interests me here is the element of mysticism and inner discipline. I grew up in a Roman Catholic world as pure and as backwoods a version as one is likely to find. Yet I'm quite sure that any intrinsic mystical element present in my parents' authentic faith was mostly subsumed in the aggressive hierarchy of the Roman Church's legalistic bent. Although my mother was devout in her daily life (as was my father, in his answering-only-to-Jesus kind of way), I felt that rules and obedience, not inner inquiry and experience, are the dominant mode or expression of the Western Church.

87 *Journey to the East* by Hermann Hesse.
88 From *The Mountain of Silence,* by Kyriacos Markides

Back in India I heard from a fellow traveler about this isolated sanctuary in northern Greece and its path of spirituality, which is said to resemble features of Eastern religions: the master/disciple relationship, and contemplative inner discipline practiced daily. This was something new to me in regard to Western religion. Here at this remote outpost of an olden tradition, that of the Eastern Orthodox Church, it is said that the spirit of the Holy Virgin Mary is benefactor, much like in my parents' southern Italian region. Interesting how men seeking spiritual communion with Deity would gather at a place where women are forbidden,[89] then go about the rest of their lives in the mystical embrace of Mother Mary. I understand the move toward seclusion from worldly desires in order to come clean of ego's hold, although I wonder if doing it *all*—including the sublime mess of sexual connection—wouldn't be a more thorough path for honest self-inquiry. Not to mention a kind of surrender to, and gratitude for, the earthly gift of body, mind, and soul complete. But there are many people with many different ways, and that's a good thing, and I'm glad of it.

Alas, I travel a modern road with a fine Danish lassie, so I will pass by this unique peninsula of monks and mysticism, of a locality where it is claimed that humans are doing their earnest best to discover and fulfill the meaning of life.

Culture Shock

I HAVE NEVER been to Europe. Yet after six months in Asia, the human ambience of this northern Greek city might easily pass for my own Vancouver's. It is Thessaloniki, Greece's second city, and the first of the Christian West on my path since Perth, Western Australia.

I walk alone, my mind ranging across nations with each step. More to the point, I stumble over feelings that I'm slow to understand, like the "shock" I felt after emerging from my room onto the streets of Canberra. The looks in passing faces haunt me and drag like numerous hooks upon my psyche. Instead of feeling comfortable in these more

---

89 The all-male residency of Mount Athos: an exception was made during the Nazi terror when the monks provided refuge for Jewish women and children.

familiar surroundings, I am burdened. Once again, by reason of like-ness, a crowd can claim me as its own. I bear witness to my own re-assimilation into a shared mental web.

Before leaving the West I had no way of knowing what a constriction this can place on the spirit of life. Yet I sensed that shadowy power before embarking on this journey. I sensed it in all the years of a home life that formed and claimed me, like a sweeping thrall, and I sought freedom from it. It is why I am traveling. Here in Thessaloniki I feel caged, and each time I look into someone's face I see him strain against his own shackles, unaware. After stimulating the shit out of me for the past six months in the East, a brief taste of freedom is gone in a blur. I am returned home into a movie of my past that would imprison my heart and mind by the weight of the social biases and habits that helped shape me. I am taken in by thought forms and emotional responses that haunt these streets like an army of unseen ghosts, and perform their strange magic for the most part *because* one is unconscious of them. That's what I feel and imagine: that I have been recaptured by the same family of invisible forces.

It's not that other cultures don't have their own forces. But when they're alien, the mechanisms of thought and feeling—the hooks—don't catch. Instead, the experience serves to entertain or to educate. At best the foreign mentality can act as a unique mirror, so that the visitor gets to see, by contrast, and by stripping away the non-essential, *oneself.* Many enjoy such feelings of freedom when visiting foreign cultures. (Others suffer deeply and hide in their rooms. I meet several in this state and I don't understand it, other than to presume their experience has something to do with a greater fear of unfamiliar surroundings.)

And so it is clear: I will return to India. I will revisit that "other" perspective. I will seek understanding on this very disturbance upon reentering the West. I'll have another look, from a different angle into that shifty, turning mirror of self. Free, if only for another season, from these ghosts that haunt me.

HITCHHIKING IS GOOD with Hayla in front. I cruise her pheromone wake as we move along athletically through Greece and Yugoslavia, on a good clip since that boot in the ass from the Pinto Pals.

An intriguing lassie is this *uber*-hot chick from Roskilde, Denmark. Back in Afghanistan I commented, with vexed curiosity, on how frequently and with seeming preference over other travelers I got approached for *baksheesh* by beggars. They would pick me out and walk straight over. Without pause she said, "Well, sure, Johnny. Even dressed like a bum you look, ummm... rich." *Yeah, I guess so.* Wanting to return the courtesy, I thought about Hayla's cinematic beauty, how we learned in school that Danes are hardworking and industrious. *Good beer and pastries, great cheese.* But flushed as I was in the heat of her alleged compliment (hardly understanding it), I said nothing.

Back in Herat, on a busy street at midday, we were accosted by an anguished youth. His broken words and shouts were not clear, but (I guessed) they spoke of an intimate interlude with her a year earlier when she'd passed through going east. Understandably upset by being cast at the center of such a spectacle, she would not talk about it. These matters of attraction and sexual tension, of forces sprung from the furnace of stars... I dig the young man's anguish, and Hayla's, too. Her predicament is that of any fresh-faced nymph: if she posts an "open" sign in her window she'll be inundated with customers, very soon if not immediately. Men are often willful, even violent, aroused by a hunger often felt and believed to be nonnegotiable, of a power beyond the personal—although we know this not to be true. And we know that the power we feel must be carried in the supple hands of compassion and connection—those of love. Hayla's look is a public force that in some way, at some times, must weigh on her, as I intuited when first meeting her on that Pakistani bus. Her *intelligence*... it seems her path is strong and steady in self-knowledge, and I'm sure there's far more than I see or can say. Yet I appreciate that it is not easy, and that her beauty is more than just beauty.

Now and then she takes her recorder from her pack and casts spiralling melodies that no doubt spin compasses somewhere down the wind. The note strings overlap and so seem to echo themselves, each a little different than the last, like mini-ragas, like shifting rivulets of numerically correct sound coursing over the bumps and valleys of my humming gray goop. Like a siren she sails me on multiple loops of rising and falling, cascading notes. *This is what made Odysseus have his men tie him down.*[90]

She tells me she was raped while hitchhiking on this main highway through Yugoslavia two years ago when she was seventeen, and that she was treated like the guilty one in the police station. It seems she isn't masking pain or stumbling over unresolved trauma; she speaks with feeling and insight. *How can this be?* Her appetite for travel is as keen as ever; it was her idea to hitchhike.

Now on the same road, heading into Mediterranean high summer, we coast in the subdued energies of yet another journey's latter days, the journey of Hayla on her plotted course homeward to Denmark, with Johnny Canucklebrain following along, en route to his sister's place not far from Venice.

The main highway through Macedonia, Serbia, Croatia, and Slovenia cuts a messy swath of numerous, manhole-sized potholes and overturned cars and semitrailer trucks through a rural landscape of shimmering yellows and oranges, greens and blues. Shawled, stern-faced women work vast fields of blooming sunflowers that undulate in the warm licks of a Mediterranean breeze. Soon my geographical sense informs me that these fairyland views beyond rusty metal bones will shift to the more neatly ordered and well-funded mania of Western Europe. A land whose rhythms, as I just learned in Thessaloniki, I'm supposed to move more naturally with. We are—both of us, incidentally—approaching gene pool central. Strange thing, too, considering how different those genes wound up looking in her and in me.

Italia, one of two countries I carry inside, the one I haven't seen yet, is up ahead a few more steps.

Son of an Italian

Immediately upon looking at my passport the customs man jerks up his head and launches a couple of eye spears at me before coming down into a steady squint. He motions me aside. I fumble in my rudimentary pig-Italiano/Calabrese: "Hey, no problem. Nice day, eh?" Hayla is already through and waiting on the other side.

90 Odysseus has his men tie him to the ship with his eyes and ears unmasked, so he can witness the power of the Sirens, in *The Odyssey* by Homer.

Further scrutiny from the guard is not unexpected. Here at the Italian border, with my surname and looks, it must be obvious that I'm connected. But he's all high-strung arrogance. *Blow a valve?* After going through more than a dozen borders, this is low drama, mildly interesting. *No worries.* I grew up on this stuff daily. It will pass over, like that cloud up there. I stand to the side and watch as the line moves along into *Italia bella (mia.)*

But the incident seems to have sprouted wings. Now three customs guys are in a booth up ahead discussing me and my passport. I know this because the one who is holding it is yelling and flinging his arms about, occasionally backhanding it with grandiose *gusto.* The other two have equally awesome points to make, their limb tossing and vocal seizures a close match. It goes on for twenty minutes. *Ah well, all in a day.* Feels familiar: my folks in the early years. Having already slipped past a few unforeseen snags on my path, I wait, expecting nothing in particular.

The first guy comes out, all rigid and twitchy. *Pissed.* After searching every micro space in my pack, he caps it off with a belligerent glare that shifts manically back and forth between my passport and my face, to which I respond with the deep emptiness of a young, well-fed calf. Ceding defeat, the customs man motions me through with a final, dismissive wave. I slip past one more snag-on-the-road.

When I finally catch up to Hayla she gives me a weird look.

Later on I piece together a quirky series of events that can account for the wacky exchange on Italy's northeast frontier. First, my given names were botched when I was born. They were supposed to honor Jesus's wild and woolly precursor on his holy Catholic day (since I was born on it) and styled *Italiano.* My immigrant mother could not be understood in the BC hospital, so things got simplified and anglicized to John, dropping the second name altogether. She didn't know; none of us did.

That is, until I received my birth certificate prior to applying for a passport at age nineteen. After opening the envelope, I gleefully told Mom, "Hey, y' know what?—my name is just John, with a 'J.' And no 'Battista.'" (There is no J in the Italian alphabet.)

"No! Tu nome e *Giovanni Battista.*" No discussion, back to kneading her huge vat of bread dough. Well, she *was* there at the time of naming.

But technically, she's wrong. It's right there in laminated plastic, government issued.

Second, Italy is possessive of its children, even of its children's children. As long as one of your parents was an Italian citizen when you were born (both of mine were), you are Italian when on Italian soil. *Hey, that's me!* By my looks and surname, the customs men must have assumed as much.

Third, Italy enforces a mandatory six-month military service on its sons. (Two years later, a similar situation results in the conscription of a Canadian-born son's son of Italy on *his* first visit to the old country. Unfortunately, this happens at the beginning of his honeymoon with his bride. He's in for the mandatory six months, during which time Fortuna farts, causing his new wife to dump him. Sad story. So sad that Canada and Italy came to an understanding of sorts, one that involves distant sons exempting themselves from army service *before* arriving on Italy's doorstep.)

I reckon the argument in that customs booth went something like this.

"I tell ya, the wormy kid's a *paisano.* We gotta grab him, *now!*"

"Come *on,* what the hell's the matter with you, Nunzio? Who the hell—what red-blooded, wine-drinking Italian father would put that *what the fuck*—'J'—in his son's name? 'John'? Fuck *that* shit! Though the little turd could use a good haircut and a bath."

"Alright, al*right!* Have it your way. It's on *your* head. I dunno anymore. Son of a bitch world's gone fuckin' crazy!"

PARTING WITH HAYLA is strained. I knew *I'd* be sad, but I thought she'd be kinda, well, aloof and such. I don't get it. She's been so cool with me. It seemed that none of it mattered—except when she smiled. Now my sorry heart reaches out and it feels... a grand gate of heaven is closing.

I say goodbye to her on a Venice piazza, seeing something in her eyes that I never saw before. Have I misread her coolness for a lack of interest? Whatever it is, I feel its rush in our eyes. It tingles on the skin, but it's not enough to melt the frozen man nor the woman before me, who longs for deeper heat just as I do. Polar attachment long conceived, how we yearn for its promise of fulfillment. I'm tossed like a stick in Gaia's surf, for this is biology's relentless power over individual choice.

And maybe it's much more than that. For it feels stranger still to be witness to it, standing over experience, heaping the weight of knowledge on the pain of loss. Sometimes I run away into words, distracting myself and the whole situation away from taking a chance and really *feeling it.* Have I allowed her "coolness" to make it easy for me to avoid jumping in?

Fuck. Fuck!

I figure we'll probably correspond by mail once or twice, then watch the thread of connection gradually fray. What might have become a different life will fade away as time passes, as our far-flung details engulf us, each in our separate dreams.

Veneto

Roma, Venezia, Firenze, Milano: these are cities of the world where a frayed traveler can get lost in the buzz. But get off the *autostrada* and I'm an alien trespassing on guarded territory. In the provincial town of Treviso, eyes dart away and heads turn in my wake. Body language is awkward and hurried. I look unusual in my hobo-Eastern garb and bearded, mop-hair look, stirring up what feels like self-conscious paranoia in passersby. But a suburban town is what it is, and this one could be anywhere in that gray expanse between the compressed surrender of cities and the artless warmth of village life.

When modern suburban locale becomes rural village I arrive in Mosnigo di Moriago, at my elder sister's place. This summer of 1976 is all about my two senior sisters and our serendipitous crossings on a certain peninsula, on another peninsula so huge they call it a continent, in the middle of a sea named for being at "the middle of the earth."

Rita's arrival synchronizes with mine. She has returned from Canada to sell her hair and beauty care business, having recently decided to move her family back to Vancouver after ten years raising two girls in her husband's village. They'd lived close to his aging parents in their winter years, but now his parents are gone. She was the deferential wife for a decade, separated from her own family in a place that would not feel like home. This return to Canada is *her* move. Her round of follow-the-leader, only just begun, has been passed over from him.

In the first seconds I lay eyes on her the faces of my mother and two other sisters shift provocatively within hers. I haven't seen her since I was twelve. When I was small she was a second mom, helping Ma in her endless workload.

Every night for a week we're up late with a bottle of wine, catching up on the last ten years. Personal changes have greatly accelerated for us both in the past year. 1976, excellent choice: year of the fire dragon, and a leap year as well.

During the days we go for drives in her maroon Fiat on far-flung jaunts into the surrounding country. Tying up business ends she provokes male acquaintances by omitting "my brother" in her introductions. At every meeting and street corner, unrequited ripples of scandal are left in our wake. *Our fair Rita cavorting around shamelessly with a young shaggy hippie?* I'm a long-haired, bearded drifter wearing plastic thongs, an embroidered Tibetan shoulder-strap bag, and paper-thin pajama pants. The dense silences, the stammering excuses, the solemn macho looks are wickedly amusing. They must assume… *When the cat's away, the mouse will play.* Befuddled thoughts crawl over the men's tense brows, and woeful pangs of dark feelings set their faces to an ugly stiffness. These are meetings in the public areas where the men are away from their wives and less guarded. Though these are inappropriate and therefore absurd jealousies, I might have eased their suffering, maybe spared the region a season of tawdry rumor by simply saying *fratello*—and spoiling Rita's fun.

As it is she chirps and flits about, as happy as a pixie in heat. In her early thirties, she's having a good time. No, she's downright gleeful. In recent times she was a local beauty queen, so there's no doubt she is of special interest to these proud conduits of manly magic.

When the visit is more friendly, usually with women in their homes during the day, we're invited inside. (Ahh, *they* will tell their tortured husbands about Rita's visiting brother, unwittingly easing their pain.) A wine-drenched reverie envelops us on an ambitious tour of Rita's social circle. Goodbyes, good wishes, and good food are generously shared at dozens of tables. As the red elixir goes in and the inner heat goes up, my eyes move dreamily over the sacramental grapes that grow outside every kitchen window, and over their daughters as well. I'm often entertained by our hosts' unguarded chatter until they realize I understand most of what they say. I understand because they are forced to speak to Rita in official (Florentine) Italian, not their (what is to Rita and to me the) unintelligible Veneto dialect, which sounds to me as much like a Germanic as a Latin language. I find it easier to understand a Spaniard speaking slowly. Likewise, Rita's and my native Calabrese is a garbled tongue to them.

In a final round of serendipitous crossings, Rita leaves Italy as my middle sister, Maria, arrives with her two young children. Maria's husband is also from the village of Mosnigo. Single Maria's overseas trip to visit her older sister a few years ago seems to have blossomed nicely.

We take a train (crowded like India but cleaner and more like a speeding metal snake) to the far south, from where my parents and the first half of their children—my four older siblings—emigrated twenty-three years ago.

Calabria

Our first walk down the lane to my mother's childhood home, where her sister Rosa still lives, is a homecoming. Nestled in the mountains of Italy's upper toe area, Serra San Bruno is the town that nurtured my parents and their families. I've never walked these streets, yet I'm deeply familiar with their collective mind. Deeper yet is Maria's connection, for this is the land of her first three years. The weekly gatherings with uncles, aunts, and cousins around a spaghetti-and-wine dinner in metro Vancouver are a tribute to this, a whole region of Italy in on the game.

As we walk, a hush of whispers and blooming of smiles ripple through clusters of women and children. The effect rolls down the lane at the speed of rumor, anticipating our arrival in a wave that moves a little faster than we do. It isn't a Sunday, we aren't riding donkeys, and no one's laying down palms, but this is the look. Glancing to my side, Maria's timorous yet awestruck face indicates that she, too, finds it all rather transporting. Maria is the middle girl, and I'm the middle boy in our brood. Yet we arrived into this life on either side of the big-sea journey that informs so much of how our family shows up in this world: the uprooting, the transplant, the relearning, the surge of opportunity, the loss, the regret, the disillusionment, the no-going-back, the cutting-edge mind blaze that set fire to ten different minds—all at once but at different stages of life. And yet more stories of suffering and hope are passed unawares along generations, some to be yanked into the harsh light of a new land by our grand move.

Last born in Italy, Maria was young enough to be "made" also in Canada. And the immigrant experience was new enough when I was born to pour a good strain of Italy into me. In the small, west coast Canadian town of my childhood our family was an oddity, a microcosm of weird-sounding, excitable, darkish folk who at times acted from a most eccentric mindset. We inhabited a world distinct from the one outside the family web and walls of our house. Even as a preschooler I was conscious of the culture inside our home simply because of its contrast with the one outside. Our private family world, unique and precious as it was in my infancy and boyhood, is an offshoot of this one: Calabria.

Rural Calabrian mountain dwellers are far from the center of Italian society. My parents often referred to old Catholic ways, like the cult of the mother-virgin Madonna, exorcism, and other more quasi-occultic practices. I arrive at the ancestral homeland of my family, a seasoned traveler with no specific plan of returning home anytime soon. The mothers of the village receive me with a unanimous, "What about your *mamma?*" accompanied by forlorn and disbelieving looks. Here *la Madonna*—mother of Jesus—is, I believe, a more popular person-age of veneration than is the Savior Himself. She is everywhere—on shelves and walls and church piazzas and in the eyes and hearts of the townsfolk. Every mother relates and identifies with her, and every son *is that very special son* . . .

Even so, I suspect that in some ways the Old Country blossomed arbitrarily in my parents' minds, separated as they were from their roots. I grew up with a view of my folks as adhering to a religious calling more fundamental than the dictates of the Vatican. Today, this is also how I see their hometown.

FOR MY FAMILY, Calabria is both memory and myth. In the early years my mother would cast away the threat of illness whenever she detected a sniffle, reading the movement of oil droplets on the surface of a cup of boiled water.[91] Her whispered prayer would stop as she gazed into the cup at the paths and diffusion of the drops. Content with their revelation, she'd dip her thumb and make the sign of the cross over the cup, touching its rim at four points and transferring the blessing with several crosses on our foreheads and chests, leaving warm, wet spots on our skin. Twenty years later on a Penang sidewalk, the devout reading of a pile of sticks by an old Chinese woman didn't feel so strange.

Back in India on the River Ganges I was struck by the posture of prayer in Hindu country, and how similar it looks to the Roman Catholicism of Italy's deep south. The upheld palms pressed together, the longing, rapt faces of the Sunday regulars cocked heavenward in the front pews, of my mother, and of the saints pictured on her entry room altar—these are postures seamlessly superimposed onto men and women praying at the holy river Ganga. The circle of prayer beads seen everywhere in India; my mom's rosary. At times, when my mother was immersed in prayer her breathing became rhythmic, and the praying synchronized with the steady rhythm of her breathing, as if the in and out and in and out was a yogic practice designed to calm the heart and mind, to instill some morsel of God's great peace. This too I saw on the banks of that river of myth, and some morsel of myself is bound up in it as I remember those nights, early in my life, when my mother taught me to pray (always for others, never for myself.) These are intriguing similarities, given the contrast between the two faiths in philosophical character and mythical form. Since India's is said to be the world's oldest extant culture, perhaps these similarities flow from the same ancient behavioral stream, evoking what is believed to be their common

91 Italia's first civilization, the Etruscans, were fond of reading omens in the natural world. They were said to have been defeated by the Romans. For sure they were overcome by Rome's military might, yet in practical terms they were more likely absorbed. Was my mother's practice of "reading" oil droplets a ritual passed down or inherited from those ancient ways?

Indo-European heritage.[92]

Walking home from church one Sunday evening, my short legs had to move fast to keep up. I was holding Mom's hand, and as we crossed the Big Park I couldn't resist staring at the first specks of blazing stars on such a vast and naked night. The large glowing disk of the moon against the deep indigo had me hypnotized for that minute of crossing the field, drawing my attention like a gaping porthole into infinite space. When she noticed my little face cocked moonward she admonished me, saying that staring at stars would give me freckles, and that I'd get tongue cankers from the moon. It was too grand to behold; awesome, perhaps ominous forces are at work in the universe. The firmament is too much like God to face directly. Maybe the universe *is* the great face of existence, the face of God. No, you mustn't look at the burning bush, or the burning sky. But I always did.

I loved and followed her, but I didn't quite believe her. Even by that tender age, I knew Mom spoke in a tongue not of the land my feet so loved. Hustling along beside her, looking up from that grassy clearing, I asked, "If God knows everything and can do anything, why is there so much sin and pain in the world?" I was little, but kids do ask. She answered in a way that, only now on my return to the East, makes some loopy sense: "God wants things to be as they are: *everything is as it must be.*" Those were strangely comforting words to a child growing astride two worlds. More than comfort, they introduced the tantalizing sense of paradox. Those words became my ally and sanctuary when opposing forces didn't make sense. I relished the feeling in the seeming contradiction that one can sin, even choose to sin, and that "everything is as it must be." I must have presupposed the existence of free will: choose to

92   In his book *Gods, Sages and Kings*, David Frawley offers a view that challenges modern scholarship by presenting evidence on Vedic India's role as a source culture for the West, and perhaps, for the world. Indeed, upon the discovery of Sanskrit's obvious connection to Greek and Latin, and considering the ancient origins of the Vedas, India was, for a brief period in the eighteenth century, seen as the source culture for much of the world. (That is, until the "superiority complex" of the Europeans re-asserted itself—my interpretation.) From the Foreword in *The Shape of Ancient Thought* by Thomas McEvilley. (Packed into this footnote is a double-mystery I will bring home, whether a door has been knocked ajar on the question of civilization's source, or on that of the personal self.)

sin or not. Yet things just happen and just *are*, and God *likes* it. I am *so* fortunate that my lovely mother dignified her four-year-old's ontological perplexity with a sincere answer.

Early on, before the genteel ways of the New World had a chance to alter the Old, Mom had us wear a cross sewn into a small cloth pouch pinned to the inside of our undershirts next to the skin. She made sure it was in place each morning, transferring the pouch to a clean shirt with quiet reverence. I remember it as a worn gray lump, slightly soiled but charged with mystical presence. I felt protected, as much by Mom's resolute care as by the pouch.

Yes, this Calabria country is stirring the cauldron of memory. The stories are many and Dad, of course, had his own to tell. He spoke of confronting the devil, who inhabited the body of a young man in the process of terrorizing the village. They claimed that he was seething in the vile energy of the Dark One himself, and that he had bent a metal pipe with his bare hands. In the throes of his contorting form he frothed at the mouth and growled obscenities while lashing out at anyone and anything nearby. Everyone was terrified.

Seized with courage that comes only from having Jesus on your side, Dad and two others dragged him a kilometer uphill to the monastery. This, he said, took the afternoon to accomplish, so possessed of unnatural strength was the young man. When the priest emerged, the whole village was present. Intoning the name of Christ, the priest exorcised the man. In a climax of "wailing and gnashing of teeth" each article of his clothing flew high into the air, one by one, as did the demons from his body and soul. Naked, he was found to be healed, and was covered with a blanket. Free at last he became as gentle as a lamb, and wept.

I don't know what to make of these stories, nor can I be certain where the stories end and "I" begin. Their language and symbols defined a way of being before I developed the complexity to reflect, *this is me/ this is not me*. This must be true for us all, even when the stories are modern ones that feature atoms and black holes, or the coveting of wealth and celebrity. No, I don't simply believe them, nor will I categorically dismiss them. I could not at their time of telling, and nor do I now as I walk the streets of my parents' hometown. These lands of my ancestors—southern

Italy—are the very lands of Archimedes, Pythagoras and Parmenides, of Empedocles and Xeno and Heracles. Their ancient stories are carried in the human folds of time, often hidden from view, just as real intelligence can be hidden in the unrefined words of an uneducated man. Is my father's personal hero myth hidden there as well, placed as it is astride a fault line where two cultures grate uneasily, one against the other?

Somewhere it is written: language is not simply a tool of communication, for it is also one of *perception*.[93] With words we describe and articulate, but as well, by their shapes and limits do we bump up to the edges of thought and even experience. And, perhaps, to the very world we share. That language is by nature a representation and not apt to describe or mirror things as they are, a.k.a. truth, is written in what have been described as the first known writings, the Rig Veda, before Hinduism developed into what it is today. Other writings allude to the same.[94] Human language itself is an unprecedented and inexplicable phenomenon in regard to one of Science's most cherished models, that of natural selection. For its origins and evolution remain mysterious.[95]

In the hills of southern Italy words describe things powerful and godly, mystical and dark, things that make sense where the supreme forces of good and evil affect daily lives.

What forms of our own social matrix elude our understanding, even our perception? Do we experience midnight-noon/Sunday/June the

93 I picked up this idea somewhere but have not found its source: that language, as well as so obviously being a tool for communication, also forms and limits, or "leads" perception.

94 Dante: "my vision was greater than our speech, which yields to such a sight"; Walt Whitman: "when I undertake to tell the best I find I cannot, my tongue is ineffectual on its pivots, my breath will not be obedient to its organs, I become a dumb man"; Franklin Merrell-Wolff in *Pathways Through to Space*: "the subject-object form, essential to language as such, can only distort the Transcendent"; Sufi writers hold that "language cracks and grows treacherous under the weight of sublime realities" (from T. Winter, "Saint With Seven Tombs," *Parabola* magazine, Fall 1997). And "don't eat the menu" from Gregory Bateson. The ancient Jews went to the trouble of making taboo any attempt at a certain naming, but the very nature of thought and language seduces us into indulging multiple brands, signposts, and categories.

95 For a provocative (if irreverent) examination of the subject, see *The Kingdom Of Speech* by Tom Wolfe.

way we do *because* we describe them so? Am I at the mercy of things and events in the world *because* I think they are more real than I am? Is (reversing) this why some play the free will game more efficiently than others do?

Watching the first moon walk in 1969 my father brushed aside what to him was deception, *propaganda,* with the comment, "Ahhh, it's all electricity." As simple as this statement made him appear, he was drawing a line, with his limited English and from his old-world perspective, between what one can *know* and what is disseminated into the collective "known" through media—through hearsay or *propaganda.* Although as a youngster I heard only the words of an uneducated old man from an outdated worldview, I now wonder whether Dad was digging deeper with his rather plain words.

Perhaps Dad's comments could be read to suggest that electricity presents something of the miraculous in its far-reaching effects—TV, city lights, spacecraft—especially as seen by one who has lived a part of his life without it, and without the education that names and describes electrons to make it understandable. Do I really know that electrons do their swapping, rushing thing when I flick the light switch? Is this knowable? Is the power of Christ and that of Satan knowable? More importantly, are the questions similar, depending on who asks, or even *not* depending on who asks?

A Hopi speaker always reveals, through grammatical markers in his language, whether the subject is directly witnessed, comes by way of hearsay, or is considered to be an unchanging truth,[96] while *our* markers reveal present, past, and future tense; and first-, second-, or third-person points of reference. Becoming aware of the largely unconscious assumptions of language might suggest some ways we unknowingly engage in agreements and, consequently, abide by "rules of reality."

My parents, bless their uncomplicated gumption, lived in daily gratitude for the great bounty of their new America. But to me theirs was a measly *lack* of choice. My understanding, my words, describe numerous choices, fantasies flung from a kaleidoscopic necklace that I barely acknowledge I'm wearing. Move my head and my words a bit, and new

96 From *The Horse, the Wheel and Language* by David W. Anthony, p. 19.

choices jump into unimagined forms, projected onto the screen called the world. My parents' words told them they'd landed the jackpot of a lifetime with just *one* picture. And they were as happy as a prince and princess with a few chickens and rabbits in the backyard, and a wine cellar bursting with the power of last year's sun.

I saw the hardship my parents eagerly endured for so little. Yet growing up in one of the most pampered generations in historical memory, I bemoaned my inability to seize the great wealth of choices within reach. I told myself: all this in a generation of change accelerated by emigration. In this case from a third-world, Roman Catholic worldview into the icono-clastic culture of suburban west coast America, circa 1950s to 1970s. I did bear witness to our different worlds, even put a satisfying word to the mix. But making sense of the reality behind the effect is not so simple.

I've merely brushed Calabria's surface with my visit, leaving my folks' cultural homeland with more questions than understanding. But weighted as any person is toward the land he calls home, I silently thank my father and mother for making the life-changing journey across the ocean to the new land.

To my beloved British Columbia.

BACK IN THE north I speak to Mom on the phone. When I tell her I won't be coming home for maybe another year, she yells and hangs up. *Yikes.* My persistent resolve to go ahead with my plans to return to the East makes it all the more clear just how detached from home I've become. But even clearer is the melancholy that engulfs me. I am deeply affected by Mom's emotion. *So how detached am I?* I was unable to describe to her the invigorating effect of travel, and that I must continue for as long as I reasonably can. I write a letter to her explaining this. I want her to understand. But also, I want to shuck off the weird guilt I feel so I won't have to carry it with me eastward.

On my way down Italy's shin I pause in St. Francis's Assisi region. In his vivid hills, which buzz with life in the sweet, sun-charged air, I ponder Francis's celebrated love of nature. As far as Catholic saints go, he's a peach. I leave Umbria and hitchhike south toward the heel and the ferry terminal at Brindisi.

I leave the land of the Etruscan (so little known and underappreciated), the Roman (so cocksure and organized), the Renaissance (so exciting and culturally messianic), the pope (so old and emperor-like), and the Lamborghini (never tried one), and a nice selection of the world's best cheeses—not to mention, paintings of Jesus.

I say goodbye to *Italia bella* as if saying it to my own mother as she cooks yet another grand meal.

11. Ancient Stream

I guess my feet know where they want me to go.[97]

Greek Isles 2, South Africa 2

From Italy's heel I take a ferry to Corinth and island-hop across the Aegean toward Turkey.

The Greek isle of Mykonos is a sun-bleached outcrop in a candy-blue sea. Its four notorious beach modes—family, nude, male, female—circle the island.

While wading in the lazy surf on Beach Nude, I turn and bump into a young lassie with strangely glistening eyes, her long dark hair shifting its fluid curls in the seawater. Her skin is deep copper, very smooth. Treading water, our steady gaze seems held in the lush buoyancy of the tepid sea. Our curious limbs probe and entwine. We have not yet bothered to speak: my all-time favorite "hello." Her face bursts numinous, a halo snatched up and popped into her mouth.

Then, as we drift along, our bodies one entangled mass, our faces inches close, my first words: "You're buzzing, I can feel it. Are you, uh, tripping?"

"No," she says, smiling. "I've been fasting for a few days." *A thousand.* Our hands wander, then our lips. Breath, skin.

She is hyper-conscious Nasha from South Africa. We walk to the end of the beach into a craggy outcrop and lay in a cozy, half-shaded nook. No schedule. We are drawn to light and shadow as they decorate our bodies and the surrounding rock.

Nasha tells me a story that rivals the freaky occultism of my Calabrian folks, a strange event in Sicily within a few weeks of our meeting: a

---

97   From the song "Country Road" by James Taylor.

crowd wailing in unison in the middle of a stormy night while she and her friend lay in a gazebo-like shack on a hilltop; a deafening "crack" and immediate silence—the crowd and the storm gone—and the effective removal of an entire Saturday from their weekend. Crazy gal. Claims to know nothing of the ways or beliefs of the locals, nothing about folds in the substance of space-time and its attendant frightening noises. Just passing through on foot, says she.

I need not know about the verity of her story, nor about whether she possesses keen intelligence and integrity, and is uncommonly intuitive—or wanders spellbound in her unique cave of shadows. Any claim to objectivity is rightly dismissed here. I'm reminded again of Mom and Dad's mystic cosmology, and how my window on it during my early years was soon overcome by the surrounding hegemony of modern science and Anglo society. As I pass from culture to culture on this global trek, the familiar bearings of my Canadian homeland fade. *Any chance for clarity?* I forgive myself my lapse in perspective. I simply listen to Nasha, allowing imagination free rein without correction and without the rational bearing so readily embraced in *my* cosmology.

I'm with her for three days, long enough for the alchemy of love to play piper to our respective nervous systems. But that mysterious alternate—detachment, reclusion—has me by the inner compass, and it points down an ancient stream that flows east, away from this paradise of beating hearts. Since my U-turn moment on the isle of Thassos, I am dedicated flotsam in that stream, and I will leave this Mykonos heaven, with or without this naturally stoned-out chick. We've already shared the fantasy of traveling together, mostly, perhaps, because we know it won't happen. A South African passport won't get far on the overland route.

The truth is, since my separation from Danna back in Canberra, I have grown deeper into my time alone, for yay and for nay. The pull of a woman's beauty is ever present for me, as it may well be for monks in caves—hey, that's probably *why* they're in caves. That week in my cruddy room of tears will not easily be forgotten. I came to know the depth of my attachment to the love of a woman, and it's here again in its infant stage with Nasha. The pattern has always been to go wherever the potion commands. Something new has begun, in fits and starts as it did with Hayla, although this new way of relating with women started with my week of reckoning in Canberra. A time of remedial singularity, one of sublime detachment (as I've heard it said) has given rise to wondrous turns of the traveling life, by which old ways seem to appear, speak their peace, and are gone. Remaining with Nasha—taking the potion—will redirect these extraordinary (I say natural) new processes.

Even so, I don't believe this one-or-the-other deal is any kind of rule, only that my own condition, my current limits, make it this way.

I'm a perfect fool when I look into Nasha's questioning eyes. There's a moment, then another… and she understands. It's done. I feel relief as well as loss when I take my rucksack and head down the road into the falling eastern sky.

THE FRAGRANT GREEN isle of Samos was home to Aristarchus, the first person known, from our Western perspective, to propose that Earth revolves around the Sun. The mathematician and mystic Pythagoras also hailed from there, before he followed that sun a little farther west to establish his mystery school in Croton, Calabria. On Samos there is a temple dedicated to Hera, mother of the gods, where it is said peacocks—Hera's own holy birds—were first kept when introduced to the West from India. Did little Pythagoras's imagination catch flight on the Indian trail of those peacocks? Apart from his famous geometric theorem, he is said to have embraced a belief in the transmigration of souls, or reincarnation. More than two millennia later, I learn his name in high school math class, but there's no mention of his Eastern worldview or "mystery school." His time was still two centuries before Alexander's rendezvous with India when, it is written, the meeting of Greek and Indian civilizations altered the course of history through cross-pollinations in science, the arts, and philosophy.[98]

98 See Peter Kingsley, his books *In the Dark Places of Wisdom* and *Reality*. In southern Italy, Pythagoras and Parmenides carried the seeds of a transcendent movement that bears signature details of the inner disciplines of India: reincarnation, the hero (or guru), the master-student dyad, and that our shared reality is an illusion to be transcended. Also, the *Encyclopedia of Philosophy* Volume 6, Parmenides, p. 49, on "The Way of Truth" and "The Way of Seeming," which seem to correspond to Vedanta's non-duality and maya. See Thomas McEvilley, his book *The Shape of Ancient Thought*.

Considering Queen Goddess Hera's fondness for peacocks, real connection between the Mediterranean and India could be much older. (Not to mention, take a gander at the look of people across North Africa and southern Eurasia between Portugal and India. Must have taken millennia for the similar look to be disseminated along that 10,000-mile stretch. *Are you Italian? Greek? Turkish? Persian? Afghani? Punjabi?* I've been taken for each of these, and others, throughout my trek.)

On Samos I meet another South African, John. His compatriot back on Mykonos, Nasha, was devoid of racism. She spoke of workers in fields on the outskirts of "Jo'sberg," and how she danced and sang with them in the land's celebrated rhythms. They laughed a bellyful at her natural affinity. "A white girl with a black soul," they'd said.

But John, although personable enough, spins tales of mystical encounters with Indian gurus who, he's happy to inform me, were "impressed with (his) noble spiritual stature." Later he goes on about the black man's native inferiority: "His brain is different, maybe not smaller, but it's not the same as the white man's. Scientists back home proved it, you know." Strange days are the few spent with the charismatic older dude from Durban, who can carry a conversation as easily as the wind carries a sigh—even though sometimes I wish he wouldn't. John's calm self-assurance in these matters of dark persuasions becomes a disturbing marker in my mind's catalog of Odd Fellas. We seemed to get along a-okay, me and the silver-tongued bigot. *A dog is not considered a good dog because he's a good barker.*[99]

I leave Nasha and John, Mykonos and Samos, Hera and Pythagoras, and skip over into Turkey.

ON THE SOUTHWEST coast of Turkey lie the remains of the ancient Greek city of Ephesus with its famous temple of Artemis, or (the Roman) Diana. It was one of several Greek cities on Anatolia's west coast, including Miletus and its influential philosophers: Thales, Anaximander, and Anaximenes. The island of Samos hugs the Turkish coast; it is visible from both Ephesus and Miletus. St. John, author of the Bible's nightmarish last book, is said to have chosen Ephesus as his place of burial.

99 Buddha.

The church of Ephesus is one of seven to whom John addressed his Revelation. It is the site of several early Christian councils that struggled with the question of Christ's dual nature. A local belief holds that Mother Mary died here. I pick up a tourist brochure and read that the Christian doctrine of the virgin birth of Jesus was established here at one of those church councils in ad 431. Though a secular state, Turkey is 95 percent Muslim, and is perhaps more forthcoming of quirky or anomalous bits of Christian trivia than, say, Greece or Italy might be.

Roaming the grounds around the great amphitheater I climb into a fig tree and dine on its fruit, ripened to perfection in the sun-spiked air. I sit perched on a branch, very still like an oversized gecko, and conjure apparitions of Roman citizens who move quietly and unseen among the gaudily dressed tourists. My Romans are taken aback by the intrusion of these cocksure yet docile, and far too numerous aliens, then put off by their ostentatious idle chatter, poor taste in clothes, and pallid, lumpy skin.

Hidden among the fig leaves I fill those Romans with me and me with figs, and watch the prattling tourists meander about filled with purpose, yet—and on this I'd bet all the figs in the Aegean—purposelessly. *Sorry, buds.*

Bus Grinds

The plan is to travel as quickly and as cheaply as possible back to the spicy cultural stew of the Indian subcontinent. Next leg: an all-day, all-night bus ride across Anatolia/Asia Minor of old, otherwise known as Turkey. It is the western-most area of continental Asia.

Throughout the day my mood has been tempered by the random rhythms of the ride. The winding, climbing, and dropping are pretty much non-stop in a landscape that cuts the sky with a million craggy knives. The vast Turkish peninsula is a choppy sea of frozen rock much like my own BC, only warmer, drier, and, not least of all, filled with Turks. The bus is comfortable enough and not crowded, a Mercedes with plush seats. Sunk deep into my seat I nod off, even though the road mimics the path of a drunken honeybee cruising a meadowland of overripe blossoms. A warm, humming capsule it is, barreling through the great out there and as well, for some who have fallen asleep, via dreamlands on the inner front. Or, goes my morbid whimsy, perhaps it is a troubled womb carrying forty or so marked embryos. Bus rides on mountain roads in Asia can arouse seesaw feelings. *Is this the one? Freedom's last call?*

I wake up at 3:45 a.m. I look around from my usual position on buses (for the last few trips I've been given seat number thirty-eight, thirty-nine, or forty, on the curb side near the back.) Snoring bodies hang limp. Who knows what phantasmagoric freak shows buzz away behind the daily veil. Moments ago I woke with an unsettled feeling, as if... *as if something ain't right.* Yet all looks fine.

Then—tip, bump, skid, thud-thud—crash! Our bus veers off the road and onto the sloped dirt shoulder on the upside, and not into the deep gully opposite. We scrape and whack along the rock face at high speed. Everyone is knocked awake in a mad chorus of yelps and cries. I hold on, noting as we bounce along the mountainside that *this time, we will live.* Holding the bar of the seat in front, I ride the heaving floor half standing, like a quick mogul run on skis. Alert and excited, and curiously ready for it, I've been awake for ten or so seconds. At fifty miles per hour it takes several jolting, crashing scrapes before the fully loaded bus grinds itself along a wall of rock to a full stop.

The shivering and the shocked stumble out into the thin, cold air to stare at a bus that leans wrongly on the side of a mountain. I wonder if I awoke at the precise moment the driver nodded off. I climb down, mulling over my peculiar good fortune, one that seems to have held trauma at bay. The men work to tip the bus back. I watch from the road as the fear-stricken are comforted; a few of the women and children are huddled down, whimpering and weeping. The men work together wielding prying tools, using brute force. The only foreigner on board, I feel I must keep a respectful distance in this hour of high feelings.

Within the hour, as the first glow appears over the east, we're humming along the highway again, forty-three wide-eyed embryos in a scraped and bent capsule.

Importer/Smuggler

At the Turkey-Iran border I'm approached by a shifty-looking, smartly dressed Iranian a few years older than me. He beckons me over to the tall wire fence that separates the two countries. It is a desolate border crossing. We talk, he in Iran with a sketchy grasp of English, and me in Turkey with a sketchy grasp of his intentions. He asks, in a hushed and hissy voice, if I want to make an easy one hundred dollars. Never mind I'm at an international border where both sides are likely to view me as an infidel. All I need to do is bring a car into Iran in my name. *Simple as mutton rice.* He infers it's a common scam: "Absssolutely no problemss to you, we do tooo many year, I promisss to you."

I recall my bout a few months ago with Hayla and the Pinto, back a mile or so down the long hill in this vicinity of Mount Ararat where danger is said to await the naïve traveler. Here is a stranger who wants something from me, moves like a human snake dressed in pimp's clothes, and makes me a promise, all in less than a paragraph. He introduces his father, a large, serious man standing by and gazing toward the distant hills. Maybe his gaze is an impatient one, but something honorable in the demeanor of the older man, who speaks no English, has me considering the proposal. After a minute of the son's dramatic pleading, his near whining, I consent. Relaxing, he introduces himself as Javaz. He says he was educated in the States and worked in Germany, "Where I have girlfriend."

He tells me to wait while they come through to the Turkish side. Then he fills me in on the rest of the deal, the hitch. We will return to Erzurum, a half-day back into Turkey, to record in my passport that I'm importing a vehicle. Sounds crazy, and I suspect I'm maybe halfway there, but I agree and trust them for now, as much for adventure as for the cash. One hundred dollars isn't much but in Asia, especially India, it buys as much as two months' traveling. It's been some time since I've replenished my stores, and given my increasing delight in life on the road, a scarcity of funds looms in the foreseeable future. A two-month extension of my magic carpet ride? *Giddy up.* Seems a more than reasonable return for what might even become an interesting diversion. Never mind that I'm doing a U-turn within a U-turn, which will result in heading in the direction opposite from my journey back to the East, smack in the middle of a not-so-fondly-remembered wilderness region. A readiness to respond to quirky turns of the road clinches my decision to go. In this sort of quasi-surrender one is more likely to sideline expectation and invite experience.

We take a taxi back into Turkey in the looming darkness. Dad decides that we will spend the night in the town of (starts with a dog, ends in a zit) Dogubayazit at the foot of the legendary Mt. Ararat. No travelers in sight, and only slithery Javaz speaks *some* English. I sleep like a babe.

The next day my passport disappears in the Iranian consulate in Erzurum. When I haven't seen it for over an hour, after handing it to some half-lit clerk, who's now conducting whatever affairs behind whatever closed doors, I conjure a larger picture with small, dorky me sitting in a phantom zone with no legal relevance. I get up and wander around the place, go down a hall or two, open two, three doors until I find a guy behind a desk. I'm quite anxious, asking pointed questions as to the whereabouts of a certain thin, black global ticket with my name on it. Alas, my fears come to nothing.

Back in Dogubayazit it's getting dark again, but this time the old man decides that we will continue on to the border. A taxi driver brings along a buddy who sits in front with him. We three cram into the back of the small cab. I've mentioned that Pops is *large*.

The driver makes what seems like an unnecessary turn off the main highway onto a dirt road. It's a black night with no moon. I see only stars, and by their absence, the shapes of mountains. It's a barren landscape and the air is cold. The two in front stop talking as soon as we leave the highway and remain silent as we drive along the bumpy, dusty track.

When we're dropped off at the border over an hour later I ask Javaz if he was suspicious of anything back when we left the main road. He said he was, and interpreting his father's sudden, spirited interjections, describes how the older man took out his knife and was poised to sink it into the driver's friend's neck "if need be, and it wouldn't be the first time I had to kill a man." The old man looks away, as if from all the goodness he once believed in. Did I say, "something honorable"?

At the Iran border the customs man inspects the car's import papers. He looks at me with suspicion, or disdain, then begins to search my pack roughly as if expecting to find an automobile hidden in there. Amazingly, he doesn't find the two extra cameras I have bundled tight in my clothes. (While in Italy, having glimpsed on the horizon the dwindling of my gold-dust trail, I sent home for my extra cameras as part of my plan to extend the noble dream by selling them in foreign-goods-hungry India. Their value should approximate another several months' traveling.) Handling my lumpy clothes as if feeling their suspicious weight, he speaks to me in Farsi with a sardonic tone while eyeing me with contempt. In the middle of this, Javaz's father passes a good wad of bills to the griping official, who swiftly pockets it without breaking character. Feigning confidence, and enjoying a moment of private humor I imagine his words: "There *is* no car in here! Foreign infidel prick bastard! Get out of my sight!" *Phhewwh!* Under the threat of a foreign jailing I muster some pretty good acting skills.

Me and my cameras, Javaz and "our" car, the crumpled bills passed surreptitiously from old Mr. Murder to the customs man—a proper little scam is neatly tucked away behind the surface of many things. Who knows? Maybe the huffy agent felt two heavy items bundled in my clothes, which is why he played out his displeasure with such drama, bouncing the bundles in his hands while speaking in Persian for them to hear—and to persuade some extra cash out of Javaz's old man's wallet.

Perhaps my good fortune took a giant leap forward the moment I agreed to their car deal proposal back at the border. *What a world! Oh, what a world!* [100]

Tehran

Javaz's family treats me well enough in Tehran. Their peculiar hospitality puts me in the ground-level basement of their home, a roomy, two-story tenement in a middle-class neighborhood. They have a small backyard/patio done up nicely in concrete and shrubs, where I sleep under an eave with the stars and a cruelly tethered chicken. I reckon it might be a pet, but within days, after reefing on its own neck every time I show up, it dies unceremoniously. *Worst relationship ever.*

On the first day, I eat with them. The sisters are gorgeous, and it's hard to not notice this. It's important, I reckon, not to look, *hmm*, three times at them. I figure twice is okay—a good compromise. Well, I guess not, since we all soon discover they don't want me sitting with their women. Never

---

100 The last words of the wicked witch of the west as she melts into oblivion, from the TV movie of the book *The Wizard of Oz* by L. Frank Baum.

mind my hippie/riffraff aura. After that initial communal luncheon they bring my meals downstairs where I eat alone. Two or three small bowls of tasty fresh herbs complement the rice, vegetable, and mutton courses. Spices, butter, and alien sauces top the scrumptious dishes. *Mmm-mm.*

One afternoon the extended family gathers on the patio, the women behind shawls. It might be a special occasion. Remembering my own family's flamboyant and heavily populated Sunday gatherings, it's hard to say. One of the older men hauls out a full-grown ewe they had stashed in "my" bathroom overnight. He slits its throat like he's done it a thousand times, cutting with thoughtful deliberation, meticulous and slow as if to savor a cherished interlude, one on one, while the beast shimmies and jerks between his legs. Little children watch its pulsating body with gleeful calm. Streams of blood squirt rhythmically from its gaping throat in wondrous, sunlit arcs. Their festive tranquility attests to the therapeutic benefit behind the grisly process. I, too, grew up witnessing the unsanctioned butchering of pigs, deer, and countless rabbits and chickens on our small city lot on the outskirts of Metro Vancouver. We were immigrant-Italian hillbillies letting it all hang loose in the Canadian West. But here in Iran, where I'm a world away from that life and knocking about like a vagabond on the outskirts of theirs, it feels like a new deal altogether.

After the head is finally severed, two boys kick it around like the World Cup's gory future. Thick splotches of blood pool on the concrete. I think it's the eerie, blank gaze in the lifeless eyes, which moments ago were tense with vitality, that especially delights the kids. The adults don't seem to mind, or even to take notice, really, that blood sprays a whirly-gig pattern all over the party.

I sit under my eave at the edge of the gathering. Reluctant to pull out my camera, I do a pretty good ink drawing of the whole affair with the sheep's carcass in the foreground. I'm sure they're ignoring me.

WHATEVER BUREAUCRATIC TANGLES are being untangled in this car-importing scheme, it takes day after *day*. I'll have to be patient with my little investment. Javaz takes an interest in keeping me entertained, or perhaps out of trouble's way.

We often take to cruising the streets in his car. Whenever he sees an opportunity to pull up close to a woman dressed Western style, with leg and knee showing, he slowly follows along, talking in a tender, low voice for a half block or so. She'll occasionally turn and smile but never say anything. Eventually, curious if only about the sheer volume of his words, I ask him, "Javaz, just what are you saying to these women?" He replies matter-of-factly, or merely tolerates my unaccountable dullness: "Oh, you know, jussst I ssay, 'You very be-*au*-tiful woman.'"

I tag along to a wedding party. As we enter, the male-only guests are sitting at a large oval table, and all as one are possessed of an awkward, bewildered, or anxious (any such combo) vibe. Quiet when we walk in, I'm sure I've made them even more tense. Necks are stiff, no one talks, and eyes twitch randomly about the room like they're all hooked up bio-electronically and there's a bad short. Laughter can be heard coming from another room, squeals of joy escaping from rapid-fire conversations—the women, of course. How we want to break free from our morbid prisons and swim, entwined in their limbs—*yes, yes, I do!* Their levity makes our unnatural quiet seem even more neurotic. On the streets, that is to say, politically and physically, the women are the more disadvantaged. But this schizzy party speaks of quite another side of things.

Or maybe the groom is bummed out for some reason. Blind guess, but it fits the picture. Alas, with sensitivity and grace, Javaz excuses us, making our weird little visit a brief one.

ONE AFTERNOON HE and two buddies meet up with three gals. One, slimmer and more attractive than the others, keeps staring at me with an anguished look. *Don't umm, know...* I look away. Interrupting everyone, she steps forward and talks directly to me with a desperate intensity, but in Persian. *Hello?* When I ask, dumbstruck yet intrigued, Javaz says she's asked me to marry her. He's quite amused, as if she just walked on stage with her skirt tucked in. This Persian babe is off the beat, clearly unconcerned with the social implications, whatever she's saying. *Is Javaz bullshitting me?* Her eyes are troubled yet clear and strong, almost hypnotic. She wants something from me. I listen, yes, but... *a-no a-speek Ing-gliss*. I wonder if she's intelligent and liberated beyond her ken, perhaps looking for a way out. I am moved, drawn to her eyes and to her courage. But not so foolish as to act out.

I'm often with Javaz and his pals, cruising the city in one of their cars. Occasionally we get high; seems like no big deal. While driving in central Tehran I look up at an ominous-looking fortress sitting atop a hill. All around the base of the hill stand squat buildings that look like army barracks. A tall barbed-wire fence encircles the complex. I query Javaz, pointing as we drive around it. "Oh, that is the palisse of the shah. Very be-*au*-tiful palisse." End of conversation.

Walking on a downtown street yesterday I noticed a government propaganda segment on TV in a home electronics store window, an eager audience standing outside. Shah Reza Pahlavi, dressed in a smart-looking gray suit, was sitting in the sleek cockpit of a fighter-bomber plane, probably a recent purchase from some Western arms pimp. Shifting levers and pushing buttons, he was as gleeful as a kid at a video game terminal, while his own prepubescent son stood by stoically.

Perhaps naïvely, I ask Javaz and his friends what they think of their Shah. From a noisy, laughing affair, our conversation plummets to the parroted, "Oh, we *love* our Shah" from each of them. They can't be sure who I really am. The lethal eye of SAVAK, Iran's covert intelligence agency, is surely resourceful enough to employ a mangy Western agent like me.

Ayatollah Ruhollah Khomeini, living in exile in Iraq and then Paris, won't show up for another two years.

Palaver

On occasion I wander the streets of Tehran on my own. One afternoon I stroll through a ritzy gateway off a downtown side street. I approach a table occupied by a solitary older gentleman dressed in a formal suit and introduce myself. He receives my somewhat audacious appearance with courtesy and grace. White haired, with a gentle face and rotund physique, he tells me he's an Iranian diplomat on holiday.

We delight in conversation for the duration of several beers in the cool milieu of the "higher," more moneyed classes. Sitting in comfy chairs in the shade of a great umbrella we speak of the relative sway of different cultures, and of how it is we enjoy, on this day, the odd privilege of perspective to even address such things. Our present circumstances, our place in our respective societies; we could hardly be more different. For an hour I'm held in a view of a meeting of minds—a razor-thin passing in a wide multiplicity of human life that goes back many thousands of years, and could continue for as many more.

But alongside the craftings of quality, both in the hotel's adornments and in our unexpected conversational pleasure, we share an illicit moment with a demonized substance: our beers. Here in the vast lands of Islam, the reputations of alcohol and cannabis are reversed from those in the West. A tall hedge is no barrier to the human noises of a sharply divergent world moving to and fro on the street, a mere few meters from our mugs.

Soccer Game

I tag along with Javaz and the guys to a soccer game. The packed stadium is fancy and new, like so many things in a society suddenly awash in petroleum moola. Oblivious as I am to the names on the jerseys, I won't be doing any cheering. On the other hand, the spectators are themselves a spectacle. We enter just before the gate guards begin turning away a steady river of fans.

One is stationed near us, visible from where we sit. Initially, he refuses entry to each person in line. A discussion ensues, with all manner of gesticulation and persuasion heaped high and mighty by the fan seeking entry. If the performance is worthy, the guard lets him in with an assenting nod. Of course, those in line behind the performer have the best seats. They await the results of the exchange in earnest, listening to every word, studying all subtleties in an effort to gauge the mood and personal quirks of the guard in order to improve their own chances for entry. It looks like blatant corruption, but it's *too* blatant, too sporting. And quite separate from the game Javaz and his buddies are wrapped up in. I'm engrossed in the socio-drama at the gate where another fan does his bit—arguing, pleading, maybe stooping so low as to beg. But alas, the performance doesn't cut it and he's firmly turned away. The guard's decision is binding and, once delivered, is not questioned. This goes on for most of the duration of the game, with perhaps a third winning entry to the already overcrowded soccer bowl.

"Sorry, we're full": this is the way of the West. Black/white, rational, tidy, and, perhaps, fair. But such is not the way at this game today. Each encounter appears as a unique situation to be dealt with on its own merit. And it is uniquely entertaining. I fancy that it reveals something of the character of each fan, and of the Iranian psyche as well. Each person seeking entry performs a drama of influence and charisma; it is an opportunity to display one's powers of reason and persuasion while the keenly observant guard stands in final judgment. Whoever wins is as fair as nature's untidy distribution of cunning, talent, and wit.

Later it is suggested by a fellow traveler that Persians enjoy an acute appreciation of the dialectical process and emotional suasion. A certain pride is taken in the skills of argument and bargaining, a pride and skill that is not so vivid in the Western mind.

Camera Thugs

Two weeks after our meeting at the Turkish border, and after repeated queries from his polite but persistent Canadian guest/business partner, Javaz takes me/him to the city bazaar to exchange Iranian rials for US dollars. Terse and impatient, his attitude spells out something like, "Oh, you want I get money? Okay, we go get money. *Fucking prick.*" He is resentful, grudging, as if conceding defeat; that handing over any money under *any* circumstance... can never be right.

I won't attempt to imagine the bureaucratic complexities that come with an official deal made between a foreigner and a native Iranian involving the importing and transferring of ownership of a new automobile from Germany, initiated in Turkey and resolved here, in Iran. But apparently, the deal is done. Mind you, I've yet to cross the Afghan border hundreds of miles away to see if I really *am* free to leave the country. *Dude, are you really so dull?*

And I still have those cameras in my backpack. Yeah, the ones I sent for in Italy and smuggled into this not exactly lenient nor observing-human-rights-laws kind of place. I reason, since I was lucky entering Iran (that border guard *must* have known) but can't count on a repeat performance leaving the country, that maybe I should sell them here in cash-ready Tehran. The new giant question mark in my passport—a whole page of Persian squiggles and stamps and a picture of a car—has something to do with my wanting to unload my (illegal) cameras here. Not feeling the *love*. The border crossing between the cities of Maschad on Iran's northeast frontier and Herat, Afghanistan... *Just who do you think you are, you twisted little Canadian infidel bug? You want to profit against the honor of Allah's own soldiers? Now it is the cameras of Satan you wish to peddle on the backs of our hungry, holy children!* A few whimsical thoughts, I'm scaring the shit outta me'self.

It's clear: get rid of the cameras. Within minutes I find that the underground marketplace is never more than the flash of a camera lens away. Somehow, my Iranian agents misunderstand (uh-huh) the price figure we're dealing with and, after the sale of my cameras, they come back (like a *doh!* afterthought) to demand a commission. They had given me our agreed sum and then left, so with their return it all looks a bit stupid. But stupid can be dangerous.

Three of them corner me in my hotel room and warn me to cough up or else. The taller, younger one steps forward. I respond intuitively with what he isn't expecting: I speak without fear or anger. "It's *your* mistake," I tell him. "I was clear on price. You were free to jack it up. I will *not* give you more." In another time or situation I might hand over half my cash, but a sense of dealer's honor has taken hold. I stand there, eyeing them with the cool poise of a (perhaps vegetarian) James Bond type. *Respond intelligently even to unintelligent treatment.*[101]

They leave, vowing to return. I leave very early the next morning. There's nowhere else to go; I'm in the only available alternative to Amir Kabir, the large budget hotel in central Tehran where all scruffy young travelers are herded. That alternative is a much smaller hotel, an over-flow joint across the street, where I'm staying.

I don't carry a weapon. No, I carry not even the thought. Not in that room, not in the dark taxi with knife-wielding Pops, and not with Hayla while being stalked by those drooling hyenas de Pinto. Carrying a weapon, perhaps even considering carrying one, would be the effect of

---

101 Lao Tzu.

a radically different mindset than the one I've enjoyed in these travels. Who knows if and how such a mindset would alter my behavior and elicit different interactions with the world at large, or responses from those three in the Tehran hotel room.

All goes well at the Afghan border. I never set eyes on "my car," but I can add smuggler and auto importer to my motley resume.

Afghanistan 2

From the west, Afghanistan appears like a mirage of the mystic past. The desert wind blows in on the shadow rhythms of chaos, and it fills the countryside with whispers, sighs, and echoes. It informs me that, as Iran fades behind, a kind of subtle cultural shift is emerging. It comes so suddenly, and the contrast is so great, that I feel it as a physical change in the air, although surely it is a mental phenomenon. As the new scene rises my eyes feel like they're coming clear, the muscles in my face softening.

In some ways the cultures of the two nations, especially in the region of their border, are similar. Both are Islamic, speak Farsi and Pashto, and share similar geographies near the edge of a vast Middle Eastern desert. What then, can account for such contrast in social ambience? Perhaps it is simply that they are two different countries, each with its own peculiar political and legal systems. Iranians are mostly of, and make up most of the Shia Muslim sect, while the Afghans, like the majority of Muslims, are Sunni Muslims.[102]

Yet perhaps a more tangible story is described by the customs buildings. Iran's: sprawling modern concrete, plumbing and electricity, late-model cars and buses parked outside. Afghanistan's: old brown shack, outhouse, maybe a donkey tied up in the back where an older-model bus comes by every once in a while.

And, as far as anyone knows, the region's deep pools of black gold do not reach beneath Afghanistan.

---

102 The two sects disagree on the prophet Mohammed's lineage, but this is disputed. A controversy surrounding the relevance of the prophet Mohammed's lineage in regard to the Sunni and Shia sects, from *River in the Desert* by Paul William Roberts, p. 191.

Going through Iranian customs heading west, as I did several months ago, is to be reorientated under the hard and critical eye of the modern realm. Iran's vainglorious facility is equipped with the tools and personnel to intercept drug smugglers.[103] Last season, traveling in the opposite direction, the first thing I saw was a schlocky tribute to the modern legal mindset, a kind of Museum of Fallen Smugglers. As the queue for Iranian customs crawled along a tight and winding hallway, travelers were treated to a showcase of past busts, with plenty of time to study the failed efforts of previous smugglers. Behind a long, convoluted bank of Plexiglas cabinetry were displayed peeled-back, thick-soled shoes, a broken guitar, a slashed gas tank, an open camera, dugout books, and more—all caches for attempted hash or heroin transport to the lucrative European market. Rumor has it that someone keeps constant watch on the queue from behind a one-way mirror. *Like candy from a baby.* Easy enough for hidden eyes to detect nervous twitches and shifty movements in rookies who assume no one is watching.

In contrast, when I open my passport at the Afghan border, the stamp that the wizened, colorfully dressed old man holds in his hand appears as a zany sample of modern toolmaking in the dilapidated old shack that is the customs building. Iran, with its newfound oil, is a nation caught up in the fever of modernization to realize the dream of becoming a "regional power." I heard it on a TV facing a downtown Tehran sidewalk, and on the streets. Afghanistan, one of the poorest of nations, operates on medieval technology well into the 1970s. Crossing this border is like stepping from one century to another. Gone is the widespread, frenetic energy of ambition-for-profit, gone are the many crass exploits of a growth-driven, technology-crazy world. Simplicity's own fresh wind seems to blow away the tarry fluff from my mind.

I romanticize a kind of mechanical simplicity, it's plain to see and easy to admit. Yet even as I relish the absence of modern clatter, I recall the bright ring of phosphor-bronze guitar strings, those deadly sounding speakers, German camera lenses, and the heavy intricacies that must be engaged and exploited to make these things available to me.

103 A small serving, perhaps, of the fruit of their liaison with the US. Yes, in the mid-1970s, USA and Iran are political allies.

SINCE REENTERING AFGHANISTAN on this return journey it's clear that my mental funk back in Greece indeed was an effect of culture shock. Until stepping away from the West I'd assumed it would be felt upon encountering stressful changes when visiting a foreign land. That returning home might trigger it as well was entirely unexpected. "Home" was adequately represented by my home culture in Europe, having just finished a lengthy stay outside Western (Judeo-Christian, "democratic", industrialized, capitalistic) culture. Leaving the West once more, I'm sure that this is what happened back in the land of Pythagoras, Socrates and Zeus.

Here in Afghanistan the sudden absence of various media frenzies, of our ubiquitous, brash hunger for consumer goods, and of our peculiar takes on social glory, changes my experience in the world. Afghanistan is a country on the edge of that shift. Coming from Europe it is the first taste of a social reality that has changed little in centuries.

Back "Road"

On the eastbound path Afghanistan's first city is Herat, my favorite each time passing through. Various cities have occupied this important center of Muslim culture, including one built by Alexander. Four crumbling minarets and the remnants of an imposing city wall dominate the skyline, the ruins of grander times that tower over today's humbler town.

This time through I hanker for less-traveled roads, with their sporadic schedules and ways. Looking at my map, a dotted line disappears a few times as it merges with the USSR border: the four-day route to Kabul through Mazar-i-Sharif. A dirt track winds through a mountainous desert along Afghanistan's northern frontier facing the Soviet republics of Turkmenistan and Uzbekistan.

The carrier is a small British four-wheel-drive pickup with heavy metal tubing welded over the box like a cage. Riders can stand between the chest-high pipes, but we lazy asses, every one, squat on the floor. At the beginning of the trip a dozen men are sitting, all cramped, every knee into every chin. The raspy murmurings of their Farsi tongue fills out a nice audio niche somewhere between the motor, the wind, and the thump-crash-bumping of the overburdened truck along the primitive road. Various pairs of squinting eyes slice at me from beneath crowns of twisted cloth. Ali Baba's *dudes*. Even though exquisite visuals are plenty, near and far, I dare not tempt what behaviors lurk behind their surly faces by pulling out my glittery camera. I must behave with respect and utter cool. This is my purest opportunity, ever, to practice the macho art of posturing. I am the only foreigner. Like them I remain unreadable, perhaps cloaking an unspeakable terror behind the hard mask. For the always-erect warrior, utter non-expression is the look of choice. And little is the choosing, so I play along.

Occasionally one of them pokes another, motioning toward me with a look of casual contempt. All subtleties have been dispensed with. I act correctly: I stare back. Getting better at practicing a routine, I give them neither fear nor aggression. Each time, they look away. Such a nerd growing up—*this is awesome!* The Afghans bear a collective persona of confidence and directness. I marvel at the feeling, or illusion, that what is present, eye to eye, is unmasked and authentic. There is little evidence of self-doubt, timidity, or skittishness.

All tough and bold one minute yet in the next, one of them takes off and rewinds his turban with the patience and fuss of a debutante at her vanity. But I don't chuckle and snigger; I don't nudge the next guy and point. One by one, like an ordered ritual, these badass dudes of the desert primp themselves in delicate silence. Each carries a small pocket mirror that doubles as a container for a green powder they use like snuff. The mirrors are tiny; only a small part of the face can be seen, so a path must be traced to get a good look, square inch by square inch. This handicap does not prevent numerous such sweet interludes along the way.

We pass through a few villages, stopping here and there to pick up a passenger or two. Never once in this candid view of rural Afghanistan do I see a woman. It would be considerably more stressful to be traveling with one now. Indeed, in this crowded truck, in this traditional Muslim region, I'm guessing that it would be unacceptable.

By evening we're in a tranquil valley. It is a lush oasis moistened by a clear river, a strip of translucent green in stark contrast to the sun-parched hills. We stop at a hotel next to river reeds that hiss like a great audience of snakes applauding our arrival. The dry wind blows hot and strong into my face and is laced with stories, as I imagine, and soon begin to believe. I could bow like the reeds, taking credit for it all. It's tough not sharing my humor with these guys. They'd probably beat me senseless.

I follow the crowd and take a seat at the open-air restaurant/hotel. We're fed a lumpy, tasteless meal they call mutton rice. I see no mutton. The hotel part: after supper the tables and chairs are removed, and we prepare to sleep right where we ate.

In the twilight, as we lie down, two local boys furtively eye up my pack and me. It is the one I traded my sleek new Western model for back in Penang. *Sigh.* I was new to the travel-in-Asia game, inexperienced and overly sentimental, so I thought mine was too pretty, too cocky. Since that day of dim judgment I've come to view this backpack as an exceptionally ugly object that violates all aspects of design, never mind my self-image as a reasonable bargaining man.

But to the boys my dull khaki blob is the snazziest thing ever. I sleep poorly, draped over it like a rag doll. Waking the next morning, intact *and* with my backpack, is a sweet gift indeed.

THE TRACK DETERIORATES. We get out of the truck a few times to cross dry riverbeds. There is no visible road. We walk along the base of a barren mountain in silence, me and these Central Asian rogues in turbans and robes. As the truck shrinks into the distance, a huge dust plume rises in its wake against auburn land and peacock sky. *See ya later, suckers!* It has to be my morbid imagination, since none of these guys speak English. Marco Polo passed by this way too, only in his day he knew not how long his journey would take. Nor did he know the location or even the name of his destination. I can drift along an unplanned reverie of the road that could last for years, seeking experience and freedom unimagined. But I cannot travel as Polo did. *As close as it gets?* I feel the loss of a bigger and more mysterious adventure.

We walk through a landscape that's lunar enough for Hollywood. Plaster boulders and giant scarabs are all we'd need for a good, schlocky sci-fi flick. The shifting colors, from the sun's rise to midday height and then its descent to darkness, create a rich palette of sultry hues, ranging from brilliant alabasters, yellows, and oranges to blues, purples, and blacks. In minutes a wrinkled terra-cotta hillside is transformed into a soft purple curtain. I turn, look back, and it's a dull gray cloud. Yet it's hard to see the changing. Info bits from high school physics appear on my screen like a jumbled alphabet. Words and hidden numbers float between perception and thought: optics, prisms, particles of dust, angle of light rays, humidity. The limitations of eye and brain, the mystery of interpretation. Reality and its representation via language and acculturated mental imagery.

But it seems that all of these measures do not reach sensuality nor account for beauty. Neither do they account for the subtlest feeling or fleeting moment of pleasure. It works wonders for many of life's tasks—build a bridge, discover a new medicine—but intellect is just one tool in the shop. Life itself is perhaps "suprarational."

The truck is now a mere speck moving along the base of the next mountain. I no longer hear the sound of its engine, just the padding of a dozen pairs of sandals in the dust. Except for the odd tuft of brown, crisp weed, the land is bare. The vast quiet of this barren wilderness is not mere emptiness out-there. The silence is also one of a different kind, one of perspective, of a quiet clarity gained after a time of isolation from the home world. I don't know where I'm going, and that's fine. *Freedom?*

But it's not without a sense of loss. Alas, I am *not* free. I remember my home, my people.

ON THE SECOND day we're crammed with more bodies. I count twenty-two men packed in tight like dinner rabbits. The heat and dust increase, and my anxiety reaches toward a new, mind-warping high. After a day cramped in an extreme squat with knees pressed into our chests, our bodies want to stretch. Demand it. And so what begins as a wave of uncontrollable shifting of feet and buttocks develops into a full-scale shoving match. Far past the point of civility, each man pushes as hard as he can. A half dozen faces grimace and drool mere inches from mine, lips parted and teeth clenched. A ludicrous mob of Moes, Larrys, and Curlys grunt and curse. I *must* push back. Caught in the madness, *my* teeth are gnashing. Music, philosophy, love—gone.

In one desperate snap I shoot up and stumble toward the back bumper, my shoes scraping backs and shoulders, ducking and holding the metal tubing. With the added burden of my overstuffed, unholy backpack, I nearly topple into the squatting mass of angry, groaning men. They yell and curse me, but they're trapped in a self-made pit of purgatory, so it doesn't matter. The boy who takes fares has kept his position standing on the back bumper throughout the trip. When I reach him he smiles, sharing a secret. From that vile pit of drooling scoundrels I noticed him the day before, his calm face a mirage of sanity. Now I stand with him, my body fully extended and reaching to rare heights where the air is clean and the view exhilarating. I feel like shouting my joy to the mountains and sky but know better than to shine upon the misery below. Getting dumped out here doesn't seem far-fetched. I peer through the dust at the mayhem, astonished I stayed there even for an hour.

On the third day, after determining we will part company in the afternoon, I pull out my camera. Several faces break into sneering grins. No words are spoken, but I catch their drift: "Sly bastard!", "Punk!", and "I should drop you and take that thing" are among the silent one-liners. I played it well, acting cool for the dudes, so I reckon I deserve the pictures. Their initial acrimony soon melts into plays of childlike competitiveness for my lens's affections, dispelling the notion of Muslims' camera-gonna-steal-my-soul phobia I've heard about from other travelers. I get shots of the men in the truck and at watering stops along the way. Hams at heart, they even set up a group pose.

Mazar-i-Sharif

In this northern Afghan city famous for its blue mosque, I befriend a couple and their male friend, all travelers from Western countries. I'm visiting them in their hotel room when a commotion in the hall grabs our attention. We open the door. Four Afghan youths move about in a state of irrepressible excitement, trying to catch a glimpse inside. Like a group of agitated hyenas spotting a limping calf in the herd, their heads bob up and down and back and forth. A lone woman entering a hotel with three men. Having heard a thing or two, they've likely jumped to some salacious conclusions. They're desperate for a glimpse of her, who should be beckoning *them* in as well, judging by their hopeful grins.

But as it is, we're merely exchanging notes on the different roads we've come along over a salutary pipeful of good black Afghani. The young woman senses their prurient interest and is visibly disturbed. Her man curses them and slams the door.

We don't talk about it. I believe that the scene we witnessed was more about "culture gap" than "gang of predators." Who knows? It could be a measure of both. Back at the Afghan border, leaving behind the technical smarts and *ka-ching* of the modern realm, I relished the ambient mechanical simplicity of this "undeveloped" country. Likewise, some in our modern societies hanker for bygone, simpler times.

Probably some things were simpler, others, not so much.

IN THE PARK next to the famous Blue Mosque I encounter a group of children, seven boys and one girl, about ages seven to twelve. The girl has not yet reached the transitions of puberty, still (but only barely) young enough to show her face in public. We spy each other from a short distance under shade trees; our mutual strangeness is the magnet that pulls them to me. I take a brochure of the area from my pack and hold it out to them. One of the older boys steps forward, and within seconds the group is entirely disarmed, crouching in awe over the glossy map, which includes various pictures of their hometown. Oohing and gasping, they don't notice me walking away.

On my way to the market area I remember I have only one key for my Western-made Guard padlock. I keep it and a simple chain for my backpack in unsecured hotel rooms and Indian trains when I sleep. I approach a man selling all kinds of colorful spices and show him my padlock and single key. It's easy to get across the idea that I have just one but want another copy made of this here key, without speaking. That is, when I have money, and those I am trying to communicate with are among the poorest and shrewdest. He points down the street, eyeing me with suspicion *and* respect. How I love the Afghans.

Walking while holding up the key for other shop owners to see, within minutes I am directed to a rudimentary metalworker a block away. The handsome, bearded old man is superbly photogenic, as is so much in Afghanistan. He pulls out a drawer that's full of all shapes and sizes of old keys and other assorted chunks of different kinds and thicknesses of metals. He rummages through the drawer looking for a key with the same blade thickness and warding as mine. Failing to find one, he compares the thickness of my key to that of various raw pieces of jagged, rusty metal. Deciding on a good prospect, he goes to work on a small slab with files, first on the grooves, holding my key next to his crude piece for reference.

Skeptical and surprised at his gung-ho faith in these simple methods I stand by, probably irritating the guy with what must appear to be casual amusement or maybe irreverent curiosity. Just when I wonder how long it will take, the old man stops working, picks up an old pocket watch, and points to where the little hand will be—two hours later—when I should return. He goes back to work only as I turn to leave.

I spend the time perusing the Mazar market observing the creative and industrious shop owners, who have so little to work with. Recalling my locksmith's meager resources I remember my own country, at the other extreme of a "wastefulness spectrum." The Afghans, by necessity, are masters at making the most from precious little. One has to look long and hard before finding any usable refuse in the dusty gravel on the sides of even busy streets. Any morsel of metal, rubber, leather, wood, wire, or string (plastic has not yet arrived) will be snatched up for raw material by some enterprising craftsman's apprentice on his way to work.

The key works fine. He charges me about forty cents, probably ten times too much. But I do not demean his impressive skill by bartering.

Chasing the Hindu Kush

Like untold invaders and explorers reaching back into prehistory, we head for the Khyber Pass in the Hindu Kush, the westernmost range of the Himalayan cordillera.

The tough Pathans control these parts—giant mountains, wild canyons, and stone-tough men. I remember passing through here a few months back on my way west. Evidently prearranged, the bus driver slowed down and stopped for a group of a dozen or so armed men blocking the road. Old single-shot muskets cradled in their arms and cold glints in their eyes, only two of them came aboard. They walked down the aisle past expensive German and Japanese cameras and gold necklaces hanging from our necks in plain view, to collect mere pennies from each passenger. It was a fee for service; the service of not pillaging completely, I reckoned. A more stable and predictable flow of people, goods, and fees is, presumably, advantageous for all. On their brief tour they took their time, studied each of us well. If they have enemies, they wouldn't be slipping by nestled among a busload of hippie tourists.

Coming from the west, the Hindu Kush rises in the distance toward a great continental divide on this most vast of continents. We rumble along on the last stretch of flat land east of Jalalabad, approaching the famous pass and the Pakistani border. I sit in the back, chasing the whole lot.

For some time now we've been followed by three vehicles, two local five-ton trucks and a camperized blue Chevy van between them. The trucks are carrying goods of some sort, probably potatoes or some other food, perhaps even contraband in the form of arms or drugs or both, or any of the above and more, or what have you, and maybe other things that I hesitate, or am unable, to imagine. It seems the three vehicles are working as a team, but the blue van looks out of place. I wonder if some misguided adventurers didn't ask enough questions when starting their journey back in Europe. Local transportation is cheap, and caring for such a valuable thing as that van would be a curse, requiring constant surveillance in most countries on the overland route. If the van is connected to the two trucks, a lucrative cargo might well be involved.

Inside the bus a serious murmur arises. I peer down the aisle and ahead into the road's distance. A large crowd stands blocking the highway up ahead. Sixty to eighty mountain men barely move aside, forcing the bus to a crawl. As we creep through the mob they thump the side of the bus with their fists and rifle butts, scowling and yelling. They're fucking pissed, but they let us pass. As soon as we do, still others poised on the sides of the highway roll huge boulders onto the road, stopping the two trucks and the van. They swarm the three vehicles, wasting no time pulling down sacks of whatever the trucks are carrying. *Were they telling us to keep our mouths shut about what we were about to witness?* Through the thick of it we speed off toward the mountains. I look out the back at a feeding frenzy amid clouds of dust.

Long after that strange scene has shrunk to a blurry speck, I still wonder about the blue van and those inside.

262

12. I Am That Bug

For all the good it'll do you, you can die.[104]

Self-guiding Whiff of Dahl

The scent of cumin has been leading me along through Greece, Turkey, Iran, and Afghanistan. After crossing thousands of miles of mountains and desert, and climbing a great continental divide on the biggest mass of dry land on the planet, we descend into the Indian subcontinent. *Lookin' for some soup, baba.*

Entering Pakistan from the Khyber Pass is to enter a distinct region of bio-Earth. Long ago, a great wafer drove up from down Australia way to ram into the largest landmass, buckling its edge to form the crust's biggest pile of debris. As well as blocking chilly air masses, the Himalayan cordillera is a barrier both biological and cultural. India and China are, globally speaking, side by side, and they are two of humanity's three greatest concentrations of population. Yet their racial and social contrasts can be attributed to the barrier formed by this kingly mound of tectonic rubble.

On the bent, weather-worn diamond of a wafer that did the ramming, a peculiar aura suffuses the general mix of plants, animals, sounds, smells, and the idiosyncrasies of its people. And—okay, I'll say it: there's something mellow about this land. It's as if the feline toxoplasma[105] swept the

104 From the song, "Everything Put Together Falls Apart" by Paul Simon.
105 *Toxoplasma gondii* has likely infected as much as half, some say 60 percent of the entire human population. Domestic cats play host to the little beasts, and humans love their kitties. The parasite appears to cause rodents to toss caution to the wind—specifically in regard to cat urine and cats themselves—thereby making them easy prey. The parasite itself does well in the mix reproductively. Many have wondered whether the behavior of humans is similarly affected. Infection with the toxoplasma has been associated with schizophrenia and bi-polar disorder. Lots of fun.

world's populations but somehow bypassed India. Here the elephants are not as big and wild as their African cousins. And in the Ganges River there can be found a docile little crocodilian—benign toward humans though it will feed on floating carcasses—called a gavial.

This land/country/civilization has spawned perhaps the least invasive of world cultures: the subcontinent's three million Jains aspire to the philosophy of *ahimsa* or non-injury to all living things, including, as exercised with a cloth mesh over the mouth, tiny bugs as one breathes. Half of India's population is vegetarian. In the golden age of the Mauryan Empire during the third century bc, Ashoka converted to Buddhism and established it as the official religion in a vast area including most of India. Navigating his newfound, enlightened worldview, he abolished the military.

But all this talk of a gentle land is beside the fact that knives and guns, mayhem, the gnashing of teeth and whatnot, are found in India as anywhere.

Yet to enter the Indo-Gangetic plain is to become engulfed in a legendary ambience. Stories, rumors, and loot gathered over millennia find their way onto the collective screen, which of course is directly wired to the personal. Gurus and jewels, *sati* or widow-burning, elephants and tigers… mystical powers. Hidden, enlightened vales. Or maybe not so much hidden as not exactly visible, one resonance to another.

But it wasn't Shambhala or Swami So-and-So that drove European explorers to circumnavigate and map the globe. It was spices: cloves and cinnamon, coriander, cardamom. Black pepper.[106]

Here rocks the cradle of Eastern religions: Hinduism, Buddhism, Jainism, and Sikhism. It is in this land that the numbers one to ten were conceived, including the great math hero, zero.[107] The universe is

---

106 Used to cure and preserve foods, this early "black gold" was so valued that it played a role in trade much as currency does. The first stock exchanges in Amsterdam and London were situated over vaults of the spice. It was, in part, control of the black pepper trade that brought power and glory to the city-state and maritime empire of Venezia (Venice).

107 With a nod to the Maya of Mesoamerica, also with a claim to zero. Of course, it might be taken as some kind of quantum prank to suggest to a Rishi of old that in the future there would exist a people, far away across the biggest ocean, whose civilization will have no contact with the Old World, who also will independently discover zero, and who will be called the "Maya." Great fun!

described in mythic cycles that tease the mind. The numbers extend, in the case of Brahma's own in-*carn*-ations, into the trillions of years (his breath-in/breath-out cover a mere few billion.)

Various traditional disciplines and studies of mind, or self, abound. The West has developed a degree of mastery over the physical world based on "observe and measure, demonstrate and repeat." The Indians have revelled in the study of *that which studies*, of the observer of the experiment; even of observation, or of consciousness itself. This is a tricky business that might just drive you *mangos*... or result in the creation of countless sects, millions of gods and the world's most ancient, extant civilization.

Or you might just catch a fast track to that rarefied club: the Enlightened set. Even though all tracks, slow and winding as you wish, ultimately get there.

LOOKING BACK, AS one travels from Greece into Turkey, a crossing of cultural significance is made: Europe into Asia, the Christian to the Muslim world. It is a turn of that great kaleidoscope, a shift in the color and hum of the backdrop of human life. I've followed a whiff of Indian soup that has lingered in my sensate memory for thousands of miles, as if it is the very scent of a certain grandeur of culture. Having come along a venerable path that weaves parallel to the Silk Road of ancient legend I am now in Pakistan, the modern designation of the lands just east of the historic Khyber Pass and the great continental divide. Once again, the kaleidoscope shifts.

I am in a different world, and *I* am different; the distinction is blurred. A blooming splendor is roused both within the journey of mind and across the ever-changing landscape. That this has something to do with leaving the West for the strange comforts of the unknown, I have little doubt.

Perhaps it is also into one's past, or one's latent aspects, that the self-as-traveler hungers for and delights in. The outward journey is likened to a "return" to an ancestral place, the East, and becomes an unexpected sojourn into the power of forgotten mythologies, symbols, and dream images. Perhaps these are the very aspects of a common heritage of culture that the modern mind has left behind with the rise of material prosperity and rapid social change.

It is only as a traveler that I speak, for even as this rich foreign land acts as the benefactor of challenges and growth for the receptive and grateful wayfarer, it is plain to see that what is novel and inspiring for me renders an alternate palette of compliance and conformity upon its own residents… as my culture does for me.

Malaise

I am light-footed, looking ahead. Feeling the brisk energies of an overall mood of desire and wonderment, I wonder where it is yet to lead me, and how it leads me on. I am not yet two days on the Indian subcontinent, heading for brunch down a city street in Peshawar, Pakistan.

In a heavy moment I'm engulfed mid-stride in a stink bomb of doubt and confusion. A dark mass moves across my soul, blocking the light of my day-to-day levity. *Why?* The sudden shift confuses; not only the bewildering gravity of this awful funk, but that I have no idea what is happening. Reason, logic—nothing. As long as I've been on the road, daily life has unfolded in dramatic turns, oftentimes euphoric. The feeling of inner prosperity is pretty much constant. Even the culture shock in Greece felt clear, in a way. Today, depression and mental fog close me in.

My gloom persists until night comes and (thankfully) I fall asleep. The next day I wake up very ill. With a vague sense of satisfaction at having gained the thinnest fluff of understanding, I reason that my smog of the previous day was the result of emotional sensitivity, a foreshadow of impending illness. Last year, while leaving Indonesia for Singapore, I came down with what had been hastily diagnosed as malaria. Since my present symptoms of nausea, high fever, and diarrhea are similar to the earlier symptoms in Singapore, and since malaria is said to recur, I assume that I carry the malaria beast in my blood and that it is enjoying a renewed and hearty swim. *Alas.* And so, ill as I am, I grasp for something better, something good. For I want to keep moving—away from the hot, grimy air of this old-world urban chaos.

I take out my trusty map. My eyes fall on the white caps of the Himalayas, then trace a path from where I sit in Pakistan's North-West Frontier Province all the way to the foothills. A town, Dharmsala, is the nearest dot at the end of the shortest route of road and rail into the hills. I fancy a comfortable rest in cooler, clearer altitudes, away from the ubiquitous blue exhaust and mind-numbing clamor of Indian cities. As sick as I am, if I keep moving, the trip should take only three days.

ON THE TRAIN to Lahore I climb up and lie on a wooden bunk, well above the lower seats toward a small margin of privacy. Cold and shaking, I note an uneasy alliance of flesh and mind, observing each as if there are two, or maybe three of me.

As the train departs, a flesh-and-mind companion appears. He plants himself square in the small compartment and stands staring, slightly upward at me. He begins to talk. No introduction. Separate he is, thankfully, but observing? Nope. Either Canadian or American, he doesn't seem to notice that I'm ill and on the edge of delirium. *Maybe thirsty?* Too weak to repel him, I tremble and offer an occasional nod. My brief moans pass as banter during his constant cackle. His pointless nattering gives him such delight as to be interrupted by neurotic fits of high-pitched giggles, which pummel my hypersensitive head in painful bursts. He is boisterous, and even in my wretched condition I find him to be an exceptionally rare and dull flowering of personhood. *Why, oh why, has the universe sent me its purest sample of buffoon at this time, on this train, when I am so weak?* The combo of his various noises, the train's pounding on the tracks, the fever in my blood... I could puke on his head. *I'd really like to.*

It's the end of the rail line near the Indian border but I need not get rid of him. On the platform my snail speed and hunched-over look wallops the sad brute into realizing I'm quite ill, after which he spins away ahead of me.

I haul myself into a horse-drawn carriage. One of the horses is a triumph of sensitivity compared with the buffoon. The steed notices me from the get-go. His head thrown back and his eyes intense, he knows I'm sick. From the first clomp of hoof I'm immersed in faith in his merciful power. Really, I am done with reason and I suspect the horse has, by some hyper-mystical quirk, appointed himself my guardian. My head bobs absently as I clutch at the carriage frame. The horse cranes his head back a few times to keep an eye on me; looks kind of freaked out by the sick cargo. *Whoa, buddy, take it easy. I was born in one of those horny Chinese horse years—I love you guys. Sorry I ate the horse meat me pappy brought home when I was a kid.*

I cross the border. A good leg of my journey to the Himalayas is done, and for a moment I savor a hopeful wad of strength that seems to grow in my stomach area. At the Golden Temple of the Sikhs in Amritsar, India, I sit in a shaded marble passage, almost passing out. I lean on a wall next to a pool of water that reflects intense, sky-filling yellows from the temple's delicate gold foil panels. *I could be in heaven, or inside the sun. Yeah, space… I am so sick.*

I shuffle over to a makeshift kitchen on the side of a walkway. Rumor among travelers has it that any Sikh temple feeds wayfarers in need without charge; my woebegone state could seal the deal. *Free mash.* But the sharp eye of the Sikh man doling out the food notes the relevant details: *backpack, camera bag, good shoes.* Besides, I'm a foreigner. *You'd better not be in need, you little gnat.* I pay. Lentil soup and unleavened bread; a little spicy, but easy to stomach. *Ahh, finally, dhal and chapattis.*

I find a hotel adjacent to the temple of glittering gold. Maybe the food made me feel sicker, or all that golden light fried a small province in my brain. Because now, deeper into delirium, I believe I'm in a good-will part of the temple complex, the whole thing a kind of floating utopia, a perfect place for me in this time of need. For sure have I been graced by a timely encounter with a society of gentle compassion, a holy wayfarer's sanctuary—*Holy good fortune, baba!* It follows that I'm invited in and entitled to stay free of charge. *Am I dead?*

My fantasy plugged tight, I refuse to pay the owner. I'm convinced that he and his sons, by asking for money, are taking advantage of a sick traveler. *The Shepherds of Utopia will not be amused. St. Peter, Ganesh—my boys.* In reality I'm as wrong as a blind man at a shooting gallery. Walking up the stairs (sleepwalking, really), followed by a trio of kindly hoteliers, I find a room and collapse onto the bed. I shiver madly but hold my moral ground as the three plead with me, an idiot Westerner who lost to high fever whatever power of reason he once possessed. I am daft.

A limp remnant of conscience is roused. I see the plain honesty in their pleas through barely open eyes, in a moment that could have been lost but instead is graced with the briefest shot of clarity. Down, down falls my cuddly Utopia of Myopia. The folly of my delusion for the past hour... *I am a sad fool, can't think... I'm done.* The father's eyes hold a look of compassion and frustration. The sons are at once patient, worried, and supportive. I pay quietly and nod away into blessed sleep. They could royally rip me off, but they don't; their goodness, at least, was correctly discerned through the fog of my delirium.

The next day, feeling buzzy and weak, I shuffle down a narrow lane looking for some kind of prescription drug to quell my misery. All kinds of business stalls crowd the tiny street: tailors and tea shops, spice peddlers and curd makers, chiselers and cobblers, candles and calendars and candies. Camouflaged among them I find a small doctor's office. Things are still thumping and trembling and spinning, but I have found the object of my quest.

The doctor tilts his head and peers at me above his reading glasses. "From where are you coming, *isn't it?* What country, please?"

I tell him about my previous bout of malaria or whatever those Jakarta mosquitoes injected into me a year ago. "Sure, yes... my parents were immigrants. I'm sure you'd also be welcome in my Canada. Doctor, sir, d'ya think I might be having a recurrence?" Cha-cha-cha-ing between Hippocratic Oath and hypocritical oaf, he's more interested in practicing English than medicine. The insouciant doctor writes, without even a pretense of diagnosis, a prescription for chloroquine, the quinine of choice used for preventing, and in higher doses curing, malaria. His mindless ease is an ill-chosen flappy jacket that doesn't look good on him. Yet he neither inspires confidence nor bothers me. Not that a lack of a prescription would prevent any pharmacist around here from dispensing whatever drug for a handful of cash. I take the prescription and drag off.

Night Train

It is dusk at Amritsar's train station. I ask around for Pathankot, the last rail stop on that shortest map route into the mountains. This will be an unreserved run, perhaps my most crowded. That queer Indian rail station anxiety is in the air.

I shuffle across the station and interrupt a uniformed railway employee, who looks very busy hauling a wagon load of luggage and boxes, to ask him about my train. He points out one that has just started rolling, stops, tilts his face to the sky and yells a few phrases in Punjabi. If a flaming vulture were to swoop in and suck the blood from his body through his eyes I would accept it along with the rest of this world's incomprehensible insanities, and move along resignedly. Loaded down by some unnamed god of traveling illness (back in India now) and a heavy backpack, I inch toward the groaning train like a deformed baby turtle toward certain doom. My foot falls upon the moving step of an overflowing coach. Another minute and I wouldn't have made it. I haul up with all I've got and park my ass on the second step. I go no farther. Even if I could afford to waste another breath trying, I can't. It's too crowded.

Throughout the cold night I ride the step, nauseous and shivering. Some angel of compassion wraps a blanket around my shoulders. I'm too weak to look up and nod in gratitude. All I can do is hold to my clawing perch and lean against the coach. My head spins and throbs. The clanking of steel wheels on rail joints beneath me is engagingly rhythmic. *Pile driving me' brain.* I wish the rocking motion would take me back to infancy and beyond, but all it does is jerk me back and forth, up and down. The speeding ground is inches from my feet. I banish the morbid thought of being punted into the darkness by some psychopath wanting a little more room. Soon enough the blanket brings a pinch of comfort. I'm as settled as can be on a humping, metal-toothed seat. In the first hour my wretched situation inspires marvel, then detachment. I make it all the way to a smile. But chuckling would hurt, and I'd puke, and *that* would hurt more.

I'm reminded of a fellow's account of *his* hell train, from Rangoon to Mandalay. (I missed that jaunt, regrettably, and second-hand memory thus substitutes for my loss.) The Burmese grant only one-week visas. Most travelers choose to endure the twelve-hour rail journey north to the nation's second and, as many say, more interesting city. The train is so crowded that once inside there's no leaving, not even to a toilet. The doors are held shut by packed-in bodies, as are those a few steps above me. Those so unfortunate as to have dysentery during the trip—as one unhappy lassie did—had to hang their ass out a window and hope the flow would spew out and away. The crowded conditions preclude options like dodging the spray, as my sorry storyteller wanted to do, being not far downwind from that otherwise alabaster ass.

Remembering his story brings another smile, and relief that I'm tucked in behind the end of the coach in case of any flying scuzz. I doze in and out of sleep.

Dharmsala

Early the next morning in Pathankot I catch a bus into the mountains. The town of Dharmsala is the point on the map I set out for three days ago in Peshawar. I arrive on a warm, sunny morning, a world away from the madness of Indian trains and cities.

I walk in from the outskirts of town, so perhaps I got off the bus too soon. By the side of the main road, overlooking a clear, spacious valley, I come upon a sadhu perched cross-legged on a giant boulder. The last traces of the morning's crisp fall of dew are all but gone. Puffs of white cumulus shift and swell over evergreen shades of conifers and tea fields, and above it all and behind him, a robin's-egg-blue sky. As I walk by, he takes a deep draw of *charis*, smiles, and greets me. I pass close enough for him to sense my infirmity; he does not offer the chillum.

I find a government tourist bungalow that's clean, so cheap it's weird, and staffed with servants. The manager sees that I'm of the untouchable sort, and as much as he might imagine refusing me lodging, quietly nods his consent when I ask for a room. Feeling rather alone and perhaps overly sentimental, I imagine a depth of compassion in his eyes. If these are self-serving illusions, I am nonetheless grateful for his kindness.

I visit the cook to plan special bland meals that I can stomach. At first I think he's compassionate, too. Then, as I make my wishes known, his face goes stupid and he smiles without speaking. After a minute he begins to nod rapidly, as if inviting me and my disease to leave his kitchen as soon as possible.

I take my bed. I don't know how this happens, but the next day a smiling blonde woman, twenty-ish and graced with the gentle and deep power of compassion, comes to share my room. Given my funky state, this is most unusual and unexpected. I have had no contact with any travelers since that boor on the Pakistani train. How is it that another person, a gorgeous woman, has come to share the room that I alone have booked? Did the manager, or the cook, send her?

Without being asked she brings me papayas and lemons from the market daily. She knows what my body needs even before I know what ails it. *She is the manifestation of the angels, baba.* By her accent I assume she's Australian, or maybe South African or Kiwi... there's a wispy softness in her speech, and my hearing is likely funked-out with the rest of me. Bad luck her coming along now—but not really. She exudes the aromatic force of great fields of roses crushed and mixed with Shakti's own goddess-grade pheromones—add hot morning sunlight and her slow, steady breath, her smile... I look on in amazement, but I see no wings. *Wait, what's that light around her head? Is that... no, is that a window behind her? Aw, I dunno, I'm wasted.* In my woebegone condition I accept her gifts of fruit, a very quiet and minimalistic conversing style, and frequent smiles that soothe my heat and spin the empty sky inside my mind. If it's possible for feminine beauty to tempt illness out and away, it will happen in this room. For three more days I lie on my cot while she nurses me.

After she leaves I recover my scientific perspective, takes less than a minute. The universe, seeing that I'm diseased and untouchable (and maybe wanting to twist me up some more after the doofus on the train) delivers the most beautiful woman available to help move me along, and chuckles indulgently.

The next day, the sixth or seventh since Dr. Whack in Amritsar, I look in the mirror and behold the golden pools of jaundice. My eyes are deep yellow. *The bloody doctor, and my own foolish presumption!* I should have said nothing. A side effect of the chloroquine I'm taking in high doses to treat malaria... well, I've heard that it's hard on the liver. My foxy "angel" did indeed bring me food as medicine.

A quick calculation: I must have contracted hepatitis in Afghanistan two weeks prior to getting sick in Peshawar. *Who might I have infected during the disease's incubation stage?* Proper thing I didn't follow my *schwing* after that hypnotic Irish chick in Kabul. I remember a couple in that very hotel courtyard. She was Australian, he, Italian. We shared a joint while I did a teeth-grittin' ear piercing on the guy with pliers, sewing needle, and flame. Probably drooled on his neck. By now they could be in Athens giving blood for an easy twenty-five bucks each.

BACK IN PAKISTAN, when I fell ill and felt compelled to flee the heat and grime of the plains, I focused on the straightest path to the Himalayas, to the first town in the foothills: Dharmsala. Though I'm familiar with the designation "Dalai Lama," I had no idea this had anything to do with Dharmsala, or that I'd be landing myself at his medical center's doorstep a few miles uphill from the town. The Dalai Lama's settlement in exile is in the Indian state of Himachal Pradesh, which lies between Nepal and the remote northern Indian state of Ladakh.[108]

In Dharmsala I learn about the Dalai Lama's exile-in-residence and that I'm a casual, ten-minute crow's flight from the Tibetan Medical Center of the Dalai Lama at McLeod Ganj, a small village farther up this very mountain. I haven't a clue about the nature of Tibetan medicine, but soon I'm on a bus heading uphill. The worst of my illness, the shakes and the nausea, is over. I relax into a debilitated yet surprisingly lucid state, as long as I keep my movements to a minimum. These last few miles above Dharmsala will be child's play after the hellish night train.

I'll soon be at rest, for a mountain road can go up only so far.

McLeod Ganj

Dharmsala is an Indian town, but the village of McLeod Ganj is almost entirely Tibetan. The bus and other vehicles come only to a turnabout point at one end of the main street. Otherwise, the village is free of motor wheels and, to the casual eye, from the rest of modernity. Affable folk go about their business among small, rustic shops on a narrow dirt street. The quiet milieu sends me back to medieval times, and my feeble state only serves to further adorn the illusion.

108 Ladakh, also known as Little Tibet, is home to a naturally intact Tibetan culture that survived the Chinese insurrection of Tibet in the 1950s. The people of Tibet inhabit a wide swath across the Himalayan cordillera from Ladakh in the west to Pemako, locale of the inaccessible "Hidden Lands" of the Tsangpo/Brahmaputra gorges.

Travelers stay in the one hotel/restaurant on the second floor above some shops. The hotel rooms are tiny; the footprint barely accommodates sidling along beside a twin bed. But this is more than compensated for by the views on either side of the building.

Inactivity is good in these days of bad blood and low energy. I spend hours at my window looking down over the back alley and long slope to the sultry plains and their infinite haze. A tribe of silvery snow monkeys passes through the treetops daily. Above them, hawks on the lookout glide on mountain breezes, dropping into trees with exquisite ease. But the master hunters' prowess is upstaged by opportunistic crows that follow and mimic with cunning flair. The crows fly right on their tails, so close that it seems a violation of interspecies boundaries. Playing the punk, out to nab what the larger birds miss?

We humans have it cushy. They say it all started with the plow: one clever thingamajig to do the work of many. Monkeys and crows work pretty hard for their grub. Millennia later and a few fields over from that first plow, this restaurant serves a wholesome variety of Tibetan and Indian foods. I'm sick and yet, for pennies a day, I get to eat as much as I want. Switch the channel and I'd be sweet pickings for monkeys and crows.

The customers in this joint are mostly travelers, many of whom smoke hash as if they're lounging in their basement dens. The restaurant tables sit along windows on the uphill side, where I spend most of my day fixed on the busy Tibetan street life below.

The occasional old man pulls into town from the mountains. Dressed in rags and animal skins, and with various implements for life in the wilderness swinging from his body, the incoming wayfarer looks like a clever chunk of mountain broken free and morphed into a human smile, now walking on two awkward sticks. Wizened, weather worn, and bearing the unmistakable countenance of transfixion, he shines with childlike awe upon entering the village after isolation in the wild, his eyes cranked extra wide by the sudden village racket. Travelers sitting near me, in their resin-induced reveries, in the seductive, cushy camaraderie of the worldly subculture of the road, seem not half as alive as these ruddy wanderers with eyes ablaze.

A town misfit stands for hours on the street below, moving along a few feet from one day to the next, looking frustrated and resentful. He wears clothes that are much too small. In the mornings he shivers and stares jealously at the Tibetans around him, who behave as if he's invisible. He looks up to my window and our eyes meet once, for a second or two. He turns away. For the next two weeks, as I sit in my spot like a pampered prince, never do I see him look back. Sometimes it's easier not to see at all.

I have nothing but time sitting out the hepatitis. I'm neither worried nor bothered by it. Instead, I employ my "untouchableness" in the service of my favorite pastime: sitting and watching. When I learned I had hepatitis, I felt my choices were either (a) fly into the coddling blankets of a Western hospital, where treatment for the disease is marginal at best, or (b) care for myself by resting and changing my diet to continue traveling. Without hesitation I chose to stay. Fortunately, by heading on that straightest path to the Himalayas, I headed straight to the Dalai Lama's clinic.

At the Tibetan Medical Center I meet the doctor, an attractive, strong-looking woman in her thirties. She comes close, looks me over and nods. With savvy use of very little English, she explains that "our medicine" knows and treats hepatitis easily, unlike "your" Western kind. She says that for Tibetans it's more like a flu, treated with a few herbs. She assures me that I'll be fine in two weeks. I'm skeptical. She gives me three kinds of dried herbs in spherical pills that are bitter and (because of their size) hard to swallow, to be taken twice daily. She says I can eat anything but to avoid greasy food and to wash the pills down with fresh mountain stream water (I use the hotel water.) I show her the vitamin B complex and "liver tablets" I bought in a Western-style drugstore in Dharmsala. She looks at them, brings them up to her nose for inspection, then screws up her face in displeasure. I trust the doctor and her large bitter pills, although for another three days I continue taking the vitamin B pills.

When I arrived in McLeod Ganj my symptoms were deep amber eyes, gray-white poop, golden-brown skin, cola-colored urine, and extreme dizziness from any slight physical exertion, even walking up two steps. I'm not sure it's the medicine, but as soon as I begin taking it I become alert and remain so for the duration of my stay. I'm easily more perky than the hash-smoking patrons languishing in the restaurant. The herbs must be stimulating my appetite, because now I eat like a dog, plowing through heaping platefuls of veggies and rice daily, even though hepatitis is said to kill one's appetite.

Every day I go for a walk. I say "walk," but it's more the look of a creeping shadow. Besides the main drag there are several short adjacent side lanes in this Tibetan village built on the saddle of a broader Himalayan slope. On one of my snail tours of the tiny, level part of the village I look through a window. Several Buddhist monks pulverize fresh greens on the floor with blunt wooden poles. On one side, round pills are grouped according to size and color, and in the middle of the room lie several piles of dried, grayish-green powders. On the other side are heaped various fresh herbs. These are the several stages of herbal pill-making, and the men quietly making them.

Buddha's Boons

I'd bet that fourteen billion prayer wheels and a sixty-hour day wouldn't satisfy these devotion-jacked Tibetans. They'd still be making and spinning more.

They say that to spin one is to set a prayer free, which counts as credit in the next realm. And that prayer wheels contain a piece of paper with a prayer written on it. The devout walk around with a handheld one that, with a gentle flex of the wrist, spins prayer upon prayer, multiplying the good message *ad infinitum*. A brightly colored "prayer wheel park" sits directly across the street from my second-floor perch in the restaurant. The old and the hopeful walk through spinning numerous small, medium, and large wheels to their souls' content. I fancy hubs and axles and clever levers enabling the ethereal magic contained within the cylinders. These prayer works are housed at waist level in a meandering line, easy even for the frail of step to navigate and set in motion while walking. The same elders, mostly women, come several times daily to spend fifteen or twenty minutes spinning hope and faith into odds on a better life.

The main attraction of this public prayer wheel center is a separate building the size of a park gazebo. Open to the street, it contains a giant, multicolored wheel. Perhaps hundreds of pieces of paper tumble inside, or maybe a single huge one is heard in the heavens as a majestic chorus. The cylinder, about ten feet high and six in diameter, takes up most of the space inside, leaving just enough room for a devotee to walk around pushing a handle to get it moving. The top half of the cylinder is painted with oversized red and gold Tibetan script, the lower portion decorated with motifs of flowers, plants, and rising suns. Always the climax of the prayer circuit, the great wheel is easily moved. I imagine a greased bearing in its hub.

An old man enters the large wheel house to find three children laughing and romping noisily inside. They run around the wheel, spinning it back and forth. The old man smiles without interfering, then turns to spin other prayer wheels. This happens again with another spinner, and another. Seems these Tibetans feel free *not* to control their children. Evidently, there is no sense of sacrilege or disrespect for the higher order of things. Like any habitual behavior, this seems a profound culture-perpetuating force.

ASHOKA, ANCIENT RULER of India's only Buddhist empire, invaded the territory of Kalinga, and it was the experience of this terrible battle that is said to have inspired him to convert to Buddhism and renounce militarism. His was, perhaps, humankind's most peaceable empire so far.

A week into my stay at McLeod Ganj I hear that some big festivities are in the offing, down the mountain a ways on a footpath in a different direction from the road in. My mental works, whatever their norm, have been laid humble by these affable Buddhists and more so, I suspect, by the bent flow of illness I now trudge through. Picturing the coming celebrations, I imagine a Buddhist hoedown; the silly word "kalingamazoid" loops into my fractured thoughts for a few hours. I settle on The Buddhist Kalingamazoid of '76. Who knows what jazzy meridians connect liver, brain, and Carl Jung's collective unconscious. For as I contemplate the forthcoming festivities, I am not yet familiar with Ashoka, nor Kalinga.

I prepare for an epic crawl. The fourteenth Dalai Lama will be making an appearance at the local monastery a half-mile away. My walk along the trail will be slow and laborious, for any increase in blood flow will stupefy my liver and produce a sudden, intense dizziness as a clear signal to *stop*. But miss this opportune Buddhist bash? I'll give myself plenty of time, and go like an inchworm if I must.

Walking down the gentle grade is not difficult, yet I'm passed by even the most ancient models on their way to the monastery. One bent old jalopy flashes me a brief and bemused side glance as he whizzes by like a Ferrari past a rickshaw.

The Tibetan Buddhist center-in-exile includes a large temple surrounded by acres of manicured gardens. On this special day they teem with monks dressed in crimson robes and bayonet-wielding Indian soldiers standing like wooden toys, all stiff and pompous in their crisp duds. Why all the guns? Maybe, unbeknownst to me, this is a notable affair, and the Indians are edgy about all the soldiers buzzing around just a few miles over in the part of China we know as Tibet.

A hum of energy ruffles the crowd: His Holiness has arrived. I've managed to squirm to the main entrance of the temple. The Dalai Lama sits cross-legged, chanting and swaying at the front of his great, loyal throng. The building is packed with monks and village folk moving in unison and chanting with their beloved master. After a period of rising, monotoned crescendo, the Dalai Lama stands and climbs, without a break in the puzzling rhythm of the chant, to a platform about eight feet higher. *Wait, is he… chuckling?* To my irreverent eye he's forgotten who and where he is and climbs toward freedom of the physical kind, vainly trying to flee the collective madness. *Everyone so attached… my children, do you not see?* But of course he knows his place, which is exactly where he sits to resume his swaying, perched on an altar at his symbolic "highestness."

It doesn't feel impudent to make light of these even-minded Himalayan Buddhists, who speak of liberation, not like I would with the Roman Catholics of my past, whose churches possess a gloomy ambience and whose claim on the affairs of your soul—which needs "saving" not liberating—feels like ominous surveillance that monitors one's every thought. With the Buddhists, such monitoring is left to oneself. And the Dalai Lama is such a chatty, laughy fellow, while the pope seems so somber.

By popular repute, Buddhism's collective soul is relatively free from the marks and smudges of inquisitions and jihads that blacken those of certain neighbors to the west. But this is doubtful. One hears inferences regarding violent conflicts with, and the subjugation of, the indigenous Bon-Po people in these very mountains centuries ago.

In any case, the setup is similar, specifically, to the Roman Catholics. Both utilize pyramidal hierarchies: a chief shepherd perched at the top, two or three tiers of governing sheepdogs, and multitudes of sheep. Perhaps the widespread tendency toward leaders and structure is symptomatic of the human condition itself, and not of any particular religion or region.

Another striking parallel is revealed in both religions' key terms: the Buddha and the Christ. For the words are also plain nouns, at least among mystics: *a* buddha, *a* christ. Perhaps these "plain nouns" carry the subliminal suggestion of the availability, in this life, of highest potential for every person.

It's clear the Dalai Lama's presence is an emotional experience for those standing near, the mountain poor. They edge their way closer, carrying me and my idle musings in the rising energy of their gasps and trembling. Their reverence for this man is profound, like that of a throng of children viewing the image of their smiling mother on a large screen after a long separation. Since this is no more than a casual look-see for me, I leave after a few minutes to make room for the more deeply involved. Hands down I'd win the Buddha's special door prize for "the most detached in the crowd."

Of course, the Dalai Lama is no mere man to them, being the present incarnation of the Compassionate Bodhisattva, a bodhisattva being one who refrains at the last threshold from attaining Buddhahood in order to aid in the enlightenment of *all* beings. Which, by definition, must include wolverines, bedbugs, sea cucumbers, and Hannibal Lector, to name a few in the running.

Now *that*—notwithstanding the question of the illusion of time—is one fine depth of compassion.

THE WALK BACK to the hotel is slow, for the path is on a gradual incline. Even a slight grade compels me to inch along, approximating the speed of a love-smitten slug.

At this pace, life is lush and *wide*. Clouds are *fast*. I see each small pebble, bits of glass, colored thread, and strangely shaped sticks. One by one they dance slowly across the stage and disappear behind the curtain. Some dried shit. *Ooh, now just look at that fine attention to form and function.* At this creeping rate, a tuft of weeds or simple blade of grass appears as a robust event. *Hey, little ant dude, wait up!* Occasionally, as air masses swing by, I stop to rest, all around me plants appearing as living explosions frozen in an earthbound instant. The peripheral forest sounds are just one sweet moment in a long-winded symphony that includes the formation of star clouds and knocking V-8 engines. I'm a conscious speck in a multitude of details that I don't normally see. I thank my sick liver for these revelations, for slowing me down from the frenzied human frequency that whizzes by this wildly detailed, intensely presented world.

Maybe this Buddha guy is having an effect on me. Maybe the Ocean of Wisdom[109] was gently lapping at my crusty shore as I stood back there, a young, irreverent foreigner, at the entrance to his temple.

EAGER TO TAKE advantage of any worthy diversion while sitting out my convalescence, I attend a lecture/class in which an eminent lama is the speaker. It appears that several peripheral events have been provided alongside the recent appearance of the Dalai Lama. Or maybe this is normal calendar fare.

Dusty sunlight streams through a small upper window in the squat basement of a stone building. I sit at the back of the room, listening with other, more devoted students. Most are Westerners with shaved heads, which alerts me to my own thick, lustrous locks and my (presumed) attachment to them. The students' general demeanor could be described as an easy combo of placid-detached-attentive. Reaching toward better observational skill, I would venture to describe my own as ingenuous-perky-hungry.

An interpreter is present. While he speaks I notice the lama's eyes darting around the room. A few times our eyes meet, but he seems preoccupied. His teaching suggests cultivating habits or virtues such as patience and moderation. Cultivating virtuous habits seems rather contrived, an errant groping at wisdom at best. Aren't they the effects of being enlightened and not the prescription for it? *But what do I know?* I'm thinking, forty days in the wilderness, years of ascetic living, getting

109 His Holiness, Tenzin Gyatso, the fourteenth Dalai Lama.

whacked on the head by a Zen master. *But these guys have been at it for centuries.* No, I mustn't put too much faith in my rookie take on these ancient, reflective disciplines of the mind. Besides, what is my preoccupation as I sit in the back? I continually scan for the female form beneath the shaved heads, hidden and beckoning for my attention, as I imagine it, from under thin folds of cloth. I am, in this way, perhaps "underdeveloped." And, well, I suppose honesty is a good start.

Is the Buddhist tendency toward analysis maybe not so good a choice for those who tend to overindulge thinking? Perhaps, I surmise, theirs is not my way, not my style of flag (as if I've made some meaningful study, and then choice, of flags.) I wonder if I'll ever go for any flag. *And just what flag do I presently fly?* I wonder if I'm too young and skeptical to take up the serious matter of enlightenment. I wonder about lamas and about llamas. I wonder about wondering so much. I exit the underground chamber, perhaps prematurely, or immaturely. Perhaps like a stray mutt. *I wonder.*

Then I wonder if the Buddhist Emptiness and belief in no-God is really just a question of semantics. *Don't believe in God but do believe in reincarnation? Interesting.* Perhaps these are devices designed to underline the non-reality of duality, of multiplicity, of the separation of self and what many label God. Emptiness might as effectively read "Stillness," "Presence," or the very Hindu "Non-duality." *Hmmm.*

THERE'S A PARTY a quarter-mile up the mountain, where I hear that some French and German travelers are renting a few buildings. Since I can't walk up a mountain, three guys at the restaurant offer to "push" me up to the party. Really. Mind you, there is no conversation going on in this restaurant without clouds of fine hash smoke permeating the mental firings. Except for mine—staying the course, of course.

The trail is wide and steep. The three take turns pushing me from behind as I lift each leg to step. This is the only practical way I can get up the trail without being carried or catapulted, so I thank them a few times, enjoying the views and this ridiculous manner of locomotion. Raise knee, raise knee, that's all I do. I even direct a serpentine path to help ease their efforts. Once there the three are exhausted. I'm feeling good and chipper.

The party is mediocre. There's an open field where travelers sit in clusters smoking chillums. Like I said, I don't smoke, for my liver is on the blink. I have yellow eyes, and I'm sure I make people nervous. Even the pretty gals look away. So I shuffle, on my own, back down to the hotel.

Shards of Wisdom

Through the thin wall separating my room from the next, I hear the clear harmonies and clever guitars of some of my favorite songs. I invite myself over and meet two couples: three Aussies and an American gal. Between songs, the first thing off their lips is an impassioned reference to their guru in Bombay, Sri Nisargadatta Maharaj. I've met various disciples, as one inevitably does in India, the world's leading source of gurus. The followers I've met so far have left me with vague impressions of a placid, drone-like vibe. Or, as in the Rajneeshees, a kind of hedonistic, ego-fueled hunger. Which, given the choice, I find easier to relate to.

These Bombay disciples exude a vitality and unaffected intelligence that seem lacking in most disciple-followers. I'm drawn by the music, so I sing along, adding harmony. I also play a few songs; we've grown from the same musical roots. Because we're in a hotel, they must play quietly. Even when they pull it down to a whisper they do so without diminishing their big emotional presence.

But I'm a stranger to the guitar I hold and the music that flares through, like *it* knows the way better than I do. Back in New Zealand I left music behind like an old skin. After weeks of carrying a guitar on my new overseas adventure, I felt its weight on my arm—in my life. Naturally, people would ask me to play a tune. But the traveling jukebox was jammed. *Why did I bring it?* I suppose I was reluctant to let go of what had brought private joy, even therapy, through my teen years. But on the road it wasn't private anymore. The guitar I carried became extra baggage, a timeworn burden. Since boyhood music came easily, as one retrieves a faculty already owned but somehow forgotten or stored, as Socrates argued.[110] But I did not take it further, not like others in my hometown who wrote songs and performed them, each

110 Plato, *Phaedo*, 72b–76b.

tapping a depth that eluded me. It was if the Muses[111] had overlooked me or worse, judged me unworthy. I was a mere dash of my father's musicality when he was my age, a minstrel for hire who played sweet emotional serenades on his mandolin to win the favor of maidens for his hometown fellow Romeos back in southern Italy.

So when a kind Kiwi pushed the buttons of the Canadian Wurlitzer he'd just picked up, the damned thing jammed. I was determined not to further taint one of the closest things to heavenly I'd known: making music. I left my guitar with some friends, then sold it within weeks of landing in New Zealand. Shedding the musician identity was a liberating act, a reassuring surprise on this brave new road of life.

But an awkward paradox looms behind that epiphany: music, by its nature, is itself liberating.

In this tiny hotel room in McLeod Ganj I play guitar, yes I do. It reminds of a pleasurable reunion with an old lover, or a psychic limb tingling in place of a missing one.

As for the four devotees, music is an extra, absorbed as they are in a world far more cerebral. They show me their Maharaj's recently published book of questions and answers, titled *I Am That.* (*What?*) I browse through a few pages. The words seem to strike the occasional small insight bell: simple, true-sounding rays of thought, or maybe shards of (what I take to be) wisdom flashing the odd laser of (what sounds like) truth. A few in my fond collection of thought bubbles quietly pop to join a growing heap of acquired, then discarded, knowledge. The so-called knowledge isn't the point. It's about old stories I borrowed and kept: joining the herd, unconscious agreements, and vague assumptions.

Yet promoting insights like these is true of many books and not a rare thing, I reason. And, tilting my head a bit, the words of this Nisargadatta sound like typical, slightly offbeat, eastern-mystical jargon. *Not sure what to think.*

And I like these four musicians/*sannyasins.* They tell me that in meeting their guru they found "a hole in the universe" and couldn't budge. Over the months they grew increasingly perplexed while chasing

---

111 In Greek mythology the Muses were the nine daughters of Zeus and Mnemosyne and were known as inspirers of creative arts in mortals.

the meaning of his words, looking to address "the nameless." They needed a holiday. When they were packed and saying goodbye, their master said something about going to Dharmsala.

I listen to what they say, but mostly I enjoy the four devotees' wit, their passion, and their music. Of course they want me to visit them at their master's pad in Bombay. I'm almost ready to move on, but I'm not sure yet if I'll be going that way.

I discover that I'm not comfortable with the concept of a guru. I was raised from infancy with a model for human perfection in the personage of Jesus, but he was said to be *the* savior, not some guru. Although I discarded that idea of specialness and exclusiveness back in grade school, it seems that my early conditioning into Roman Catholicism might have left a shadow, as evidenced in my squirmy reaction when faced with the idea of an eastern guru.

At least Castaneda's Don Juan had the appealing, impish qualities of the trickster, and an air of preferring not to bother at all with the dull, pesky Carlos.

WITHIN A WEEK and a half of taking the Tibetan herbs, my symptoms are almost gone. The doctor was right. Two and a half weeks after my visit to her clinic I throw on my pack and hit the road. You could say I was foolhardy to travel sick for three days across the grimy plain, hang limp on a horse carriage, and cling to an overcrowded night train to catch a bus... just to get myself into the mountains and their cooler, clearer climes.

But with the unexpected discovery of the Tibetan Medical Center of the Dalai Lama, the urge to keep moving resulted in a real boon.

The Greco-Aussie and I in the Himalaya

Traveler and locals on smoke break, Himalaya

Children on trail, Himalaya

Me on an Indian train

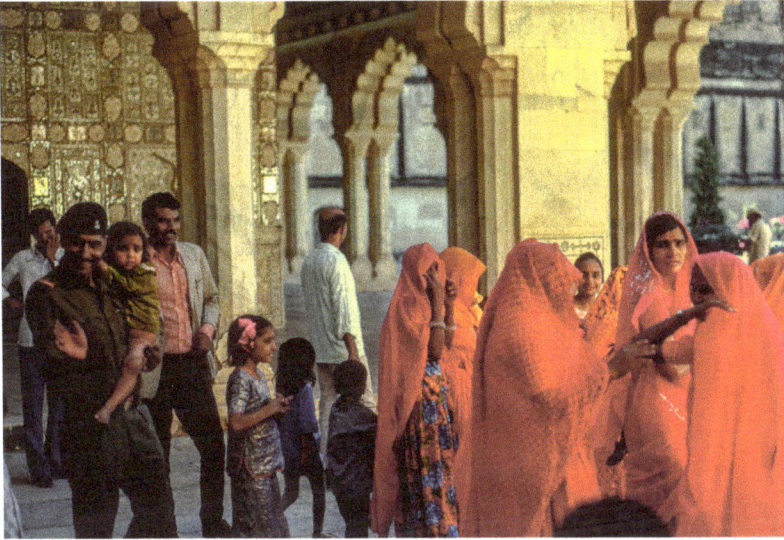

Cop reacting to my camera moves, Red Fort in Delhi

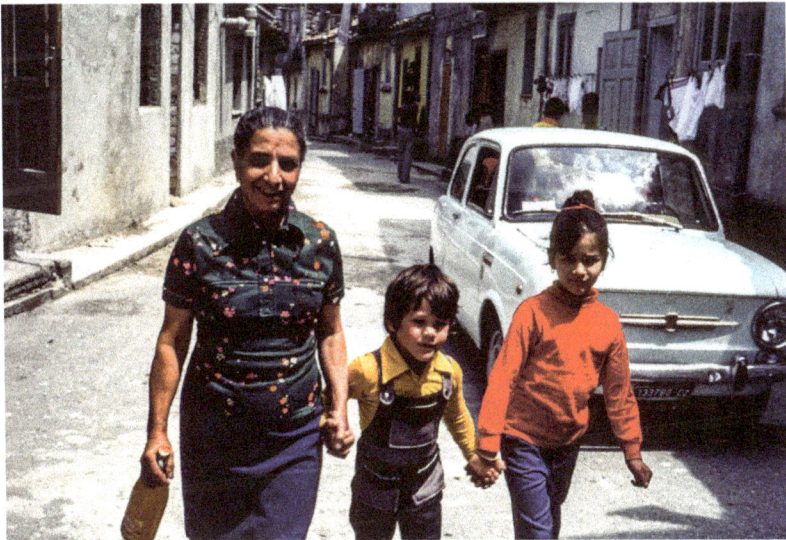

My Zia Rosa and my sis's kids, my folks' street in Calabria

Tehran children

Family gathering in the back yard, Tehran

Northern route to Mazar-e-sharif, Afghanistan

Men running for our 'bus', Afghanistan

Road disappears on the northern Afghan route

Bus break en route to Bamiyan, Afghanistan

Faces missing, Bamiyan Buddhas

Hash Man

Band-i-amir Lake, central Afghanistan

Ancient minaret and goats in Herat

Town square in Mazar-e-sharif

Blue Mosque, Mazar-e-sharif

Children all agog over a brochure of their town

Men and camel, Kandahar, Afghanistan

Monk saunters by in Dharmsala, India

Young women like my camera on a Goan beach

Nisargadatta with children in Bombay

On a beach in Corfu, Greece

13. Goa

children crying and colors flying[112]

Wanderlust

After plundering Goa in 1514, Portuguese sailors returned to their king with never before imagined treasures, elephants included. More recently, say, the last half of the twentieth century, Goa's enduring appeal became a lure on the world travelers' beat. The late 1960s saw the arrival of a first wave of those who took to the road and marched into India, but this time, unlike marauders from the past, they weren't interested in treasures of the physical kind. They were "the first generation of foreigners to visit nonviolently and without greed."[113] Goa had become Grand Central Dreamland for a new kind of landlubbing traveler, a mere few years after Portugal was booted out in 1961.

Just before I left Canada, the so-called energy crisis made it clear that what had been loosely called the Sixties were done. Some said they were long gone back in 1967 with the Death of Hippie ritual in a Frisco park, others when Martin Luther King and Bobby Kennedy (along with political hope) were shot dead in 1968. Others preferred the killing by hired guards at the Rolling Stones' Altamont concert at the end of 1969. The Beatles' break-up the next year added to the perceived shift.

But for many of us, the 1960s' turbulent *zeitgeist* flared on into the early 1970s. By the time I went overseas in 1974, disillusionment had already dulled the spark in many a youthful eye. My own small-town streets saw the creeping in of harder, addictive drugs, and a growing

112 From the song "After the Gold Rush" by Neil Young.
113 From *A Season In Heaven* by David Tomory.

distrust of mainstream society, and each other. You might say this down-turn in spirit was the inevitable consequence of new ideas taken on all at once and too quickly, and of the tendency to slip back into old patterns.

Yet as that peculiar energy of renewal and celebration waned in America and Europe, it took to the road in Asia. Anyone so inclined, and those like me who stumbled into the stream by happenstance, were enabled to continue enjoying the philosophical mood of that notorious decade. We self-serving, pleasure- and oftentimes truth-seeking wander-ers were the unwitting emissaries of a hopeful energy—eager and motley, naïve and lofty. The pouring into Asia of so many young, disaffected, yet idealistic travelers was, perhaps, that of a cultural offshoot looking outward. Dissatisfaction with and mistrust of consumerist, polluting, individualist interests, and plain-old curiosity, steered us through the afterglow of a decade into the pop culture of the East. It was about con-sciousness and self-inquiry; about rekindling faith in some basic values that seemed to have been sidelined by the guiding stewards of the increas-ingly mercantile home world; values like honesty and love, beauty and freedom. I was not ready yet to settle in and take one of many sanctioned, prearranged positions in the worldly machine. And I was cozying up to ideas that blew open certain rooms in my mind; inscrutable yet intriguing ideas like transformation and transcendence. I was wondering whether they were mere ideas or whether they were real, and if they were, what they might mean.

In short, the 1960s partied, passed out, and a bunch of us, still a little high and not ready to call it a night, grabbed a rucksack and hit the road. I doubt that timing is *everything*, but we did get caught in one of its fine tailwinds. Thousands from affluent countries took the slower routes "on a shoestring." Timeworn trails wove random patterns throughout south-ern Asia between Australia and Europe. Places like Kabul, Kuta Beach, Ko Phuket, and Katmandu became the geographical destinations of a certain cultural wanderlust. With such localities so rich with experiential potential—reminiscent, it might be argued, of olden ways in us moderns' own recent past—it wouldn't be long before "cultural offshoot" became oblivious to the trunk it grew from. Anyone wandering that dreamy tangle of paths would eventually feel the pull of its strongest magnet, the largest concentration of vagabond expats anywhere. Goa became *Goa* as people spoke of it, and because they were arriving there daily in expectant droves.

Goa is where the mythology of travel, of becoming unstuck from the home culture—not merely traveling but living a life "on the road"— becomes most visible. At least for me. It is in Goa that I hear about the first intrepid pioneers of The Road To Katmandu during the mid- and late 1960s. It is here that I feel nostalgia for something I could not experience, for a mode of travel long gone, to the mysteries of the East. It is in Goa that the picture of bourgeois wannabe posing as intrepid adventurer comes into focus. I, who am one of thousands in this second (or third) wave, have found my way to India along a path of glittering pebbles, placed and made visible by the slippery graces of hope and desire.

And it also is here that I catch an uncanny glimpse into what is often blithely referred to as madness, and of the homeless, nameless *sadhu* inside me.

SITTING PRETTY IN the Himalayas with my health wondrously restored, I'm ready to spring upon my own treasure trove of cultural charms. Keen and expectant, I head south.

Within days I find that wanderlust has leap-frogged ahead of full recovery from hepatitis. I moved on from McLeod Ganj too soon, too fast. Dizziness and nausea force me down. I pull into a comfortable tourist estate on the plains at the edge of the foothills, not more than 200 miles along.

I share a room with a chipper Aussie with eyes the color of a shaded Mediterranean cove. He sells me his Swedish gasoline camp stove for seven bucks. He's a good champ, his eyes a-sparkle as he speaks with passion about knowledge of the spiritual kind. We share an interest in some Western authors with an Eastern bent, exchanging books; Alan Watts, Aldous Huxley, and John Lilly come to mind.[114] *The Tao of Physics* by Fritjof Capra was published just last year. My Aussie friend is particularly engrossed in this new fusion of East and West. We are impressed with each other, and maybe, ourselves. At this point I'm not sure "knowledge"

---

114 Alan Watts: *The Book*; Aldous Huxley: *Moksha*; John C. Lilly: *Simulations of God, Center of the Cyclone.*

and "spiritual" quite fit together, though I'm not sure why. My mind is like a jumping monkey always on the move, and hard to get behind one hundred percent.

But never mind, cuz Aussie bloke is off on a siren trail after a petite red-haired Vancouver beauty who passes by our door. Surrounded for a moment by children of Van is the blue-eyed lad from Oz, first a sick dude with cool books, then a hot babe more compelling than any book.

In the pleasantly dry countryside I'm approached by a tall, fine-looking Indian, thirtyish. He wears white robes, a trimmed beard, and an earnest demeanor, as if a bizzaro Jesus has found me. Other than his curious wish to be accepted as my guru, he is soft-spoken and remains respectful. Evidently, he's shopping for disciples, and perhaps he sees in my debilitated condition a good and easy bargain. I tell him, "Thanks, but I'm just passing through." The rookie guru is focused on his goal, which is to say, searching, acquisitive, and with a pale shade of anguished wisdom-in-waiting. *Rather un-guru-like,* methinks. I embarrass myself.

THE STOVE I bought from Aussie Bloke is a key item on my way to health. *And good timing, aye.* The slight nausea that pulled me in for a rest indicates the need for further action. Without pausing to think about it, I'm drawn to the market and its colorful vegetables. *Thanks, Popeye, thanks, Mom.* I pile them into a billy for a slight steaming, acting on the unarticulated belief that this will unlock many wonderful nutrients, making them easygoing for my flagging liver. But not too much heat; don't want the soft, mushy stuff. After each such meal I feel clear-minded and good. My eating pleasures are rounded out with fresh fruit, curd, fish, and rice (and, of course, chai and maybe the odd cookie.) My vitality is so pumped every time I eat the veggies that I'm back on my feet in just two more days.

Having provided no follow-up course of care, the Tibetan doctor must have had considerable faith in the efficacy of her medicine. I keep taking her wondrous herbs and store a bit away for curiosity's sake. *Giddy up, mama.*

Monkey on the Run

Hardwar is a holy city that sits at the feet of the Himalayas. Word on the street, the toddler Krishna sprouted wings and took off over India after mischievously nabbing a flask of milk from Ma, and in his care-less toddler haste he spilled four drops. One landed near Allahabad, two down south somewhere, and one here in Hardwar. Every three years on a twelve-year cycle, a great meeting and celebration takes place in each of the four sacred spots, the truly grand Hindu parties called Kumbha Mela. As a matter of fact, one is just getting underway down the plains at Allahabad, at the confluence of three rivers, the Ganges and the Yamuna, where one can find the present-day city. The third is the ethereal Sarasvati, a mythic river not quite so visible (not unlike the third eye between our two common ones.)[115]

But wait. I recall a Hindu folk drama. Shiva the destroyer, the supremo macho deity, Lord of Lingam—big hard dick of the cosmos, really—was returning home one day. But he didn't know that while he was gone his lonely wife, Parvati, had created a boy from clay to keep her company. A good boy, he stood guard as his mother bathed. Then Shiva returned. Enraged by this young punk presuming to stop him, the Great One, from enjoining his wife, he cut off the boy's head. Confronted by her sudden anguish as the little body lay bleeding, he ordered his goblin attendants to go out and find a head, *pronto.* I don't know how reincarnation and attachment to material form works with gods, never mind the mechanics of linear time ... Anyway, it seems that time was indeed an issue, so his men were outta there and back in a flash—with a young elephant's head. Shiva grabbed the head and plonked it onto the boy's neck. Parvati was overjoyed. She just *loved* the new look. Now *everybody* loves Ganesh. He's the wisdom and good luck guy, and a good-looking sort.

Marvelous stories. And a wonderful locale, where this holy little city of Hardwar sits on the banks of the Ganges between Himalayan toes. But I'm just stopping for a connector train, just passing through.

I step off the train and marvel at the great number of monkeys loiter-ing around the busy station in various groups. I've never seen so many

---

115 Yet modern studies in archeology suggest, supporting the written works of the ancient Vedas, that the river did indeed exist in bygone millennia at the end of the last ice age—potentially re-christening an early human civilization the Indus/ Sarasvati. From *Underworld,* by Graham Hancock, p. 162–165, and *Gods, Sages and Kings* by David Frawley.

monkeys. Clustered idly in trees and on top of bench shelters, they know the place is holy and that humans will remain at their best behavior. A good place to hang, for sure, this sacred town. And the train station? Always an interesting crossroads of journeys and dreams. These monkeys? Good observers of the human sideshow, this much is plain to the observer. Adepts in the inquiring ways of Advaita Vedanta they likely are not, but I'm noticing how they're noticing me noticing *their* noticing. And so I avert my eyes, having encountered, once or twice before, monkey folk trouble that started with just this kind of circular mental folly.

My energy is way up; those herbs and veggies must be potent. I start jogging along the platform on this clear morning of sharp light and great vision, as if I have somewhere in particular to go. I bound along like a happy giant on some effortless jaunt across Pipsqueak Valley. Looking up and ahead I spot a medium-sized rump protruding past all the others, drooping off the edge of a shelter roof. *Come on, lazy-ass, pick it up a notch.* In one of those moments that seems to happen just ahead of one's conscious participation in it, and with my rhythmic bounce egging me on, I spring upward and slap it, good and hard.

Okaaay, didn't think this through... Shit. My short history with monkey folk rips a mad-flash avalanche of anxiety; my juvenile act will not go unpunished. Howls of indignation rattle the station. I keep running, faster now, as I look back at the shocked faces of first the insulted individual, the smaller, then the larger "boss" beasts. A thirst for vengeance spins their heads this way and that as they inform one another of the intrusion, the unforgivable violation. My running like the guilty perp I am is all they need. I turn again; several bosses have given chase and are gaining speed, the little guys bouncing in their wake. They are *fast*. Now at full sprint, I veer toward the station's restaurant across a big lawn, abso-*freakin*-lutely needing the glass door fifty feet ahead to be open. It's 8:15 a.m. Running madly across a clearing with my lopsided backpack, dozens of enraged monkeys a few feet behind and closing fast...

My timing is keen, right down to the precious second. The glass-and-metal door closes slowly with a final sharp *clunk* on a crowd of shrieking-mad monkeys putting the brakes on hard, denied and stopped, left outside. Huffing away, I stand for a few seconds looking at the bewildered faces of the restaurant workers, then at the monkeys screaming on the other side of the glass behind me—a murderous simian crowd enraged with unrequited vengeance.

The place is empty, probably just opened. The workers look at me, then at the hopping-mad monkeys. To their bewilderment I should add doubt, consternation, mistrust, and finally, judgment: *We are believing the monkeys, sir. We will be serving breakfast now.* Flustered, relieved, and a little awkward (and yes, hungry), I sit down for one of those good, if predictable, railway station meals.

If the door had been locked, well, there'd be no eggs for Mr. Johnny Canucklebrain this lovely morning of unplanned beginnings. And tomorrow's local headline: Traveling Numbskull Spanks Monkey, Hospitalized By Hanuman's Guard. Assuming, of course, the monkeys hadn't fully dismembered me, I'd bet on honorable mention in later editions of the Darwin Awards.[116]

THE ROADS ARE multiple and without preference, the usual situation on whatever crossroad I happen to find myself. Kumbha Mela is in the wind and gathering at the holy rivers. Millions are walking, and millions more are talking.

And shitting. It will be a while before I'm fully recovered from the hep. As I ponder a mega-scale brew of human bodies, with no plumbing and all the unseen galaxies of riotous scum... *yikes.* The question of hygiene more easily wigs me out these days of reflection and recuperation. Posters of smallpox-scarred faces are displayed all over India on utility poles, at railway stations, and in restaurants. It's a government drive to stamp out, to the last germ, a plague that in 1974 killed *between* 10,000 and 20,000. That's only two years ago, and a misplaced tally (conservatively) of five thousand or so human lives. A year before that, thousands more (exact number hazy) died in a malaria epidemic. At Kumbha Mela, the micro-beasts themselves will be partying.

On the other hand, Goa's intrigue evokes scenes of wholesome hedonism, nirvana dreams, and a tropical playground. I head south.

---

116 *The Darwin Awards,* by Wendy Northcutt.

Three Times Lucky

But first I'll return to the incomparable city of Benares and compare it to the last time I was there. I add a 1,000-mile eastward zigzag to my 1,000-plus-mile southbound route.

And I find that I am in a different city.

As personal history fades and trusty references go into hibernation, my eyes see through a different light each time while visiting even the same place. "We do not see things as they are, we see them as we are."[117] Bilbo Baggins, that distinguished veteran of otherworldly travel, did not say that, but he did observe, "Wherever you go, there you are."[118]

"The real journey of discovery consists not in seeking new landscapes, but in having new eyes." Marcel Proust said that.

Occasionally, these old/new eyes get tired. Today I feel a peculiar melancholy, unclear and restless. Existential heebie-jeebies? Jealous little Catholic imp on my shoulder, spooking around since my hasty exit from altar-boy duty to join the new religion of A-theism? Now all bedevilled over my recent fascination with Indian culture? *Offa me, you little roach.*

Hepatitis *frightis*?

I walk down a squalid lane. Off to the side, a dead rat lies belly up. Around here it's no big deal. I turn a corner and see another. Then another, and another. Dead rats, aren't they competent carriers of disease, playing host to all kinds of little buggers? Why so many? And if *they're* dying, how does this augur for their less adaptable, bipedal neighbors? Didn't I just shake off something like liver plague?

The book *The Plague*[119] begins with a doctor in a North African city noticing a dead rat here, a dead rat there... I recall a health pamphlet in Oz that warned of the possible persistence of plague "in pockets in Pakistan, India, and Southeast Asia."

Early the next morning I leave Benares for the third time.

IN DELHI I collect my mail and am stunned to learn that my buddy Rick was killed in a crash. I check my passport; I want to know where I was

117 Anais Nin.
118 *The Hobbit* by J.R.R. Tolkien.
119 *The Plague* by Albert Camus.

when it happened. It might have been the day, not a month earlier, that I fell under a cloud of confusion coming down with hepatitis in Pakistan. With the news of Rick's death, dispelled are the entertainments of mind I've so faithfully cultivated on the road. I'm snapped back to an earlier time… Back in grade seven it was from him that I first heard about Eastern mysticism, about crazy ideas like plants being sentient creatures. That's when we did the blood-brother thing. It was at his urging; he had us both promise to contact the other from beyond death, whoever goes first. We were close; he kept me on my ethical toes. But he wasn't perfect. He was sorely competitive with me—girls, music, school—and was always there to notice whenever I indulged a moment of dumb pride. I remember how I disrespected him once, played the bully when we were younger. He didn't deserve it, and I wound up hating myself for that. He was good to me, and his honesty was good for me. And I see now that I hunger for more such direct criticism, so rare in my life when it aims true. I miss that artless honesty. With his death I feel strangely shocked, and emptier.

A couple of things Rick said during our teenage years have stayed with me. The famous question: "If a tree falls in a forest and there's nobody to hear it, does it make a sound?" His answer, which took me many years to come around to: "No. Sound isn't 'sound' until our ears register it, otherwise, it's just waves of potential energy."[120] And on the question of heaven and hell: "Hell is simply separation from God. Like here on Earth."

A few times I've faced and accepted my own untimely demise on dangerous mountain roads. Travel is risky business in wilderness Asia. When it came to death as in, might-just-happen-today, everything in my experience shifted. At least by surrendering the whole shebang, my normal consciousness was like a spell broken, and it hit me, an "amplified now"

---

120 I suppose the question is both a mechanical and a philosophical one. The one refers to the eardrum and the phenomenon of sound (which requires one); the other asks the question, "Do objects exist, or can we know they exist, if there is no perception of them?" One could say that the question itself posits the existence of trees, forests, air, and the like, so why not sound? Perhaps it comes down to the definition of sound, and of perception (how our senses limit and "define" what we *think* we see), and might also probe into the nature of solipsism. (If a tree falls and no one's there, does it make a sound? My thought at the time: *Dunno. Wasn't there.*)

that filled the canyons of fear that would claim me, the gullies and chasms right there outside the window. With the unexpected detachment from life itself, I was perhaps released from the burden of living. Accepting one's own conjectured death is something—yes, it most surely is.

But the real death of a loved one resets my existential poise. *Wake up, Johnny! Your skin, now tingling with grief, will one day rot from your bones!* I keep moving, wondering how going anywhere ever mattered. *All those (s)miles.*

But going home is nowhere in the picture. Pushing into a third year on the road, I've dispensed with the usual reasons for going to this place or that, or for leaving. Home buddy Rick is gone; his funeral is long done. I'm on the other side of the planet. I doubt anyone expects my return; they don't even know where I am. My good health is still a new and fragile thing. A rest on the beaches of Goa, a retreat from dense cities and personal gloom, feels … exactly right. I'll rest under tropical shade trees for as long as I wish. It will be a good convalescence.

Can it be true, Rick?

Maya's Eden

I arrive at Vagator Beach and behold, from the top of a cliff on a breezy afternoon, the cover shot for heaven's feature brochure: *Welcome, all ye souls of beauty and unending love. Let us start our tour at a little place called Goa, shall we?*

I scoot down a path into a palm-leaf tea hut and take a seat amongst a dozen other travelers. Someone plucks a weird local instrument; no canned music. Semi-nude gals and guys from all over the West sip tea or pass a chillum. Eyes are listless, yet also intimate and bold, in several of the gals, at least. It is warm and dry, but not hot. All is quiet except for the sounds of waves breaking and washing the sand, and the rustling of palms high above us. Like on that south Thai beach, travelers have stumbled upon a most obliging playground for exploring hidden dramas.

A tall, thin, pale dude a few years older than me walks in. He talks as he enters (Australian.) His gait is loose, even flaccid. His eyes appear somewhat glazed and dull yet they are, at the same time, keenly aware in a most peculiar way. His drawling mouth moves all slack and unevenly, as if driven from several loose joints away. Incoherent words bounce senselessly from ear to ear to ear. He talks but it is to no one, or it's to anyone. His tone is snide, the content wide-ranging and everyday-oddball. Behind the surface haze his eyes are steady and suggest a kind of lazy but penetrating force. Yet it's obvious (I have already decided) that he moves in his own abject continuum.

But what, exactly, is so obvious? Sane, insane—their meaning is... I'm just not sure.

Referencing my tattered sack of memory-bits it seems that we've had a love/fear thing going with insanity: either we banish or imprison it, or we exalt it as mad genius. That is, when it comes packaged with uncommon talent. We are unclear on the relationship between sublime acts of creativity and sheer madness, or we assume there *is* such a relationship. We hold to a "hoary belief that the horrors and the splendors are inseparable, that one is the precondition of the other, that to paint like Van Gogh you have to cut off your ear."[121] Seems that all such beliefs and understanding I previously held have now lapsed, if ever they were mine. *Weren't they, in fact, borrowed from family, village, and the hoary beyond?* Today I know only that I must assume nothing on the matter.

Meanwhile, Mr. Aussie Everyman moves down his own hair-raising road with his crooked walk and nonstop blather. The more I listen, the more I see it's not so different from the endless yakking in *my* brain, whenever I bother to take a good look. Which I've just started doing lately.

Settling into this new Eastern thing, my first response is calm detachment. This word-salad chef seems harmless. Soon I'm overcome by casual compassion for outcasts and derelicts everywhere. *Sip tea, nibble cookie, watch Mr. Oz.* Others in the tea hut frown and fidget as his rambling spews on unabated.

His casual chatter soon balloons into brash assaults aimed at each twitch and squirm, from one person to the next. What first appear as nonsensical word strings are transformed—perhaps with imagination, perhaps not—into descriptions and comments about the twitchers and frowners. Our bizarre oppressor appears to respond aptly, and

121 From *Ghost in the Machine* by Arthur Koestler, p. 312.

bewitchingly so. His words shift character and content as he moves from person to person, as if reading them one by one. It's a fantastic performance of mind-bleed mischief, bordering on maniacal/magical. After their turn in his personally delivered echo ramblings, two gals up and leave, one after the other, in fits of pique and embarrassment. In the front-row view from *my* easy chair, insane has become an oblique state of tainted grace, possibly un-fucked-up, but fucking everyone else up just the same. He isn't crazy; he's just an asshole stuck in a weird, unholy place, disconnected from everyone. *Telepathetic.* He continues around the room; I am smitten. *I'm here, brother, I await my turn!*

But he doesn't see me. He walks by as if I'm invisible. Looks straight through as his eyes pass over to the next person. I watch them closely, of course, but they don't even flinch. I'm the only one he skips past.

I feel a bit special, maybe geeky-special. And kinda ripped off. *Man.* All I did, by way of suspended judgment, was to simply look right back at him. *Like a mirror.*

Ms. Cow

When left to fend for themselves, cows will occasionally display a cunning that rivals that of the average dog. Perhaps the odd mad genius frequents these beaches of play and plenty. The free cows of India, the cows of near-joy, are known to put that seamless intelligence to good use as hunters of one of their favorite things: paper products.

Early one morning on Vagator, while the first pot of chai brews on the flaming kerosene, the tea hut owner and a young Ms. Cow match wits. She pokes her head through the door and spotting a yummy *hors d'oeuvre* (wall calendar), she looks around to see if anyone's watching. She is so alert that the rest of us, except for the busy owner/cook, appear decidedly bovine. Taking the hanging morsel as fair game she lunges for it. Familiar with cow rhythm and perhaps wise to the odds, the cook leaps from the kitchen and fouls Ms. Cow's attempt with a swat. Larger, more complex brain wins once, then twice. Three times—no contest.

Now Ms. Cow, perhaps chewing on fresh info regarding the human rhythm, hatches plan B. She stands behind the tea hut wall for a longer while, very still, out of the cook's (but not my) sight. For a good minute and a half, maybe two, she stands quietly. Not an ear twitch. Maybe she's thinking, maybe not. Or maybe she's waiting for Skinnybrain Biped to . . . *forget.* Is our young lady's poise one of scheming patience? Cunning?

Indeed, in one quick motion, my lady genius does a rapid one-eighty around the end wall to snatch her snack and flee, chewing as she runs, the calendar crunching smaller by the second, with dumb old Brainstick chasing and cursing.

Bom Shankar!

Bom Shankar! Bom!

This is the greeting I hear on beaches and trails. *Who is this Mr. Shankar? Does he own a sitar?* When the smoking chillum is raised, someone (always a guy) shouts it: "Bom Shankar!" It is ritual and invocation for the sacramental inhaling of *charis* smoke. In this idyllic, fledgling culture of travelers from the world over, an element of worship is borrowed from the host Hindu culture. Of course, to combine hippiedom and its impromptu music and dance with the world's finest hash for dirt cheap, entertaining, no-pressure eastern religion (comes with the hash for communing with divine energies) and a nudist social setting with great food—and no rules or cops—is to provide a perfect milieu and seductive primer on worship and devotion for any young, hedonistic drifter. In this case, the closer you get, the worship and devotion looks a whole lot like . . . getting naked and getting stoned on the beach.

Many *sadhus* mingle freely with foreigners on the Goan beaches. Chillum smoking and weird jam sessions, at least, are taken to with great enthusiasm by both groups and have become daily fare. The detachment educed in a life of wandering, with its feeling of "being in but not *of* the world," as the Sufis say, adds to the charm, if only happened upon circumstantially by the traveler. The sadhus have renounced the ways of the world, and we travelers have left our personal ones behind. As well, the sadhus are seemingly always male and subject to the steady lure of fair, naked tourist gals. Though their lives have been given over to the spiritual quest, some trace of maya's carnality persists here and there . . . traces of a carnal attachment that might be fully experienced to be *truly* transcended... *a reasonable enough, hard-to-disagree-with working plan, baba.*

The sadhus I've met on these beaches adhere to the cult of Shiva, god of destruction in the Creator-Preserver-Destroyer Trimurti of Hinduism. Shiva is also the god of creative and sexual energies, of the rivers, the forests, the Himalayas, and the moon. *Not bad.* He is the god of yogis themselves. By smoking charis, sadhus attune themselves to a greater rhythm, feeling the energies of life and breath directly. Homage is paid frequently—"Bom"—to Shiva, the god of change itself. Some longtime travelers adopt the saffron robes and material renouncement of the sadhus, attracted as they are to the energy and character of the Shivites. And not least of all, to the hash-as-sacrament deal.

At sundown on the beach, with massive bonfires and dancing and such, the hash-as-sacrament deal comes in handy. Guitars strum away while sadhus wail or knock or blow on rudimentary instruments. The result is an eerie, appealing dissonance, a mock symphony with offbeat cohesion that makes my head tilt like one of those clever mutts upon hearing an odd note in the wind. I'd bet that even the crustiest music academy snob would come around eventually with reluctant curiosity, then longing.

A few Shivites pounce around the fire, poking it with long poles. Others continually haul over logs and stumps like mesmerized drones programmed *to burn it all.* I expect they'll arrange it as they like, then sit down to enjoy it with the rest of us. Not so. The battle/love affair with the flame demands turning logs for hours, getting stupidly close. *Feeling the burn.* They grunt, heave, and whine, their faces contorted in prolonged fits of anger and pain. My Hinduism-For-Dummies take: the camouflage of *samsara* enacts the drama of *karma* on the fiery, illusory wheel of life, death, and rebirth. It is invigorating, and sometimes it hurts. *It is my dharma, baba.*

And what a workout.

A Day at Little Vagator

I've been rambling 'round the adventure of "life as you wish, sahib," India. As such, my mental framework seems to have taken a sharp tilt. My senses, as the trusty allies they must be, are taking it easy and lately, they seem merely along for the ride. In the past, only psychotropic plants have been so accommodating of such a departure from the civil norm. And for a Western traveler in the East, such a departure, by definition, is experienced as a further move into unconventional social territory.

For many travelers, the beach life sojourn remains of unknown duration. Personal history, familiar boundaries, the clothing rule—are all but faithfully departed. Not a drop of alcohol nor any recorded music to be seen, drunk, or heard. I've stumbled into an effective simulacrum of Lotusland.[122]

I plant myself on Little Vagator Beach, a tiny cove shaded by palms and pampered by a faithful ocean breeze. Three grassy terraces rise up from the sand in a gentle, concave arc. On each step sit several palm-leaf huts that local kids build and sell for three or four dollars at the beginning of each dry season, as Western travelers trickle in from all over India. Once bought, the hut is yours for as long as you stay. Of course, you can sell it or give it away anytime. The monsoon will wipe it out in a few months anyhow, after which the kids will rebuild and resell. A grass-hut restaurant offers tasty meals for pennies. All this for a dollar a day. But I'm a big spender. Some days I'm well into *two bucks*.

For simplicity I carry as little as possible and sleep on the beach; perhaps the ancient tradition of asceticism has found resonance with me. I'm drawn to the softest spots, the longest shades. My favorite: a comfy pocket of tousled sand next to a gentle rise of boulders a good ten feet from the high-tide mark. I sleep with a cotton sheet, T-shirt, G-string, and a pouch with enough money for a week or so. The names "John" and "Canadian" top my meager heap of possessions. I haven't seen a clock or a mirror in weeks, and I suspect their unprecedented absence has begun to noodle my brain into a curious, plastic ease.

The sand is molded into whatever shape one prefers. In the darkness of the first new moon I bury my passport, money belt, and camera next to one of those boulders, the one with the sly, bulldoggy face.

In the morning the first alert is sound: waves breaking on shore, a rooster or a dog. The numinous transition of dark into light, of

122 From the Lotus-Eaters in *The Odyssey* by Homer, and what our balmy and idyllic corner of Canada, its extreme southwest coast fringe, has been nicknamed.

subconscious wanderings snagged on conscious markings, slowly shifts to the daytime realm. With so little to encumber me, I often wake up smiling. The cool sea air, at perfect ambient temperature, and the cozy hum of land systems pamper my excellent, comfortable body, providing a fleeting reference from which to recall life-as-it-is. Still in early shadow, I get my bearings by the pounding of surf and the carefree rustle of palms way up high. In the absence of real world concerns I wonder, in these first moments, not only where, but *who* I am. This single shot of amnesia is a rare pleasure, a casual alchemy refitting the works of memory and focus. And it's further tweaked by the gentle reminder that never was there a guarantee even of waking up.

The intense sun has long since chased my shadows down the beach. It burns now from high above and blasts me from a sea of sand it spent all morning cooking. Barely awake, I rise to my hands and knees. Civilization's buzz is a half-day away in several cities where homeless children, cripples, and lepers scratch along miserably. Scarcely a morning passes that I don't remember this awkward fact. I reach out from my protective cover of "responsible innocence," real or imagined, a notion I find useful given my more than favorable accident of birthplace. I hope that the road from innocence to cynicism, if one were ever to find me, is long, slow, and ultimately, unnavigable.

I visit Map'sa town every other week or so for banking, mail, or to accompany someone. Whenever a memory strip of that Indian urban scene rolls through I'm reminded how disproportionate are the boons given us, depending on who, when, and where. The cool fact is, this self-indulgent life of unstuck travel has reached a pinnacle of decadence on this very beach. And so I amble on all fours into the surf, naked. *The sea will wake me.* A bourgeois dropout, a morning dip in Freedom's backyard pool.

After a morning swim I make my way to the watering hole at the beach's crown for morning ablutions. Buckets of fresh water, pulled up from a deep natural pool, wash the salt and sand away.

"Hello, good morning." It's disorienting in these inelegant early moments to be standing, naked and wet, with several traveling strangers. Our bath is communal, co-ed, and open-air. In this normally private affair of tending to one's personal comforts, there's a hint of bashfulness and intimate trepidation (rarely seen around here), eyes held a little longer in one another's, as if away from other, more sensational places.

Every morning at about the same time an old cow arrives at the watering hole and waits until someone with a measure of compassion offers a drink. Over several days our timing moves into synchrony and I develop a marginal fondness for her; for I have become her trusty bucket man. She laps back two or three buckets full (as other travelers wait their turn), then continues in the same direction, day after day.

One morning, in a spirit of inquisitive goal setting that I haven't felt the likes of in months, I decide to follow the old dame. She plods along, sneezing and shuddering, taking a long and tortuous route up through a sprawling village area under shade palms, an extensive area still unavailable to automobiles. Madam Cow stops along the way at other watering holes and marketplaces where merchants throw scraps of edible garbage, the charitable donations to an obviously dependent beast. Sometime later, when her route begins to arc around toward the curvature of the coastline, and my pity for the wretched, winded beast becomes wearisome, I leave her, satisfied that she must travel the same path daily in a successful cycle of bare-bones sustenance.

Back at the beach I think about Canada, about my father and the effort he has made for so long to gain edible scraps for his large family. Then... *need I, or will I ever go back to this place, this "home"?*

THE MOST SQUALID part of beach life is the daily poop. Farther up the ridge is an outhouse with a deep hole bored into the earth. But the hip beach folks look upon it as a nasty pit of non-integrated filth.

The ocean, on the other hand, offers a more palatable disappearing act. The beach is tiny and flanked by rocky outcroppings. It is on their rough slabs, at low tide, that many leave their droppings. Word on the beach: *the ocean eats everything up.* Several defecating apes, male and female, squat three or four feet apart, strategically aligned so that one does not directly face another. The area is small, particularly when the tide creeps in. And I kinda believe it; the ocean probably *does* eat things up. Especially in less-populated days. Later, swimming in the hot sun, you might notice the odd little flotilla like a foul devil trespassing in God's Holy Pond.

Mornings fill the tea huts with travelers from any part of the world affluent enough for its young to dream *and* scrape together some cash, basically Western Europe, Canada, the US, Japan, Australia and New Zealand, with a few rare ones from South Africa, Israel, and Romania. Sipping tea, eating porridge and fruit, there's always a pair of eyes or limbs to read. Not to mention the other natural wonders of surf, sun, sand, and green that wash through the senses and rinse away any remaining traces of life's toils. Even in the morning, chillums are going around. It's usually late afternoon before I join in. Great soil for cult sprouts, and occasionally, I spot someone given over to tilling his own special garden.

A half dozen swims a day. Lads and lassies, all nubile, all handsome. Volleyball in the sand: half-crazed monkey folk jump naked into the sky, flappy parts bouncing on a crazy-whip action. Bra or bathing suit: much too weird for paradise. Dress code: naked = excellent; lunghi = cool. It isn't long before an embryonic society, even one in which rules themselves are *verboten*, begins developing, as if by compulsion, its own silent codes. Barely noticeable is this at first, but alas, it's all the same. Full circle, short trip.

I pull out my veggies. Still feeling the effects of my bout with hepatitis, I make good use of the camp stove I bought from that spunky, blue-eyed Aussie up north. A day missed is a day with sagging vitality. And two days? I've tried, three times now, putting away the stove and veggies. Each time, after little more than a day, I feel the weakness and dizziness return, with the odd pang near my liver. Perhaps I am one suggestible monkey. But I suspect that if I am to remain in India, I need to carry on the good work started by those Tibetan herbs in nursing my liver back to health. The nutritional clout of a large mass of veggies each day seems to do the trick. I buy three or four days' supply of carrots, cabbage, green beans, beets with greens, tomatoes, onions, garlic, potatoes, turnips, cauliflower, yams, chilies, and whatever else I find. My billy brims with a dozen or more veggies. My slumping liver, vitality, and general well-being all enjoy a sharp boost each time I eat this deluxe mix.

From a distance others can see that I'm up to something. My reputation as steam-mate spreads rapidly. I dig a hole in the sand more than a foot deep for my breeze-sensitive stove. A hungry, perhaps undernourished wayfarer wanders over and sits. Barely a word is exchanged. I hand over half my vittles. Despite the extravagance of copious clouds of hash, always a-puff nearby on these beaches, they walk away high on the benefits of this barely cooked fare. I feel it too, with a mind clear and still and a belly beneficially full. They know I always make enough for two. The same person never comes twice in a row, nor do two show up at once. Once in a while it's someone I've never seen before. We do it every day.

I put away my stove and break into an easy jog, feeling strong and free. A cow that's been snooping in one of the huts looking for some tasty paperbacks or letters to munch jerks back her head with a terrified look. Caught in the act, she turns and runs in the direction I'm already heading. Aiming for the next beach anyway, I keep running. The poor cow gallops ahead of me, fleeing the wrath of the human menace. A minute later when her energy is spent, she turns to face me, her legs spread out to keep from falling over in her weakened state. She stands her ground, battle-ready challenge in her eyes, pulsing shafts of hot breath pumping her nostrils like twin steam exhausts. Laughing, I run a big arc around her. She stands there gasping, too far gone to look up.

But I'm soon back, just before sunset, at my favorite beach where all the good musicians hang. Every day at this time, a neo-primitive celebration erupts. As the sun transforms into a cosmic orange fire-egg, all bloated and mesmerizing and sucking ever closer to oblivion beyond the hazy curtain between sea and sky, between thought and no-thought, we all gather in a large circle for the pranayama-chillum boogie. Bongos, guitars, recorders, pump organs, bells, harmonicas, and other weird local instruments loop and climb together in a wacky crescendo. A few energetic nymphs dance in the breeze, invoking the natural grace of mating pigeons (it's the sand.) Only after the last fiery spot blinks into the hazy, lazy ocean do the mounting tensions wane.

And there's more music to be played and enjoyed, more chillums to be filled and sparked, more timeless philosophical stews to be stirred and shared as the indigo of night deepens and absorbs us all. Before morning comes I crawl away, as overstimulated, fatigued, and useful to this world as a keyed-up toddler.

Clocks and Mirrors

Here in Maya's Eden, clocks and mirrors have all but disappeared, giving way to a peculiar lightness of being not usually associated with normal adult humans (except for maybe the Pygmies, before the tall villagers moved closer to the forest with their plantations and weird religion.[123]) In their unexpected absence, the clock and the mirror are revealed to be all-engrossing, their overall effect approximating hypnotic fixations in the modern mind.

One might not suspect how big a shadow is cast by the sly mirror. You might say it's not the mirror but the desire to look into it that matters. So pervasive is this effect that only complete freedom from it will unmask its power. I haven't seen my face for a month, and I don't miss it. My comb has eight fingers and two thumbs, and the light in anyone's eye serves as a faithful reflection. Perhaps some of the beach people have small ones tucked away, but I haven't seen any.

And the clock? If one's immediate needs are simple and accounted for in the foreseeable future then time, like some lazy dog, will retreat into the shade of the daily scheme of things. *Chronos* gives way to *Kairos*. *Remember? Remember when you were small?* If the condition persists, and one need not assess, measure, or even notice it (for so long!), the shapes and textures of time begin to morph. After weeks of living in the acute present, "ten minutes ago" or "ten minutes from now" become absurd quirks of the mind-as-it-was. Yesterday and tomorrow are quaint insanities, or at best, fantasies, notions worth little more than a quiet chuckle. A speck of awareness then wonders of itself, "Who are you, bud? Brother, sister, do you not also feel this?" It is languorous, dreamy, seductive. Moments expand, taking personal orientation with them. And noticing only seems to enhance the effect.[124]

When one afternoon I ask, in the spirit of imp or class clown, "anyone know what time it is?" there is no verbal answer, just a smile and a few

---

123 From *The Forest People* by Colin Turnbull.

124 For a provocative and profound exploration of time beyond my simple chronos/ kairos take, one that challenges fundamental assumptions we in our modern mindset tend to make about the absolute nature of its left-brain, tick-tock-linear mode, see *The Dance of Life* by Edward T. Hall.

half nods as the beach fellas acknowledge, in silence, the comic empti-ness of my mock question. One guy—perhaps less stable than most as he bumps along the rush of mental changes that this unrestrained beach life seems to enable—shoots an intense, sidelong glance my way as if I have invaded and am deliberately messing with his mind.

There's no need to gauge or engage seconds, minutes, or hours. The sun rises, crosses the sky, and sets. The moon does too, looking a bit different each night, bigger, then smaller, until it disappears. The dual drama is both sufficient and perfect. How long can this last? *You wouldn't ask.* The passing days are constant in ebb and flow, light and dark. Experience connects to the great out-there; our physical senses cleave to the cycles of nature. *Kairos.* Simpler animals, when they're not on the hunt or being chased, must know this lucid freedom. *An eagle, a horse.* It's as if a bygone mode of the human mind has been reactivated.

That's not to say there isn't a background eye keeping watch. I figure on two things for sure: every person knows that they are "me", undis-puted; and it's always "now." Not much, but hey.

And now back to *chronos,* for that background eye does remember. Much has been stored that can entertain the mind, as details (such as banking hours) bubble to the surface like strange bits of flotsam. For example, the artificial nature of time measurement that results in various calendars. Apart from the BC/AD (or BCE/CE) Christian one, there have been Mayan, Jewish, Egyptian, Chinese, Aztec, Roman, Incan, Mesopotamian, and others. Each is an attempt to make sense of the daily dance of moon and sun, which don't exactly jive with each other, or with any of the planets. It's a mess out there, as if a primordial wad of cosmic goo was flung blindly in a careless fit. The resulting chaos has had groups of priests and proto-astronomers draw up some pretty good charts. *But what did they know?*

On the beach we don't use any, yet we always know when to party.

"TO PARTY" ALWAYS includes a great deal of hash smoking. Bom Shankar has become the preferred demigod of our snug expat subculture of sexual freedom, good food, hash, and music, all acoustic and live. Add trendy, Eastern pop philosophy on the fly…

After several weeks of rather excessive toking, the effects of the high-grade indica resin seem to be cumulative. And with beach culture synergy upping the brew, they begin to resemble those of mild doses of classic psychedelics like psilocybin mushrooms or peyote. This occurs to me one afternoon as I walk along the shoreline and react, by giggling madly, to the sudden breaking of small waves on my feet as if they are a rushing phalanx of cackling fish-squirrels lashing at my toes with electric tongues. Is this mere entertainment, or could it be the precursor of a certain unhinging showing up in me?

An early word for psychedelic substances was psychotomimetic, meaning psychosis-mimicking. I've never before seen such an amplification of the relatively mild effects of hash. Is my unexpected giggle-fest related in some way to certain individuals I've seen wandering these beaches, naked and tormented, even though I've not seen any of them smoking?

The black indica resin is indeed strong, usually Manali from up in the Himalayan foothills. The best in the world, they say. On the beach it is cheap and wildly abundant. (But as I've noted, there is no booze; perhaps it's just not psychedelic enough.)[125]

Here on the beaches of Goa there appears to be a high number of personal identity fractures in which verbal and emotional connection with others is broken. It's as if the normal ego—the sense of a separate self that at least adequately interacts with other separate selfs—has lost its defining edges and is unable (or no longer cares) to maintain conventional boundaries: the agreed-upon signals of me/not-me.

Come to think of it, nowhere else have I seen such large numbers of travelers in one place, providing, perhaps, a first good look at the overall hippie-traveler picture. We are those who have chosen to cut ourselves loose, in a more significant way than most, from the physical and psychic controls of our homelands. Does this make us more vulnerable, less stable? Or are a higher number of unstable individuals drawn into the anonymity of this fringe reality? Is something in this renegade subculture triggering out-of-the-ordinary states of mind in an

---

125 At least I haven't seen any in my stay of several months along the stretch of northern beaches from Anjuna to Little Vagator—although much of that time was spent on L.V.

otherwise tolerably unstable minority? Is it always part of any culture's duty to pull in these loose strands that might become pathologically "unstuck", as say, they might more readily tend to do in an ungoverned, faraway place?

Does Goa, with its lure as a quintessential travel haven and aura of beauty and freedom, somehow exert a peculiar, destabilizing effect on the minds of all dream-struck travelers? Vulnerable, stable, and the lot?

Rajneeshee

Houses are available for rent within the village-like expanse that sprawls throughout the adjacent lands above the Vagator and Anjuna beaches. Some travelers group together to share the five- to ten-dollar monthly rate. There's no electricity, but kerosene lamps are fine. No running water, but a communal well is never beyond a laundry's haul away.

On a winding path I come upon a big, roomy house, fancy digs in these parts. It's the home of a dozen or so orange-clad devotees of Bhagwan (God, or as some allege, master of the vagina) Sri (holyish tag) Rajneesh (Lord of the Night.) Later he is called "Osho." Evidently, this house serves as a politico-spiritual center for his followers in Goa. Back in the West, back in the 1960s, we heard of Hari Krishna and Maharishi Mahesh Yogi with a little help from the Beatles. This Rajneesh is the latest Big Guru Dude to hit the West with such a mind-licking splash. Few are surfing, of course, and many are gathered to take in the view. I lounge in the sun-dappled cabana of involved/not involved.

The wearing of a man's portrait on a necklace by all members of a group seems behavior fit more for drones than for autonomous beings of love. *Just sayin'.* For this, the necklace and orange robes, is the uniform of the Neeshees. A certain hive-mind/control aspect of the committed follower makes me uneasy, having grown up in the penumbra of evil- and/or God-fearing Catholicism. Not to mention being emotionally traumatized by one or two very bad sci-fi horror flicks at an inappropriately early age (admittedly, this is my own shit.) Nonetheless, I find the Neeshees to be a lively, intelligent lot compared with disciples of some other gurus I've met on the road. The eyeful glimmer of a healthy libido and unrestrained body language is refreshing and easy to relate to.

Inside the Neeshees' house, loudspeakers blast His Darkness's wise-ish, almost melodramatic tone in every room. I hear snippets of interesting messages from (what I could swear are) various sources. *Forgive me if I'm wrong, Bhagwan,* but the words seem well thought out, with an eclectic range of verbal images. It's not that I don't appreciate what he's saying; I'm downright *inspired* by things he says. And it's not that I expect to hear something entirely new. Many would agree that wisdom jewels from across all lands are mined, throughout millennia, from the same vein. Makes sense.

But for whatever reason, my ears are not so receptive to the same phrases. *Bhagwan, I want to hear* your *words, so I can hear them better—so I'll know they come from* you*, the teacher.* A charismatic, a self-made, selfless man with a grand following? I don't know. When he speaks he sounds, to my ears, like a "learned" man.

Maybe if there weren't so many Rajneesh eyes in huge posters all over the house looking down at me, and maybe if those eyes weren't so apocalyptically self-aware, so gloomily voracious... shades of Zoltar the Magnificent.

Later, while discussing the merits of joining a like-minded group (and the intrinsic properties of color) with a young American lassie, I look down at the orange robes that barely shroud her petite, comely figure.

"But why orange?" I ask. "Why not... green?" *Green is pretty great, after all.* We're standing on the beach, and the horizon is on her side.

"Sunsets... are orange," she offers in a tone that begins as thoughtful and cryptic but turns hollow and inane by the time it reaches my ears. I ponder the blueness of the sky...

Sure, there might be a good reason.

I ask about Rajneesh himself and learn that to meet him at his ashram in Poona one need pay twenty dollars—easily a month's wages for the average Indian—and wait for three days. Only then will one have paid the full price for a brief interview in which he assesses and perhaps accepts you into the hive (after renaming you, which is part of the bargain.)

Anyone willing to pay top dollar, wait three days to see Mr. Guru for ten minutes, then take on a new name, would already have invested considerable faith in the story (or they'd be a reporter or a writer.)

The merely curious, like me, do not possess the tenacity to bother. *Mr. Bhagwan, sir, forgive me once more...* for I come away believing Rajneesh's meet-and-greet setup is an effective device for separating sheep from goats, for gathering an unquestioning flock.

And yet I must jump off my horse once more, to admit that I believe some good work is being done. The Rajneeshees I've met seem to exude a courage for inner inquiry and a strength in exploring visceral experience, on a path that I haven't, perhaps, felt ready to take just yet. With their consistent example of hungry-eyed expressiveness, I wonder whether I avoid taking such risks with mind and body, and lean in a bit too far toward the safe perspective of observer.

A Cat and a Snake

A quick movement catches my eye off to the side of a trail. What looks like a large house cat is fighting with a snake an inch in diameter and at least four feet long. My camera ready, I creep to within ten feet of a dramatic interspecies battle. The cat rolls in the red dirt, holding the snake with claw and fang. The snake wriggles and hisses, biting the side of the cat's face with wide, ugly jaws. Great gods in disguise—*a Hindu folk drama unfolding in the woods just for me! Yippee!* It hardly seems like a cat and a snake would be play fighting out here on a trail well away from any sign of human domesticity. Not that that would necessarily account for anything here. It's a good shamanic (at least a Kodachrome) moment.

When I raise my camera for a few quick shots they freeze in mid-battle, their heads suddenly turned toward me. *What the...?* Perhaps my lens reflects a mesmerizing glint? They remain in that pose for almost a minute. A huge, iridescent eye in the middle of my face? I am gripped by such grave presence that I am frozen too, and do not dare release my noisy shutter. They are a mere few feet from me. In our collective quiet they relax, untangle their fighters' grips and recline, *together,* in the dirt. The cat licks her paw and washes her face, her eyes aloof slits. In less than a minute her thrashing energy has been transformed into comfortable lethargy. Likewise, the snake lies still. Is the snake sleeping? *What does a sleeping snake look like?* They are body upon body and there they remain together, as if cuddling while they doze.

I snap a few mediocre pictures and continue on. I don't know what to think. That the scene I just witnessed is unconventional or even incredible seems clear enough. Yet there is no real clarity in saying so. I'm left without any reasonable way of framing it.

Have I been graced with a portent? If so, its meaning clearly eludes me. And yet any further thinking on the matter might easily delude. Is it just magical thinking? I consider the beginnings of Hinduism, with all those animal gods. And shamanism, sometimes described as our earliest social system going back for untold millennia, by which everything possesses spirit and meaning. Like those early myth tellers might have fancied, the performance back up the trail has something to do with worlds that don't fit—a cat, a snake—but soon will in some cozy synthesis that will fill the gaps in my spotty understanding. Has the cyclops in my hands, by the sorcery of light in a multi-coated "third eye," made lambs of lions?

What can be said of the reality of what we see when our eyes, wide with wonder, act also as magnifying glasses, or distorting mirrors?

The longer I stay in India the more comfortable I become with ideas that once were wild, ideas like reincarnation and mystical powers (*siddhi.*) When an untenable idea is accepted as plausible, will evidence begin to appear and then accumulate? And then take the shape of the idea itself by its preconceived projection? These days it's become common pop-mystic fare: our preconceptions shape, by choice (conscious or unconscious), how we describe, and even see, what is real.

It has been said that in the growth of scientific knowledge one paradigm shifts to another, and one generation's understanding gives way to the novel inter-connective ideas of the next. Science moves through cycles this way, with evidence that gathers to explain the hitherto unexplainable, evidence that can no longer be ignored or refuted.[126] Looking back over a few such cycles it's clear that we have a tenacious habit, at any given time, of acting as if we understand a whole lot more than we actually do. Each mini-age looks

126 Trained as a physicist, Thomas S. Kuhn moved toward the philosophy of science, resulting in *The Structure of Scientific Revolutions,* one of the most cited academic books of all time.

back upon the blinders of the last with self-assurance and so-called clarity, which turns out, by the next round, to be not-so-clear. As it slowly and awkwardly unfolds in the collective, so it goes, I reckon, in the personal.[127]

We like to think we see things as they are out there. Is it possible to be objective? We do observe things; this we can say for sure. But who observes? Shall we observe that too? My cat and snake have presented the unclear in clear light, having placed mystery on a flat-earth platform so I can walk around and look at it. I get to see ignorance—the general variety, for sure. But specifically—and more relevantly—mine.

Perhaps it's not so amazing that a cat and a snake in mid-battle would do an abrupt ceasefire, cuddle up, and fall asleep together when a large biped with a great shimmering eye approaches. *Perhaps.* The distinction between mystery and the explainable makes for a dodgy line.

Sitting around a fire back at the beach, I want to tell my friends about my Disney-shaman scene. As awkward and opaque as the encounter was—a brainy feline, a legless reptile, me off to the side with a gleaming tunnel of glass in the middle of my head—I feel I must report it. How can I resist? I feel like talking about it just to hear it myself.

Right away it isn't hard to spot one or two personal paradigms jiggling, eyes twitching and heads bobbing. The serious American chick with long black hair wonders aloud about some heady *siddhis* on the loose. The pretty ginger British gal, now speaking of *chakras* and *dharma*, rides a wave of trendy ideas and new experiences that unfold like a wondrous, psychedelic flower as she tells her story and explains mine. The cool Italian dude imagines ego vanishing before his eyes, while its unholy stroking is what *I* feel... as well, that regrettable aftertaste. Maybe one day I'll learn to forgive myself my trespasses.

---

127 I suspect that the above mentioned "refuting" by the current custodians of Truth—as well as the inevitable, subsequent willingness of many to fall in line—are subject to the old tricks of preconception, compliance, and control. I tend to think of this complex of behaviors as a collective inner beast in the service of guarding old kingdoms of thought, a beast that would deny, by the sway of visceral power, any new idea that would shake the kingdom's foundations. I imagine how we might befriend, and perhaps tame this beast. Reflect upon it, understand how it governs by fear. And how this fear not only deprives us of new paths of discovery, but also bends the very light that grants us perception.

The next day, the American with long red dreads walks up and says, "You don't have a whole lotta karma left, man." I say nothing, just look back at him, vaguely understanding the suggestion that karma is like some kind of ethereal baggage, that it registers only as psychic or spiritual weight, and that I presently appear to him as rather light. *Could you mention my sweet nothingness to those hot Swedish chicks over there?* He has no idea (and I feel no need to detail) what a rather simple laddie I am, all things considered.

Like a random whirl of child's breath from chilly Labrador into a typhoon that Shiva would be proud of, my little report has grown with flair. Cats and snakes spar in the woods—*yeah, I guess.* And we beach folk see simple things in mystical bursts of sweet divinity. I imagine it all, an egoless cyclops lurking in the jungle, taming wild animals with a simple look. And I *want* to believe, I want this wondrous mess of desire, perception and contradiction to be nothing but beautiful, delightful truth.[128]

Yet the ruse of human pride is the slickest trick of all, as I am discovering. Clearly, it's the one to watch.

Reina

One evening, I look toward the north end of Little Vagator at the moving silhouette of a naked woman coming our way in the twilight. Not an unusual sight in Goa, and certainly not an unwelcome one. Her appealing figure stirs my interest, but so does a ragged sway in her movement. As she comes closer I recognize Reina, a German gal I met a few weeks back on the ferry from Bombay. She seems to recognize me.

On that overnight boat ride we were immediately drawn to each other. She exuded a powerful sensuality and heightened awareness. She sat close and looked straight into me, her eyes like dark little fires. Within a minute my arm was around her waist as her words danced circles around mine. The old wooden ship slipped across a sultry, quicksilver sea as we lay together on that warm night, as she looked around and observed that "everyone except us is only half alive." As self-serving as this sounded (her German likely would have been more graceful), I

---

128 *The psychotic drowns in the same waters in which the mystic swims with delight,* Joseph Campbell.

looked around and agreed. In that moment, Reina's presence, how she drew me there, made it look that way. *Naturally,* I thought, *we're stoking a hot little flame...* and everyone else is tired and settling in for the night. But I couldn't (and didn't want to) disagree with this unusual and lovely woman. We lay together, talking through the night with such ease as befits longtime lovers.

The next morning after the boat docked I left, heading down the street. I hadn't considered any mode of travel but going solo since the evening I discovered, on that Greek isle, that I would return to India. My drive was resolute. I didn't know why, and I couldn't have defended my action; all I can say is that my legs moved sure and swift. I looked back once at Reina standing in the middle of the street. After that day I forgot her.

A couple of weeks later I saw her in a beachside restaurant with two guys. My guess is they were compatriot Germans; doesn't matter. I stood at the entry of the restaurant staring, and went no farther. Reina was behaving in an uninhibited, almost boisterous manner. She was laughing as she danced seductively among the tables while receiving (and enjoying) the fixed and heavy attentions of the two dudes. I was surprised by this unexpected turn, and repelled by the guys' sedate yet voracious energy. The way they looked at her, their eyes following her every carefree move, like their intent was predatory. I despised them. Maybe I exaggerated my protective fear in my own mess of jealous feelings and nostalgia for our unusual connection back on the ferry. Reina didn't see me; I had come to check out the scene at Colva Beach. At least I don't think she saw me. I left quickly, overcome as I was by complex and oppressive feelings. Perhaps I felt some guilt about leaving her on the street that morning. And I was utterly repelled by the two guys. *Assholes.*

Now she approaches in the warm twilight, naked, not even carrying a bag. *How far has she wandered?* I walk toward her and she recognizes me. But she's not the same person I met on the boat over a month ago. There's something abject in the way she carries herself. Her eyes are set in a dramatic moment of loss. Pain is covered over by a glaze of isolation, but only barely. And she doesn't talk. Back on the boat she did most of the talking, and I was captivated. *How, and why, has she stumbled into this mute and dissonant zone?* Like the Aussie in the tea hut, like others, she seems to have lost her bearings. *Social? Personal?* Adrift yet bound, she ricochets between isolation and pain.

She stays close to my side like a child who has found a safe spot in a dangerous zone. I take her to the restaurant hut. As she sits nibbling at her meal of fish and rice a friend drapes a cloth over her shoulders. After dusk falls she huddles against me in the sand. Our first meeting on that boat was not so long ago; her smooth skin, her body's hypnotic aura, all but overwhelm me. But the contrast in her condition... this time it's eerie. I guess, for verbal communication is nil, that she remembers something, lying so close to me. I feel a rush of blood but there is conflict and confusion. She's naked, and I might as well be; I'm wearing only a few square inches of flimsy cloth that both contain and magnify my heat. I am being drawn in as if by foregone hardwiring. Or, as I sink further into my own discordant story, I'm carried in the pull of two magnetized bits that seek to turn this disconnected world toward unity, ecstasy—however I might want to spin it in this fractured space between desire and madness.

I touch her tentatively—once, twice. She does not reciprocate but keeps whimpering and moaning. *Is it... now louder?* A freaky psychological chasm separates us; my confusion and lust, her messed-up state.

In an instant the so-called hardwiring, the "program"—glitches and collapses. From this moment I am her protector. She trembles like a child as I hold and comfort her. The only sounds she makes are lone syllables and those incomplete moans, and half whispers that disappear back into whatever experience she is struggling through. Those whispers... she's afraid, yet she remembers. It seems she barely manages to maintain a common psychic bearing with me; our brief connection that night on the boat seems to have left but a trace of safety. She needs something—*I want to help.* For how long can I be invulnerable to the magnetism of sexual heat? *I don't know.* To help someone back to mental and emotional health, if it's possible, must be an enormous task. I'm not sure I want to take it on, and I'm not sure I'd know how. I feel like a failure for being so limited. Afraid of my own capacity or lack, and sinking into despondency with a fear that cripples me.

Fuck! I will help Reina find her strength. *I must.*

Deeper into the night when she must think I'm sound asleep, she frisks around my body, perhaps searching for money. That, of course, has been buried for weeks now, not twenty feet from where we lie. I remain still; she relents and again snuggles close.

At breakfast the next morning she seems more at ease, but still, she is mute. Her face and her eyes have softened; the terror has returned to its hiding place. When our eyes meet I imagine her smile somewhere inside her, how it had enticed me back on the boat. And how it surely must be as real, right now, as yesterday's terror. But there is little in the way of response, and little I can be sure of.

Later when I'm away for a few minutes, she disappears.

Wild Man

Another naked one appears, this time from the other end of the beach. A man with angry eyes and a bushel of crazy-black hair bounds along the rocks toward us. He growls and hisses, his spit flying through the sun's rays in pretty arcs. He appears so wild and unhinged that the beach people are keeping clear of what looks to be his projected path. Exorcism would be the order of the day back in *Cattolico* Land.

I sit in the tea hut reading a book by the anti-guru, J. Krishnamurti.[129] His reflective words seem to induce a quiet appreciation of the natural world around me. I look up at this wild man who approaches with the grace of an enraged wolverine, then back at my book. Starting with Mr. Oz, I've seen a half dozen travelers wandering recklessly in these lost jungles of mind. So this latest example, although the clear leader in dramatic impact, lacks the surprise element of the first few. Besides, my gut says the "wild one" poses no threat, and that the best medicine is in interacting normally, with dignity. My inclination is to respond foremost to his intact creaturehood and humanity, then take it from there. For some reason part of me just doesn't fully buy into the cloaks we wear, or the fear of so-called insanity.

Perhaps he senses and is drawn to my "benign indifference." Snarling at those nearby, he stomps straight to me, in stark contrast to Mr. Oz in this very tea hut when I first arrived. He lands on the bench beside

129 *The Second Krishnamurti Reader* by J. Krishnamurti.

me and peers fanatically into my book, leaning on me as if there's no space or distinction between our bodies. Raining sweat and smelling like a fishy forest, his breathing wheezes past a fortress of clenched teeth onto the pages and over my face. Partly because I wonder how Krishnamurti's words will fly, and partly to ease him back a notch so I can once again smell the ambient perfume of life, I offer him the book. He takes it like a famished hyena, his eyes and nose stuck into a page. A minute later he leaps off to a pile of boulders ten meters away. He parks himself on top, his back to the tea hut. Hunched over like a large ape, he clutches the book and remains motionless. I give him twenty minutes or so. When I get the feeling he might soon be bounding away again, I walk over.

"Hey, I haven't finished reading it myself." I speak to an intact creature, and in this I know he hears me. He looks frightened, angry, and guilty, barely contained behind the tight slits of his eyes. "You can have it when I'm finished." I place my hands on the book as his clench tighter. The process of extracting the book from his grip is slow and forced. I take it from his hands and then pause, looking into his fear-stricken eyes. His face is full and crazed, as if all the anguish in his life is spring-loaded, ready to snap. In my periphery I sense many eyes, large and still. I've seen how fanciful notions will spring from scant evidence and proliferate wildly. Surely some have already sprung from this little drama, quickened in the wake of Reina's immediate cleaving to me, and before that, my cat-and-snake story. And now my calm handling of this flipped-out ape man... My grasp of the gab is not so sure in the face of such novel and embarrassing group dynamics that are so difficult to understand, never mind talk about. I'm just trying to get my book back while respecting the guy; seems simple to me. Reina and I felt a con-nection on that boat, but something grave must have happened to her since I saw her last. It just didn't occur to me to explain to everyone that we'd met before; it was so intense, minute by minute. And the cat and snake? *Good luck with that one.* The public spectacle makes me deeply uncomfortable. It's eerie. A trendy mini-culture is being shaped daily on this beach, and hey, *I'm no fucking Krishnamurti.*

Having come to these beaches intent on a long, easy convalescence, I got more than I bargained for. The primitive, sexy paradise I stumbled into has made mutant dreamers of common travelers. Each one flies a magic carpet woven with desire and illusion, super-charged in an atmosphere of uncommon permissions. On this beach of pleasures I yield to unprecedented freedom, real or not. But I am still weak from illness. I've come into an unusual state of mind, the benefactor of new behaviors I didn't know were in me. I'm unwilling to assume I know things I probably don't, and I ask new questions, like, "What *is* sane/insane?" In the wild man I behold a person flawed in a big and public way, but simply flawed, as we all are in this pain-imbued world. "A personality... lies behind the psychosis," said elder Carl Jung.[130]

And that particular personality needs to know he's overestimated *this* personality's generosity. I turn around, book in hand and (like Bobby D. said) I don't look back.[131] The plainness of it is, I don't fear the wild man.

ODDLY, FROM THAT moment, the wild man doesn't see me. He growls this way and that, never speaking, acting out the bad-tempered chimp. He walks past as if I'm invisible, his eyes not even flinching, as if the light bouncing off my physical shape bounced into some phantom zones between colors. Like Mr. Oz in the tea hut, like the gangs on that Old Delhi street.

Nonetheless, when I finish reading the book, two days later, I take it to him. He is at this moment cussing and slobbering at a gal—just arrived, backpack still on—and hasn't seen me coming. I tap him on the shoulder, startling him. My popping back into his reality disorients and confuses him. I'm less than graceful in my timing, but also, I've been watching for a few minutes and I feel sorry for the poor new arrival he's scaring the shit out of. I'm also optimistic: I wonder if he's caught in an awkward place between his snarling (the psychotic chimp) and the peace in Krishnamurti's words (his intact human self, as per Jung's inclusive assertion).

He takes the book and bounds away. A few hours later he returns it to me, never saying a word but nodding coherently, ever so slightly. Incongruent with his behavior up to this point, the subtle nod—and the simple act of returning the book—is evidence of a perhaps buried social savvy. The old human self.

130 From *Memories, Dreams, Reflections* by Carl G. Jung.
131 *Don't Look Back* is an early film about Bob Dylan.

A little later, he disappears.

I SIT ALONE on a grassy bank looking out over a sea of flickering jewels—rubies, emeralds, diamonds. A mirage of glory appears and disappears on the tip of each wave in the afternoon's long, golden rays. A warm breeze carries the ocean's numinous beauty into my pores, through my hair and over the countryside. Occasionally, like today, I walk along the shore and find a cushy spot away from the area where travelers hang. I want the quiet, the space. I want to observe my own inner workings: what's going on apart from this uncommon milieu, this unprecedented gathering of wayfarers that itself affects each of us in a novel way. The group thing. It's been two weeks since the wild man's exit.

Two figures approach. He has returned, accompanied by an older man. And here's something new: he's fully clothed, and he's walking. No bounding, no growling. He is transformed. *Dad picks up the mask that son carelessly tossed aside, helps strap it back on.*

I say, "Hi." He greets me with excitement and speaks my name. *He knows my name.* It's the first time I hear him talk. Back in his mute madness, he heard our words. He tells me *his* name, introduces his father... who has come all the way from Israel to rescue his son-gone-bananas on a whacked-out beach in India. Sadness and compassion are set deep in the father's eyes. He looks to be in his early fifties, but I have a feeling the circumstances of this day make the lines in his face look deeper than they should. We're alone, and I'm glad of it.

The son has reapplied the veneer of the common mind, donned its time-fashioned cloaks. He's going home; there's nothing much to say, a sentence or two of small talk, an awkward goodbye. His tone is all longing and loss, as if we've been close. The father dropped whatever his life demanded of him and crossed an ocean to love his son, complete package, in this world. And now here they are, with me at a road's end. It's clear that the wild one has come looking for me, hauling Dad in city clothes a quarter-mile up the beach.

The father nods; it's time. As they leave, the son turns to face me. For a second his eyes go manic and his body tense. Instantly, he phases back. Then back again, like a genie wanting to break out. They leave quickly, he looking over his shoulder at me like a child being taken away. The symbolic reversal is as perplexing as it is disturbing. With the father firmly leading, the wild man's frightened, luminous face disappears behind a shrub against the translucent turquoise of the Arabian Sea.

Mystery of the Jungled Mind

A chick with long dark hair runs through the camp screaming and crying. It seems that no one understands her, or has the will to try. The next day I wonder about her, so I go back to the same spot. She's been given food and clothes and now sits still, mute and withdrawn. In answer to the questions in mine, it is evident that something is left undone by the terror in *her* eyes.

A tall Greek man, indulging his version of The Asshole, approaches on the rocks, naked like the others. As the weeks pass, so does this musician friend's sense of connectedness with the rest of us, until he wanders the shore laughing and talking to someone we don't see. A mad German is said to be living alone in a cave up north past all the beaches. On an inter-village path I meet a slight, pale, ghost of a girl, just arrived with backpack, who begins to trail me like a zombie. It is upon those first visceral stirrings of eye contact, and the plunge into intimacy implicit, that I tear my eyes away from hers and deke out down a side path. A certain "hollowness" in her look and manner feels wounded and lost, and I have to say that the question of helping her arouses in me not only feelings of incompetence and insecurity, but also a disquieting pull toward what I might not really know about myself.

Indeed, the ones who bother me most are the sure-footed dreamers who aim to lead the way, their confident gloss locking compulsively into the lonely ones' drifting holes of desolation.

IT OCCURS TO me one day, as I walk the shore away from the crowd toward my solitude, away from our little society into a swirl of mad thoughts and chuckle fits, that I might be lagging behind the "others," *but I can see the jungle from here.* Subtle markings of madness like this could snowball if left unattended. So I begin, in earnest, to attend to them.

Attend to them? Keeping an eye. Looking at, observing. What else to do, join the wild ones? Considering *that* alternative—a trip through social and personal limbo with no promise of a return ticket—this self-monitoring is my trail of pebbles, my vital cord.

Could being conscious (and not in denial) of our own potential madness keep us "in balance"? And even from going there publicly? Might this sense of self-observation be related to how others see and connect with us? The suggestion has been made that consciousness—*con scire*, to know *with*—is, in fact, *inter*consciousness: we are conscious by being conscious together.[132] Are the lost souls one encounters so frequently in Goa merely suffering from a partially severed psychic connective tissue that binds us all? Perhaps the bane of the (post)modern human can be explained, in part, by our once unquestioned identity in the tribe having disintegrated over the last few centuries. The tribe's compulsion toward unexamined compliance is also diminished, at least for some, and we can be thankful for this. Yet a heightened sense of individuality can foster the illusion that we are special, which further promotes the sensation of alienation, of being separate. Or *un*-special, insignificant, meaningless. Is it the coin flipped? Same old ego with its back to the mirror? Perhaps the complex, modern ego finds specialness in a more clever, or hidden way. The questions are easier to ask than to answer. A few troubled wayfarers, or "lost souls" have crossed my path, and my brush with the forbidden territories has been limited and brief.

When I first came to India's Malabar Coast I stood on the bluff overlooking the whitecap-streaked blue ocean and lush palms swaying on Vagator Beach below. A minute later I walked straight into the light and the sands of what had been half hidden in a subtle layer of mind: a primal paradise, perhaps conjured privately, but more likely with a generation, a culture—or the whole human family. Freedom? *As you wish, sahib; stay, police no come.* An abundance of willing sexual partners. Make love on the beach under the stars or in the warm lick of sea under blazing sun. Sing, dance, wander at will, an aimless pilgrim. Excellent food for pennies, heartfelt music. The intellectually stimulating company of travelers from all over the world under luminescent

132 Rupert Sheldrake, from the magazine *What is Enlightenment?*, vol.6 no. 1.

palms and warm-as-a-womb surf. The royal clock and faithful mirror: *your sorcery ends here.* The Goans themselves exude a benign aura; they are remarkable in their tolerance of the audacious young foreigners who flock to their beloved home. Indeed, without their casual openness and fine hospitality, their self-assured grace, the phenomenon known as Goa would not be.

After a time, and for some, one does not merely wander anymore. The frame of reference, the place you started from—home, memory— have fallen away. One might wander even from wandering itself.

We have been conditioned to believe that we are tainted mortals in a cruel and vicious world, while at the same time fed morsels of paradise visions. Religious scenario or Hollywood fantasy, doesn't much matter which. *Here it is, sahib, what you came for.* And so the mind begins to bend. But will it be to liberate, or to enslave?

In this land, an ancient spiritual tradition refers to the visible human realm as *maya,* illusion, often described as a dream we *will* awaken from. How strange to stumble upon one's private dream, within the greater dream, perhaps, only to cross an unmarked boundary into a jungle of unknown effect… as have more than a few strays along these beaches into neurosis, madness, psychosis, whatever we might call it. I too came to that jungle's edge and peered in at those wandering inside, each isolated in a thicket of their own. I saw my essential similarity to each of them. Turning back, I saw also how those behind me—we who call ourselves sane and normal—function as a group, for yay and for nay. In comparison to the wild ones we are drone-like, slavishly and unconsciously adhering to agreed-upon behaviors (not altogether a bad thing, I must assume.) In some basic way, the wild ones have slipped away from our shared state. To what degree is this shared state a collective entrancement that we anoint with the authority of normalcy, of sanity? Each culture with its own version—each casting a jaundiced eye upon the next?

I looked into the jungle again and saw versions of myself running loose in there. *Did I turn away too soon, in fear? Does a deeper human experience avail those whose courage permits a closer look?*[133] Seems we all own a mask,

133 For two very compelling "memoirs of madness", see *Darkness Shining Wild* by Robert Augustus Masters and *Darkness Visible* by William Styron

and it fits so well we hardly know we're wearing one. Until it knocks loose and we begin to tinker and maybe try taking it off.

Mask or no mask, *there but for the grace...* Those who are judged as broken need this non-condemning view more than they need the measure of "normal." Carl Jung: "The crucial point is that I confront the patient as one human being to another."[134] The *crucial* point.

A thread of memory reaches back to a small book, *The Politics of Experience*,[135] which must have had a greater influence than a high school kid could imagine; one that would later guide him around odd protrusions that pop up unexpectedly on the evenly raked paths of our world. We chart a common map of experience, limiting what we take from the spectrum of greater potential, then tell ourselves that these limitations are necessary for the sake of civilization as we know it. Is it so? Perhaps it is, and this—a curbing of what we are permitted to express and become—is the cost. We build super highways of thought—philosophical, scientific, religious. Just as a highway must eliminate whatever grows in its path, the intellect tends to fear what is not in the clearing. *Dreams and symbols, gods and demons.* Can we have another look, maybe sit with it? *Daniel, with his lions?*

It can be scary, the power of connection and compassion that abides healing, a glorious strength that is surely everyone's birthright and will soften the eyes of a madman. But it's not fantastic. There were moments when I stepped away in fear. I was taken aback, looked again, and then deeply moved by the profound effect of simply facing each of them. Is a modest degree of compassion, or connection, enough to remind of one's unnatural singularity, of what we are (and never stopped being) beneath the pain? Perhaps I was threatened by the power of direct connection, and the implication that so much of how I normally interact with others is, by comparison, a shallow probing of the greater depths that are available within and among us. And that those shallow interactions and stories are what is so normal in the world.

134 From *Memories, Dreams, Reflections* by Carl G. Jung.

135 In his book, R. D. Laing questions our concept and experience of "normality", and suggests that those we call insane or mad are unable to be reined in by the "straitjacket of conformity" that modern society fits every child with, and that in this way our potentialities are sharply reduced.

To recognize the integral self in one who ails is not so amazing, not really. That the recognition itself promotes healing seems clear enough. As simple and as natural as the starting point of safety and trust. What is the nature of the healing effect, of one person and another? Is it simply the unimpeded action of what is often described, by mystics, as the essence of life itself—of what we call love?

And what of those brief but crucial passages we call transformation? *Our deepest fear is that we are powerful beyond measure.*[136]

That this is, evidently, rare in our world, *this* is what I found—and find—truly scary.

Anjuna

If Goa is Asia's Freakville, then Anjuna Beach is its hippest downtown beat. A mile or so of narrow golden beach fronts a village area shaded by a sprawling plantation of coconut palms. For the visiting traveler, it is the center of fashionable and commercial activity for a larger area that includes several beaches to the north and south. On a per-capita reckoning, it seems that musicians flock to the Vagator beaches; junkies and the Children of God prefer to hang downtown. A bona fide locus of Western indulgences, Anjuna reminds of my own society's frayed edges.

The meeting of cultures is in full swing, for we have come from many places. The Goans themselves are a pleasant intermingling of India and Portugal, of the Hindu and the Catholic worlds. Perhaps the Goans and we travelers share a certain perspective. Looking west out to sea, the small state of Goa is closed in on all sides by the vast multiplicity of Hinduism. Portugal was evicted in 1961 and the "hippies" arrived a few years later. Perhaps we Western travelers were a welcome sight to the Goans.

One morning I bound over the rocky cape from Vagator to the north end of Anjuna into the first tea hut. I squeeze in at the end of a bench.

A guy strums a guitar, a Goan girl and her American boyfriend sit next to me. She speaks of straining under opposing forces, for she has acculturated into the modern mindset, and her folks will not accept her

---

136 From Nelson Mandela's inaugural speech, taken from *A Return To Love* by Marianne Williamson.

foreign hippie beau. A young woman from Bombay speaks up. She left a life behind, describing how her new one began by risking a meeting with a young man of choice, and not the prearranged one. By merely touching feet under a restaurant table, somewhere in the sprawl of that vast city, they'd leapt into a new life. Here they are, this Goan gal and this Bombay lass, mingling naturally with us in the palm tree shade, just as our pasts and dreams cascade throughout our conversations.

Down the beach, chillum-sharing groups of travelers pound the sandy plains of euphoria. It's the usual mediocre guitar and bongo while Goan children scamper happily about. A tall Indian with long black hair and dressed in colorful shawls strolls along the sand carrying a wicker tray from which he hawks assorted coins. I stop him, this being the first coin seller I've encountered. Poking through his random heap I isolate four or five silvery ones that stand apart from the rest on account of their irregular shape and ancient look. I pick what appears to be the best of the group and pay five (!) US dollars for it. Having started at a price of seven, he will not budge any lower. He behaves as if it is of high value, of course. I will take this unusual prize home to my father, who enjoys collecting coins.[137]

A swap meet is held every Sunday on the beach, organized by and for the benefit of travelers. That is, until the Goans figure out we've been getting away with something other than simply evading the repellent forces of our respective homelands. And that something involves the exchange of goods, services, and—aha!—the local currency. The administrators of order (and accounts payable) decree the swap meet be moved to the road. And start collecting a fee from each seller. After some initial bellyaching we do what we're told, for this is the way of the world and we are, evidently, still in it.

And enjoying it immensely.

A WOODEN STAGE is tucked into the small crescent at the south end of Anjuna. This is party central for several adjacent beaches. In the past two months there have been parties at full moon, new moon, Christmas, Boxing Day, New Year's, and on a few other nondescript nights.

137 Years later, with a little research—long after my father has passed—I learn that the coin is from the early Parthian Kingdom of ancient Persia, in the second century bc.

Word on the beach: once upon a time the rock band The Who, after visiting Anjuna, left behind a band's worth of instruments and a sound system for all to enjoy. Urban myth? A lockable cement building stands near the stage where the equipment is kept, so who knows? The caretakers, whoever they are, act like hippie commandos and hover around the stage area in an atmosphere of celebrity/authority. The "innest" of the in-crowd, and a difficult circle to penetrate, if anyone should be so crass as to try. That young travelers are driven to form cliques—driven to *identify with*—is both puzzling and discouraging. Or amusing, depending on my mood. At other times I feel I glimpse a different scene—a harder scene with hard drugs and hard knocks. *Hard faces.*[138]

Late one afternoon I walk from Vagator across the shrub-covered cape to Anjuna. I hear sounds; I imagine snakes. I've been fortunate to spot a few from some distance, larger than the benign garters back home. But other than the one who snoozed with a cat in the presence of a friendly cyclops, I haven't run into any on these trails, and I don't want to. It's cobras and their victims that I hear about on occasion.

There's no reason to expect a party at Anjuna today; it's not a full moon, nor a new nor a blue one. It's not even a weekend, though that would hardly be on anyone's mind here in the Tropic of Timeless, where days of the week and such have fallen away into the forgotten flotsam that smacks up relentlessly against the eroding banks of memory.

I climb down from the cape and stop at the tea hut. The ubiquitous guitar is passed around; time noodles on without aim. As Big Yellow Sky Dragon cools to amber, a constellation of flickering lights answers in kind from way down the shoreline where the stage sits at the far end.

Curious, I rise. On my way I'm joined by others; a few walk ahead. In the twilight, with the gentle lapping of waves at our feet, our migration recalls a semiconscious response to a master signal, like those unfortunate descendants of ours in that early H. G. Wells sci-fi classic.[139] We are spaced-out layabouts, walking in unison like the drone-humans in that movie, a bit friskier and more curious maybe. Call us Lazy Lemmings or Savvy Salmon.

138 The infamous "Bikini Killer", Charles Sobraj, is said to have been hanging around Goa at this time.
139 *The Time Machine* by H.G. Wells.

We're under a spell, alright, but the real magus is license pushed by desire (and a nominal reserve of cash.) Hints of ecstasy are all around as we walk, and in some flickering lights down the beach, we see many things.

We arrive to find that a group of Goan merchants has prompted this, by now, appreciable gathering. They've set up their food, drinks, and trinkets on blankets near the stage. Each has placed a lit candle in the sand. They've done good business catering to ravenous freaks at all-night parties over the last few weeks. And this evening, since the air and the sea (not to mention their pockets) are still and expectant, they decided to throw one themselves. The only occasion is the one the Goans have created. It works, and we don't mind. Because now, *it's time to party.*

Out come guitars, flutes and bongos. The concrete bunker is unlocked, and electric equipment is hauled over by eager rock 'n' roll dreamers. *Time keeps on slippin'* through the *lunatic... on the...* stage's sound system *so you (think you) can tell, heaven from hell.*[140] At the worst jam sessions in unrecorded history, every person on stage is the lone star, and the state is always "my turn." By 3:00 or 4:00 a.m. some semblance of a groove descends upon the stage as if from some deeper, ego-defeating realm. *The Muses relent.* The early, insufferable noise is transformed into dreamy, loosely woven instrumentals. Dancing, naked forms reflect bio-sensitive moonlight through retinas and into bloodstreams. The forbidden feast, all the delicious poisons. We go headlong, hungry and beguiled. I am pulled along the serpentine movement of dark and light, of hovering crescents and bobbing shadows on smooth, luminescent skin. I am thrown deep into fires that are the laughing eyes of swaying young women, drawn into galaxies of pleasure, appearing, disappearing, each unnamed star moaning its approval. We are charged and mesmerized by life itself.

What unfocused, hedonistic beasts we have become.

All the while, Goan children move through the crowd, taking money and delivering drinks, and not least of all, learning the strange ways of these colorful and libidinous foreigners.

....

140 "Fly Like an Eagle" by Steve Miller; "Dark Side of the Moon" and "Wish You were Here" by Pink Floyd.

LIKE MANY OTHERS, a young Indo-American sadhu keeps returning to humble Little Vagator from the much flashier Anjuna. As it often is, it's for the good music.

He returned to the old country from middle America a few years ago, immersed himself in its ways, and took Shiva quite seriously. Having donned the ocher robes he crisscrosses India, hopping trains and walking the smaller tracks between villages, following his *dharma* as it manifests a path before his eyes. Occasionally he encounters, as a sadhu is said to do, unexpected pleasures of the flesh in the vast countryside of an ancient land.

Often present at the unrestrained delights that are Little Vagator's impromptu beachside jams, he listens well when I pluck a guitar, more mellow than the usual hyper *thwangs*. He tells me I don't have much anger or hard feelings to transcend, and that it's a function of this or that chakra. *Hmmm, chakra.* On the other hand, I have no reason to doubt his sincerity.

On a brilliant day, in the nearby town of Map'sa where foreigners cash traveler's checks or shop for supplies, I see him standing on the street outside the post office. His pose is straight and expressionless, his eyes fixed on a distant point. *Or is it an inner, non-point?* He has a postcard addressed to the USA. He holds it high on his chest. It lacks a stamp.

The sadhu has no money, no attachments. He "possesses nothing, and nothing possesses him."[141] Even now, this postcard might be mailed simply in compassion for loved ones. The sadhu sends a postcard to relieve suffering, not from the compulsion of personal attachment. An explanation that abides the higher calling expected of a sadhu is easy to conjure.

I go in, buy a stamp for the States and hand it to him. He takes it, his eyes softening for a moment. A subtle acknowledgment of the giver, of the impersonal bounty of Vishnu yet again in the act of preservation. I'm sure he recognizes me on the edge of his focus. But I'm not sure how deep and steady is the sadhu's *pranayama,* or how awkward the young American feels.

Yet his stance is true to his calling. They say a sadhu must never beg, and that he must take only what is freely given.

---

141 An alternate of "He does not possess wealth; it possesses him" from Benjamin Franklin.

Jungle Lake

to see the world in a grain of sand
and heaven in a wild flower
hold infinity in the palm of your hand
and eternity in an hour[142]

IT'S TIME TO go for a walk. Word on the beach: a whacked-out, ill-tempered German is said to be living in a cave, feral-hermit style, just past a remote shoreline. A group of squatters is camped around a lake that sits right next to the last beach up north.

Early one morning I check my pack at Little Vagator's lone eatery hut. The family who runs the place stores travelers' belongings for a small weekly fee, as well as for the main benefit of keeping us hanging around buying their tasty meals. But I don't trust the arrangement quite enough for the dense-value items: traveler's checks, passport, camera. I pass the spot in the sand where I buried them over two months ago. Wondering how long I'll be gone I hesitate, reinforcing the image of the handsome pattern of boulders framing Bulldog Rock adjacent to my precious cache. I turn and walk north along the shore, playing foot games with the waves.

I carry twenty bucks in a money belt (plenty of cash for a few more weeks if I'm prudent.) My thin lungi/blanket and T-shirt are folded over it. My proud baggage is covered by about twenty-three square inches of worn muslin, and when a little puffed in the presence of a comely traveling chick, it's easy enough to move my T-shirt over. Asses look bare with this local style, but mine is partly hidden by hanging clothes, a modest measure for around here. No need to wear the lungi on the beach, just like the local fishermen. As well, the minimalist crotch-patch style is borrowed from them.

My only map is the verbally sketched "a day's walk to the north." After a pleasant stroll along a pristine stretch of beach I come to a wide river mouth. A small dark man with peaceful eyes waits in a canoe-like vessel for one or two more passengers. In good faith I pay the small fee before crossing.

---

142 From *Auguries of Innocence* by William Blake.

As we glide over the water I find that I'm a passenger aboard more than just a rudimentary wooden boat. The peaceful man and his vessel are bene-factors of a passage into a new region, one that is more than sand and sea and coconut palms. I am cut loose like the blue meanies cut me back in Kuta but this time, without help from the plant realm, the passage is gentler.

The membranes of life pulse and breathe as the boat slips along. Fragments of beauty are strewn across water, land, and sky. The world buzzes and sighs. It crawls and flies and swims in freely moving bits of stories, hunks of myth, and look-see symbols that blink on and off, teasing my capacity to catch sight of them. They pop into vistas conscious and personal, and maybe unconscious, archetypal. The river, like my thoughts, is in many places at once, always emerging, always disappearing. Trees that reach skyward at the water's edge are the frozen, transmigrated tributaries of the same deep river. *Coming from, and going where?* Indeed, along the fine design that unifies their branches and the veins under my skin? Look—birds fly upward and chase each other like toddlers, then splash apart like a fountain. Are they thrilled, as I am in witnessing their art? The surface of the water; what kind of barrier could mean such different things, say, to a fish and to my hand? It's a puzzle with no problem, no solution. Hints of meaning vainly seek descrip-tion in pictures and words, a mysticism for dummies. *Look deep into the water, as far as you can.* My shifting reflection spills the secret: *identity left behind, back at the surface.* There surely is value in Reina's and the wild Israeli's isolated sojourns. My heart and mind are still bound up in their stories—something arcane yet common to us all. It appears that I go along a different path, a more common one. Yet my hunch is that it is already written in pebbles up ahead, in her style, in his, the telling of stories from future and past.

I step from the boat and continue along the shore. The world arrives each moment on a zillion trails of ancient light. I am fortunate. I have done little to earn such laughter from the breeze, to walk past sanity, sanctity, and still be free to keep walking. Tears of wonderment, of grati-tude, and of sadness, rise and fall. I'm not so sure of their reason or their source, but I hold it all here inside my smiling skin, at a place with no address at the edge of the world.

The warm sand and tepid sea disappear into forest mist, blue upon green upon gold. Huts are visible through the coconut palms as is, occasionally, the shadowy movement of Goan villagers among the trees. They notice me, of course, a glance here and there. But it's unimportant; they're busy, and I've become unstuck from the already unstuck business of travel. For I am no bother to them, and little is their bother to notice me. For several hours as I walk into the sprawling afternoon, I meet no one.

A great tower of rock juts into the Arabian Sea. I clamber upward on a mission, waves crashing below. It occurs to me that getting to the top of the world is permitted. I bellow out with a power that startles me, the raw howl of a stranger clear across the ocean, a caged beast whose voice I don't recognize. It's a gut-cry gone flesh and bone, back to stone and into the sea, a long overdue scream from the night of spiders and dreams.

By late afternoon I come to a small tea hut on the beach. Two Western gals, each wrapped in little more than two square feet of colored cloth, walk slowly along a sunlit path. They smile in my direction. *I must be close.* I chase my hunger and take a smooth tangent alongside their swaying hips. A young prince in a Hindu myth,[143] confused and hungry and unable to resist the self-induced spell of the maiden-goddess, wanders for eons, passionate but enslaved through a wonderland forest of his own making. Walking the trail along the sun-dappled, sparsely wooded beachfront, drawn into the theater of their beauty, I think I remember his life.

This is a fishing village area so serene that I feel I've walked clear out of the age of money and machines. A few hundred meters up the beach is the place I set out to find early this morning.

Somewhere down the road, will I reemerge along the partialities of my homeland? As the guy who can't read stones, and who will no longer remember ancient myths?

A NARROW RIDGE of sand separates a small lake from the choppy ocean. Across the pond a trickling stream drains a thickly wooded crevasse that rises gently inland between two semi-arid hills. Along the water's edge and up the dense valley on winding trails, travelers loll about. Some

---

143 From Tripura Rahasya (*The Mystery Beyond the Trinity*), an ancient Sanskrit literary work.

swim or wade in the lake. One frolicking pair splash a bit and laugh quietly as they couple in the water.

Many appear to have settled in comfortably. Sleeping holes are fashioned from logs and leaves, in bushes, and in old hollow stumps. Homes have been made among the tangle of giant roots, some up in trees. In one elaborate nest near the edge of the jungle, a young French mother and her man live with two toddlers in several rooms carved from the foliage. It is a neo-retro settlement, a straggly remnant of counterculture spirit transplanted a decade down a faraway place. Seemingly cut off from modern life the people here have, in a way, found simplicity. Yet packaged goods are handy at dinnertime.

Some like me are casual visitors, here for several weeks or so. But there are more than a few permanent travelers in India making their winter home here in Goa or Kerala, and moving north to various Himalayan locales like Nepal, Kashmir, and Ladakh for the summer. And some of those perennial travelers are no doubt here at this wilderness valley and lake by the sea.

Viewed from the sandbar at the beach, the valley across the lake looks deceptively small, nothing more than a patch of green. But the real size of the narrow jungle is impressive, going inland so far as to become a distinct environment itself. The sounds of surf and people are a roaring symphony compared with the stillness of the forest. Walking the darker, humid trails that braid alongside the creek recalls the Amazonians' fabled quietness of movement. When meeting others on those trails, we moderns naturally adapt the same delicate step and silent demeanor.

Tree or No Tree

Farther up the valley stands a most splendid tree.

An ancient banyan has spread out over decades, maybe centuries, creating an environment only of itself. Like a Vedic riddle, it is a tree but no longer *is*—yet it's the only thing in sight. The six-foot-diameter central trunk is long gone. Vines that circled it when it was mature and hard have grown thick and hard themselves, some two to four inches, and serve as a convenient spiralling ladder going up twenty feet or more and spaced nicely for climbing. Within the giant coils grow younger vines, spirals within spirals, a two-tiered, concentric triple and quadruple helix on the wild side circling skyward. Like a metaphor for materiality itself, this whole phantom tree is composed mostly of space. It is perfect for this place, this moment, and for this mind that defers to the ways of a land and civilization partial to riddles that trace eccentric circles over shifting maps of reality.

From this awesome centerpiece more than a dozen huge branches, as thick as two feet, grow horizontally in every direction. The great mass of these daughter limbs cannot be supported by the trunk—which is nonexistent—nor could it by any trunk anywhere. Instead the branches are borne by a small forest worth of trees that dropped to the ground as weeping tendrils seeking sustenance a long time ago with the original tree, then thickening over time to their present massive dimensions. I look around; all the trees in this part of the forest aren't trees at all but giant overgrown tendrils connected to, and holding up, the *larger* horizontal branches above. These vertical and horizontal limbs create a network that one can easily climb and walk around in. It is spacious enough to accommodate three homes in the air twenty feet apart, room enough for the comfort of relaxed squatters. I tour the middle and upper reaches of this arboreal world without disturbing these neighbors of the air. I'd stay much longer in this fantastic airy land so high above the forest floor, but I'll soon be snooping into someone's room if I stay.

I stand on the seashore, looking north. The narrow beach dwindles until the land rises sharply in a series of low mountains that reach into the sea. This is perhaps the northernmost of the Goan beaches. From here, where this most reclusive tribe of travelers hang, the beaches of Goa stretch for fifty miles to the south.

Looking again toward the shoreline of misty hills I remember the German. His cave is said to be farther up the beach, hidden behind a ridge and isolated, like its resident mind is said to be.

I turn around and head south.

Pigs of Heaven

The village of Benaulim, adjacent to Colva, catches my roving fancy for a week or so (at forty kilometers long, Colva is the most magnificent of the Goan beaches, some say in all of India.) Here one can rent a room and live among the Goans, a ready hospitality that I've encountered nowhere else on the subcontinent. Of course I've seen only a small bit of what is India, and there's no doubting the kindness of Indians all across their country. Yet I've felt, in most places, that I am "other." It is said that when you enter Goa you leave India behind. The commonality of Christian heritage, brought here by sixteenth-century Portuguese colonists, might account for some unexpected affinity.

Three months on, I still feel the after effects of hepatitis, although I feel stronger with each week that passes. I continue to use my gas stove several times a week. All those rich veggies.

Sitting next to the beach, Benaulim village spreads luxuriantly among tall coconut palms. Pigs of all sizes wander about ungoverned, enjoying a sub-society of their own. Wells and toilets, each used by several families, are evenly dispersed among the huts. The watering holes serve as meeting places where smiling villagers go about their daily business, yakking happily, washing clothes and carrying water.

On the other hand the toilets double as diners for the pigs. Cleverly designed for this dual purpose, the concrete base consists of a few steps that lead to a squatting spot on a small platform. One's droppings fall into an angled chute, accessible to a pig's snout from the back. For privacy, the platform is rimmed with palm-leaf walls. Behold the "pigloo."

After a few visits to these (presumably) ecologically sound toilets (do we want it back in the soil, or in the pig?), a young one follows me over. Earnest and purposeful, he scoots along close to me as if to avoid attracting attention. *The brainiest of the bunch, my little buddy,* that kind of look. The last thing I see before dropping my pants is a moist pig snout, sunlit, quivering, and waiting with quiet patience at the bottom of the chute. A second later it's a diabolical, drooling maw with nasty fangs aimed ominously close on my hanging softies. As soon as they begin, these daily interludes become times of surreal anxiety.

Soon enough I cause a noseworthy stir in the village's porcine subculture. The secret is out; my rich diet has made irresistible fare of my superfluous pap. When I walk toward the toilet, a fight breaks out among three or four of the largest brutes until Top Hog trots over to await the sweet mash. After my sphincter is licked by the rough tongue of a particularly hasty one, I bring a weapon. I poke and whack at their faces with a rough stick once or twice, and they learn to be patient. I snap a picture. *Bad.*

And so it comes to pass that I move down the shore. Too bad, too sad for that community of lively porkers tucked into the palms on that fabulous beach down the Malabar Coast.

Bobby

Bobby is from California and fancies himself a budding guru. Even before he's a full-fledged guru he's seeking disciples, like the rookie guru up north. Says he just came from a consummating retreat with *his* guru, a disciple of Sri Yukteswar, who was the guru of the renowned *Autobiography of a Yogi* author Paramahansa Yogananda.

Bobby says his master told him he'd soon be ready to start a following of his own. When he all but proclaims himself a Buddha, saying that wherever he goes children follow him chanting "Bud-dha, Bud-dha", those on the beach dismiss him as a self-absorbed crank. Bobby wears a crew cut and denim cutoffs, the strangest of the strange in this mid-1970s beachside subculture of nudity and untrimmed hair. His short do and denim are one-offs here, pink jelly beans floating in a bowl of dhal.

When Bobby shares a chillum and bubbles over with the typical giddiness of the newly stoned with the rest of us, it's clear that he's contradicted himself. Earlier, he claimed to inhabit a spiritual state beyond the effects of even powerful psychedelics like LSD. A disgruntled Frenchman calls his hypocrisy and leaves in a huff. Bobby meekly explains that he can choose to share in others' states of mind. But he speaks with the thin hesitation of one who fumbles for an explanation.

I'm impressed, however, with his impromptu musical sojourns. He plays the same drawn-out song, something about being "on the border." He strums and plucks and sings several guitar and vocal parts with rare gusto in an oddball outpouring of musical coordination. Seems it's the one song coming out of him: on the border between sanity and liberation, of this world and some other. He was singing when I first saw him, his eyes like a child's—believing, energetic. Right away I liked him. *Flying straight through the gates of freedom on the wings of this one tune—go for it, Bobby!* Later, I discover it's an Eagles song he kept twisting and turning.[144]

My tendency to hear out even the strangest birds, and to delay judgment, has Bobby hopping high on his spiritual horse, persuading me to follow. Even with all the Eastern ideas I've been exposed to in a year, the idea of a guru still seems an acquired taste. Sure, Christian doctrine came with its own ultimate guru, Jesus. As a child I had my doubts, and today I still have neither accepted (nor rejected) the notion that meeting a guru or master, even if they do exist, is an inevitable consequence of seeking life's meaning(s).

I like Bobby. I don't want to simply rebuff him (confrontation issues), so instead, on several occasions as we talk, I (a tad manipulative) lead the conversation elsewhere (a skill I developed growing up a placid yet cunning nerd in the middle of a large, highly emotive family of extroverted toughs.)

On a morning perfect in temperature and light, Bobby and I sit in the tea hut at Vagator. He's on about my spiritual readiness and this or that chakra, and his service to me, the perfect disciple, *yadda.* This is the third or fourth (and getting old) time. He's more urgent, less patient. I haven't seen him work so hard getting that guru thing off the ground; his master *did say.* Hope is fading on what he must have seen as a great bargain on a keenly receptive soul. Now as the real picture fills in, I suspect that disillusionment is threatening his wannabe vision. I haven't been brutally straight, but neither have I been dishonest. And I do enjoy his childlike let's-make-a-new-world energy.

Then, in what seems an entirely separate moment during the height of his entreaties, he shoots me a look that appears off-color and dissociated, and feels premeditated. His eyes flash distant, queerly goat-like, with a cold intensity that leaves me feeling like I've been... violated? It lasts for a couple of seconds after which, as if spent, he up and leaves. I feel scrambled, disoriented. My belly button throbs inappropriately.

Somewhere in the controversial Carlos Castaneda writings, Don Juan describes a psychic trick he used to "imprint" and draw in the dumb apprentice Carlos. Does there exist some esoteric device used by

---

144 "On The Border" by the Eagles, written by Henley/Leadon/Frey.

would-be gurus in a land that has passed on all manner of psychic disciplines for thousands of years? I wonder, as I remain in the tea hut feeling spooked, why I feel I just dodged an arrow. Right after Bobby shot me the look, didn't I catch a glimpse of extremely weathered ruins of a lost, proto-ancient civilization in the incoming tide? Have I gotten too close to that border? Am I climbing the fence? I've seen others become unhinged; am I so immune? Did Bobby's rookie effort run amok to result in these rambling mind loops?

Maybe I've gone soft, imagining mystical bogeymen in nothing more than a weird, exasperated look. I'm thoroughly flummoxed, but after a few minutes of sitting, breathing, and peering across the ocean into unknown possibility, I feel good. I'm grateful to be who I am, whoever that is, and whatever should happen.

With that, Bobby gives up on me. Does he continue his search for disciples and his own guruhood? In this tropical lotus land, where souls wander aimless and receptive, there's as much chance as anywhere that he'll find it all.

FOR SEVERAL WEEKS running I've said to my new friends, "Maybe I'll stay another week." When I finally do leave, my decision is made in a moment, and I tell no one. I put away the letter from home I just re-read for the third or fourth time, and down my last gulp of chai. I take my pack from the restaurant and walk over to Bulldog Rock, digging up my valuables in the light of day, taking impish pleasure as others look on. I pull up a sealed plastic bag containing my passport, money, and camera, then turn and smile at those still watching. As close as I've grown to more than a dozen travelers on this tiny beach, I'll probably never see any of them again. Without a goodbye, I walk toward the road where a bus comes by every once in a while.

Standing alone, I'm conscious of how little I possess. I count my good health (the post-hep weakness continues to fade) as the best on a small list that includes a scrubby backpack and a small Canadian booklet that enables me to move in the world with relative ease. But I also have time. Time, the continuum that claims everything, the trickster who'll toy with your senses as soon as you stop paying attention. The illusion of its abundant supply is on sweetest offer for travelers, especially those who have lost sight of traveling's end.

At once, from within the bush next to me, come the sounds of snapping twigs. Out of the tangled growth stomps a thrashing, panting, Bobby. It is illogical—and preposterous—that anyone would fight the dense underbrush like this. Why didn't he come along one of the many paths? In the excitement I forget to ask. It's as though, in a moment of sudden urgency, he caught wind of my departure and made a beeline straight to me. Ludicrous. Impossible.

He launches a wildfire blast of log-jammed words and phrases; blurts out that he's relieved to have found me before I left. *What? I just decided to leave with the morning's last cup of tea! And you came from the opposite direction! Through the bush!* His timing is uncanny; I haven't seen him since he gave up on me more than a week ago.

He tells me things I wouldn't have guessed he had the sensitivity or mental acuity to perceive. He describes my psychological and emotional condition. *Not bad.* The stage of life and spiritual journey I'm at. *Cool.* He speaks of my light "karmic debt" and how I'll be treated on the road… and to beware of certain strangers who will, like parasites, look to harm me in my cleaner state. *Weird-ass shit, baba.* And he tells me a secret of cosmic proportions he makes me promise never to tell a soul. *Okay.*

It's amazing that he finds me on this day, minutes before the bus arrives, and less than an hour after I decided to leave. Amazing, too, are his flood of insights and deeply serious manner. He speaks in a spirit of serving, as if helping to prepare me for the next part of my journey. *Still no guru, but man!*

This secret thing: he says he learned it from *his* guru. I won't say much about it (I promised), but I reckon it's intended as a key to revealing mysteries great enough to spin the cosmic *yugas*; a profound recipe of poetic sound, a lure toward growth, a holographic Zen kōan. An uncharted synthesis in Hermann Hesse's *Glass Bead Game*.[145] A simple but truthful word drawing, a description of the mechanics of all-that-is. *A clue to the cat-and-snake drama? Sigh.*

But no sign of sudden enlightenment, the one topic that informs this civilization. Is Bobby on his own road to this enlightenment, or

145 Also known as *Magister Ludi.*

are his words nothing more than diluted takes on big ideas, those of a dissipated mind on a rudderless journey? Staring at this impassioned, perhaps delusional, would-be guru next to the tangled thicket he just emerged from, both views play in my mind. I look into his eyes, then into the dense bush, still amazed he climbed out of it. In an eerie way, one mirrors the other. For a moment, as I look steadily into Bobby's eyes, I see the faces of the wild man, of Reina, and of other stray psyches wandering unhinged along these sublime beaches.

But when Bobby was telling me his secret, I thought I saw something more. For a split second his eyes looked cracked, divided—between the imperfect, foolish man he appears to be and an unknown depth that draws and holds me. It is the power of a way of being that I know little about, other than that I... yes, I *hunger* for it. Somehow, I see this in Bobby's awkward leap toward the guru life, in his freakish burst from the jungle tangle, and in his tall words of service to me. Words one might hear on any street in any town in this enduring land of the traveling soul.

The bus arrives. Bobby barely has time to say the things he wants to say, and he struggles between sentences. His eyes dart about like he's trying to "remember everything," even as I climb the steps.

"Thanks, Bobby."

I look him good in the eye, once more, as the bus groans into gear.

14. Hole in the Universe

I stepped into an avalanche.[146]

Where to Now, St. Chris?

Backing up a day... I receive a first message from my father. He is sixty-one, I am twenty-two. I pause in my tracks, to see and to understand, as best I can. Tomorrow morning I will leave the beach life on what feels like a spontaneous urge; Bobby will come crashing out of the jungle to where I stand and wait for a bus. After re-reading the letter I ask, "Where am I in this journey, this life?"

EVERYWHERE I LOOK, people are tangled in a web of survival needs, like my folks back home. To travel as we do on these charmed and archaic roads is still a rarity. We've taken a serious break from the home world, even dropped out of it. At times I feel like a stranger carrying a familiar passport. We travelers can get to looking quite indulgent, even to ourselves. Complacence, pride and pretension, and entitlement lurk like thieves in the shadow of so-called freedom. *What is my purpose here? How shall I give back?* There is conflict, a malaise of privilege. Must we forsake the feast only to find hunger again?

I left home because I wanted to break free from the constraints of the home world, and that's what I believed I did. *But there is no "breaking free," not in this world, for you need food, and trains, baba.* It is, perhaps, a turn of the devil's bargain.[147]

146 From the song "Avalanche" by Leonard Cohen.
147 From the song "Woodstock" by Joni Mitchell, likely drawn from the legend of Faust, in which he traded his soul to the devil in exchange for knowledge. Or, as various groups have acknowledged in the pervasive condition of suffering in the human world—from Buddhism to A Course In Miracles—Earth's "meat circus" is one tough gig.

I found, as I imagine most travelers do, that the world submits: once its faithful stooge, you become its honored guest. Other than choosing where to go and when to eat, and buying tickets and rooms for the night, I need not *do* anything. Avalanche up ahead? *Oh, hey.* One behind? *Chill, man.* I am unaccounted for and without obligation, wide-eyed *and* blind, moving like a shadow through brilliant days. Grateful for this life, it matters little where I go. A general direction is in the shifting breeze but the path of the unmoored is capricious, looping and zigzagging, this way and that. Odysseus was manipulated and his path all jumbled *because* he was trying to get somewhere. And so Mount Olympus's finest can't scramble the unattached traveler, for the road ahead is defined only by where our feet happen to fall. *When you don't know where you're going, any road will take you there.*[148] One can become unstuck even from the idea of traveling. *A good traveler has no fixed plans and is not intent on arriving.*[149] When that stubborn gatekeeper stopped Lao Tzu, well, the story goes that he had arrived even before he'd left.

Have I arrived, finally, at the place where Billy began, at Auckland Airport with a few dollars in hand, a one-way ticket to adventure booked on a flight, as he put it, "faster than the speed of mediocrity"? A lucky break in the generations? Unearned favor in a lopsided world? Calm before the storm of the turning of worlds, just as our eyes come clear enough to catch a glimpse of the last turning? A cycle of *yugas*, as the Hindus say?

Many moons ago on a dusty highway in Oz, the tumbleweed of expectation came loose from the snag of knowing, and a working holiday rolled away into the sweet unknown. The follow-up has just recently appeared, here in Goa: the question of ever returning home has become moot, as time itself teeters and wavers, then slides along like a slipping clutch between awareness and action. Moments expand and disappear, taking personal experience with them. Thinking itself becomes a loopy-wise exercise, with emptiness a frequent visitor, or a prankster. Or something too fine to recognize, as the Buddhists might say.

---

148 Paraphrased from Alice's conversation with the Cheshire Cat in *Alice In Wonderland* by Lewis Carrol.

149 Lao Tzu.

In realizing that I might never go back "home" I discover that it's okay now, to go there. Only in recognizing that it's okay does it become clear that it previously was *not*. The act of surrender comes bearing a gift: from deep in a sea of funk a single blossom emerges, and a petal falls. Government of Canada is stamped on the underside. *So long, and thanks for the almighty papers.*

We move in pairs or we move alone, it doesn't always matter. I am mystified daily by the numerous faces encountered and left behind, each one as detailed and focused as mine. Every one as "me" as me (can't get over this one, probably never will.) Connection—yea or nay—with each who passes by in this spectral world, with every pair of eyes that draws me in and reflects some essence of everything I think I am, or am worth, or imagine myself to be. Everyman, the hero's billion faces.[150]

Throughout my time in India I have been eerily drawn to the sadhu's anonymous quest. *Everyman.* The renunciant's vow is the polar opposite of ego-puffing cults Celebrity and Fortune, flaunted everywhere in the neo-modern West, on screens and in magazines, in churches and in classrooms. Yet they are magnified —made real—only in the lens of longing inside each of us. And not peculiar are they, perhaps, to nation nor culture. Even sadhus are subject to the wily glory of ego, as I move closer to glorifying them, and their wandering path that leads like a serpent and tempts me so.

There are ways a traveler can earn the small amount of money needed for survival in India. Stuff from one place is worth more somewhere else. Some do hash-rubbing runs from Himalayan valleys; the mark-up in Goa for European tourists is astronomical. *Aw, who am I kidding?* I'm about as entrepreneurial as one of those water buffalos down on the Ganges.

A few travelers disappear into the continuous stream of untold, nameless ones. *Now I'm listening.* Throw on an orange loincloth, take a staff, a vow of silence, let the dreadlocks go. These most tolerant of traveling paths grant the fair-skinned convert entry to the ultimate dropout life: that of the wandering ascetic. With my dark complexion they wouldn't even blink. I could join the stream as a bright-eyed devotee of Shiva or Vishnu or Whoever. The dharma might require, for some undeclared period and purpose, not to utter a sound. Something tempts

150 Refers to *The Hero with a Thousand Faces* by Joseph Campbell.

me... Further along from Kuta's mind swim, the useless, brittle skins might just keep falling away. *Yes, let all your burdens go.*

In Middle Earth, Gandalf said, "All that glitters is not gold, and all those who wander are not lost." I can't be lost, for being lost implies somewhere to be lost from. The traveler's checks and passport could stay buried in the sand...

I HAVEN'T WRITTEN home in three months. In the letter I just received from my father, he said that he's "tired of knowing my son travels the world." He knows what it's like. His nickname in Calabria was *Bruno d'India.*[151] His father and grandfather went on various journeys over sea and over land. Remembering this hurls me into a current or a "field" of self, one of unnamed links that govern more than we know. Like bleed throughs in identity, the patterns and connections question our sense of self-determination and individuality. We acknowledge connections to past and future through the stream of DNA, yet there seems to be another that is non-material, something about systems of inherited experience. Something, perhaps, about the traveling soul.

Dad's tone sounds serious, maybe urgent; it's hard to tell with relayed words. The timing is surprising, and yet not-a-surprise. Truth is, I am freer in responding to his odd words; ignoring them would be to turn away, to *resist*.

With Dad's letter it becomes clear: I will honor our connection, branch to roots. Or, in this mess of clashing metaphors, I will let go the hard edge of my own reasoning to move in a current within a greater field, one that I can't define.

I will leave this pseudo-paradise, this sumptuous beach of broken masks and adolescent dreams.

And so I turn toward Canada. Which is *that* way, or (spin 180 degrees) *that* way. Since I initially came from the east it seems natural, indeed

151 In my parents' home town, and in their time, it seems that everyone had a nickname. When I asked my mother about the meaning of my father's alias, she said that his "rich spirit" was the reason. In humble Calabria, India represented a land of untold riches, as it likely had for centuries across Europe. (In 1700, India's share of the world economy was a whopping 27 percent; by the time the British departed it had shrunk to 3 percent. From *Inglorious Empire* by Shashi Tharoor.)

proper, to zig back, follow the sun, and continue west like a zillion hatch-lings before me. Overland once again, fly from Europe. I'll head north, hang a left at Punjab, and cross the second half of time zones of my tour around our crusty little fireball—but in a fraction of the time.

It will be simple and graceful, like tying a shoelace.

Bombay

It is midday when the old ferry docks in the inner city. Before I get as far as the nearest street I stop and look around. I'm in an empty lot next to a foothill pipsqueak in the shade of greater peaks. It is that most modern of Indian cities: downtown Bombay.

Mmm, hungry. I drop my pack, pull out and light my gasoline stove. I fix myself a dose of vegetables grande, hunched like a predator over his first meal in days. Since my illness upon arriving in India over six months ago, my self-served discipline of food as medicine has become my functional trade-off for not flying directly into the safety blankets of a European hospital. It's likely that the rapid efficacy of the Tibetan herbs made this deal possible, enabling me to continue traveling. Today, down at the waterline in the shadow of Bollywood, a skinny creature eats alone, and no one seems to mind.

From the waterfront straight into the buzz, I bump into someone in the middle of the street. It's the Scot-Kiwi Ali, a Zen Buddhist from many pleasurable evenings of song and surf in Goa. A fine musician and conversationalist, Ali has a charming manner fit to the traditional image of the quintessential, itinerant minstrel. Back on the beach, songs seemed to bloom from within him as naturally as his smiles. Tall, red-and-wispy-haired, he's kind, intelligent, and clear-eyed. Often seen wandering the sands with guitar in arm, women were unabashedly drawn to him.

He taught me a Scottish jig and reel on the mandolin that I bought from an old luthier in Panjim City. I learned a few of his songs. Ali said he didn't think of them as *his* songs at all; he felt they came to him "from somewhere." Could I be so selflessly romantic with songs that might "come" to me? He had no reservation about letting strangers learn them, exemplifying a level of freewheeling generosity and utter lack of possessiveness that was new to me. I would proudly show him to visiting reptilians, who would discern a higher value in these chatty, succulent bipeds. And then, of course, not eat us.

We are excited by this chance meeting on a busy street. After a short chat we're surprised to discover a mutual association with the four Nisargadatta devotees, the musicians I met up north the year before in Dharmsala. Ali is, just now, on his way to their hotel room, just a few blocks away.

We cram into their room and sing songs—Ali's, theirs, and more. These are the ingenuous, mentally stimulating *sannyasins* from my convalescence in McLeod Ganj. At their urgings, Ali and I agree to join them for a visit to their guru's pad the next day. The prospect of encountering a "real live Buddha" seems a peculiar and opportune turn, if only for it coming during my latter days in India.

AS I LEAVE the *sannyasins'* pad and walk to my hotel, the number of people living on the street is bewildering. Anyone with the sufficient hope and gumption required to break free from the feudal world of landlord and peasant in India's vast countryside must have arrived here tonight, drawn by the city's inexorable magnetic force. A national election (the one that will bring down Indira Gandhi) is due in days. Many have poured in and are sleeping on sidewalks and traffic islands. Every space large enough is occupied by a human body. When I arrive at my third-floor room, the tops of freight trucks and sundry flat surfaces are all taken, covered with the sleeping homeless like a layer of oversized vermin fallen from above in a ghastly, moonlit world.

In Indian cities these multitudes include a staggering number of beggars. Some are able-bodied, giving the impression they've settled into a comfortable vocation. Others are frail and downcast, *really* begging. Some are children, and some are aging. Many are crippled, maimed, or diseased. In the city I often see lepers, known as such by their blunt, flaking, and often bleeding appendages, once recognized as fingers and noses, ears and toes.

India is known to be a creative provider of sensational and infamous sights. They come as a shock to visitors who aren't mentally prepared or emotionally resilient. The odd one will take the next plane back to Europe or Australia after one or two shell-shocked days. A fellow Canadian in Goa described how, after an initial stroll on a Delhi street, he quarantined his ailing sensibilities in his hotel room for a week. In Benares a moody Frenchman spoke in a melancholy and dissociated tone while describing the "holy man" he saw die on the blessed River Ganga, leaving this world in a blaze while sitting on a raft in the lotus position, his hands in his lap held upward with fingertips pressed together, eyes closed, back straight, the flames consuming him as they would a cardboard mannequin.

There—a sickly man with a one-inch-high, pus-and-blood-dripping volcano on his face. And over there—a young, energetic boy with one clear eye, the other a crater-pocked, golf-ball-sized semi-globe protruding from his face and festering with the same yellow and red juices, the whole mess obscured by dozens of disease-sucking black flies. With his sudden movements as he runs about, an expert squadron is frequently jerked airborne for brief, arcing flights away from, but always back to that ripe, weeping eyeball. *Man is born free, but everywhere he is in chains.*[152]

Taking a continental flight into India can tear away a veil all at once—the cushy veil adorning one's own home culture's perceptual gates. On the overland routes you hear stories, foot by mile, and over time those stories exert appropriate, psychic adjustments: the strange action of attuning you with the tools of hearsay, imagination, and familiarity, otherwise known as preconception. An effective barrier, balm, or booster—*your choice, mister.* Coming into India on land can accomplish the nifty job of gently uncloaking one's familiar veils over time.

If the profusion of beggars in Indian cities teaches me anything, it is this: my resources will vanish today, maybe tomorrow, if my money belt is tethered to a tender heart. After a few days of succumbing to my tender heart at incessant calls for *baksheesh,* yielding coin after coin to outstretched hand and sullen eye, the simple numbers guide me with conscience unfettered past the entreaties of the able-bodied. It is weird (but necessary) to remember a harsh picture: the first- (second-?) and third- (maybe fourth-?) world imbalances, by which I am sitting, through

152 J. J. Rousseau.

no merit of my own, at the fat end of the world banquet table. I calculate the scraps I will toss to which cripple, leper, or mother with babe. And calculate I must, reserving my donations for those who appear to have little other choice.

In a Muslim part of town at dawn one day, the real beggars, those who cannot work, are out in the middle of the main street. They don't beg, for there is no need. This is their time: the first hour. It would be an unnecessary cruelty to have them wait; their morsels are assured, right at the front. Out crawl the crippled, some dragging legless bodies on leather pads in the dust; some, it is said, deliberately disfigured at a young age to be raked of their "earnings" by ruthless syndicates. *Is this why, after I offered a meal the other day to a persistent boy, the restaurateur was so ill at ease for the whole time we sat and ate?*

Out come the diseased, the lepers creeping from shadows. The merchants and other residents emerge from doorways to offer scraps. The local community is kept running smoothly; everyone will have enough for another day. The beggars don't beg this early morn, and they take no more than needed. Greed could serve no end in this transparent mode of social welfare.

The same spirit will greet tomorrow's first hour. And if it doesn't arrive? May the next turn of the *meat wheel*[153] be smoother rolling.

The World, 1977

The US invents the neutron bomb.

A baby mammoth frozen in ice is discovered in the USSR.

Forty-seven years after they were invented, PCBs are outlawed because they tend to throw wrenches into the works of immune systems, motor skills and memory, and play roulette games with gender.

CFCs are banned in the US.

Writing is traced back to 10,000 bc in Mesopotamia.

153 From *The Dharma Bums* by Jack Kerouac.

Voyager 1 & 2 shoot into the firmament; the rings of Uranus are discovered. First photo of Earth and moon in a single frame from 7.75 million miles away.

Hydrothermal vents with creatures that live on Earth's energy, not the sun's, are discovered in the Galapagos Rift.

The last wild case of smallpox reported in Somalia.

With queer timing, 14 percent of gulls on a certain island off the California coast are found to be lesbian.

Fiber optics pioneered.

Balloon angioplasty surgery pioneered.

Albert Hofmann (discoverer of LSD) and associates present evidence that the ancient Greeks used a form of LSD extracted from a fungus growing on grasses in the Eleusinian Mysteries, in which the participants saw visions.

Three years after optimistic scientists send out their message-in-a-bottle, the "Wow" mystery on Aug. 15: a signal is detected, for a mere seventy-two seconds, that for many still stands as our best evidence yet for ET (see "The World, 1974," chapter 1).

ALI BHUTTO is elected prime minister of Pakistan, then overthrown.

In China, Deng Xiaoping returns to power after years of "rehabilitation," then introduces Western-style market incentives and promotes foreign trade. (Totalitarianism plus capitalism. *Yikes.*)

President Carter pardons American draft dodgers.

An exodus of "boat people" leaves Vietnam.

Sadat visits Israel.

Quebec goes French.

Pol Pot rises to the surface.

In France: the last execution by guillotine.

Amnesty International receives the Nobel Peace Prize for its work in Northern Ireland.

Steven Biko dies in a South African jail.

NEW YORK CITY blacks out, looters loot.

Soweto riots; the UN condemns apartheid in South Africa.

In the US, the "Protection of Children Against Sexual Exploitation Act" is passed.

Studio 54 opens.

Son of Sam—mail guy David Berkowitz—is arrested.

Indian birth-control program is halted by scandals over botched operations and forced sterilizations.

State funding of elective abortions halted in the US.

After years of government resistance, South Africa finally gets TV.

AFTER STARTING IT at the age of twenty-five, J. R. R. Tolkien's first work, *The Silmarillion*, is published posthumously, four years after he dies at the age of eighty-one.

First edition of the Nag Hammadi Library is published

Star Wars, Saturday Night Fever, Annie Hall, and *Close Encounters of the Third Kind* are released.

Rumors, Aja, Peter Gabriel, CSN, JT, Running on Empty, My Aim is True, and *The Beatles at the Hollywood Bowl* are released. The Sex Pistols, The Clash.

The Love Boat and *Roots* are big on TV.

Elvis Presley—they call him "The King"—is dead.

MURDER ON THE Hippie Trail: Charles Sobraj, "The Bikini Killer," "The Serpent," along with various accomplices, kills as many as twenty travelers on Asian roads in the mid-1970s.

In Vancouver, Paul Watson leaves Greenpeace to found the Sea Shepherd Conservation Society.

Construction of the partially subterranean Damanhur, a unique artistic and spiritual community in the Italian Alps, begins in secret.

Taylor Camp, vestige of the hippie dream in Kawaii, Hawaii, is burned down by authorities.

The personality of Eckhart Tolle, a suicidal, ex-professor of philosophy, by his own telling dissolves and is rearranged, and he becomes a street guy. Later, a world teacher.

Kingdom of Nirvana

It's the glitziest shopping center in the known world. The goods are so varied, the displays so captivating, that window gazing itself can enthrall a lookie-loo like me.

At the big mall of guru malls, India, I hear all about them: Raj Neesh, Muktananda, Aurobindo, Ramakrishna, Yogananda, the several-thousand-years-old Babaji (who shows up unexpectedly over the centuries in youthful form), Ramana Maharshi, Krishnamurti, the Maharishi Mahesh Yogi, the old breatharian lady (who needs only to stand in the sun with moistened skin for nourishment), weird little Dalai Lama stories, the coming of Lord Matreiya... even a potent Catholic equivalent in the diminutive figure of Mother Teresa. The names are many and often on the lips of wayfarers. Down south, Sathya Sai Baba is said, with his magic touch, to materialize copious amounts of holy ash, or some other substance, perhaps flower petals or merely their sweet scent—wherever he places the tips of his sacred fingers. This and other paranormal exhibitions, trickery or not, bring in thousands, year in and year out.

I carried no expectation of such mystic attractions during my first approach from the Far East, only a vague feeling I would trudge along a daunting, dense, and grimy road to emerge into the stark territories of a Middle Eastern desert. Coming back from the West, I knew well what lay ahead, and I hungered for it—the clamor, the smells, the food, the unknowns hidden behind every preconception and idle thought, and not least, my unaccountable feelings of sheer attunement with this ancient land. Of course, by then I'd heard a thing or two on the other-worldliness of Hindu holy ones.

Yet I'm not inclined to follow up on any leads. Images of snake-oil-peddling, circus sideshows have followed me since Professor Marvel, then my local priest, shook my faith in charismatic authority under any banner: clergy, salesmen, Dr. Knowledge. Never mind the duality of my immigrant family milieu, one that blasted top-down authority to smithereens, resulting in an eager receptiveness to the idea that societal truths are merely relative. So I'm reluctant to suspend mistrust. Raised in a mystical, old-world Catholic home only served to deepen my sense of the power of belief, or disbelief. I became skeptical regarding their unpredictable, and especially, their unconscious ways. And I have inad-vertently plumbed certain shadowy depths enough to admit that it's possible I could still harbor some Satan- or God-fearing, otherworldly triggers that lurk below without my official consent.

So it seems prudent, even reasonable, to question motives for offer-ing, or seeking, spiritual redemption in such a wide-open marketplace as India. More than once have I been seen as ripe fruit for the picking by aspiring gurus, whose aspiration itself evidenced not-so-much their being a guru as an awkward simulacrum, or worse, contradiction. Or worse, a hypocrite.

Perhaps my reluctance to explore some of the more intriguing stories shared among travelers on the road borders on negligence. I hear accounts of wondrous and anomalous goings-on, but I pass them by on a pathless quest, as if I go by chance and not deliberation. Since one could spend a lifetime exploring the many gurus and ashrams dotted around India, it follows that something of interest, even without aim, eventually would be encountered.

Like running into Ali on that Bombay street, who leads me to the four devotees and their Maharaj.

SO IT IS: I will visit a real live Buddha.

But what does it mean to possess the cosmic consciousness that R. M. Bucke spoke of more than a century ago?[154] Does a Buddha's view include schemata to the workings of Jung's synchronicity and collective unconscious? A spin on the mathematical poetry of fractals? A love glue strong enough for lambs and lions... *cats and snakes*? Or a master lexicon to connect the ramblings of all those unstuck, moonstruck strays stumbling throughout Goa's beaches of pseudo-paradise?

Is a Buddha one who has merely awoken from our dream-like state, from *maya*?

Christian theology primed my young mind to accept such ideas before I could think. Transformation, redemption, spiritual awakening, living in truth and love—all are ideas that point to a "realizable otherness." In Bucke's view, this would mark the presumed territory of our next stop on the evolutionary train. Or perhaps it's simply a continuous unfolding.

Contrasted with the drab, suffering tone of our normal way of civilized being, this otherness, and its evidence for transformation, leads me along like a siren's song. Putting aside categorical rejection of such notions by entrenched "scientific" materialistic thought, how could we not be interested in this possibility?

Before I could read a book, I was strangely smitten by this notion one evening in *the* epiphany of my entire childhood. It was triggered by seeing Jesus in a Hollywood movie, of all things, at home with my family, age seven. The man from Galilee was transformed from a Catholic, only Son of God (who peddled salvation/damnation as the ultimate ultimatum) into a woke-up human, nothing more. As this living-room melodrama kept my family fixed on (we could have been kneeling before)

154 The book *Cosmic Consciousness* by R. M. Bucke.

the TV, a beam of love shone through all the suffering and madness. One simple man seemed to know who he was, his purpose, and what really goes on in this mad tangle of beauty and agony that we call the world. It was the first time I perceived, or imagined, sanity. Perhaps all that really happened is that I created a story to make sense of a world that felt insane. I had hitherto loathed something about it but could not afford to be conscious of it, not until there was something to contrast it with. From that day forward, something inside me relaxed. Cuz now there was something to look forward to: sanity. *In myself.*

So, I was a good Christian kid for most of my childhood (Christian, I suppose, if rejecting the doctrine of saved/damned doesn't summarily disqualify.) When I was eleven our priest, saddled with "corrupt love" for his altar boys, was the unwitting benefactor of yet another worldview transformation. I quit his unholy church and became an even better "scientistic atheist" for a good seven years (practicing *that* religion to the delight of a supporting cast of math and science teachers.) Then the 1960s sponsored a meltdown of knowledge—church and textbooks included. It's no wonder the road beckoned.

Conversion after conversion: age seven, eleven, seventeen, then add a few years and set sail to foreign lands. Maybe this Bombay Buddha will recognize a kindred stray, a kid brother.

Occasion to linger at the altar of the cult of personality (namely one's own) comes in many guises to any twentieth-century, latter-days kid. After each visit to that heady and bedazzling altar, as anyone who knows what they're doing must do, the golden calf of ego is rebuked. But it reappears, again and again, as firm and proud as ever. Dismissing its external trappings—organized religion, celebrity, and success worship—is far easier.

And here it is again, charming me into thinking that this old wise guy holds for me a special shine, even though he's not yet cast his earthly eyes my way.

BUT NO. *Me no shop.*

And neither is this Nisargadatta (natural data) dude out to sell anything. The story goes that by diligently following the instruction of *his* guru, he one day "fell from the tree like ripe fruit, never to return."[155] His transformation or enlightenment was as obvious as ripe fruit to those around him. He said that nothing had happened, only that he now sees things as they are.

Nonetheless, many gathered around asking questions at his *bidi-*making shop. The number of his seekers grew to the point of blocking the narrow road and disrupting the neighborhood. Turning the business over to his family, he moved from street level to the flat upstairs. The crowd followed and stayed. Content to remain in his loft in Bombay, he is said to have turned down the offer of a wealthy man to build an ashram for him somewhere in the Himalayas.

By and by my friends, the four devotees/musicians, became a daily part of that crowd and got stuck for five months to the enigmatic human magnet called Sri Nisargadatta Maharaj. Going a little crazy and needing to give their third eyes a rest, they decided to take a holiday from the serious business of enlightenment. Before they left, the master spoke: "Don't forget to visit Dharmsala." They didn't know why. They went there anyway, and that's where we met. They were in the next room making music—music I loved. I knocked on their door.

And now, five months later, in their hotel room and between songs, they tell me his cryptic suggestion had made no sense. When I show up in Bombay, they remember "Dharmsala."

I will go see this Nisargadatta guru dude, who seems to align people like some force on iron filings.

Avalanche

And now, I will again speak of things I have no good explanation for.

One morning, early in 1977, Ali and I follow a motley assortment of travelers and Indians off a busy side street in Khetwadi, a district in the dense expanse of Bombay's vast sprawl. We climb something between a ladder and stairs up a tight passage next to a bidi shop. At the top I slink by discreetly, jumping the queue like Quiet Tigger as others pause to lower their foreheads to a pair of bare feet that belong to a thin old man

---

155 As for many of his sayings, I'm not sure whether I heard the translation in his loft, or read them later. But they are the words of Nisargadatta Maharaj.

sitting cross-legged and very erect. I feel awkward for not observing the prostration custom when visiting a holy man or guru, but I'd feel more awkward doing it. I'm a newbie to this world of mystics and masters, not wise to the value of such concepts as guru or (except for Popeye's *salami, salami, baloney*) "to prostrate." I sit near the back, a safe distance, hoping the old sage either hasn't seen or isn't bothered by my indiscretion. About twenty others fill the smoky loft.

Nisargadatta always asks newcomers why they've come. Inquisitive to a point just this side of indelicate probing, his eyes seem to sear his question past the usual pleasantries to an honest place inside. Yet I manage to hold on to a safe wall of defenses in answering, "just curious." He nods and looks away, unfazed by the predictable façade, I suspect. The truth is, although I'm here by virtue of the persuasive urgings of the four musician-disciples, I also bring a private story. This includes the vague yet fanciful notion that one is at a reasonably high spiritual level, whatever I, or others, take this to mean. But I don't dare think the words, for the ego's ruse must not offend the intellect's more sophisticated (and fundamentally shallow) decorum. What I hold dear, without admitting it, is an experiential resume, my worldly shine, as evidenced by: the math, the music, the babes. Enlightenment—could it be that far off? Monkey brain could be "thinking" these things while "one" might not want to notice. In retrospect, I'd say that in some way I have always loved myself, despite there having been many superficial, hedonistic moments.

I settle in alongside the rapt followers of an old Indian sage whom others proclaim is a Buddha, a Christ, a *gnani*: a liberated, self-realized, enlightened one; in the kingdom of heaven, the state of nirvana; one who has attained *samadhi, moksha,* God consciousness, cosmic consciousness, liberation, illumination, emancipation, Enlightenment. One who has awoken from the thrall of *maya*. Those around him say all this and more. All *he* says is that he knows who he is, and, would you like to find this out for yourself?

I sit somewhere in the middle of Bombay, comfortably anonymous, basking in the presence of this "cloud of dust rising from the water,"[156]

156 And "the roar of waves heard over the land," Zen sayings.

immersed in my own mirage of glory, *a real special little snail.*[157]

One moment I buzz away in heightened complacence—self-absorbed, dull. In the next Nisargadatta shoots an X-ray look, a true arrow past a dozen shoulders and ears that crashes my narcissistic swoon, a sledgehammer to the third eye. Our eyes lock, or maybe his grab hold of mine for a couple of seconds. I see with *his* eyes, and it resets my own capacity for seeing.

Torn open, walled-in, exposed—all this do I feel. Yet these are mere words. Within moments I'm burdened with more self-seeing than the sum of years before. The compression of a master view, beyond the previous constraints of who I believed I was, rushes in as a conscious storm, a deluge upon my speck of a mind. It is the crush and boom of a new order of awareness. What I see is *me,* the one who sees. And *how* I see: the old get-ups, the games, the ego machinations. Mere phantoms. It hurts, but not really—mere words again. More like a gaping rawness all at once, the doofus clothes I've worn so proudly, torn and loose and worthless.

There is no threat or mal-intent. On the contrary, I'm granted extra vision. His eyes/my eyes have pierced the mental veils, the hallowed self-images. My discomfort is felt for *what* is seen, and because my seeing itself is transformed. But not by the look itself. If it's judgment day then *I* am the judge, my borrowed sight some kind of hurting light that leaves no shadow.

With his "look" I'm through a needle's eye into an experience that is, to use an indirect term, non-ordinary. My cranked awareness is many orders more powerful than the usual everyday/ordinary. Perhaps it's a taste of his "huge." And it stretches me thin, more comfortable as I am in my small. A mole gains sight, a worm wakes up with legs, that kind of thing. I'm wonder-smacked just shy of passing out. If I'd been mainlined with the juice of psilocybin mushrooms, these leaping sensory proportions would make sense.

And I'm not gonna say *he* did it, cuz I don't know that. Is it him doing something to me, or my hiking to and putting myself in the path of an avalanche? It feels bloody important not to ride the pendulum

---

157 In his book *Eight Little Piggies* Stephen Jay Gould explains how any snail could be the progenitor of a whole new population, as evidenced by "evolutionary radiation" into isolated valleys.

from the fog of narcissism (which brought me to his loft) to some follow-up guru delusion.

When I leave Nisargadatta's loft I am oppressed by an amplified mind, or some condition I have no clue about—or, it seems, control over. By their attentiveness it is clear that my friends—the four devotees, a couple from London and Ali—see that I've been struck by lightning.

Absorbed in this new agony of raw sentience I walk away from them into the chaos of midday, big-city India. They don't stop me, and I don't look back. Nisargadatta reached in and cranked the intensity knob. My voltage is doubled, tripled. If I could find that knob, I'd turn it down. I'm compelled to bear witness to a plurality of thoughts and feelings that are maybe firing at the speed of neurons.

It is awesome, and pushing close to unbearable.

I WALK THE streets of Bombay for the rest of the day like a clear-seeing zombie. The ignorance and numbness in passing faces—I'm aghast. I know, I'm supposed to see the transcendent beauty of perfect spirit in every Being of Glory. But no, it is the mask of the world that I must see, the one I've worn my whole life.

Until the next day I eat nothing. I'm too deep into the psycho-turbulence of an unprecedented state of mind to be concerned with or even notice something so base as hunger. It is as though I alone am awake, and in the act of continual walking, I flee. But from what? From this multitude of sleepwalkers who drone on by? Or goats with their cracked-out eyes and chickens, poor things, that move like broken toys? I see/feel the quality of mind all around me. Halfway through the day I stop to watch a middle-aged woman walk by. She doesn't see me (methinks), but in all the miles I walk, she looks different: not so ignorant, not so numb. The fabric of the world is altered by the light of Diogenes' lantern as she moves through it. *Aw, who am I kidding?* It's probably just me wanting and needing to make some sense, to see something different.

Don't know if I *want* to turn it down, whether I dare sacrifice this sublime agony... If I could find that dang knob. I have never experienced such a barrage of information and emotion except by swallowing a psychedelic bomb.

By late afternoon I'm weary, but the burden of consciousness and meta-consciousness persists and keeps me moving. By 10:00 p.m. I'm in my bunk, still captive to this heightened rogue state.

I FALL ASLEEP. But weirdly, I remain aware. I dream and *watch* the dreaming, unnatural as this sounds. During the night I see my body lying on the bed. I see a dream rise, subside, then another come and go. I see myself sleeping, my body shifting. The night isn't a long time, and it isn't short. Time has lost its pivots—it isn't *time*. How can this be—to be aware behind the sleeping and dreaming outside any sense of time? The "witness" (as I will *later* learn about in Nisargadatta's words) observes all transitions, all states simultaneously. (*Ha! Simultaneously!*)

In the morning I watch as the body/mind awakens, gets up, and drifts like a phantom to the shower. In the sensuality of water over skin, in surrender to the pain of psyche and the pleasure of flesh, in a lower-chakra spasm as I desperately pleasure myself, the spell is broken. An alternate reality slips away in the descent. I come in for a smooth landing, sinking, shrinking, back to regular old me. I am relieved, finally, of the massive weight of an expanded self. I feel safe and, by comparison, numb.

Also, *lesser*. And now, already, the memory... *the loss!*

The effect of Nisargadatta's look lasted from 11:00 a.m. yesterday and through the night until now, twenty-three hours later. Where is free will in this? What just happened?

Man. I am *so-o-o* hungry.

Whodunnit?

Perhaps I'm fortunate to have come into close contact with several psycho strays in Goa just before arriving in Bombay. Their hyper-separation within our small beachside subculture was the key element of their condition, or so it seemed. Our little beach life came together as a mini-society removed from the generality of the traveling life, which itself is defined by a broader separation from the home world. The compounding effect of separation upon separation perhaps leads to an intimate view of certain forsaken territories of the psyche, where I reckon the personal reality of the psycho strays happened to get stuck.

Of course, this is a simplified view as it appears from my perspective, and does not take into account the life experience of, say, Reina, or the wild Israeli, prior to their arrival on Little Vagator Beach.

Here in Bombay, often described as India's feature window on the West, I walk the edge of that forsaken beat once again. Muddling around a city poised between ancient ways and modern days, between opulent ostentation and abject poverty, for a couple weeks I shuffle along its uncensored multiplicity as if in a psychic stupor. I step aside, catch a bigger glimpse of the general human madness, knocking about the vaguest notion on the matter of waking up. In our time-pressed space it now seems rather astonishing that we are governed by these convictions: that we each are separate from others, and that we *are* awake. Like a spell or entrancement are these assumptions cast upon us in the enthralling mirror of the world.

And that is where I am today. This is the hardest thing to grasp about the kingdom of nirvana. It suggests that all things personal, and the experience of the passing of time, is limited to a narrow band of all-that-is; and that it tends to appear limitless and all-inclusive—and self-evident—when you are immersed, with a multitude of others, within that thin band.

I STAY IN Bombay for a month, looking at and listening to Nisargadatta as he answers the mostly flaccid questions of his many visitors. From my position of separation (persistent habit) and dull judgment (tiresome indulgence) I puzzle over what, if anything, sets him apart.

He gives mantras to a visiting couple and they leave, satisfied. When his regular disciples question him about his (unexpected) action, he says a mantra was all they wanted. Another asks for a mantra. "What do you want with a mantra?" he replies. He indicates to a seeker, when asked, that the smoking of *ganja* is insignificant. Later my friends tell me he once forbade a mentally unstable young man from ever going near any, issuing the command to abstain like a dark little Führer. It was presumed that Nisargadatta meant to redirect the man's slide toward schizophrenia, and that *ganja* or *charis,* in his case, was quickening the slide.

In my desire to understand, I seek to reconcile these conditional responses with the daily *pujas*—lively, devotional rituals—that he conducts for his more traditional followers, those who expect these scheduled rituals within whatever religious system they maintain, in this case, a rushing rivulet of mainstream Hinduism. It has been said that when Paramahansa Yogananda visited Ramana Maharshi, the celebrated sage from South India, he did so with the intention of seeking counsel before embarking on his famous trip to the West. He asked, "What shall I tell them?" Maharshi's answer: "It depends on who's asking."

Nisargadatta appears to have little interest in others' preconceptions, or their thought constructs. When he is brought the brand-new, two-volume hardcover edition of his book of questions and answers (titled *I Am That*), all he does is glance at the covers, turn them over, then put them aside. At a presentation in which he is honored on a stage in a small auditorium (I don't understand a word of it), he up and leaves after noticing something to the side behind a curtain. He is promptly rounded up and seated in his place by a devoted drone. Earlier, when he was being escorted in by a gaggle of loved ones and pundits, he took the first empty seat he saw, in the audience near the back. Apparently unable or unwilling to tune in to others' mental concerns, he has the look of a wiry and perhaps senile old man. As youthful as he appears, and moves, he *is* elderly, and I wonder. But with him—the strong, clear eyes, his simple and direct words—I must keep looking.

During my visits to the loft the only notable thing I see besides his animated, almost electric energy, is his physical suppleness. After two hours of squatting, *my* youthful body is cramped. The room is low, but he is considerably shorter than me and can stand freely. When he does it is with the ease of a child after sitting still for the whole time, every time, no jerky shifting around like me. He's eighty-one, and I'm twenty-two. Looking for clues, I am *Mr. No-clue McGoo.*

Love says, "I am everything." Wisdom says, "I am nothing."
Between the two my life flows.[158]

"NICE CAMERA, CAN I have it?" He smiles an odd smile, but... *did he just ask for my camera?* A Zen master whacks a dumb student on the head.[159]

158 Nisargadatta
159 From the *Tao of Physics* by Fritjof Capra, p. 128, and specifically, the story of the master Huang Po's exchange with a student.

Jesus curses a fruitless fig tree.[160] I don't get the camera bit either. I don't respond, but I keep snapping, not ready to let go of the snazzy thing that came my way under a darkly auspicious Aussie sky many moons ago.

In India there's a saying: "Easy for a poor man to renounce material wealth." Regardless of where one places on the affluence scale, self-knowledge is tricky business. I'm not sure what I'm ready to renounce, and I reckon I'm neither rich nor poor. Or I'm either, depending on who measures. I'm working-class Canadian; my folks own a house or two in a modern country. But given that we have enough to eat and a roof to sleep under, attachment, I now understand, is the real game. One could be attached to having few possessions, or to poverty itself. One might be proud of one's rags, just as another is proud of his or her riches. Or one might be attached to the idea of detachment. Or imprisoned by the quest for freedom.

As I move about with my sure finger on the clicking shutter—and an unsure grasp on the meaning of possessions and attachment—I know I'll *not* give Nisargadatta the camera. At least I won't be attached to it *and* be without it. A small serving of "know thyself"[161] is half chewed, halfway down, a lump in my own throat.

And maybe he just wanted to take a picture of goofy old me.

Either way I'll soon leave Bombay, attached as I am even to my unclear grasp of things.

THIS ENCOUNTER WITH Nisargadatta marks my first inkling and sensation of the entire human shebang as dreamlike, with a few billion sleepwalkers crawling semiconsciously on the surface of a beguiling and beautiful, yet fear-drenched planet. The dreamlike view that drifts in and out of my consciousness of late corresponds to Nisargadatta's teachings on nonduality, the study of Advaita Vedanta. It's not surprising, considering the gravity of my experience on the day of meeting him in his loft, that the character of my perceptions has shifted. It brings me to a view that provokes confidence in my own seeing, yet I'm filled with exhilaration, and trepidation, in facing such a rewiring of reality's soft-core motherboard.

160 Matthew 21:18.
161 Socrates

And so I tell myself that all I can do is bear witness to it all. That I will feel whatever there is to feel, inside and outside, in utter honesty and acceptance. And that I will not pretend to know what I do not know. Like a mantra, I hear this one often in the echo chamber of mind. Mine is a simplified view, a reduced telling of myriad things, my willingness to ponder such grand vistas surely exceeding my grasp of them. But regardless of my uncertainty it's clear, with my perplexing sojourn in Bombay, that I have been interrupted by, and now walk, ever so slowly, toward the predilection of those we call mystics.

What do I make of it all? Where do I stand?

Whatever the answers, I am drawn toward inquiry of the riddle of self, of existence plain. And the necessity of love. It is love, after all, that moves one forward, is it not? The love of "truth", the love that draws me to every laughing or crippled soul encountered on this singular path through successive shiftings of worldviews—Roman Catholic, atheist, guru-Jesus, pan-spiritual. A path that meanders along lush lowlands between lofty conceptual cliffs I barely can see: between time-bound needs and timeless enigmas, the visible world and invisible forces, between the finite—what I hold in my hands—and the infinite, what I can only imagine. Between death and its ironic emissary and accomplice, life. Whether death is real and final, or a collective mirage integral to the rules of the game of this earthly sojourn, I am left with the conviction that it is love, even as we might imperfectly know it in our human lives, that puts a spark to any, and to all of it.

EVERY DAY FOR the past month, after meandering aimlessly around Bombay's inner-city waterfront district, I end up at the same restaurant. Chai is delicious just about anywhere in India, but it's this traveler's hangout in Colaba (and their yummy lemon-cream cake) that pulls me in. It has become my trusty but brief pleasure in a time of psychic turbulence and restless melancholy. My running philosophical dilemma is chased by a dense gloom that is never far away, making these moments of sipping tea and eating cake amongst passing travelers ones of (almost) carefree frivolity. In the fog of my malaise they seem even decadent. I assume I will be home relatively soon, and I feel I am more a child today than when I started this trip. I feel drained of goodness and clarity, and shallow in morale.

Yet as grim as I feel, I am a Canadian traveler in Bombay. I could wallow in my funk, but the fact remains: many choices are available to me. And so, as I often do, I wonder how I must appear to those who call these streets and back alleys home.[162]

One morning I feel, from across the restaurant, an unsettling flicker at the edge of my field of vision. It is the gaze of Reina, the German lass I met on the overnight ferry from Bombay to Goa, and subsequently, on the beach of dreams where I'd been squatting with other travelers for several weeks. I remember how on the boat she exuded a vibrant aura that drew me into her earthly delight, the disturbing scene with the two guys at Colva Beach, and how she arrived on Little Vagator—naked, mute, mentally fragmented—and stayed close to me for a day before disappearing again.

Today in this Bombay restaurant we glance across solitudes, nervous and hesitant. She's wearing a new set of good clothes, and one of the popular faces of the sane: stifled and rigid, with the odd wisp of anguish rolling through like a ghost hitching a ride on body and soul. Back on the boat when we'd first met, if it wasn't for all the other travelers surrounding us on deck, I would have followed her into deeper waters. I was smitten with her physical beauty and her charismatic intelligence, and especially, with her lushly intimate vibe that enveloped me within minutes.

Why did I leave her standing on the street the next morning?

I wouldn't have been able to had we gone deeper. When I saw her dancing in the Colva restaurant, my immediate, dark feelings toward

---

162 Regardless of my own troubles there is a sordid scene, perhaps not far from this very restaurant, where the suffering is of a different order. Mine is a melancholia of means; with money in my pocket I can go where I choose. Later I will learn about a Bombay underbelly where real girls on display in real cages peer out, eye to eye, into the decadent hunger of morally depraved men. Men who stroll along narcissistically, shopping the cages; it is a wretched fringe of the world-wide sex trade. These girls, often pubescent, are "captured" from perhaps well-meaning parents in villages by hustlers on the promise of work in the city. See *Empire of the Soul* by Paul William Roberts, Ch. 7. I'm guessing that traveling women can fall prey as well.

the two guys tell a story. I felt loathing toward them, guilt inside myself, and a protective fear for Reina and the part I might have played in how things seemed to be unfolding for her. And then, without even approaching her in that restaurant, I left her again. On the beach when she showed up, naked and traumatized, I concluded that I would do whatever I could to help her find health and safety. And then *she* left.

Today, raw anxiety is set in Reina's face, as it was with the young Israeli when we parted. Her once carefree passion, then deeply traumatized condition, is bound up in meaning that escapes me. Throughout these travels I have become aware that my attraction to women borders on a level of desire and need that is rather more like "addiction." And it's unnerving that where once our bodies and minds had briefly ignited and come alive together, an immense distance now looms. To feel such distance in the faded shadow of intimacy, with the unknown circumstances of her trauma, blackens my presumed innocence. Love, *the only spark*, is hidden away. But why? I want to solve this mystery, I want to purge her of her pain and me of my ignorance and terrible fear. Whatever happens between and behind two pairs of eyes in such a charged moment, I can't say. But I am dumb, and my mind is heavy.

When I look back at her, I feel that immense distance and I'm unable, for a minute, to move. Reina looks good; her clothes, at least, are new, and she's well-groomed. On the surface, or by appearance, something restorative seems to be happening. But is it?

I rise from my chair and walk out of the restaurant. As if from one timeline into another, I walk like a wraith into the bleeding light and crushing sounds of the city. I walk away from my capacity to help, from my will to perceive and let in the miracle of redemption. I walk away from a woman who might need me or want my care—indeed, one who could help to release me from my own straitjacket of numbed-out fear. Alas, I walk away from unknown gifts, perhaps from a life unborn. I turn away from the evidence—whatever it means and wherever it might lead—that has gathered and deepened with each time we've crossed paths.

I don't know much, but I know this: Reina's eyes across the restaurant today, the wild Israeli's as he was led away by his father back in Goa, and the single shot Nisargadatta sent me through a psychic wormhole with—the look in their eyes, all, are fixed inside me.

I leave Bombay the next morning.

I HEAD NORTH. My sights are now set on home, way over yonder in the hinterlands of the Far West, my family's own sweet spot in good British Columbia. My existential tilt-a-whirl is still spinning, and I think there's a loose belt in the works. The hyperactive gremlins at the controls are fun-loving sadists with no plan on easing up anytime soon. As I turn toward the last stretch of my precious gold-dust highway, my US dollars grow leaner with every mile.

After leaving the epicenter of a quake you get to view its effect on the surrounding country. In New Delhi, the Bombay jolt's wider effect looks ghastly, a world that feels debased, insipid. This time it's not culture that shocks me, it's the whole mess of the human movie—history, chocolate, greed, sex—all of it. Our overcrowded, planet-wide party is in violation of some fundamental, existential bylaw written in the language of love.

On the streets people bear heavily the group mask. The spark in their faces, what's left of it, is perverted and buried beneath it. They whiz by like phantoms, the odd one pausing in shell-shocked glee to taunt the speck of sanity I believe I still safeguard in my shaky view. A pageant of sorrows, hidden and not-hidden, as in any city. It is a dim view indeed, and I don't even *want* to see, for my eyes are sullied by their own seeing. My journey homeward feels like the dispirited jerkings of a sad zombie. It is surely by some God-sent grace that I remain oblivious to the disco and punk music that presently plies the West's airwaves or I might be driven to the outskirts of madness and deposited in its decaying rubble.

The truth is not always beautiful, nor beautiful words the truth.[163]

It's a sunny day in the park at Connaught Place. An old woman offers deep ear cleaning. *I could use a deep head cleaning, ma'am.* I sit and watch the twinkle-eyed ancient extract moist, hairy, black, frightfully *huge* wax globs with a tiny spoon from deep within the ear of a charming traveling chick. Someone else steps up for a turn. *Oh, woman, how I wish you would scrape the grime from my soul!* The shrivelled crone's

163 Lao Tzu.

vigorous digging (cutting, snapping noises) puts me off. I leave the scene without taking advantage of the great local prices.

I go slowly, bumping against a handful in a multitude of broken stories. A motley parade of Indians eke out a living on the edges of *their* worlds. There—a snake charmer with his eerie shadow music and doped-up cobra. Fortune tellers, office workers, cobblers. An organ grinder with a rhesus monkey hopping happily as if in a jungle. A boy hawking trash trinkets that no one wants, another peddling street drugs, another, incense. Women offering massages, young girls with stoic faces carrying babies as large as themselves. Simple entrepreneurs selling papayas or mangos, upping the price along the few blocks they've carried them from the market. And beggars begging, disfigured and in an assortment of shapes and endings. Today, they all look the same. It's Team New Delhi, and a fine day for a masquerade.

From this head-beating multiplicity emerges an American musician I knew in Goa. He walks straight up, smiling. I'm glad to see him, like an old friend dropped from the sky bringing hope and clarity to my downcast mood. Back on the beach we enjoyed soulful maneuvers on the wings of many a tune. He developed a special fondness for the old mandolin I found in a Panjim shop, and he wanted to buy it from me. I couldn't blame him, but I held on, even though he played it better than I. I'll pass it on to Dad, the real mandolin player, when I get home.

"What's up?" he asks. I describe what I see. His face stiffens, and his body slumps. I ask, and he says he knew one or two others like me. "I know the space. You're on acid—what you see—you're on acid, man." He's not talking Hoffman/Owsley.

"Those... 'others'?" I ask.

"They're dead, man. Fell into the fire."

"Oh."

With the word "dead" I'm tossed into one of those turbulent river rapids of being. I say goodbye to my friend and walk away into the resigned chaos of big-city India once more. The human games, the seesaw dualities, are flaunted in broad daylight: death and birth, pain and love, mind and matter... healthy/sick, rich/poor, good/bad, yes/no. All march in the mighty parade of beautiful confusion. I build one on the spot: life + entropy = zero. A formula, a triangle. Not fitting in. *Special.* I'll build it a shrine, strong in my mind, for three is strong, strong enough for a shrine. India is a hothouse of shrines, for living and dying, waking and dreaming, and I'm here again, looking for Sri Zero in his native land. Words come and go; I hear their scrambled echoes in the graffiti-scrawled hall my mind inhabits like a hermit crab. I savor their jive and perfect nonsense, wandering this city of scoundrels and pawns, my feet tracing circles and snakes and point-blanks.

I've wandered a physical path for some time now, but I'm also borne on a slippery wind of words along a twisting loop of faith, my own *Möbius Trip*[164]. Seeing two sides as one, *making* them one. *Sane, insane.* In the shadow of the big boys, coaxing Einstein's Godspeed and the quantum quandaries into an easy tango. It's always been that way, carrying emotion into the streets of reason, watching Mom and Dad duke it

164 A "Möbius Strip" is a mathematical value and yet it represents a paradox. As a physical object it is simply a long rectangle with one end rotated at 180 degrees and joined to the other (some conveyor belts are shaped this way so that there is only one continuous surface area, resulting in even wear and longer life.) I reckon that the Möbius Strip is always inside/outside; either up or down; at once forward, sideways, and back-to-the-start; and, as if in salute to what only mystics venture to speak of, it demonstrates that "two are in fact one." For me the image captures the essence of my conflict as a result of all the ways I have been bounced and stretched along this journey, culminating in my rendezvous with sane/insane in Goa, and the psycho-spiritual wormhole-encounter with Nisargadatta. The conflict shows up, finally, in the push/pull of the seemingly opposing, but Möbius-tripping views of reality as represented by the explorations of scientific materialism, and what could be called the metaphysical sciences, or the disciplines of consciousness. Even venturing to name this "other" realm of knowledge underlines the gravity of the dilemma: the first is sanctioned by society at large; the second is either marginalized (by the first, which occupies the current "truth throne" in our modern age) or, more often than not, it remains a private exploration. Each discipline is the bearer of a "temperament" of consciousness, and they are as different as any two cultures of mind that occur in our world—thus their seeming "oil and water" predicament, and my own personal conflict. For one focuses on the bits and pieces of what we perceive with our five senses, resulting in the grand edifices of our modern civilization; the other with more elusive energies in both the world and in the individual, invoking an awareness that is said to plunge directly into the nature of reality. Symbols that persist through millennia and across cultures (or pop up in our dreams), the non-linear nature of time, and a connecting principle between all of us—these are the conceptual and experiential signatures of what the metaphysical disciplines seek to explore.

out along stories that didn't even begin with them, wooing logic along the drunken walk of ego, knocking good and bad between the meat circus and blessed sleep... wondering how that legendary sword slipped into the bloody stone without splitting any atoms. *All that empty, wavy space we're on about.* Some storyteller way back then saw the zero behind the one behind the two—he just *knew*. And he knew that with his story we'd eventually stumble onto atoms and crack their mythical emptiness with the sword of inquiry, *everywhere, all things entangled...*

My musical friend and his solemn words—I'm into the fire, dumb and burning, here and gone with every breath.

Asshole 2

The next day I enter a shop looking for a screw and some epoxy glue to mend my mandolin. A burly Indian stands straight and tall behind the counter. It's one of those gray mornings; the spirit of humble fire is lost in the drab of my stiff, ungrateful face. How things change, one day to the next. Neither is the shop owner all smiles. Who knows why I'm so moody. Maybe I got sad, then pissed, when I opened the wooden case I just dropped to find it in four pieces. My beautiful mandolin! Not to mention yesterday's whirlwind tour through our beloved earthly purgatory. I can't fathom it anymore. The carefree travel coming to an end, the once sultry and silver-tongued Reina, all shrunken and compressed into a tight fit of melancholia. *Did I play a part? Is she on a camouflaged road to "higher" self?* Nisargadatta's gargantuan wrench in my puny personal works, Dad expecting me home. No, I don't care for any of it.

I indulge my low mood. When I speak to the shopkeeper, my voice lacks common respect.

He counters with a flat "No." *Ooh, too quick, too hard.* Is that "No, I don't have it, get lost" or "No, I won't serve you, you fucking little prick"? Well I just can't tell. My manner slides from impatience to the condescension popular among, well, assholes, especially traveling assholes. *Nature has given us two ears, two eyes, but only one tongue.*[165] These sage words don't come to mind just now. I continue to tempt the hulking shopkeeper with my arrogant nattering. In an instant his eyes come alive to reveal a wise

165 Socrates.

and feisty demon come down from the Himalayas to take possession of his body, grab me by the T-shirt, and pop me in the nose—not too hard, not too soft, but with just enough force to set me right without damage.

I should have acknowledged the steady eye. Shoulda noticed the large forearms.

Out to mend my mandolin, I let the Asshole out for another peek. I leave the store screwless and glueless, and with a sore nose. *Enjoy yourself, it's later than you think.*[166]

Pride/humility, pleasure/pain, devils/angels. That damned duality in all things. Our illusions and creations, day by night. Around here they call it *maya*. "I Am" and the world of multiplicity, the sexual/spiritual dance of Shiva/Shakti: the Hindu big picture. I think about the Asshole and my speck of free will, about genies and their magic, about the marvel of transformation, the grace of redemption, and how crazy, wide open it all is.

Within this great multiplicity, and on this day, it is prudent that I tuck the asshole back inside Johnny-the-good-boy. Yet there is little doubt that both characters are alive and kicking.

I think, *I am one lucky dude.*

Quietly, I say, "Hold on, Dad, I'm coming home."

Freedom to do what one likes is really bondage, while being free to do what one must, what is right, is real freedom.[167]

---

166 Socrates.
167 Nisargadatta.

15. Overland 3

A cloudburst doesn't last all day. [168]

A Smile from a Veil [169]

We sit in the shade of a tree sharing a snack of fruit and delicious bread at the side of a quiet street on the outskirts of Ghazni, now a sleepy town a few centuries downwind from the great Mahmud and his unforgettable exploits. It is midday, hot sun. The she of we is Vonnie, a sensuous, genial gal with hypnotic eyes from a fruity valley in Kiwiland.

Down the parched road a billowing foursome approaches. In the desert breeze their black cloths flap like the foul wings of the wraiths of a new apocalypse. They each wear a single head-to-toe tent-like garment that hides even their faces, a mesh window for the eyes deemed adequate for public jaunts. On city sidewalks it's been good fun making a surprised face in the last moment of "eye contact." You couldn't see hers, but you knew. *Oh, you knew.*

When the four are directly across from us, they stop. Wife #1, I reckon, walks over. She lifts the veil from her face. She is beaming, about thirty-five. Her eyes are warm, piercing beacons as she talks in her own language, in a kindly voice, to Vonnie. We don't understand a word. It is a voice of courage in forsaken times, a bold gesture that leaps over a cultural wall to declare a sisterly bond. Her symbolic message—she must know that we can't understand her—speaks of her love for Vonnie's freedom. This young woman from a strange land travels with a young man and shows her face and her arms to the world.

---

168 From *All Things Must Pass* by George Harrison.
169 From *Wish You Were Here* by Pink Floyd, written by Waters/Gilmore.

The woman reaches over and gently caresses Vonnie's face, replaces her veil, and crosses the road toward her three comrades-in-waiting.

BACK AT INDIA'S northwest fringe, a massive, mad-swirl civilization behind me, I felt quiet and pensive. The sober, early steps of a third overlander, the last zag in a 5,000-mile back-and-forth... I left Italy last year with a strong yearning to head back East. The ways of my *paisani,* familiar yet muddling, were tossed anew into my personal brew of cultures: Italy, Canada, the States, Britain, and now newbie India. How? *I don't know; it just is, baba.* Canada is a bicultural nation, with England and France the old-country players. Way west in Vancouver, raised in an immigrant-Italian home... not much of France in my neck of the woods. I leave India a second time filled with much that has yet to be sorted.

At customs an old Sikh officer searched for my stamp of entry into India, taking his time, touring the pages of my passport like a nice book of postcards. Back and forth, ho-hum, flip, flip. Finally, he closed it and handed me my passport, saying, as if informing me of something: "I'm sorry, but you have not *been* in India," his face dead straight.

"What?" *Come on, old man, what are you talkin' about?* I'm still *in* India, just walked from deep with*in* India. I flipped the pages and found the stamp. Steadily and slowly with standard procedure, the decadent old nerd stamped my book, his bland face looking up to the next in line.

On the road one hears snippets of odd and interesting things about what's ahead from travelers whose path is met headlong. It's 1977—no surprise to encounter a buffer space between India and Pakistan. Yet I was surprised by the short stretch of road that had to be walked, for no vehicle would enter the limbo zone of denial. It's as if two great countries sit facing away from each other, with all roads on either side, well, denied. Most international maps have the Muslim states of Jammu and Kashmir, where the northern reaches of both countries converge, contained within India's national boundary. Pakistani customs are said to confiscate any such maps if found. Early that morning I made sure to bury mine deep in my pack. It's only two years since tens of thousands of prisoners of their brief war were released, since East Pakistan declared itself Bangladesh and separated from what remained as Pakistan in the west. The political scars are not yet healed. The quarter-mile nether land is one massive political and psychic Band-Aid.

Mmm, wuzzat smell? Along our short walk, aromatic cannabis grew green and bushy and neat like well-groomed gardens. *Smell that shit.* We stared good and hard, we five or six travelers who didn't know one another but who happened along at the same time on the same day wishing to cross the same border in the same direction. Who knows? Given the usual lowbrow nationalistic mudslinging, it doesn't seem out of the question for them to plant the weed, entice, then nab anyone dorky enough to grab a free inter-country sample. *Who tends to these gardens?*

We walked the odd, quiet road, no one speaking, as we left Hindustan to enter Islam.

Afghanistan 3

Colorful, archaic, and rugged Afghanistan.

On the long trek west, my feet know where they're going, as if duty bound. Yet this country of dry mountain wilderness and lush river oases, and the townsfolks' medieval ways, will charm and grab and hold you, and keep you for a spell.

This time Russians, under the brand Soviet, crawl all over the place in buzzcuts and suit stylings from the silent movie era. Don't recall seeing so many of these awkward dandies last time through.

The arrival of strangers is not new for the Afghans. Their landlocked country has been invaded repeatedly over millennia. Perhaps starting with Vedic kings in the distant past, then from Darius I of ancient Persia and Alexander the Great to Genghis Khan, and Islamic groups and later the British—numerous hordes have marched through with spears or swords or guns. Central Asia is on a timeworn path from Europe, the Mediterranean, and the Middle East to the riches—physical, cultural, mystical—of India and China.

But remember, Afghanistan had its own time of greatness in an empire wider than Babylon's, reaching from Persia to India. By the eleventh century, Mahmud of Ghazni had it up to *here* with foreign pricks running the show. But after a historic fifteen minutes[170] of despotic glory, Afghan style, the tide of invaders kept coming.

My first time in Afghanistan was a year ago; I don't recall seeing any Russians. The second time, not four months later on my way back to India from Europe, it didn't take long to notice the odd pack of Russians buzzing around officiously in their own mental zone on Afghan streets.

Now, this third time through, another nine months along, the number of Russians has ballooned. They move about in groups, unabashed and with purpose, attracting the attention not only of travelers but also of local merchants. The city Afghans, like city folk anywhere, don't warm up quickly to strangers. Also, I am something like an infidel and had better know my place while visiting their homeland. Even so, the Afghans always seemed up for good, authentic connection.

Now the street merchants nudge me slyly with hidden elbows, motioning with narrow gaze and point of chin toward the Russians, as if *we* have *them,* and their alien weirdness, in common. As if to say, "Look at these cork-suckers. Who do they think they are, coming to my town like they own the place? Forkheads." With the recent proliferation of Russians, the Afghans are letting me know *they* know what's going on, and that *we're* much closer to being on the same team. Yes, my genes are pure Mediterranean, a near cousin to the Afghans, but I'm ragged up like a swashbuckling hippie.

Two years later when Soviet troops invade Afghanistan there is little doubt the Russians will be in for more trouble from this small, undeveloped country than they bargained for. From remote shadows in untold craggy mountains, the Afghans would be ferocious—and fight to the last, if necessary.

BACK IN GOA I reset my compass on a letter nudge from Dad, then had my personal reality deconstructed in the solar wind of a Bombay storm *à la Nisargadatta.* My so-called knowns are down to lean cargo—a sorry cache of lumps and hunches dangling from my hip like an old sack of

---

170 "Everyone will be world famous for fifteen minutes," a notion popularized by Andy Warhol, a satirical tribute, methinks, to we moderns' obsession with celebrity, and our short attention span.

nostalgic junk that I used to call interesting ideas and other near-cool things about me.

This is not how I imagined returning home. I was supposed to be brimming with learning and experience, walking tall in the heady strata of purpose and meaning. *Worldly.* Instead I feel isolated, moody, scattered. After such a wild ride it doesn't make sense. Why I should feel so diminished on my way to reuniting with family and friends after close to three years… the loss of a dream? Disillusionment? The hangover after a prolonged high by the novel stimulations of "elsewhere" and "otherness?" The wilted scene in Delhi as the dark shadow of the exotic; I am one in a multitude of travelers ducking away from slotted duty at home and now, staring down the last long road: no rainbow, no gold. Aligned, at last, toward the final frontier—the interior self—to discover a vacant, unkempt spirit. As if I've wandered, slow and aimless, only to hit a big, featureless wall. Yet I've found a hole and I look in. And it stares back. So now I turn around—end of the world, whatever.

I remember some wisdom-words, paraphrased: those events in your life that come unforeseen and unexpected are the most meaningful, for they are communications from the Self— which will, if necessary, ignore the conscious oath of nonviolence in order to wake you up.[171] I sense the tingle of truth in these words, yet I don't feel any consolation in them.

While passing through the breezy, subtropical city of Kandahar, I go walking for its trusty therapy, as walkers do. And yet, when you're a visitor in a strange country where the citizens are sure to see you as otherworldly, the benefit of that therapy can be lost on the lack of blending in. For this is what I desire on this day, to move about unnoticed. Instead I feel like I'm wearing flashy neon clothes that, paradoxically, render me transparent, so that these men and children, even the dogs, immediately see through my unfocused wandering right smack to the question, "So why *are* you here, you godless dick?" They aren't hostile; it's just that they have heartbreakingly clear eyes. And the dogs—*oh, the dogs.*

I walk through a residential area that resembles a thriving hillside hobbit village in an arid setting, the folks a bit taller and wearing rustic turbans. And smoking hookahs. There are no paths in this sloped part

171 Nisargadatta.

of town, so I find myself walking over mounds that turn out to be the roofs of homes, dusty hobbit homes after a great shift in climate—no gardens, no ale. I walk softly, and no one seems to mind.

Except for one particularly ravenous hound. He starts with a few casual barks aimed my way. Then it's as if he suddenly notices something entirely loathsome about me, for he explodes into a drooling frenzy of growls and machine-gun yaps. A few seconds before Dog Demon spotted me, I noticed an old man noticing me, sitting in the shade surrounded by frolicking children, his amusement growing unaccountably as his eyes followed my walking arc over his next-door mound.

With the dog's transition from recognizable companion of humans to lathering hellhound, the old man's amusement is transported into rollicking laughter. I continue walking casually as if nothing untoward is going on, as if my one-act play will overcome the surrounding drama on the strength of "ignore and it'll go away." As *if.* Between the flailing dog, the scampering children, and Old Man Hyena, I feel like I'm moving through a David Lynch favorite or some dignity-stripping half dream that I'm glad I forgot to transcribe. The dog is *choked.* He darts forth and chomps my calf, evoking long, extended yowls of cascading laughter from the old man, his face thrown up to the sky as if to capture every morsel of ecstasy that Allah would rain down on this pure and blessed day. *Do the Muslims have demons? Did one follow me out of India?*

Moved by a twitch of compassion (I assume), the old man leans forward and points to a gnarled stick between gasps for breath. Abandoning the placid mode, I grab the stick and swing madly at the beast of purgatorial agony, who turns back into a dog and scoots away behind a mound.

The incident leaves me with a bite mark shaped in a nice "J."

But thankfully, with no rabies beast in my blood. I worry for three days about slow death by monster virus, then forget about it.

IT'S NO ACCIDENT that each time I enter the vast Muslim region on the overland route I'm befriended by a fine lassie seeking companionship. The comfort and safety afforded her by hooking up with a man in this sexually regulated region is all but essential. Of course, her company is no burden for me. A week ago Vonnie picked me out from across a

Kabul teahouse teeming with young, wander-struck travelers. Awkward but appreciative, I welcomed her to share in what had become, in a moment, adventures in parallel. *Yum.*

Heading west from Ghazni we whiz through the rest of Afghanistan, Iran, and Turkey. Having been through these parts twice before in the last year, I don't mind. We pass through Greece like it's an interesting part of town, a 'hood we're fond of. We're on a good clip now, won't be hanging around.

We head straight for the small town in Calabria where a handsome young Bruno Michele once picked soaring melodies on his mandolin with his wizard fingers, wooing the gorgeous Marietta Elizabetta and eventually, having me, the fourth of six sons, eighth child of eleven in total. The first three didn't make it past childhood, resulting in a fine, robust brood.

Calabria 2

I gaze into the frothing wake, hooked on the sea's unrestrained power and beauty. The more I look the more I get the feeling it's *me* who's restrained, hovering in a liminal place just this side of *gaga*. Right now, holding on to the rail with a killer grip and slitted eyes, I fancy the ocean to be a living passion, its depths a playground for the relentless game of X and Y as they drown in absolute pleasure for suffering, ecstasy, and for eternity. Their anguish and joy are transmuted into a wild, electric-blue froth at the surface, available to Vonnie and me, among others, and barely visible to the human eye.

This fabled middle-of-the-earth sea is ringed by the old worlds of Carthage and Rome, Greece, Palestine and Egypt, and the Minoans, Phoenicians, and Etruscans. Malta, Asia Minor, Spain and Venice. It bleeds hypnotic blue love through the sun's interactive gold, and up, up, up into the sky. *Why is the sky blue, Daddy?* Dad would speak with crazy passion (boasting, actually) about the bluest of blueness of these Mediterranean waters. He spoke, his eyes spoke, his arms spoke a piece for the rest of us. I thought it reckless exaggeration. Today it teases my mind, flaunting his wild claim and taming the irreverence inside me. *Look, Papa, now* I'm *telling the stories.* The madly shifting reflections have become floating leaves of light, then globs of real gold that move like quicksilver dragons in the swaying valleys between waves, between the small, crude kingdoms of men. *They all will be released, drawn into the great peacock sky.* Their transient shimmer has made boring, dead stuff of what I remember of jewelry.

How much is the allure of diamonds, gold, and rubies married to the experience of possessing them? Does the power of beauty become simply power? These rocks are called precious, a word related to "price" and, therefore, to possession. The sea gold cannot be possessed, but one *can* be stricken by mad beauty. Or with the "possession of possession." Tibetan monks spend days and weeks creating highly intricate mandalas with colored sand on the floors of temples, only to be wiped away after their beauty has been but briefly known. In the West we are enriched by works of genius, but we also cherish and possess these works, as do the artists, oftentimes leaving evidence of attachment and ownership with a large, bold signature that has little to do with aesthetics. This fluid sea gold is alive, and those jewels, well they're just frozen old chunks. *Now just you look at all that gooey gold!*

With Vonnie on the other side of the ferry, a fetching nymph (another Kiwi) saunters over to where I'm standing at the deck's edge. Fortuna has decided that today I will not suffer a minute without a bonny Kiwi lassie by my side. This one smells divine, like the strange fruit of an awesome new planet. Without introduction she is pressed by my side, our bodies already humming a common tune. In a quiet, sultry voice she tells me of her adventures with powerful men in Egyptian palaces. She's been a mistress to several. I listen, of course, but *hey, whatever, baby.* Her story exudes a pure sexual force, so a part of me is keen. *Alas, what a fine cloud of venom* sang the little spider.

One eye on her wily maneuvers, the other held fast by the spell of golden sun and churning sea dragons, ancient love riddles and the great blue of life… the young lassie's awkward attempt at seduction is matched by equally graceless verbal noodling on my part. Somewhere between Mr. Sultan *Schwing* McGoo and the Great *Sha Na-Nile*, I smile. I show her *my* palace: my super-magic, electro-turquoise light show with *real gold* in it. *Hey-ya-ha? Ha?* Wink.

She plunges a disdainful eye into mine, pauses for a long, cruel twist, then turns and leaves. *Nice.*[172]

BEFORE BOARDING THE ferry, Vonnie and I spent several days on the west coast of the Greek isle of Corfu. Along with a congenial lad from the South of France, we walked up the shoreline from a small village and camped just beyond the elastic tentacles of tourism. Back in the village, foreign yet familiar, a sun-browned, contented old man beckoned us to his shady grape arbor and wine hut for a glass of red. He looked me over and set his face to the question: "Why do you look like one of us?" My answer, "Italia, Calabria," drew his first words: "Calabrese... Greco spaccato" (his take on Calabrese, my parents' home lingo: spoken, in Italian, for "broken Greek"). Face, hand, and eye dances filled in the blanks.

I recalled a grade-seven history map with parts of the Mediterranean, from the western shores of Turkey to southern Italy and Sicily, settled by Greeks prior to the flourishing of the Etruscan and Roman cultures in central Italy. During the first millennium bc and beyond, southern Italy and Sicily were referred to as *Magna Graecia*, which in Latin means "Greater Greece." To the Greeks, it was *Megale Hellas* (same). The people who lived in a group of Greek cities along those coasts were known to the Greeks as *Italiotai* and to the Romans as *Graeci. Go figure.* It's probably why southern Italians, darker in complexion, look more like Greeks than they do their northern compatriots.

The cities grew in wealth and power and became important centers of trade and of Greek civilization. The philosopher Empedocles and the great mathematician Archimedes—as well as the mythic hero Heracles—were from Sicily. Pythagoras and his mystery school, and the Eliatic (Parmenides, Zeno) school of philosophy were established along Italy's southern coasts. Today the University of Magna Graecia is located in Catanzaro, capital of both Calabria and Catanzaro province. Italia/Italy takes its name from the Greek *Italoi*, which means "worshippers of the calf." The name replaced the local *Vitulo* of the Catanzaro area, going back to the Iron Age with archaeological evidence of the worship of the statue of the calf. This might suggest a link to earlier civilizations

---

172 "It is amazing how complete is the illusion that beauty is goodness," Leo Tolstoy, *The Kreutzer Sonata.*

in Crete and Asia Minor and perhaps to an era that predates our modern, patriarchal cultures. I say this by way of scant evidence, for sure, but the depictions of a freer feminine expression in Minoan art and in Catal Huyuk in Turkey, both of which are said to have been bull-honoring cultures, and in the art of the Etruscans, provoke my earnest imagination.

Today we are headed for that handsome, spiked heel of southern Italy en route to Calabria, the land that nurtured the flesh and minds of my parents. Brindisi, a port town on the back of that heel, lies ahead a few more miles across the southern Adriatic. It will be Vonnie's first visit to Italy, and my second. Approaching the deep end of my gene pool, I suppose I should be feeling something.

OUR SHIP DOCKS alongside a giant pier. Dozens of dockworkers stand as one without moving, watching us from the next pier across a rectangle of seawater. Even at a distance, the sweet madness of yin/yang's charge is as easy to read as green-yellow-red. As the tourists keep coming, day in and day out, the workers feast their perpetually hungry eyes. By this simple carnal measure, we are one.

In a moment one of the workers raises an arm and erupts in a tirade, sarcastic and scathing, something about fat-cat tourists and his honor, calloused hands, virility, and such. A southern Italian knows the value of the performance, his rant rapid-fire and profuse. A nervous guffaw wafts through our crowd. Without pause, and channeling a response burned in from those precious early years, I step forward and give him the ol' hand slap on the outstretched bicep, Italian for "Up yours—this far!" Dockworker Man is silenced. Cries of delight on our side, stalled disbelief on theirs. My uncanny resemblance to a few of the characters in Leonardo's *The Last Supper*, combined with the far-reaching effects of Vatican spook have, I believe, worked their common magic once again. Just the same, I'm glad we're separated by a gigantic, moat-like slip. A fitting scene, I reckon, for entering the homeland.

Calabria spreads from Italy's arch to the end of the big toe. Vonnie will be in for an unexpected treat; the human flavor of backwoods Calabria is reminiscent of rural, southwestern Asia. The DNA stylings, the hegemony of the official religious order, the distrust of modern Western ways—a complex of social qualities make Calabria more akin to Turkey, the Middle East, and even places as far away as Kashmir, than to Dusseldorf or London.

From Brindisi we hitchhike up the heel, across the arch, and into the hills to Serra San Bruno, from where my folks emigrated twenty-four years ago. My mom's sister, Rosa, remains in the hometown, having waited till her late fifties to marry. Unencumbered by raising children or devotion to a husband, Rosa has enjoyed the freedom to serve her community. Spry and cantankerous, a kind of unwitting feminist pioneer, she reigns over a complex of occupational identities including seamstress, nurse, scribe, adviser, mentor, and elocutionist of letters. That she is respected and trusted by her fellow villagers is plain to see. Walking the town's narrow lanes last year with her and my sister Maria and her two children was like touring Her Majesty's domain. Moving alongside her brisk pace we were met with sincere greetings from townsfolk at many a doorway: "Rosa! Buongiorno, Signora Rosa!" The deferential manner shown to this tiny woman was resolute and sweeping. Most looked past me, Maria, and her kids—obvious strangers—to proffer respect and salutations to Rosa. Although I'm sure they got a hungry eyeful of our backsides as we continued along.

This time Vonnie and I arrive in the central plaza at 8:00 a.m. Too early, I reckon, to go calling on my aunt. We sit on a bench and share a snack while girls and old women in black scurry past, trying to get a good look at, and then quickly away from, something foreign and gossipworthy. Perhaps we will wait until 10:00 before walking to my aunt's flat.

But within minutes the hunched, shawled figure of my Zia Rosa appears in a far corner of the piazza. She spots us and shoots straight across the stone like a giant arachnid. Pulling back her shawl, and zapping me with Medusa's freaky ice she scowls, "What you've done to *me!*" She is referring to our undignified arrival in the square like vagabonds, but most of all to my having shamelessly brought a single woman who isn't (among a good list of other interesting points) wearing a bra—a scandal akin to publicly associating with a Jezebel. *Cool.* Leaving us barely enough time to put away our bread, Rosa hauls me across the piazza, her pulling me and me pulling Vonnie down a narrow alley lined with rudimentary row flats.

Once inside, she launches into a whirlwind of domestic burdens related to our arrival and, I suspect, to her own cherished insanities. The irascible Rosa explains, with the charm of an evil queen, that she'd heard about a foreign couple hanging around the square like gypsies. I've heard how fast news travels by ear in small villages. *The girls and old women scurrying about the piazza.* She declares she knew at once that it was me. I go to tweak her cheek (as so many Italian big mamas did when I was small and defenseless), thinking it might soften the mood. She deflects my impudent arm—whacks it good—and keeps talking.

She tells me (she knows no English, speaks directly to me in Calabrese) to clean up and put on something respectable. We are wearing thongs, pull-string pants, and skimpy cotton shirts from India. I catch an eyeful of Vonnie's smiling nipples through the thin fabric as if they're the most prominent points in *Magna Graecia*. In Calabria you might be out of work and crying the blues, but you don't leave home without clean duds and a good 'do. The imperious Rosa derides our absence of fashion savvy by giving me some pressed slacks and a shirt—and ignoring Vonnie. I look at frowning-Vonnie, then wash my hands by raising them almost as high as my eyebrows.

Queen Rosa decrees that I will sleep in the common room with Zio Antonio. She will share the double bed with young-Vonnie. At first I think she's joking. Obviously, she wouldn't. I picture her and Vonnie together—two women separated by opposing shields of culture and a forty-year gap. I look at the incredulous, starting-to-get-the-picture-Vonnie, and stage my surrender with a lame-ass smile.

The impetuous Rosa moves with dizzying agility between the two rooms, preparing the beds like a super-large, deeply troubled ape-bird. Protests are futile, though I take the odd limp shot. Rosa's decision is as binding as the elastic that strangles her hair into a bun. The neighbors will know that no un-Catholic hanky-panky will happen under *her* roof. Sin of that magnitude comes with shock waves felt for miles and years, and would reverberate for generations in every tender leaf of the family tree.

During her remarkable nest building she occasionally halts inches in front of me, glaring into my face like a powerful witch. She talks nonstop, with great purpose and force, recounting the Calabrian folk doctrine that a boy and girl must never be left alone. For like a spark and dry leaves they will ignite into an evil fire. *An evil fire!* And there will be no chance of controlling it. *None!* It sounds as convenient as it does screwball-truthful. She and Antonio haven't been married long; her pet drama is probably overcompensating for all the nookie she's been getting.

But what a handy crafting of reason, I reason. *If it's true that you can't control your libido, then why try? And, no responsibility! Yay!* Have these sly old Calabrians granted virtual license for illicit flesh swapping? In the Old World you have marriage without divorce, and perhaps veiled permission to follow one's momentary throb. *The fire cannot be stopped.* No need for the whole range of intellection that comes with personal conscience, choice, and, uh, responsibility (this is where the omniscient superpowers of organized religion come in handy, no?) *Besides, controlling your passion isn't manly, yeah?* But never mind, we're all one by common biology, and there's much I don't know about my old *paisanos'* ways. Navigating the sexual powers at the social level isn't always among our strong points, no matter the place or time.

Walking the winding lanes of Serra with Vonnie is a contrast to last year's visit with my sister Maria. This time the comments are hushed, the looks stern and aloof, a parallel to the vibe I encountered when venturing out from my Afghan hotel with or without a gal pal. Perhaps the "free woman" is a threat similar in character to the small-town Catholics and the Muslims on my path. I reckon most cultures unabashedly indulge gender chauvinism. Perhaps mine and Vonnie's freewheelin' egalitarianism epitomizes to these old-worlders what makes us moderns so strange.

WE HAPPEN TO be visiting Serra San Bruno during the annual Festa di San Bruno, which includes a parade up to the hilltop monastery and a spectacular fireworks display.

Serra San Bruno's fireworks are pyrotechnics of a new vision. Their nonstop staccato intensity is maniacal. But even more, it's their shocking proximity to the crowd. Normally, fireworks displays are detonated far away, and *way* up high. These can be very exciting, but they remain a phenomenon occurring away-over-there, a mostly visual treat that is comfortably separate from the viewer.

But not here. The fireworks explode a mere thirty to forty meters distant, giving us a sensation of being right beside, almost *inside* them. We are forced into a trot-step, back and forth motion as part of a wiggling mass of gasping revellers in ebb and flow, body upon body, providing an excellent illusion of personal surrender. Oohs, yelps, and sighs—I look at Vonnie, at her face that glows wonderstruck. We are like babies, awe-struck at the display of shape, color, and motion.

Our orgy of psychedelic delight seems to have dissolved certain barriers. We drift in the afterglow of a satiated crowd, blending easily into a people who normally maintain a strong resistance to outsiders.

Retreating from the crowd, we lean on a railing that circles a stagnant pool next to the monastery. In the pool stands a statue of the town's patron saint, San Bruno, his stony face cocked heavenward in reverent agony. Perhaps there's a drainage problem, for the water reaches his belly. Vonnie comments on the unintentional monkish symbolism, observing, with a tinge of sarcasm, that "he was probably frigid from the waist down anyway." I doubt it, judging by horny priest scandals all over the monkish realm.

But she probes me for a reaction. The knowing glance she flashes me says it all: we're hot for each other, and she mocks my monkish choice. I've kept my hands off Vonnie, an act of restraint I haven't always been able to pull off in my travels. I'm beginning to see that I'm not as free lovin' as much of my generation claims to be. I want it to be more, like some spiritual fairy tale, like the Church's promise of heavenly two-as-one. If I'm a fool caught within outmoded illusions of romance and matrimony, so be it. I don't know if there's a higher love that can be found in dyadic embrace on this monkey-farm planet. A vision in which carnal love plays alongside soul-driven growth toward non-duality, a mélange of ancient Vedic teachings and the Romeo and Juliette, Helen and Paris stories: sounds pretty awesome to me. A big, juicy idea, *for that's how I like 'em.*[173]

---

173 And yet in exalting our lover, perhaps we separate ourselves from them; this has been the hidden story in my fitful dance of love in these travels. Indeed, as the years pass after my return home, as I raise three children with my good wife for twenty-three years and then receive the incomparable gift of becoming a grandfather... apart from surrender to connection itself, there is little I can truly say I've learned along the multi-layered quest of dyadic love.

I won't deny it: what is plain to see is the pull of biochemistry, as strong and as primitive as ever. Yet I can't seem to shake it; there's something about the downgrading of my dear vision, of what love might be, and of how it often shows up characterized merely as a beastly drive—that doesn't turn my crank. Especially the closer I get to the whole woman and real intimacy.

Whatever way it is framed in this precious sack of meat and mind, this bonnie Kiwi lassie isn't following the old scripts, not the Church's, not the movies' happily-ever-afters. Vonnie is a sassy reminder, contrary to the gender-centric biases of a generation of biologists, that Ms. Egg has much to say about who gets in, and when, despite Master Sperm's fabulous projectile talent.[174]

A WEEK IN Serra San Bruno is enough to arouse in us both a fanciful yearning for the mythical light of modernity. As we leave, the irrepressible Zia Rosa grabs my arm and ravages my little-boy psyche with a harsh *malocchio*. "If it wasn't for *her*," she hisses, "you wouldn't get away so easily—not yet!"

I thank my good fortune in bringing the audacious young Vonnie with me.

Dante Town

We hitchhike up the Italian shin, stopping briefly in Roma on our way to Firenze, where Vonnie looks up a brother and sister she met in India the year before. It's my turn to play guest, and the reversal is complete: her friend is of the aristocratic cream of Firenze, the flip-side of my folks' peasant culture in the mountains of the deep south.

Leo and Gina inherited a vast estate, including vineyards, a winery, and a mansion with classical carvings and paintings on the lofty ceilings. We stay in a comfortable, sprawling library strewn with several sofas and

---

174 Back in high school I reflected on the current biological take on the matter: that the winning sperm gets in. I had my doubts, for a cursory look at the surface of things can be deceiving. In hallways between classes, it appeared that the male's more active advances trumped the deal, but really, I thought, it's the female who decides. And so, by sway of the maxim "as above, so below" I concluded that somehow the egg must play an active part in choosing which sperm gets in.

various chairs. It's the biggest private library I've ever seen, eighteen- to twenty-foot ceiling. *I could live here.*

On the day of our arrival one of Leo's friends pops by. Dino is a well-drawn sketch of the jet-setting, Euro-trash fop. His played-up energy intends to sweep his audience into bristling excitement as he enacts the agonies and ecstasies of his career-pilot plaything excursions in Ethiopia. Traces of crusty European colonialism persist, it seems, to this day. Italy, unlike youthful up-and-comers France, Spain, England, Holland, and Portugal, got as far as Ethiopia, discovered a certain fragrant bean then high-tailed it home, eager to work on a new pleasure-promoting gadget, the *espresso* machine. I figure Italy's past exploits over millennia resulted in a certain resigned world weariness in matters of empire building, and the discovery of the black nectar served up a higher satisfaction by that time. Older bro Greece didn't even make it out of the harbor. But I digress.

Dino's verbal drama describes a free-fall dream as he flies his airplane over African landscapes. *The ecstasy—oh, the agony.* Lodged in an aristocratic worldview, his lot is the prize of few who are, by reason of birthright, more privileged than the many. I, the bourgeois woulda-been, stand by gazing over shelves of books in this splendid library, some of them perhaps centuries old and making an embarrassment of anything going on in this room today. The dude is all psycho-baggage and charisma. He is glamour and culture, his airplane the nuts-and-bolts extension of his self-propelling ego. No, I don't like him, don't like the testicular stink nor the faux sophistication he spews. Like me, he is more interested in Vonnie's earthly dimensions than in any of the claptrap crowding either of our small heads. I'd rather hear three honest words on this than the emotional and intellectual junk flying around the room. *All one, we are, by this simple measure.* Okay, bud, *breathe.*

Speaking to Leo, Gina, Vonnie, and (least of all) me, the well-groomed, well-heeled dick leaves in a multiple orgasm of promises, best wishes, and exceedingly saccharine goodbyes.

LEO TREATS US to a night on the town. We are an elite within an elite. I sense the cocky, self-assuredness of a town that sparked the Renaissance, the reawakening of Western culture after centuries of European intellectual and artistic *wank*. The other day as Vonnie was taking in a little more than I was willing of the profusion of museums, I asked a man on the street about Firenze's local tongue in my own garbled Calabrese/pig-Italiano. "We have no dialect," he declared with smug pride, taking in a view of all Italy, including me, down the aquiline ridge of his Florentine nose, never mind the peninsular divide of the Apennines. The city-state or republic of Firenze (Florence) is where the modern language was taken from, in Dante's native tongue.

We are escorted by sleek black cab to a posh restaurant. Our long table is a horn-of-plenty spread. Vonnie and I have little problem pleasuring our vegetarian preferences. In our pop-hippie garb we're like Judas and Mary Magdalene cavorting around town with the money lenders behind Jesus' back. In all, about a dozen have met up at this great trough of pleasures. The strata of society we've cozied into isn't clear until one or two in our company are beseeched for autographs by adoring fans from other tables. Violin-wielding little men are upon us at once, offering sugar-sweet melodies with which to chew, swallow, digest, and fart. Some restaurant patrons at other tables, mere mortals, watch us with what feels like obsessive hunger. *The envious person grows lean with the fatness of their neighbor.*[175] So long ago, a wise man spoke of what I see today. The imbalance, the sordid symbiosis of inferior/superior, feels eerily familiar. But why? Who knows, but there's an acrid aftertaste. Being treated like a royal baboon is no delicacy. *Something here I loathe.* Perhaps it's the classist separation, or the coveting and protecting of what turns out to be the make-believe values that trump this world.

Or perhaps my distaste for the royal treatment is drawn from what some call racial memory, or what others might think of as a queer little déjà vu of the reincarnational heebie-jeebies. In any case I feel it strongly. To lose one's anonymity as these Italian celebrities have? No thanks. Leo has expressed serious reservations about his inheritance but he fits the part superbly, as any Hollywood royal baboon would conjure.

Like Vonnie and I, Leo and Gina are in their early twenties. Their inheritance also has made them fugitives of that same good fortune.

175 Socrates.

In Italy, as in other parts of Europe, the rich are occasional targets of leftist revolutionaries—the Red Brigades or *Brigate Rosse* in Italy, the Red Army Faction in Germany—sometimes by kidnapping, sometimes by assassination. Upon receiving their inheritance, the two took a timely trip to India to think over their new double-edged life, and that's where they met Vonnie. Leo explains that although he wishes to sell the fortune, Italian law forbids dividing up historical estates such as theirs, and they are bound to sell it only to Italian nationals. These limitations make him feel stuck, he tells us, "as if trapped in a cage of gold."

Naturally, the food and wine are divine. As absurd as my offering to pay our way seems even to me, when dinner is finished I fumble for my measly nano-lira, on cue in a programmed proletariat *pathetico comedy*. But Leo's subtly flexed brow and gently raised fingers settle the score with grace.

After dinner Leo takes us to a nightclub. We walk into the dim underbelly of an inner-city building. The scene is similar to what one would find in a fancy club back in Vancouver, only it's slicker, more Italian. But there's something else. I wonder if so much time has passed, or whether this flashing, thumping oddity of music and dance is an Italian development. I creep through the mannequin crowd watching the rhythmic, pseudo-sexual pumping of the dancers. The music seems to induce a stolid hypnosis with its heavy, perfectly timed bass drum dominating the sound. It's as though the music "dances" the people. The year 1984 is still seven years away yet this is a den of drones, for only drones could be so uniformly styled, both in movement and in dress. Those who aren't on the dance floor peer and leer in obsessive eye moves that lash at the speck of sanity to which I cling.

I figure my momentary malaise might be a recurring taste of culture shock, as happened on my return to the West over a year ago in Thessaloniki, Greece. I look out of place in my long-haired, bearded, hobo-hip costume of the world traveler. But I can't get my mind off the soul-stripped music that I assume the youth of my ancestral homeland have produced by disfiguring good old rock 'n' roll. This new industrial Latin version is all dazzle, its spirit as dead as its beat is rigidly measured.

What I didn't know is that I'd missed a significant twist in popular music while tramping around the East. This queer music isn't a mutant form of Italo-rock. It is what's playing in clubs all over the West, and it's called disco. (And, as I later discover, some of it ain't half-bad.)

BACK IN NEW Zealand, Vonnie had been an art student. Her special interest in the great masters provides me with a well-placed tour that I'd probably be oblivious to without her. In the Vatican and in Florence I love tagging along, viewing Michelangelo's this and Raphael's that. Lucky for me, the power in these works cuts across educational and cultural barriers. Standing before the *Pieta* or gazing at the Sistine Chapel ceiling I'm a Neanderthal in awe, eyes agog and jaw all slack. I'd bet that even a passing cocker spaniel would feel something.

But after several hours of luscious beauty, painting after sculpture after architectural marvel, I lose my cultural bearing and my senses falter, unable as I am to absorb another morsel of what is offered. I am aesthetically numb and maybe, a little cranky. I stand among the most renowned works, yearning for a child's guileless scribble, my eyes pulled into random folds and shadows in the clothes of passersby. While Vonnie looks at something old, important, and beautiful, I escape to the street, drawn upon a heightened affection toward the unordered debris and grime at my feet.

THERE IS ONE last stop for Vonnie and me before leaving *Italia bella mia*. We've seen the old-world hills of the deep south. We've had a fling with the upper crust in uptown Firenze. Now we're in for a quick lick of the working class in the Po River valley of the industrious north.

Mosnigo is a small village in Treviso province near Venezia, stomping ground for both my older sisters' husbands. My senior sister, Rita, and her family moved back to Canada during the last year, so their place remains empty. It is the ground-level third of a triplex shared by her family and those of her two brothers-in-law. I am welcome to stay, and I bring the fair Vonnie.

Not much happens in Mosnigo. The brother living in the floor above has the usual spermatozoon glint whenever he asks, in sniggering tones, about Vonnie and her nubile package. I try to be gracious, feigning a deferential, macho-friendly poise. We are an unmarried couple, unchaperoned, sleeping under the same ceiling. But we are outsiders, and, I suppose, tolerated. Nonetheless, I feel the hot sparks that arc wildly in the village's collective mind. We are culturally insulated, yet we hear the snaky whispering that follows our lazy meanderings of the clean, narrow streets. We see the tight-lipped, steel-eyed matrons who wait on us. We see their puffy, judgmental forearms, the large meat cleavers, and their disapproving thwacks on cutting boards.

But after Serra San Bruno, *meh*. Mosnigo di Moriago—milder breeze, same wind.

HITCHHIKING NORTH FROM Italy we stop for a few tasty beers in Germany. In Amsterdam we turn a corner and get a red-light peep. At the edge of the property next to the street, hookers sit in Plexiglas booths lined with an ingenuous display of action snapshots of their trade.

I go to a bank, collect $400 "telexed" from Canada to pay Vonnie the money I borrowed back in Afghanistan; she trusted me for thousands of miles. We part most amicably over some delicious rye bread, exchanging addresses. I reckon I'll never see her again.

AS I GUESSED it would, England bears an easy resemblance to New Zealand. Mother Britannia is older, cooler, more crowded, and a bit more, hmmm... self-impressed? *Hey, hey, Mama.*

I'm on my way to look up a couple, Caragh and Dragan, who I'd met in India. I arrive at a proper middle-class neighborhood in Rickmansworth on the outskirts of London. Caragh is a white-skinned, black-haired English lass and Dragan a tall, steady-eyed Croatian from Split. Both are consciously exploring out-of-the-way experiential avenues, one of which led to Nisargadatta's loft in Bombay, where we had exchanged addresses.

During the week at Caragh's folks' estate we enjoy some great games of croquet. Another birthday (my twenty-third) passes, this time, unnoticed.

Dragan and Caragh are married in the backyard. At their request, I shoot the photos. Somehow the negatives get ruined. I do hope their marriage, unlike those negatives, has good chemistry, develops within the wonders of contrast and balance, and lasts well into the next century.

They might have gotten married on my birthday, which would explain why I forgot about it, what with all the hoopla. Later in the year I will forget how old I am for the first time.

Twenty-three, a prime number, becomes my sentimental, all-time favorite.

16. Dream

a carousel of time[176]

Souvenir

Early evening, deep summer. I'm eight years old, walking alone on a neighborhood street. I smell what I love—the sweet tang of cottonwood—and I love what I see: the gentle rise of jungle up the Burke Mountain slope toward the snow-fringed shapes of the Coast Range skyline. They are the mountains of an unsaid, grand silence, one that seems to easily absorb the quaint bustle of my little town.

Mid-stride, and with a sudden surge of inspiration, a few simple words pierce the fog of a boy's daily concerns: *three years away from home*. It comes as a whisper, or maybe not. Or a phrase of thoughtless banter in an empty room. Yet it evokes a yearning, calm and deep and mysterious. The words (gone now) leave an energy that is not strange, but also feels entirely new. Like an *a priori* message in a bottle, it's about a journey, a significant departure from all I'm familiar with. The experience is without precedent or reference. Its strangeness, and my young mind, are not helpful in examining it; I'm not inclined (or perhaps equipped) to reflect upon it. Does it get stored in the mind? A word souvenir? In it there is a feeling, as if it is a *new* feeling, of taking my small yet captivating existence into something *other*. For sure it's an admission of ignorance and of facing it steady on, even savoring it. Implied is the question of what I am, apart from the world that knows and defines me. And a suggestion, still unarticulated yet specific, that the home world, by begetting and bearing witness to one's every

---

176 From *The Circle Game* by Joni Mitchell.

thought and action, befogs a clear view of... the viewer. The combined influence of all and everything is suspect. It's the Calabria/Canada thing again, each story assuming it's the valid one, with me on the sideline watching the show. The "message", the words, came along on a light breeze, clear and explicit. But it is soon forgotten.

Facts are accumulated by effort, but truth reveals itself effortlessly.[177]

Already an avid map gazer, I am in awe of the grand, humming mess of the natural world, a raw wild that provides both a stunning backdrop and a complexity that is powerful, unpredictable, and sensuous. The homeland that nurtured Billy, Jona, Danna and me is a deep and luxuriant wilderness. Our town and the big city are but self-conscious specks engulfed in a brilliant profusion of forests, rivers, lakes, islands and sea. Fold-crust mountains curl north to east in the morning distance, in blue majesty, always there to remind of the marriage of chaos and wonderment. Not remarkable in altitude, yet they are cloaked in a jungle so tangled and treacherous as to inspire stories of murder and a secret gold mine tucked in some crevice a few peaks in, up a river valley, just several miles from town as the crow flies. Legends speak of fortune seekers vanished in its quest, some from down the coast in California, all driven on the craving for mammon.[178]

Our dot on the map, like hundreds more across the land, is the hopeful crawl of modernity into a woodland so vast it rings the planet. It is a hope that is spiked into the very soul of our town, in each of our homes, heated as they are with the Earth's own vapors by the prodigies of science.

Yet it is the fringe of this forest wonderland that my buddies and I are committed to penetrating on a daily basis. Perhaps we'll discover a

177 Ramana Maharshi, early twentieth-century South Indian sage.

178 From the book *Slumach's Gold* by Antonson/Trainer/Antonson. It refers to the Lost Creek Mine of the Coast Salish man named Slumach, the legend of whom is based on his being seen around New Westminster, BC flaunting gold nuggets in the late nineteenth century. His mine was believed to lie somewhere in remote mountains north of Pitt Lake. Slumach was hanged for the murder of a female inn worker in 1891, and many believed he carried knowledge of a rich gold deposit to his grave. Attempts to find the mine ended in mysterious deaths and disappearances on several occasions, giving rise to the belief that Slumach cursed the mine's location. It is also said that exaggeration and sensationalism crept into early journalists' desire for a good story.

new land deep in the jungle with full-grown, half-naked women from my brother's *Playboy*s, or maybe we'll find an old shed with snakes hiding under rotting boards. Delicious blackberries and salmonberries; tadpoles, frogs, and bloody salmon. The whisper of a new river pulling us in through the darkness between trees. Glorious Nature, free of the human buzz, serves as an antidote to the hierarchical and emotion-flogging ways of home, school, and the street. *Bigger than us all.* The forests and mountains that surround us are eerie and, I reckon, never ending. This, paradoxically, also seems to assure that the world is somehow "good." My being in, and maybe a part of this fragrant vitality we call life *has* to be good, cuz that's how it feels. The concept of infinity lifts my smallness as I gaze into the jagged horizon from the top floor of our home, and by our boyish push through the underbrush. Our scruffy little gang is drawn in beyond the end of many a road, lured by black shadows and weird sounds. "Infinity" becomes our mantra. We toss the word back and forth like a cerebral hot potato as we thrash through the bush, giddy from its transcendent power. "Infinity! Infinity!" we shriek as we whack at branches, feeling like pirates but sounding like geeks. We play with—we tease, within ourselves—the emptiness and fullness at the edge of the world.

"BC" is a symbol for the hazes of prehistory, but it is also the name of our homeland. Brobdingnag, Gulliver's land of giants,[179] is thought to have been placed by its eighteenth-century writer somewhere along this coast, where trees grow like the blue whales of the plant kingdom. At the time, this region epitomized the remote unknown, for it was still unexplored by Europeans. Certain old maps in the school library don't recognize our coastline. Along with a chunk of Australia it is simply missing, a fact that does not elude my trail-blazing eye (as it probably did not elude Swift's.) This status as one of the planet's last tracts of *terra incognita* (a Euro-centric term) gives our local wilderness—and daytime adventures—a credible pang of uncertainty.

When European sailors finally did arrive it was one of the last fronts of the meeting of worlds in the Columbian exchange. English ships came and went as late as the early 1800s seeking trade goods with

179 From *Gulliver's Travels* by Jonathan Swift.

indigenous nations. As a boy, I knew not of the local king, Maquinna[180] nor of his people, the Nootka, who lived along the westernmost of our coasts on the far side of the big island. They were a unique people who ate well, enjoyed music, played games, and created haunting art and the enlightened tradition of potlatch.[181]

We four—Billy, Jona, Danna, and I—are European by ethnicity, recent transplants to this land. We were born here, all, and this underlines a strange and difficult conflict: our belonging here, and that of disparate mythologies, the colonial and the aboriginal, still reluctant to blend, like oil and water.[182] From age fourteen till I began this trip I crisscrossed, by thumb, this land of cut rock along numerous paths every summer. Yes, I feel it as *my* British Columbia, and I hope I am able to share my love for this land with the First Nations people.

Yet it was the explorers I learned about in grade school—Marco Polo, Cristoforo Colombo,[183] and Giovanni Caboto—who, in my boyhood

180 See *White Slaves of Maquinna* by John R. Jewitt

181 Among the aboriginal peoples of the Pacific Northwest potlatch was a gift-giving tradition, a feast, a vital part of a whole economy that, in a way, redistributed wealth. A leader's wealth and power was demonstrated by throwing a great party and giving away possessions. Potlatch also served as the overarching ceremony for births and naming, deaths, marriages, and the passing on of rights and privileges from chief to eldest son. (from Wikipedia, referencing *The Story of the Masks* website.) Potlatch ceremonies were banned by the Canadian government, sure evidence of the clash of values, held dearly, by different cultures. Only in 1951 was the ban lifted.

182 The First Nations of these lands have always held a deep fascination for me. Indeed, I've felt a conviction that what is missing in the matrix of the modern worldview—and to pathological effect—is epitomized in the more inclusive and less rapacious worldviews of the First Nations. My hope is that our modern civilization will play catch-up on sorely missing values, those of honoring the land that nurtures our bodies, for one, and that one's well-being is synonymous with one's tribe's—for seven generations—for another. I offer thanks for the flourish of a human reality I have barely skimmed the surface of and which has existed in this hemisphere for millennia. The peoples of the Americas were more numerous and complex than was assumed (until recently) by colonizers, as revealed in *1491* by Charles C. Mann.

183 My elder brother likes to point out that every time C. C. signed his name he traced six circles, which might have gone to his head—and earned him a place in history books.

imagination, offered a palpable link to my own so-called ethnicity, and especially, to my fascination with the unknown. Terra Incognita (unrecognized or unknown land) is a term drawn in my parents' own tongue. The experiential language of the Italians follows on a long and proud cultural legacy. The Romans overcame and absorbed their compatriot and mysterious Etruscan[184] neighbors to dominate much of the world known to Europeans at the time. The artistic and philosophical surge of the Renaissance in central Italy reawakened European cultural pre-eminence, and (putting aside my personal take on the matter) the hegemony of the Roman Church continues to hold sway over the psyches of many millions around the world.

My parents, uneducated Calabrese themselves, were proud of their move to the Far West, of owning their own home with electricity, indoor plumbing, and central heating. But it was the vast complexity and seeming intelligence of the wild canopy of life that had *me* spellbound. Without knowing it, my folks moved to the edge of one of the planet's grandeurs of wilderness. So vast and dark is this temperate forest as to contain beliefs and stories of an elusive man-ape. Whether eyewitness fact or mythical metaphor, both the First Nations and recent arrivals speak of encounters with the Himalayan yeti's overseas cousin, sasquatch. And so in one generation the dreams and sensibilities of a southern Italian family crossed an ocean, genuflected to a new credo of the unknown, and did a cultural 180.

As we nerd-youths slash through the bush, I pick up on subtle tricks of the English tongue, its peculiar points and paths of focus, taking cues from my buddies and storing details of their lingo and personal flair. I learn the extra-serious game of correct Canadian behavior alongside the daily fun of bushwhacking. At home I observe my family's antics: beheading chickens, whacking rabbits, and fists slamming the kitchen table with almighty force in the glow of God's good wine. I look across our yard, next door at self-composed Mr. "Canadese" mowing his perfect

184 The Etruscans are unique in their artwork for the frequent depictions of women in positions of power, at the heads of tables, and so on, and for their many scenes of smiles, joviality, and happiness. Their language has long eluded modern scholars' attempts to decipher it; I'm not sure how complete their efforts have been.

lawn, and his missus tending her perfect flowers. Looking askance at the lowbrow wop shenanigans next door, their smirks of condescending amusement glaze their eyes and puff their faces. Even before I could form sentences, my eyes barely reaching the windowsill, I saw the two worlds, was witness to two different kingdoms of thought and behavior. Both kingdoms would vie for psychic space. The crazier, more exciting one was contained within my home. But I learned, or decided, that my best gamble would be in aligning with the more self-controlled one: the surrounding Anglo hegemony. Food and love came from my folks, but a bigger picture determined a choice, all without words. Words that could reach only so far in an uneasy place between worlds. Can free will be willed unknowingly? Perhaps understanding is not the product of words, even though its expression, and therefore reason itself, is tied to a lingual structure.[185]

The world outside carries authority, of this much I was sure. My family is a speck of a different color in a bigger, paler, more genteel world. *We* are different—we, the weird ones. Soon enough I discover (or decide) that I do not quite belong to my parents' world. But nor do I to this *Canadese* one. Perhaps this is the reason the phrase "three years away" appeared and mystified me on that day. Perhaps this is what afforded me the perspective to cast doubt on the authority of any single worldview, and what seeded the discontent and the curiosity to want to leave everything that "the world" would presume to define in me.

Next question: How big, exactly, *is* the world?

JUST TURNED TWENTY-THREE. I'm in an airplane halfway across North America on the last leg of a 'round-the-world tour. For the first time since I thought it, and quite suddenly, like a mask yanked from my whole self, I remember the three-years-away boyhood moment. Stored for all that time, it's the perfect moment to pop back in. To have forgotten it for a generation, then have it recur at the end of that very

---

185 I paraphrase, by way of my own bias, these words from A. Einstein: "Innovation is not the product of logical thought, even though the final product is tied to a logical structure." Perhaps the arrow of intuition can cover vast ground that only later does analysis attempt to make sense of and measure.

thought come true... I'm inside one of those ornamental bubble worlds you hold in your hand and turn upside down, the myriad silver flecks the bits and pieces of my timeline tossed into suspension, floating in a liquid sky. *Do you have the patience to wait until your mud settles and your water is clear?*[186] What choice? At least I can see my mud clearly.

Did I program or will myself to do this trip long ago? Or did it just happen because I thought it, and I'm a big dumb ape who follows whatever clever story happens to stick? Do "free will" and "just happen" cooperate? Are they beasts in conflict, circling each other like hungry dogs from opposite sides of town? Do they meet illicitly when we sleep, slipping into our feeble minds to tango like drunken Buddhas when we dream, tossing us the odd symbol, heads thrown back in mountainous laughter at questions like these that arise in the flatlands of our dull, waking minds?

Those boyhood words spook me good and deep as I cross the planet above the clouds in a bird-shaped metallic beast. For a moment the sweeping illusion of past-present-future is cleared. I simply exist. A minute later I'm looking back at it, savoring its scent like a passing hungry dog.

We enter thick cloud banks caught on the great cordillera of North America's western third, the last barrier to Lotusland.[187] Still buzzing with unresolved thoughts and feelings, I doze off.

A Zillion Packets of Light

A sudden murmur wakes me. I sit up and look out the window. Through sleepy eyes and parting clouds I spot the twin bridges of Lougheed Highway crossing the Pitt River[188] and up ahead, my old neighborhood. Dazzling sun rays have arranged themselves into multiple fans of

186 Lao Tzu.
187 Named after the "lotus eaters" in Homer's *Odyssey*, who indulged in the fruit of the lotus and became indolent and dreamy. It has been the nickname for BC's balmy West Coast (what unites Canada? Snow in Vancouver, as they say)... where the locals hang out lulled by the land's beauty engaged in such non-productive endeavours as water and snow skiing, snowboarding, kayaking, mountain biking, and hiking—at any time of year. For me, Lotusland conjures the lovely, large white flower representing both the fecund brilliance of the land and our earnest dabbling in the philosophies and fashions of Eastern lands and their mystical traditions. The lotus flower is a recurring symbol in ancient Hindu and Egyptian art and religion.
188 Before our modern, cable-stayed bridge, two two-lane bridges spanned the river.

smoky light that appear and disappear in the caprice of blowing mists, all superimposed over leviathan cloud shadows creeping across the lush landscape. Within seconds I'm looking down at the very streets of my first twenty years, where Shaughnessy Street crosses the Lougheed and the CP Rail tracks: my dear old PoCo.

We pass over my hometown toward Vancouver International Airport. Up ahead Vancouver Island is a sharply defined range of mountains, separated from the mainland by shimmering slivers of quicksilver, the Georgia Strait. We come in from the east and angle down past the skyscraper-packed West End and thickly wooded Stanley Park. Together they form a polarized figure eight, an oversized infinity symbol that jogs the mind in echoes of ancient teachings. The city and the jungle, the one and its shadow; duality that is so damn real in this world, the only one in sight. Shiva's arms have snaked their way around the globe and his gremlin fingertips noodle across landscape and sea and into my brain, reminding me not to forget my visit to his land. Long rays of afternoon sunlight flicker across Vancouver's glassy skyline through swooshing clouds, splashing my retinas with intense golden flashes, brief shots of clarity that brace the habitual dullness of that dang real world… could be the end of a storm, the beginning of a calm spell.

REENTERING ONE'S OWN country in grubby garb after a lengthy absence will rouse suspicion at customs. In all my border crossings, only Italy paid special and unexpected attention to my arrival (the JD "Canadian importer of automobiles incident" at Iran customs was expected.) At Vancouver Airport, on home's doorstep, I am again taken aside for a thorough search. In a dirty side pocket of my backpack the man in crisp duds finds a small leather pouch with irregular, dark-brown balls in three pill-like sizes. They're wrapped in clear plastic and smell like aged, spicy greens. *Nice.*

"Oh, I know this looks suspicious. You must think it's hash, but it's actually a sample of Tibetan herbs that worked wonders on my hepatitis a while back. I decided to bring some home and have it checked out." I speak with unabashed ease. The man is silent, proper, very Canadian. But he itches and twitches, and his owly eyes are fixed on a picture of law and order, good and bad, wanker customs duality business. The others in the lineup are wide-eyed as well. Our little drama, the predictable ruffling of genteel feathers, amuses. They take the herbs away for closer inspection. After fifteen minutes they're returned, and I'm waved in without a word.

Outside the airport I feel no urge to fall and kiss the ground. It's neither mystic nor emotional. I move forward as I look back. New Zealand and Australia: strange sibling lands, my journey begun on the flip side, Down Under. Java, Bali: lush islands teeming with humanity where something called culture screams awake and at the same time, falls away. India: where my jaw drops on an unaccountable sense of returning, where the meanings of home, self, and even time begin to lose their sharp definitions. Italy: the birthplace of my emigrant family, barely recognizing me in my new-land Anglo adornments.

And now Canada, my native land. *Thanks, on behalf of me and my folks, for the permissive immigration policies.* I grew up never quite feeling like a "regular Canadian", but here I am, belonging to it as it belongs to me. On the bus from the airport, the country of my birth is one more on the list I've had the good fortune to visit. Entered only minutes ago at the bottom of that list, it reemerges where it always was: at the top. Not until visiting other lands could I appreciate the scope of my homeland's beauty—newly cut, rugged, and canopied in a most wondrous and luxurious biota. British Columbia. Even the blueness of the sky and the variety of cloud pictures are bracing in depth and clarity. Quite unlike anything I've seen. Culturally, it's similar to New Zealand and Oz, but with a distinctly American buzz. The bus driver is friendly; a few "East Indians" stare. Hmm... many seem to have moved to Vancouver while I visited *their* homeland. Some recent arrivals notice something, as if they sense I've just come from *there. My face has a different look now.* The words come and go as I glance at my Tibetan bag and Indian pants, the visible evidence of a more subtle effect.

Back at the start, I simply showed up at the ticket counter, then showed up at the airport; the rest seemed to just happen. Looking back, flashes of moments on the road are all that are left. But not really.

Bearing the bulk of my tattered backpack one last time, I walk up a street named like a northern Italian lake to a home I've never seen, my folks having moved during my absence. It's Sunday night at 10:00, early July, just as these particular longitudes pass into the deeper shade of Earth's luscious curve.

I knock. Something is ending and something beginning. Sure, that can be said of any moment, but *this* one... I stand in front of the door, sure of even less than I've grown accustomed to. Freedom? The cliché is probably true: a prisoner could be freer than one who drifts unbound.

The door opens, and I'm greeted by my younger siblings—my now womanly sister and my brothers, who have acquired deep voices and square faces. In a moment the time and distance missing between us whips through like an ethereal whirlwind. I remain anchored by their eyes and by our connection even though, near the end of that time and distance, I cut loose from home and all it ever meant. *Ahoy! A zillion packets of jolly light dance and zing among us!* I savor the rush of familiarity, the utter mystery of reunion after so long. I savor the gasps, the dizzying wildfire of all the untold signals in our smiling faces and hidden goo. Out here at the far end of an old but newly arrived dream, a few easy footsteps do one last jig and wrap it up nicely. As far as dreams go it was a good one, a loose run across an ocean or two, a few coastlines, valleys, and mountain ranges and through numerous faces... *each one as "me" as me.* And I came along only *one* path.

I stand at my folks' front door as my personal reality of three years disappears into vaporous memory. As galaxies turn, as DNA everywhere opens sleepy eyes or hunkers down, or unpacks its bags at another fork in another road... as my stomach plays chicken with my brain...

As little packets of light flush our hungry faces I say, "Hi," and step inside.

Epilogue

THE SLIGHTLY OLDER INDIAN GUY NUDGES ME, POINTING TO BIANCA, sitting in the next row. "She's a good-looking one, isn't she?" I agree. I just met Bianca and Mary as we scrambled onto the airplane, leaving their native Australia from Perth and heading north into Southeast Asia. The guy's not being lewd or macho. He merely observes her beauty, and is likely referring to my own keen interest. Even though I've been gone from Vancouver for over a year, it seems my journey has just taken off. With this short flight I will leave the land of the English tongue, and the West, for the first time. My own parents did a brave migration to a new land just before I was born in it. I have come by way of New Zealand and Australia; these are faraway places, for sure, but they are sibling nations to Canada. Today we fly to where even my imagination is reluctant to go. It is easier to imagine the secrets of Bianca as I watch her. *Who is she? Might we laugh together?*

"Where do you go? And from where have you come?" The wise-ish Indian dude with the gentle-smooth voice has already disarmed my traveler's anxiety. I want to understand his questions, maybe what's behind them.

"Oh, I'm from Canada, and I'm, uh, heading through Asia on my way to Europe."

"Canada? Why then, do you go?"

I know he is asking for more than I am able to say just now. *Why do I go?* It's what my ex-girlfriend asked just before I left. Then, at least, I aimed at something deeper: "Well, not for a holiday." Today, on this stopover flight to Kuala Lumpur, his question leaves me nearly dumb. But I grab and stumble around a few words... to *explore, experience,* to be *exposed, expanded.* With each word his eyes grow... sadder. He feels something I don't understand. Strangely, I *feel* it, but clear perception is elusive. It might be his lands I plan to tromp through on my way to... *expression, experiment...*

He looks at me as if for the first time. It feels like he sees through me, sees something else. His eyes are still and strong. Compassionate too. I feel it, believe it, but I don't really get it. Not yet.

Softly, he says, "Go home."

Acknowledgments

THANK YOU...

To the friendly staff at Friesen Press, and to Eva Dominelli and Ryan Quiring for their help with my old photos. To my daughter Eva especially, who filled in sundry gaps in my handling of the whole process.

To Clearmind International... it was "P2 Prac" class and the Odyssey workshop that really kicked my ass into getting this book thing off the ground.

And to all those who suggested, in their way, that I might have something of value to offer by way of the written word:

George Zebroff, under whose tutelage I first became aware, way back in grade nine—a mere peek, really—that I might write something worth writing.

To Randall Crow, Pam Dominelli, John Mansell, Lois Peterson, Rick Mansell, Sean O'Leary, Geraldo and Sandra Dominelli, Jim Olynyk, Nora Weber and Carol Waters.

To Alice Hung, Wendy Noel, Saira Kenwal, Rebecca Criswell, Mellie Fricker, Brad Martin, Duane O'Kane, and Robert Ellison.

And to Susan Keetley who, with her gentle encouragement, showed me how to string and tune my guitar with nouns and verbs.

Thanks to all these fine people.

And I want to thank... those lucky stars.

References

Alighieri, Dante, *The Divine Comedy* (14th C)

Anthony, David W., *The Horse, The Wheel And Language* (2007) Princeton University Press

Antonson/Trainer/Antonson, *Slumach's Gold* (2007) Heritage House Publishing, Surrey, BC

Baker, Ian, *The Heart Of The World* (2004) The Penguin Press, New York

Baum, Frank L., *The Wizard Of Oz* (1900)

Blair, Lawrence and Lorne, *Ring Of Fire* (1988) Bantam Books, New York

Blake, William, *Auguries Of Innocence* (1803)

Blanchet, M. Wylie, *The Curve Of Time* (1961) William Blackwood & Sons Ltd, Edinburgh

Boo, Katherine, *Behind The Beautiful Forevers* (2012) Random House, New York

Boyd, Pattie, *Wonderful Tonight* (2007) Harmony Books, New York

Brody, Hugh, *Maps And Dreams* (1982) Pantheon Books, New York

Brunton, Paul, *A Search In Secret India* (1934) Wexford College Press (2013)

Brunton, Paul, *The Short Path To Enlightenment* (2014) Larson Publications, New York

Bucke, R.M., *Cosmic Consciousness* (1901) Innes & Sons (1969) E.P. Dutton & Co.

Campbell, Joseph, *The Hero With A Thousand Faces* (1949) Bollingen Foundation, Pantheon Books

Camus, Albert, *The Plague* (1947). Penguin Books (1960), England

Capra, Fritjof, *The Tao Of Physics* (1975) Shambhala, Boulder, Colorado

Carroll, Lewis, *Alice In Wonderland* (1865)

Castaneda, Carlos, *The Teachings Of Don Juan* (1968) University of California Press

Castaneda, Carlos, *A Separate Reality* (1971) Simon & Schuster, New York

Chapman, Marina, *The Girl With No Name* (2013) Pegasus Books, New York

Chatwin, Bruce, *In Patagonia* (1977) Jonathan Cape, Ltd., UK

Chatwin, Bruce, *The Songlines* (1987) Viking Penguin Inc., New York

Cruttenden, Walter, *Lost Star Of Myth And Time* (2006) St. Lynn's Press, Pittsburg

Danaos, Kosta, *The Magus Of Java* (2000) Inner Traditions, Rochester, Vermont

David-Neel, Alexandra, *Magic & Mystery In Tibet* (1929), Penguin (1971)

Davis, Wade, *One River* (1996) Simon & Schuster, New York

Davis, Wade, *The Serpent & The Rainbow* (1985) Stoddart, Toronto

Densmore, John, *Riders On The Storm* (1990) Delacorte Press, New York

Dispenza, Joe, *You Are The Placebo* (2014) Hay House, Vancouver

Donner, Florinda, *Shabono* (1982) Delacorte Press, New York

Dylan, Bob, *Chronicles Volume One* (2004) Simon & Schuster, New York

Everett, Daniel L., *Don't Sleep, There Are Snakes* (2008) Pantheon Books, New York

Farrow, Mia, *What Falls Away* (1997) Doubleday, New York

Fermor, Patrick Leigh, *The Broken Road* (2013) John Murray (Publishers), UK

Frankl, Viktor E., *Man's Search For Meaning* (1959)

Frawley, David, *Gods, Sages and Kings* (1991, 2012) Lotus Press, Twin Lakes, USA

Furst, Peter T., *Hallucinogens And Culture* (1976) Chandler & Sharp Publishers, Inc.

Goldman, William, *The Princess Bride* (1973) Harcourt Brace Jovanovich Inc.

Gould, Stephen J., *Eight Little Piggies* (1993) W.W. Norton & Co. Inc., New York

Grof, Stanislav, *Realms Of The Human Unconscious* (1976) E.P. Dutton & Co. Inc., New York

Gurdjieff, G., *Meetings With Remarkable Men* (1963) Pan Books Ltd.,(1978) London

Hall, Edward T., *The Dance Of Life* (1983) Anchor Books/Doubleday, New York

Hancock, Graham, *Underworld* (2002) Crown Publishers, New York

Hesse Hermann, *Journey To The East* (1956) Picador, New York

Hesse, Hermann, *Magister Ludi/The Glass Bead Game* (1943) Germany (1969) Holt, Reinhart & Winston Inc., New York

Heying, Heather & Weinstein, Bret, *A Hunter-Gatherer's Guide To The 21st Century* (2021) Portfolio/Penguin, Random House, New York

Homer, *The Odyssey* (8ᵗʰCentury BC)

Huxley, Aldous *The Doors Of Perception/Heaven & Hell* (1954) Harper & Row Publishers Inc., New York

Huxley, Aldous, *Moksha* (1977) J.P. Tarcher, Inc., Los Angeles

Janov, Arthur, *The Primal Scream* (1970) G.P. Putnam's Sons, New York

Jewitt, John R., *White Slaves of Maquinna* (1815)

Johnson, Robert A., *We* (1983) Harper & Row Publishers, New York

Jung, C.G., *Memories, Dreams, Reflections* (1961) Pantheon Books/ Random House, New York

Jung, C.G., *Synchronicity* (1960) Bollingen Series, Princeton University Press

Kerouac, Jack, *The Dharma Bums* (1958) The Viking Press

Kerouac, Jack, *On The Road* (1957) Viking Penguin, New York

Kersten, Holger, *Jesus Lived In India* (1986) Element Books, Ltd., Dorset

Kingsley, Peter, *A Story Waiting To Pierce You* (2010) The Golden Sufi Center, California

Kingsley, Peter, *In The Dark Places Of Wisdom* (1999) The Golden Sufi Center

Kingsley, Peter, *Reality* (2003) The Golden Sufi Center, California

Koestler, Arthur, *Ghost In The Machine* (1967) Hutchinson Publishing Group Ltd (1975) Pan Books Ltd., London

Krishnamurti, J., *The Second Krishnamurti Reader* (1970) Penguin Books, England

Kuhn, Thomas S., *The Structure Of Scientific Revolutions* (1962) The University of Chicago Press

Laing, R. D., *The Politics Of Experience & The Bird Of Paradise* (1967) Penguin Books, London

Lamb, F. Bruce, *Wizard Of The Upper Amazon* (1971) Houghton Mifflin, Boston

Lao Tsu, *Tao Te Ching* (6th Century B.C.)

Lawrence, Grant, *Adventures In Solitude* (2010) Harbour Publishing Co. Ltd, Madeira Park, B.C.

Leary, Timothy, *The Politics Of Ecstasy* (1970) Paladin

Lehmann, Herman, *Nine Years Among The Indians* (1927)

Lilly, John C., *The Center Of The Cyclone* (1972) The Julian Press, New York

Lilly, John C., *Simulations Of God* (1975) Simon & Schuster, New York

Lipton, Bruce H., *The Biology Of Belief* (2005) Hay House, Inc.

Lofting, Hugh, *The Story of Doctor Dolittle* (1962) McClelland & Stewart Ltd.

MacLean, Rory, *Magic Bus* (2006) Penguin Books, London

Mann, Charles C., *1491* (2005) Alfred A. Knopf, New York

Markham, Beryl, *West With The Night* (1942, 1983) Houghton Mifflin, Boston

Markides, Kyriacos, *The Magus Of Strovolos* (1985) Routledge & Kegan Paul Ltd.

Markides, K., *Homage To The Sun* (1987) Penguin Arkana, England

Markides, K., *Fire In The Heart* (1990) Paragon House, New York

Markides, K., *Mountain Of Silence* (2001) Doubleday, New York

Masters, Robert Augustus, *Darkness Shining Wild* (2005) Tehmenos Press

Matthiessen, Peter, *The Snow Leopard* (1978) Viking Press

McEvilley, Thomas, *The Shape Of Ancient Thought* (2002) Allworth Press, New York

McKenna, Jed, *The Enlightenment Trilogy* (2010) Wisefool Press

McKenna, Terence, *True Hallucinations* (1993) Harper Collins, New York

McTaggart, Lynne, *The Intention Experiment* (2007) Simon & Schuster, New York

Merrell-Wolff, Franklin, *Pathways Through To Space* (1973) The Julian Press, New York

Morgan, Marlo, *Mutant Message Down Under* (1991, 1994) Harper Collins, New York

Morrow, Susan Brind, *The Names Of Things* (1997) Riverhead Books, New York

Mukerjee, Madhusree, *The Land Of Naked People* (2003) Houghton Mifflin, New York

Nisargadatta Maharaj, *I Am That* (1973) Chetana, Bombay (M. Frydman transl.) (1982) Acorn Press, Durham, N. Carolina

Newby, Eric, *A Short Walk In The Hindu Kush* (1958) Harper Collins

Northcutt, Wendy, *The Darwin Awards* (2000) Penguin Putnam, New York

O'Rourke, P. J., *All The Trouble In The World* (1994) The Atlantic Monthly Press, New York

Olsson, Suzanne, *Jesus In Kashmir: The Lost Tomb*, (2002)

Person, Cea Sunrise, *Nearly Normal* (2017) Harper Collins, Toronto

Plato, *Phaedo,* (4th Century BC)

Plummer, Rachel, *The Rachel Plummer Narrative* (1926)

Ramana Maharshi, *Talks With Ramana Maharshi Vol. I-III* (1972) Sri Ramanasramam, Tiruvannamalai

Rampa, Lobsang, *The Third Eye* (1956) Martin Secker & Warburg Ltd., England

Roberts, Bernadette, *The Experience Of No-Self* (1993) State University of New York Press

Roberts, Paul William, *River In The Desert* (1993) Random House, New York

Roberts, Paul William, *Empire Of The Soul* (1994) Stoddart, Toronto

Robertson, Robbie, *Testimony* (2016) Alfred A. Knopf, Toronto

Rogers, Carl, *A Way Of Being* (1980) Houghton Mifflin Co., New York

Rosolie, Paul, *Mother Of God* (2014) Harper Collins, New York

Rousseau, Jean-Jacques, *The Confessions Of Jean-Jacques Rousseau* (1783)

Saint-Exupery, Antoine de, *Wind, Sand & Stars* (1939) William Heinemann Ltd.

Segal, Suzanne, *Collision With The Infinite* (1996) Blue Dove Press

Shankar, Ravi, *My Music My Life* (1968) Simon & Schuster, New York

Sheldrake, Rupert, *A New Science Of Life* (1981) Blond & Briggs, London

Simon, Carly, *Boys In The Trees* (2015) Flatiron Books, New York

Simon, Ted, *Jupiter's Travels* (1979) Doubleday, New York

Smith, Patti, *Just Kids* (2010) Harper Collins, New York

Stewart, Stanley, *Old Serpent Nile* (1991) John Murray (Publishers) Ltd., London

Sting, *Broken Music* (2003) The Dial Press, New York

Styron, William, *Darkness Visible* (1990) Vintage Books, New York

Swift, Jonathan, *Gulliver's Travels* (1726)

Terzani, Tiziano, *A Fortune Teller Told Me* (1997) Three Rivers Press, New York

Tharoor, Shashi, *Inglorious Empire* (2017) Scribe Publications, Australia

Tolkien, J.R.R., *The Lord Of The Rings* (1968) George Allen & Unwin (1991) Harper Collins, London

Tolkien, J.R.R., *The Hobbit* (1937) George Allen & Unwin (1966) Houghton Mifflin, New York

Tolstoy, Leo, *The Kreutzer Sonata* (1889)

Tomas, Andrew, *Beyond The Time Barrier* (1974) Sphere Books Ltd., England

Tomory, David, *A Season In Heaven* (1996) Harper Collins, England

Tree, Isabella, *Sliced Iguana* (2001) Penguin Books, London

Turnbull, Colin, *The Forest People* (1961) Simon & Schuster, New York

Ward, Tim, *What The Buddha Never Taught* (1990) Celestial Arts Publishing, Berkeley

Walls, Jeanette, *The Glass Castle* (2005) Scribner, New York

Watts, Alan, *The Book On The Taboo Against Knowing Who You Are* (1966) Penguin Random House, New York

Watts, Alan, *The Joyous Cosmology* (1962) Vintage, Random House New York

Webb, Jimmy, *The Cake And The Rain* (2017) St. Martin's Press, New York

Weil, Andrew, *Marriage Of The Sun & Moon* (1980) Houghton Mifflin, Boston

Weil, Andrew, *The Natural Mind* (1972) Houghton Mifflin, Boston

Wells, H.G., *The Time Machine* (1895)

Westover, Tara, *Educated* (2018) Hutchinson, London

Weyler, Rex, *Greenpeace* (2004) Raincoast Books, Vancouver

Wheeler, Tony, *Southeast Asia On A Shoestring* (1975) Lonely Planet, Australia

Whitman, Walt, *Leaves Of Grass* (1855)

Williamson, Marianne, *A Return To Love* (1992) Harper Collins, New York

Wilson, Brian, *i am Brian Wilson* (2016) Random House, Toronto

Wolfe, Tom, *The Kingdom Of Speech* (2016) Little, Brown & Co., New York

Yogananda, Paramahansa, *Autobiography Of A Yogi* (1946) Self-Realization Fellowship

A Course In Miracles (1975) Foundation For Inner Peace

Tripura Rahasya or The Mystery Beyond The Trinity (1971) Sri Ramanasramam, Tiruvannamalai

The New Testament

Genesis, Numbers, The Old Testament

The Books of Enoch

Who is the Drug King of the Golden Triangle? Journeyman Pictures (You Tube)

Story of the Masks (Web Site)

Printed in the USA
CPSIA information can be obtained
at www.ICGtesting.com
JSHW072004111024
71355JS00018B/84

9 781039 124110